International Institutions and Socialization in Europe

Since the path-breaking work of Karl Deutsch on security communities and Ernst Haas on European integration, it has been clear that international institutions may create senses of community and belonging beyond the nation state. Put differently, they can socialize. Yet the mechanisms underlying such dynamics have been unclear. This volume explores these mechanisms of international community building, from a resolutely eclectic standpoint. Rationalism is thus the social theory of choice for some contributors, while others are more comfortable with social constructivism. Still others combine the two. This problem-driven perspective and the theoretical bridge building it begets are the cutting edge in international relations theory. By providing more fine-grained arguments on precisely how international institutions matter, such an approach sheds crucial light on the complex relationship between states and institutions, between rational choice and social constructivism, and, in our case, between Europe and the nation state.

Jeffrey T. Checkel is Professor of Political Science at the University of Oslo and Research Associate, Centre for the Study of Civil War, International Peace Research Institute, Oslo. His research and teaching interests are international relations theory, European integration, politics in the former USSR and West Europe, and human rights. He is the author of *Ideas and International Political Change: Soviet/Russian Behavior and the End of the Cold War*, and he has published widely in leading European and American scholarly journals.

T0371192

International Institutions and Socialization in Europe

Edited by

Jeffrey T. Checkel

University of Oslo

CAMBRIDGE UNIVERSITY PRESS
Cambridge, New York, Melbourne, Madrid, Cape Town, Singapore,
São Paulo, Delhi, Dubai, Tokyo, Mexico City

Cambridge University Press
The Edinburgh Building, Cambridge CB2 8RU, UK

Published in the United States of America by Cambridge University Press, New York

www.cambridge.org
Information on this title: www.cambridge.org/9780521689373

First published 2007

A catalogue record for this publication is available from the British Library

Library of Congress Cataloguing in Publication Data
International institutions and socialization in Europe / edited by Jeffrey T. Checkel.
p. cm. – (International organization; v. 59, no. 4)
Includes bibliographical references and index.
ISBN-13: 978-0-521-68937-3 (pbk.)
ISBN-10: 0-521-68937-6 (pbk.)
1. European federation. 2. International agencies–Europe. 3. Socialization–Europe.
4. Group identity–Europe. I. Checkel, Jeffrey T., 1959– II. Title. III. Series.
JN15.I624   2007
341.24′2–dc22   2006031549

ISBN 978-0-521-68937-3 Paperback

Contents

Part III. Critique, Conclusions, and Extensions

Preface

Over the past decade, there has been a notable and welcome shift in research on international institutions. If early work was preoccupied with showing that institutions mattered in world politics, more recent research explores the processes, mechanisms, and conditions under which they matter.

The present collection is part of this trend. Since the path-breaking work of Karl Deutsch on security communities and Ernst Haas on European integration, it has been abundantly clear that international institutions can – under certain conditions – create senses of community and belonging beyond the nation state. Put differently, they may socialize. However, the mechanisms and processes underlying such socialization dynamics have been less clear. It is precisely the latter on which this volume focuses.

In exploring these mechanisms of international community building, our emphasis is resolutely eclectic. Rationalism is the social theory of choice for some contributors, while others are more comfortable with social constructivism. Still others combine the two. This problem-driven perspective and the theoretical bridge building it begets are the cutting edge in work on international institutions and in international relations (IR) theory more generally. For sure and as our two concluding essays argue, middle-range theory of this sort faces challenges of its own, especially at the levels of research design and methods. Yet, by giving us more fine-grained arguments on precisely how international institutions matter, such an approach sheds crucial light on the complex relation between states and institutions, between rational choice and social constructivism, and, in our case, between Europe and the nation state. To employ a bit of IR jargon, it is "both/and," and not "either/or."

Our eclectic approach also generates significant empirical payoffs. Employing a variety of theories, methods, and data sources, the chapters in Part II offer fascinating, richly detailed, multicausal stories of how NATO, the European Union, and

The essays in this collection originally appeared as a special issue of the journal *International Organization* (59,4, Fall 2005), which was itself the fruit of a larger collaboration on "Europeanization, Collective Identities and Public Discourses" (IDNET). IDNET was generously funded by the Commission of the European Union, through its Fifth Framework Program under the Key Action for Improving the Socio-Economic Knowledge Base (Contract No. HPSE-CT-1999-00034).

other institutions may socialize states and individuals, thus building new senses of belonging. However, a key phrase in that last sentence is "may"—for socialization does not always occur. Indeed, one of our central findings is that regional institutions in Europe socialize less than our theories and popular accounts would suggest. This is a striking result, one all the more important in a Europe marked by the twin processes of supranational polity building and enlargement.

Thanks are owed to many individuals and institutions. In Oslo, the ARENA Centre for European Studies at the University of Oslo played a central role. I thank its co-directors, Johan P. Olsen and Morten Egeberg, as well as its administrative leader, Ragnar Lie, and former executive officer, Kristin Eikeland Johansen. At the European University Institute, where the Robert Schuman Centre for Advanced Studies hosted two workshops, thanks are due especially to Sylvie Pascucci and to the Centre's former director, Yves Mény. In Brussels, Angela Liberatore of the European Commission's DG Research was a very helpful administrative and intellectual resource. At *International Organization*, Lisa Martin, Thomas Risse, and Rebecca Webb played key roles in a rigorous, but fair and efficient, review process.

Finally, I thank Cambridge University Press, where Barbara Chin and Robert Dreesen have ever so patiently answered my many queries and requests.

Jeffrey T. Checkel
Oslo, Norway

Contributors

Jeffrey T. Checkel is Professor of Political Science at the University of Oslo and Research Associate, Centre for the Study of Civil War, International Peace Research Institute, Oslo. His research and teaching interests are international relations theory, European integration, politics in the former USSR and West Europe, and human rights. He is the author of *Ideas and International Political Change: Soviet/Russian Behavior and the End of the Cold War* (Yale University Press, 1997), and he has published widely in leading European and American scholarly journals. His current project – a collaboration with Peter Katzenstein of Cornell University – explores the politics of European identity construction from a variety of disciplinary perspectives.

Jan Beyers is Associate Professor in the Department of Political Science at Leiden University. His research interests include European policy making and interest group politics, the interaction between public and private actors, and the study of political elites more generally. His publications have appeared in a number of journals, including *International Organization, Journal of Common Market Studies, European Journal of Political Research, Comparative Political Studies, West Europeon Politics*, and *European Union Politics*. Currently, he is at work on several large-scale comparative research projects on the Europeanization of interest groups and political agenda setting.

Alexandra Gheciu is Research Associate in the Department of Politics and International Relations and a Research Fellow at Somerville College, both at Oxford University. Her research interests include international security, international relations theory, international socialization and the politics of humanitarian intervention, and post-conflict reconstruction. She is the author of *NATO in the 'New Europe'* (Stanford University Press, 2005) and of several articles on the international practices of reconstruction of failed states. She is currently at work on a book for Oxford University Press that examines European security institutions and the "war on terror."

Liesbet Hooghe is Professor of Political Science at the University of North Carolina at Chapel Hill and Professor in Multilevel Governance at the Free University of Amsterdam. Her research interests are in theories of European integration, multilevel governance, political parties, political elites, and public opinion. Her recent books include *The European Commission and the Integration of Europe: Images of Governance* (Cambridge University Press, 2002) and *Multi-Level Governance and European Integration* (Rowman & Littlefield, 2001, with Gary Marks). She has published widely in American and European journals, and she is currently editing two journal special issues, both on the topic of Euroskepticism.

Alastair Iain Johnston is the Laine Professor of China in World Affairs in the Government Department at Harvard University. Johnston is the author of *Cultural Realism: Strategic Culture and Grand Strategy in Chinese History* (Princeton University Press, 1995) and co-editor of *Engaging China: The Management of an Emerging Power* (Routledge, 1999) and *New Directions in the Study of China's Foreign Policy* (Stanford University Press, 2006). He has a forthcoming book, tentatively titled, *Social States: China in International Instiutions*. He has written on socialization theory, identity in politics, strategic culture, and China's participation in international institutions, among other topics.

Jeffrey Lewis is Assistant Professor of Political Science at Cleveland State University. His research interests include international relations and European integration theory, with a current focus on decision making in the European Union's Council of Ministers. His articles have appeared in a number of leading journals, including *International Organization, Comparative Political Studies*, and *Journal of European Public Policy*. He is currently working on a study of elite socialization among Central and Eastern European newcomers to EU decision-making institutions.

Frank Schimmelfennig is Professor of European Politics at ETH Zurich. His research and teaching interests are theories of European integration and international institutions. He is the author of *The EU, NATO and the Integration of Europe: Rules and Rhetoric* (Cambridge University Press, 2003); co-author of *International Socialization in Europe: European Organizations, Political Conditionality and Democratic Change* (Palgrave Macmillan, 2006); and co-editor of *The Europeanization of Central and Eastern Europe* (Cornell University Press, 2005) and *The Constitutionalization of the European Union* (*Journal of European Public Policy*, Special Issue 2006).

Michael Zürn is Dean of the Hertie School of Governance and Director of the Research Unit "International Institutions and Conflicts" at the Social Science Research Centre Berlin (WZB). His research interests include theories of international regimes, international institutions, and governance beyond the nation state. He has published widely in leading international journals and presses, most recently co-editing *Law and Governance in Postnational Europe* (Cambridge University Press, 2005).

Part I

International Institutions as Community Builders

1

International Institutions and Socialization in Europe

Introduction and Framework

Jeffrey T. Checkel

Is Europe different? For many theorists, policy analysts, and politicians, the answer is obvious: "Of course!" Europe's degree of integration, level of political community, and pooling of sovereignty far outstrip those seen anywhere else. If there is any place in the world where the nation-state would seem to be in retreat, it is in Europe. Moreover, recent years have witnessed a seeming acceleration of the continent's "specialness." A common currency has been successfully introduced, a constitutional convention held, and a (supranational) constitution is now being discussed and debated. This all looks and sounds more like federalism and supranational polity building than the anarchy and Westphalian system that have so fascinated theorists of international politics over the centuries.

As with many headline stories, this one, which emphasizes Europe's *sui generis* nature, is overstated. Yet, as most would admit, there is something to it; Europe is different. Contributors to this volume do not so much disagree with this claim as approach it from a different angle. Leaving the scripting of headlines to others, we are—to continue the journalism metaphor—the investigative reporters, working down in the trenches, exploring the how and why.

Europe is thus our laboratory for getting at some bigger issues concerning the relation of institutions, states, and individuals. When do international institutions create senses of community and belonging? If and when this happens, what does it mean for individual and state allegiances, interests, and identities? What processes underlie such transformative dynamics? What happens to the national and domestic in such situations? These are big questions, ones to which we still have incomplete answers. The latter, to give away perhaps the central punch line of this volume, will only come when we more systematically explore the relation between states and institutions, between the national and supranational, and between rational choice and more sociological perspectives.

Contemporary Europe offers a wonderful opportunity and setting for exploring such relations. The past decade has seen the (already rich) alphabet soup of international institutions of Western Europe extended eastwards. In the early 1990s, organizations such as the Council of Europe (CE) and the Organization for Security and Cooperation

3

in Europe (OSCE) moved quickly to expand, offering membership to numerous transition states in Eastern Europe and the former Soviet Union.[1] More recently, the North Atlantic Treaty Organization (NATO) has done likewise, albeit on a more limited scale. Even for the European Union (EU), once a laggard in this race to expand, enlargement to the east became a reality in May 2004.

This institutional activity in post–Cold War Europe has not escaped the attention of social scientists. Students of what might be called the new comparative regional organizations have explored its effects.[2] Likewise, EU scholars have begun to study how the EU's policies—notably, its application of conditionality—are promoting domestic change among the transition states of Eastern Europe.[3] Renewing and reinvigorating an earlier neofunctionalist line of reasoning, Western Europeanists are once again examining how participation in the institutional structures of the EU may affect the interests and identities of state agents.[4]

A common theme running throughout this work is the socializing potential of international institutions. This volume makes that theme explicit. We examine the conditions under which, and mechanisms through which, institutions in Europe socialize states and state agents, leading them to internalize new roles or group-community norms. To paraphrase Ruggie, the challenge for us is to ask—and begin to answer—"what makes Europe and its institutions hang together."[5]

This disaggregation exercise is essential if we are to better explain the striking variation in socialization outcomes across contemporary Europe. Why is it that one can talk of the Europeanization of German national identity, but not British?[6] Five decades after the European project began, how is it that prominent Europeanists can still vehemently disagree on the socializing power of the Brussels bureaucracy?[7] Why is it that some states in Eastern Europe and the former Soviet Union are quickly socialized into the dominant values of the West, while others are laggards?

In addressing such puzzles, our contribution is fourfold. Theoretically, this volume explores the mechanisms of state/agent socialization from a variety of analytic perspectives, including social constructivist, rational choice, and social psychology. We do not pretend to offer a single theory of socialization; rather, we emphasize the development of scope conditions. In theoretical terms, the volume's goal is to offer middle-range theories of socialization.

Empirically, this theoretical diversity helps us capture the complex reality of contemporary Europe, where a variety of mechanisms are socializing states and individuals/groups within them. The authors in this volume thus analyze the socialization potential and practices of several different European institutions (EU, NATO, CE, and OSCE), and do so in both Western and Eastern Europe and at the macro (state

[1] Farrell and Flynn 1999.
[2] See Acharya and Johnston 2007; Schimmelfennig and Sedelmeier 2002; and Schimmelfennig 2003.
[3] See Grabbe 1999 and 2001; and Kelley 2004.
[4] See Egeberg 1999 and 2004.
[5] Ruggie 1998.
[6] Katzenstein 1997.
[7] Compare Wessels 1998; and Laffan 1998.

socialization by European institutions) and micro (individual agent socialization) levels.

Methodologically, each contributor addresses a series of operational issues— how to recognize socialization; the development of empirical indicators; what counts as good data—and theorizes in terms of scope conditions (when and under what conditions a particular socialization outcome is more likely). Attention to such questions improves the validity of individual contributions, while also helping to place the nascent socialization literature in international relations (IR) and EU studies on a more systematic footing.[8]

In policy terms, our findings speak to important debates among both European and international policymakers. For the EU's ten new member states, which joined the Union on 1 May 2004 and are highly protective of their sovereignty, a key question is whether membership will lead to a diminution or, worse yet, loss of national identity. Our results suggest this is unlikely. For an international community that has devoted much time and effort to helping the formerly communist states rejoin Europe, an important issue is whether conditionality and incentives, or diplomatic suasion, or some combination thereof best promotes domestic change. Our findings strongly endorse the use of mixed strategies that combine different policy instruments.[9]

The remainder of this introductory essay is organized into five parts. In the first section, I introduce this volume's research questions and concepts. Second, I briefly survey the state of the art in the EU and IR socialization literature. Third, I highlight the particular causal mechanisms of socialization explored in this volume. Fourth, I address methodological and design issues. In the concluding—fifth—section, I preview the empirical studies and the critiques/extensions that make up the core of the book.

International Socialization: Questions and Definitions

The central question we explore is whether international institutions have the ability to socialize agents in contemporary Europe. Contributors view international institutions as both formal organizations (working groups of the EU's Council, for example) and specific intergovernmental organizations (such as NATO or the CE). Our agents—the targets of socialization—include both individual policymakers and states.

We adhere to a classical definition of socialization—one with deep roots in sociology and symbolic interactionism—whereby it is defined as a process of inducting actors into the norms and rules of a given community.[10] Its outcome is sustained compliance based on the internalization of these new norms.[11] In adopting community rules, socialization implies that an agent switches from following a logic of

---

[8] See Johnston 2001; and Caporaso and Jupille 1999, respectively.
[9] See also Kelley 2004.
[10] See Dawson and Prewitt 1969; Alderson 2001; and Hooghe 2001b, chap. 1.
[11] See Siegel 1965, 1; and Johnston 2001; see also Ikenberry and Kupchan 1990, 287–92.

consequences to a logic of appropriateness; this adoption is sustained over time and is quite independent from a particular structure of material incentives or sanctions.[12]

Yet there is more than one way in which agents may follow a logic of appropriateness.[13] On the one hand, agents may behave appropriately by learning a role—acquiring the knowledge that enables them to act in accordance with expectations—irrespective of whether they like the role or agree with it. The key is the agents knowing what is socially accepted in a given setting or community. Following a logic of appropriateness, then, means simply that conscious instrumental calculation has been replaced by conscious role playing. We call this Type I internalization or socialization.

On the other hand, following a logic of appropriateness may go beyond role playing and imply that agents accept community or organizational norms as "the right thing to do." We call this Type II internalization/socialization, and it implies that agents adopt the interests, or even possibly the identity, of the community of which they are a part. Conscious instrumental calculation has now been replaced by "taken-for-grantedness."

It is important to keep the two different types of internalization in mind when analyzing socialization. Both represent a shift away from a logic of consequences; both require a logic of appropriateness; and both capture distinct aspects of the socialization dynamics observed in contemporary Europe.

If the purpose is to theorize socialization processes, however, we also need to ask when a shift to internalization occurs, and how. The former requires that one distinguish between situations in which change results from socialization and situations in which it is induced by a calculation of costs and benefits. When do actors switch from a logic of consequences to a logic of appropriateness? To ask "how" is to think about mechanisms, with three highlighted here: strategic calculation, role playing, and normative suasion. In turn, these suggest three modes of rationality that may contribute to socialization outcomes: instrumental, bounded, and communicative.

Some may be surprised by our inclusion of (instrumentally rational) strategic calculation because it invokes images of self-interest perceived as alien to a socialization model. In reality, though, this is a matter of dispute, with one recent review arguing that how "dispositions become anchored as part of an individual's identity [that is, internalized] and how they shape this person's preferences and behavior towards new objects or issues are matters of debate."[14] Given our problem-driven perspective and our concern for integrating diverse analytic traditions, we are thus open to the possible role of each form of rationality.

The purpose of this analytic disaggregation is to explore questions of scope and domains of application. When, and under what conditions, is a particular mechanism more likely to lead to Type I or Type II socialization and internalization? Table 1 summarizes this volume's analytic goals.

---

[12] March and Olsen forthcoming.
[13] I thank Thomas Risse and Liesbet Hooghe for discussions on the following.
[14] Hooghe 2001b, 15

Table 1. *Analytic Goals*

- To explore the ability of international institutions to socialize states and state agents in contemporary Europe
- To theorize and document a set of socialization mechanisms as intervening variables linking input (international institutions) and output (socialization outcome or internalization)
- For each mechanism, to articulate and empirically test a set of conditions (scope conditions) for when it is more likely to produce internalization (Type I or II)

Institutions, Socialization, and Social Agents: The State of the Art

Until recently, scholars in both IR theory and EU studies have undertheorized social-ization. Within IR, neorealists and neoliberals have had little to say about such dynamics. Neorealists invoke the term, but their usage is at odds with standard defini-tions.[15] They tend to conceive socialization as a process of selection and competition, whereby states are compelled to emulate the self-help balancing behavior of the most successful actors in the system. Over time, all actors thus come to share realist behavioral traits. However, the emergence of such commonalities has no connection to the social context within which these states operate, and is driven by no process of internalization.[16] Neoliberals, from their side, rarely mention socialization. More generally, social interaction, internalization, and the study of preference change have not been a central focus in their research program.[17]

Socialization plays a much more important role in the work of the English School. Here, international society—and not international anarchy—is given top recognition; it is conceived as a highly social setting capable of socializing states.[18] Unfortunately, scholars in this tradition—because of their holistic ontology and an avowedly nonpos-itivist epistemology—have paid little attention to theorizing either how socialization occurs (mechanisms) or its end point (internalization).[19]

A similar state of affairs has confronted students of the EU. While the early neofunc-tionalist work of Haas and others hinted at the EU's powerful socializing role, theoret-ical underspecification and methodological challenges hindered empirical research. The exact micro-mechanisms behind notions of spillover were never clearly specified. Difficult issues of self-selection—that is, that national officials heading to Brussels may already be highly pro-European—were never fully addressed.[20] This was and is unfortunate, for the EU's densely institutionalized structure would seem an ideal laboratory and "social soil within which actors' preferences might be transformed."[21]

---

[15] For example, Waltz 1979, 127–29.
[16] See also Johnston 2001, 489–90.
[17] Martin and Simmons 1998.
[18] Bull 1977.
[19] See also Alderson 2001.
[20] See Pollack 1998; and Martin and Simmons 1998.
[21] Caporaso and Jupille 1999, 440. See also "The Brussels Consensus," *Economist*, 7 December 2002; and "Cracks in the College," *Economist*, 13 September 2003, 32.

Despite this background, the good news is that the past decade has seen a revitalization of socialization research by both IR theorists and Europeanists. This work has a strong focus on the role of institutions in socialization, but views them in two distinct ways: as promoters or sites of socialization.

Institutions as Promoters of Socialization

One strand of research views institutions as promoters of socialization in public arenas. In an important sense, this work by IR constructivists builds on the arguments of the English School regarding the socializing effects of international society; its added value comes in systematically explicating how and when such effects occur.

A volume edited by Risse, Ropp, and Sikkink represents the state of the art in this area. The book offers a five-stage model for explaining the process through which international norms have socializing effects at the national level. Empirically, the model traces the ways in which norms shape the politics of human rights change in a number of different settings.[22]

The editors' approach is strongly influenced by work on social movements, however, and this unintentionally limits the pathways through which socialization is theorized to occur. Its starting point need not always be the social protest mechanism emphasized by Risse, Ropp, and Sikkink, in which national elites react in a calculating, strategic manner to movement pressure. Socialization can also begin via a process of social learning, in which state agents learn new roles and interests from the start and in the absence of social mobilization. Though the Risse, Ropp, and Sikkink model hints at this pathway, with the role it attributes to persuasion and arguing at certain points, it remains underdeveloped.[23]

Institutions as Sites of Socialization

Addressing the problems highlighted above is another strand of socialization research that views institutions as sites of socialization for individuals. Here, Europeanists and a smaller group of IR constructivists have taken the lead. They theorize how state elites, in insulated settings where social pressure is absent or deflected, adopt multiple roles. This builds on a long tradition of research in IR theory and negotiation analysis that emphasizes the socializing effects of international organizations and institutions on the individuals who participate in them.[24]

Several Europeanists have explored the socializing effect of repeated meetings over long periods within EU institutions.[25] These studies often employ rigorous quantitative analysis. However, their tendency to operationalize socialization purely in terms of the duration of contact risks neglecting the qualitative context of these meetings.

[22] Risse, Ropp, and Sikkink 1999.
[23] Checkel 2000b for details.
[24] See Haas 1990; and Chayes and Chayes 1995.
[25] See Beyers 1998; Lewis 1998; and Hooghe 1999 and 2001a. See also Beyers and Dierickx 1997 and 1998.

Indeed, prolonged contact in sessions marked by intense bargaining is likely to have quite different effects on actors than meetings devoted to puzzling and joint problem solving.

Responding to such criticisms, a second group of Europeanists addresses this qualitative dimension and its relation to (possible) agent socialization. Arguing that the small size and expert focus of many EU committees promotes deliberation and common puzzling, these scholars portray socialization as being driven by Habermasian dynamics of communicative rationality.[26] However, a lack of attention to research methodology makes it hard for other scholars to ascertain deliberation's causal role.[27]

At this point, the EU literature intersects with the work of IR constructivists doing work on socialization within international institutions. With a strong focus on agency, these scholars explicitly theorize the mechanisms of socialization hinted at above. To accomplish this, some draw on Habermas,[28] others seek to operationalize social learning concepts,[29] while still others emphasize dynamics of persuasion and social influence.[30]

The Multiple Mechanisms of Socialization

Building on this research, the contributors to this volume seek to better specify the various mechanisms of socialization, viewing them generically as "a set of hypotheses that could be the explanation for some social phenomenon, the explanation being in terms of interactions between individuals and other individuals, or between individuals and some social aggregate."[31] Typically, mechanisms operate at an analytical level below that of a more encompassing theory; they increase the theory's credibility by rendering more fine-grained explanations.[32] Mechanisms connect things; they are "recurrent processes linking specified initial conditions and a specific outcome."[33]

We thus seek to minimize the lag between international institutions and socializing outcomes—the adoption of new roles (Type I internalization) or changes in values and interests (Type II internalization)—at the individual or state level. As mechanism-based accounts are in principle "quite compatible with different social theories of action,"[34] our starting point is to highlight three distinct mechanisms connecting institutions to socializing outcomes: strategic calculation, role playing, and normative suasion.

[26] See Joerges and Neyer 1997a and 1997b.
[27] However, see Pollack 2003.
[28] See Risse 2000; and Lynch 1999 and 2002.
[29] Price 1998.
[30] See Johnston 2001 and forthcoming.
[31] Hedstroem and Swedberg 1998, 32–33.
[32] Johnson 2002, 230–31.
[33] Mayntz 2003, 4–5. More generally on social mechanisms, see Hovi 2004; Tilly 2001; and Mayntz 2003.
[34] Mayntz 2003, 9.

Strategic Calculation

Strategic calculation[35] has deep roots in rationalist social theory. While incentives and rewards can be social (status, shaming) as well as material (financial assistance, trade opportunities), one might expect both to play some role in the socialization process. After all, if they are operative in other aspects of social life—as one knows to be the case—it would be odd if they were absent from socialization dynamics.[36]

When this mechanism operates alone, there can—by definition—be no socialization and internalization. No switch from a logic of consequences to one of appropriateness has occurred. Agents are viewed as instrumentally rational. They carefully calculate and seek to maximize given interests, adapting their behavior to the norms and rules favored by the international community. However, as argued below, it is possible that what starts as behavioral adaptation, may—because of various cognitive and institutional lock-in effects—later be followed by sustained compliance that is strongly suggestive of internalization and preference change. Given the desire to disaggregate the socialization process, it is thus still important to include a role for this first mechanism.

Under what conditions are incentives and rewards likely to promote behavioral adaptation? Contributors to this project theorize several possibilities, all of which emphasize the importance of political conditionality in the socialization process. Defined as the use of material incentives to bring about a desired change in the behavior of a target state, conditionality is the quintessential incentives-based policy. It has long been a favored instrument of international financial institutions such as the World Bank and the International Monetary Fund (IMF).[37] More importantly for this volume's purposes, European regional institutions have used conditionality in the process of Eastern enlargement.

Conditionality's role can be explored more specifically by considering what Schimmelfennig calls intergovernmental reinforcement. Intergovernmental reinforcement by reward refers to a situation in which an international institution offers the government of a target state positive incentives—rewards such as aid or membership—on the condition that it adopts and complies with the institution's norms. This is a classic use of political conditionality. Transnational reinforcement by reward refers to the same process, but now directed at nongovernmental actors in target states. Given these definitions, behavioral adaptation in line with community norms is more likely under the following conditions:

- Targeted governments expect the promised rewards to be greater than the costs of compliance (Intergovernmental Reinforcement).

- Targeted societal actors expect the costs of putting pressure on the government to be lower than the benefits of conditional external rewards, and these actors are

---

[35] I present the hypotheses and scope conditions for each mechanism in abbreviated form; detailed discussions can be found in the individual contributions.

[36] See also Hooghe 2001b, chap. 1.

[37] Checkel 2000a, 2–9.

strong enough to force the government to comply with the international norms (Transnational Reinforcement).[38]

These propositions are clear, and fairly easy to operationalize, and they capture an important part of an international institution's domestic impact. At the same time, their social-theoretic foundation limits the analysis. As with all rational-choice scholarship, the ontology is individualist, and core properties of actors are taken as givens. While we agree with others that the ontological differences separating rationalism and constructivism are often overstated,[39] the former is nonetheless ill-equipped to theorize those instances in which basic properties of agents are changing (Type I or II socialization).

Role Playing

This mechanism of socialization has roots in organization theory and cognitive/ social psychology. Agents are viewed as boundedly rational. It is not possible for them to attend to everything simultaneously or to calculate carefully the costs and benefits of alternative courses of action; attention is a scarce resource. Organizational or group environments provide simplifying shortcuts, cues, and buffers that can lead to the enactment of particular role conceptions—role playing—among individuals.[40]

When role playing occurs, the shift from a logic of consequences toward a logic of appropriateness has begun, as it involves noncalculative behavioral adaptation. Organizational and group environments trigger roles, in which a degree of "automaticity" governs individual behaviour. Agents adopt certain roles because they are appropriate in that particular setting. However, no process of reflective internalization driven by communicative processes has occurred. In our terms, the socialization outcome is Type I internalization.[41]

Drawing on a rich laboratory-experimental research program in social psychology,[42] contributors to this volume advance a set of scope conditions emphasizing contact in small groups as a stimulus for Type I internalization. This allows them to provide carefully argued support for the old neofunctionalist claim that prolonged exposure and communication in European institutions promote a greater sense of "we-ness," as well as socialization dynamics.

More specifically, contributors argue that the internalization of new role conceptions in line with community/group norms is more likely when the following conditions hold:

---

[38] Schimmelfennig, this volume. On the link between incentives/conditionality and domestic politics, see also Kelley 2004, chap. 2.

[39] See Fearon and Wendt 2002, 53–58; and Caporaso, Checkel, and Jupille 2003b, 11–15.

[40] See March and Simon 1981; and March and Olsen forthcoming.

[41] We make no assumption that the adoption of new role conceptions necessarily leads to better outcomes. Indeed, there are interesting parallels between work emphasizing this mechanism and earlier research in social psychology on groupthink, which focused on suboptimal small-group dynamics. Checkel 2001, 563–64.

[42] Orbell, Dawes, and Van de Kragt 1988, for example.

- Agents are in settings where contact is long and sustained, and it has some significant duration.
- Agents are in settings where the contact is intense.[43]

However, such arguments must control for the fact that individuals entering a new institutional arena are in no sense free agents; they are embedded in multiple domestic and international contexts:

- Those agents with extensive previous professional experiences in regional or international policymaking settings are more likely to internalize supranational role conceptions.
- In contrast, agents with extensive domestic policy networks who are briefly "parachuted" into regional/international settings will be less likely to internalize new role conceptions.[44]

These propositions begin to control for the self-selection and presocialization that bedeviled earlier work in this tradition.[45] The validity of these propositions is further bolstered by the degree to which they overlap with insights drawn from other research traditions. This is particularly true of symbolic interactionism, in which scholars have theorized multiple embeddedness in terms of role conflict.[46] Olsen makes a similar point in regards to the Europeanization literature, which explores the impact of the EU on nation-states.[47]

This work on role playing not only marks an advance on earlier studies, it also captures an important, if understudied, dynamic in international politics—one different from the instrumental or normative ones. Individuals and states take on roles because it is easier socially, as opposed to only and always acting strategically and instrumentally. Yet these roles may later become taken-for-granted habits, without any conscious act of persuasion (see below).

This suggests a subtle, but important, difference with the normative suasion mechanism. If role playing is at work, agents will comply with group/community norms, but in a nonreflective manner. That is, if asked about the source of compliance, they—after conscious thought—might answer, "Well, I don't know whether it's right or wrong, it's simply what is done and, I guess, it's a habit of mine by now."[48]

---

[43] Contributors operationalize intensity with some care—defining it, for example, as the number of committee meetings attended plus the number of informal contacts outside these formal sessions. They also design their research to distinguish the independent causal effects of duration versus intensity. Beyers, this volume.

[44] One can also conceptualize embeddedness in organizational terms. See Egeberg 2004, in which organizational specialization and affiliation are used to develop additional hypotheses on the adoption of new role conceptions in European institutions.

[45] See Beyers, this volume; and Hooghe, this volume. See also Martin and Simmons 1998, 735–36.

[46] See Stryker 1980; Meyer and Strang 1993; and, for an important application to international institutions, Barnett 1993.

[47] Olsen 2002.

[48] I thank an anonymous reviewer for pushing me to clarify these points. Methodologically, this has implications for the types of (process-oriented) questions we should be asking in socialization studies. Zürn and Checkel, this volume.

Normative Suasion

Recent work by IR constructivists adds a communicative understanding of rationality to the instrumental and bounded versions illustrated above. Drawing on Habermasian social theory as well as insights from social psychology, these researchers claim that communicatively rational social agents do not so much calculate costs and benefits, or seek cues from their environment. Rather, these agents present arguments and try to persuade and convince each other; their interests and preferences are open for redefinition.[49]

Recall that role playing presupposes an agent's passive, noncalculative acceptance of new roles evoked by certain environmental triggers. When normative suasion takes place, agents actively and reflectively internalize new understandings of appropriateness. If asked about the source of compliance, agents— after conscious thought— might answer, "Well, this is the right thing to do even though I didn't used to think so." The switch from a logic of consequences to one of appropriateness is complete, and the result is what we label Type II internalization.

These insights give new meaning to the idea of international institutions and organizations as "talk shops." Arguments and attempts at persuasion—"talking," in popular parlance—may change the most basic properties of agents. If the strategic calculation mechanism views language as a tool for self-interested actors to exchange information or engage in signaling games within institutions, then normative suasion embodies a much "thicker" role for it, as constitutive of agents and their interests.[50]

Most would agree that persuasion operates in international institutions. Indeed, two practitioner-scholars with considerable experience in the world of diplomacy describe it as a "fundamental instrument" and "principal engine" of the interaction within institutions.[51] While perhaps overstated, the real challenge has been to operationalize this common-sense insight in ways that allow for systematic empirical testing.[52]

Contributors to this volume address this gap, articulating a series of scope conditions under which persuasion-socialization dynamics occur. In particular, they suggest that arguing and persuasion are more likely to change the interests of social agents and lead to Type II internalization when the following conditions hold:[53]

- The target of the socialization attempt is in a novel and uncertain environment and thus cognitively motivated to analyze new information.[54]

- The target has few prior, ingrained beliefs that are inconsistent with the socializing agency's message.

- The socializing agency/individual is an authoritative member of the ingroup to which the target belongs or wants to belong.

---

[49] See Lynch 1999, chap. 1; Risse 2000, 6–11; and Checkel 2003.
[50] See also Adler 2002, 96–98.
[51] Chayes and Chayes 1995, 25–26.
[52] See Checkel and Moravcsik 2001; and Moravcsik 2001.
[53] See Lewis, this volume; and Gheciu, this volume. More generally, see Zimbardo and Leippe 1991; and Brody, Mutz, and Sniderman 1996.
[54] Put differently, agents are viewed as communicatively and not boundedly rational. With the latter, they would be much more likely to filter or ignore new information.

- The socializing agency/individual does not lecture or demand but, instead, acts out principles of serious deliberative argument.
- The agency/target interaction occurs in less politicized and more insulated, in-camera settings.

The chapters that follow provide significant empirical support for these propositions and scope conditions. Yet problems remain. Most importantly, there is typically an element of overdetermination in analyses testing for the effects of arguing and persuasion, with several interacting variables leading to socialization in a single or perhaps two cases. Greater attention to research design and use of cross-regional comparisons can mitigate this problem.[55]

Cautions and Caveats

There are three cautions for the reader. First, when highlighting the effects of these differing mechanisms, I have followed common practice by arguing that socialization becomes deeper and more stable as one moves from incentive-based (behavioral adaptation) to normative mechanisms (Type II internalization). Indeed, social theorists have argued that preference shifts promoted by suasion should be more enduring than those promoted by incentives and strategic calculation. With the latter, newly adopted behaviors can be discarded once incentive structures change; with the former, they will show greater stickiness, as actors have begun to internalize new values.[56]

Yet this hierarchy of effectiveness can be questioned. Research on self-persuasion and cognitive dissonance suggests that internalization can occur even in the absence of any attempts at persuasion. Consider individuals who, for purely strategic, incentive-based reasons, begin to act in a certain manner; at some point, they will likely need to justify these acts to themselves and others. As a result, a cognitive dissonance may arise between what is justified and argued for, and what is (secretly, privately) believed. Laboratory and experimental work suggests that human beings have a tendency to resolve such dissonance by adapting their preferences to the behavior; that is, they internalize the justification.[57]

There is also growing empirical evidence to suggest that what starts as strategic, incentive-based cooperation within international institutions often leads at later points to preference shifts (Type II internalization) and, thus, to more enduring change. For example, Kelley finds precisely this pattern in her research on the Baltic states, European institutions, and minority rights. In several instances, she uncovers evidence of an initially highly strategic and instrumental process at work, as state elites carefully calculate how to change laws to ward off pressure from the EU, CE, and OSCE. Yet beyond the formal changing of laws, Kelley also finds evidence of changing practice and sustained compliance—patterns indicative of deeper socialization effects.[58]

[55] See Zürn and Checkel, this volume; and Johnston, this volume.
[56] Hurd 1999.
[57] Zürn and Checkel, this volume. This appears to be the implicit psychological dynamic behind Elster's oft-cited argument regarding the "civilizing force of hypocrisy." Elster 1998. See also Fearon 1998, 54.
[58] Kelley 2004.

It is therefore more useful to view the three socialization mechanisms as nominal rather than ordinal categories.[59] Many contributors to this volume implicitly adopt such a perspective, when they emphasize primarily one mechanism—role playing, say—to the exclusion of the others. This has clear benefits, for example, in allowing the analysis to flesh out and empirically test how a particular mechanism works in practice. Gheciu's study of NATO and normative suasion is exemplary in this regard.[60]

Second, a focus on social mechanisms raises a micro/macro problem. To explore mechanisms often implies an emphasis on the micro level—in our case, of specific agents operating in institutionalized environments in Europe.[61] Yet some, including many IR theorists, would be more interested in micro-macro linkages. When does individual attitudinal or role change result in a shift in state policy? Do state policies and practices change in ways consistent with newly learned roles or preferences?

We address this issue in two ways. Some contributors establish positive correlations between socialization at the individual level and later changes in state policy. Others go a step further, advancing a causal, process-tracing argument that connects socialization mechanisms to changes in policy.[62]

Third, readers should view our discussion of scope conditions as preliminary. In some cases, this is because they are inductively derived from our work. In others, they are deductively derived but are tested with qualitative and quantitative methods that differ from the laboratory-experimental orientation of the original research. In his contribution, Johnston suggests specific research-design strategies for addressing these problems.[63]

Summary

The starting point of this volume is as simple as it is straightforward. International institutions are social environments; participating in them may socialize states and state agents.[64] Our stress on the multiple mechanisms leading to this endpoint marks a new analytic turn for work on European institutions, on which most research to date has emphasized either their constraining[65] or constitutive effects.[66] We see both at play.[67]

Our focus on causal mechanisms and the embeddedness of social agents in multiple contexts—national, subnational, as well as international—marks an advance over earlier neofunctionalist and social constructivist theorizing. Rather than employing vague

---

[59] That is, there is no assumption that they are in any particular order. Keohane, King, and Verba 1994, 151–55.

[60] Gheciu, this volume. Of course, such an approach also has drawbacks—namely, in neglecting how the three mechanisms may work in combination to produce a socialization outcome.

[61] Mayntz 2003, 1.

[62] See Gheciu, this volume; and Lewis, this volume, respectively. See also Zürn and Checkel, this volume.

[63] Johnston, this volume.

[64] See also Risse-Kappen 1995a; Barnett and Finnemore 1999 and 2004; and Wallander 2000a.

[65] See Keohane, Nye, and Hoffmann 1993; Moravcsik 1995 and 2000; Kopstein and Reilly 2000; and Wallander 1999 and 2000b.

[66] See Soysal 1994; and Banchoff 1999.

[67] See also Zürn and Checkel, this volume, on dynamic approaches to the study of European integration/socialization; and Hooghe 2001b.

neofunctionalist notions of spillover, we theorize specific socialization mechanisms (strategic calculation, role playing, normative suasion) and examine them empirically. In addition, and again in contrast with neofunctionalism, there is no normative agenda driving the analysis.[68] The empirical studies demonstrate that the socializing effects of European institutions are uneven and often surprisingly weak, and in no way can be construed as shaping a new, post-national identity.[69]

The micro-level perspective we offer complements recent constructivist work that examines socialization from a macro perspective. In addition, this volume develops arguments that better specify the international learning or social learning often stressed by constructivists to capture the constitutive impact of international institutions.[70]

More generally, by stressing mechanisms and scope conditions, we contribute to the development of middle-range socialization approaches.[71] Ever since Merton's pioneering work in the late 1940s, social theorists have argued that such theories can only be constructed by elaborating mechanisms that shrink the gap between input and output.[72] In turn, this requires one to minimize use of the "as if" assumptions that play such important roles in many studies of socialization and of international institutions.[73]

Methods, Design, and Approach

The five empirical chapters in this volume offer detailed studies of particular instances of attempted socialization in both Eastern and Western Europe. All follow a similar template, beginning with an introduction in which authors highlight their socialization puzzle and provide background and context for the European institution(s) on which they focus. Next, the theoretical argument linking institutions to state/agent socialization is briefly summarized. In a third section, authors spell out their particular mechanism(s) of socialization and suggest conditions under which they expect it to operate. A fourth section introduces the data and justifies the methods employed. In a fifth and most important section, contributors relate their socialization account. These accounts make up the heart of each essay and of the volume as a whole.

In telling their socialization stories, authors address a threefold analytic challenge: (1) to establish the presence of socialization mechanisms and the conditions of their operation; (2) to assess whether internalization (Type I or II) actually occurred; and (3) to ask whether socialized actors behave differently than either they did before they were socialized, or than nonsocialized actors do. Put differently, the authors examine

---

[68] Caporaso 1998, 6–7.
[69] It is surprising because contemporary Europe is a most likely case for such dynamics. See next section.
[70] See Adler 1997; and Adler and Barnett 1998, chap. 2.
[71] See Johnston, this volume; see also Alderson 2001, 429.
[72] See Merton 1968, chap. 2; see also Mayntz 2003, 3–4.
[73] See Checkel 2000b; Sterling-Folker 2000; and Wendt 2001, 1028–29. Our stress on mechanisms and a commitment to reducing reliance on "as if" assumptions in theory development can furthermore be viewed as a substantive contribution to the scientific realist research agenda. See Wendt 1999, chap. 2; and Wight 2002, 34–36, 43. I thank an anonymous reviewer for discussion on these points.

whether a shift has occurred away from a logic of consequences and toward a logic of appropriateness.[74]

Regarding the methods used in this volume, several points should be stressed. For one, many contributors employ the case-study technique because it is especially well-suited to establishing scope conditions and examining causal mechanisms.[75] In addition, each author uses a number of tools and techniques to enhance the reliability and (internal) validity of his/her study. These include: reviewing and justifying the data or data set; discussing the proxies for operationalizing and measuring key variables; explaining the qualitative or quantitative methods (or combination thereof) employed to draw inferences about socialization processes or effects; and considering alternative explanations or using counterfactual analysis, where appropriate.

A number of contributors use process tracing as their main method. This means that they examine "whether the intervening variables between a hypothesized cause and observed effect move as predicted.... Put another way, process tracing looks at the causal mechanisms in operation in a case."[76] In executing this method, authors triangulate across multiple data streams, including interviews, surveys, secondary literature (newspaper reports, scholarly analyses), and primary sources (archival materials or confidential meeting summaries).

Recall that our dependent variable (DV) and socialization outcome is the degree of internalization. Depending on the author and socialization mechanism at work, this is measured in slightly different ways. For those stressing the strategic calculation mechanism, the DV is sustained compliance with the norms and rules favored by the larger (Western European) community, where it is this consistency—regardless of rewards or sanctions—that is taken as an indicator of socialization and internalization. Authors who examine cognitive role playing operationalize the DV as the adoption of new roles consistent with group norms. In our terms, such adoption is an indicator of Type I internalization. Finally, contributors exploring the normative suasion mechanism define their DV as the adoption of new values and interests consistent with those of the international community; such change is taken as an indicator of Type II internalization.

In all cases, the DV is then measured through quantitative techniques, qualitative techniques, or a combination of both. Two examples highlight how this is carried out in practice. In his study of socialization in Eastern/Central Europe, Frank Schimmelfennig begins with a correlational analysis of party systems and norm compliance, establishing a temporal connection between norms and policies favored by European institutions and their domestic adoption. Next, he switches to a qualitative process-tracing technique to establish causality, demonstrating that cost/benefit calculations by domestic actors were a key force in the early stages of the socialization dynamic.[77]

Hooghe, in her examination of socialization within the European Commission, constructs a data set consisting of surveys of Commission officials, as well as nearly

---

[74] I thank an anonymous reviewer for discussion on these points.
[75] See Bernauer and Mitchell 1998, 7, 22; and Bennett and George 2005.
[76] Bennett and George 2005.
[77] Schimmelfennig, this volume.

150 follow-up interviews. In addition, she uses Eurobarometer polling data to control for preexisting national-level attitudes. After introducing a number of carefully constructed control variables, Hooghe uses quantitative techniques to test for evidence of socialization and internalization in the Commission.[78]

Regarding design, one important point needs to be addressed. Readers familiar with the comparative regionalisms literature[79] or work exploring the IR/institutions nexus[80] will immediately recognize that Europe is a most likely case for socialization. Why did we make this choice? Simply put, we do not yet have a good sense of how, and under what conditions, socialization occurs.[81]

Thus our most-likely-case design is justifiable. It allows us to map and identify the various causal paths leading to socialization.[82] Indeed, if the goal is to establish a roster of socialization mechanisms, such a strategy would seem indispensable at this point. At the same time, our selection of cases allows for significant variation in terms of both institutions (NATO, EU, and so on) and the value of the DV (the degree of internalization). Moreover, we further contextualize the latter by exploring instances in which socialization appears weak (chapters by Beyers, Hooghe, and Schimmelfennig), exploring instances in which it produces not an either/or replacement of roles and interests, but a more complicated layering of them (contribution by Lewis), and by drawing on socialization research in other regional contexts in which very different types of institutions are at work (discussion of Asia in Johnston's essay).

A final, more general point concerns this volume's basic approach, which is problem-driven. This leads to a pragmatic understanding of ontologies, in which they are not viewed as "manifest truths . . . [but as] tentative empirical assumptions about actors, taken for purposes of pursuing a particular set of theoretical questions about political behavior."[83] Put differently, our goal is to develop substantive middle-range frameworks, and not to engage in arguments at the level of social theory. The volume's strong emphasis on scope conditions can be read as an endorsement of the former at the expense of the latter. We well appreciate that there are big and (possibly) unresolvable issues dividing proponents of choice-theoretic, rational choice, and economic approaches from scholars who favor sociological and social constructivist perspectives.

Yet we are also aware that from a problem-driven, empirical perspective, such divides rapidly begin to melt away. The starting point of the analysis moves from "either/or" to "both/and," with the latter pushing questions of scope and domains-of-application to the fore. Since we observe calculative, role-playing, and persuasive mechanisms at work in the process of socialization in contemporary Europe, intellectual honesty demands that we capture these facts in our theories.

---

[78] Hooghe, this volume. An arm of the EU's statistical service, Eurobarometer conducts surveys on a regular basis in all member states.

[79] Hemmer and Katzenstein 2002.

[80] See Weber 1994; Risse-Kappen 1995b, chap. 1; and Pevehouse 2002, 529–30.

[81] See Alderson 2001, 416; and Johnston 2001, 492–93.

[82] Bennett and George 2005.

[83] Lepgold and Lambom 2001, 28.

This common-sense perspective is gaining adherents within both subfields to which this volume speaks. In IR theory, one now sees a growing number of calls for "both/and" theorizing. Much more importantly, these scholars are beginning to develop arguments for how one can integrate the ideational and the material, game theory and social constructivism, strategic-choice and cognitive perspectives, other-regarding and self-interested behavior, and the like.[84]

Students of the EU also now recognize that the way forward is not to revisit the decades-old battle between intergovernmentalism and neofunctionalism. Rather, the challenge is to develop more complex approaches that capture both the constraining and constitutive aspects of the European project.[85]

This stance of ontological pragmatism, and the (attempts at) theoretical bridge building it inspires, have practical implications for the way in which authors deal with alternative explanations in the empirical essays. Most importantly, they spend less time engaged in the standard practice of demonstrating that other, alternative accounts are inconsistent with their data, and more time thinking about bridge building consistent with the empirical evidence.

Consider two examples. In her account of socialization dynamics in the EU Commission, Hooghe connects consequentialist and appropriateness logics via what one might term a domain-of-application approach, in which one theorizes conditions under which particular processes and dynamics are more likely.[86] In particular, she argues that socialization and internalization are more likely to shape preferences on international norms when these are general and close to individuals' core beliefs, while strategic calculation and utility maximization will influence preferences on international norms that materially affect career chances.[87]

In contrast, Gheciu's essay on NATO and socialization dynamics offers what might be called a temporal-sequencing argument, in which different mechanisms and logics are fitted together over time to more fully explain a particular outcome.[88] For example, while she stresses the ability of NATO to normatively persuade policymakers in applicant countries, this ability is premised on a (temporally) prior calculation by these same countries that NATO is central for managing their relations with the United States.[89]

These empirical efforts at bridge building are later complemented by a conceptual analysis undertaken by Zürn and Checkel. Engaging in what they call a double interpretation, the authors take each empirical contribution, deconstruct it (identifying its causal mechanisms and scope conditions), and then reconstruct and reinterpret it

---

[84] See Katzenstein, Keohane, and Krasner 1998; Finnemore and Sikkink 1998; Odell 2000; Lepgold and Lambom 2001; Alderson 2001, 431; Lebow 2001, 547–59; Hemmer and Katzenstein 2002, 599–600; Fearon and Wendt 2002; and Snyder 2002, 9, 12, 37.

[85] See Checkel and Moravcsik 2001; Olsen 2001 and 2002, 27–28; Tallberg 2002; Caporaso, Checkel, and Jupille 2003a and 2003b; Smith 2004, 99–103; and Checkel 2004, 241–44.

[86] Caporaso, Checkel, and Jupille 2003b, 21–22. See also March and Olsen forthcoming, 21–22.

[87] Hooghe, this volume.

[88] See Risse, Ropp, and Sikkink 1999, chap. 1; Caporaso, Checkel, and Jupille 2003b, 22–23; and March and Olsen forthcoming, 22–23.

[89] Gheciu, this volume.

from the point of view of both rationalism and constructivism. This exercise not only allows them to offer reflections on the right places to build bridges, but also to tease out the finer differences between rationalist and constructivist frameworks.[90]

Organization

The remainder of this volume is structured as follows. The core is five empirical studies that examine the socialization policies and practices of various European institutions. These are followed by two essays that extend and critically assess our arguments along theoretical, methodological, and cross-regional dimensions.

Empirical Studies

The volume begins with a chapter emphasizing the strategic calculation pathway; next comes a chapter that combines the strategic calculation and role-playing mechanisms. A third chapter explores the role-playing mechanism, while two chapters examining normative suasion come last. This order is not only consistent with how the mechanisms were introduced above, it also proceeds from the least to the most complex understanding of socialization (and rationality). Given this structure, scholars and students reading across the essays can thus more easily evaluate the utility of our disaggregation exercise, with its emphasis on multiple socialization mechanisms and their conditions of operation. The following are descriptions of each empirical study.

Frank Schimmelfennig, Strategic Calculation and International Socialization: Membership Incentives, Party Constellations, and Sustained Compliance in Central and Eastern Europe.   Schimmelfennig articulates a rationalist starting point for understanding key aspects of socialization in the transition states of postcommunist Europe. In particular, he theorizes strategic calculation as an initial and crucially important socialization mechanism, in which international organizations offer material and political rewards in return for the adoption of norms and policies, but do not coerce noncompliant governments. Empirically, Schimmelfennig substantiates these propositions with aggregate data on the development of liberal democracy in the states of Central and Eastern Europe, and with process-tracing case studies on Slovakia and Latvia.

Liesbet Hooghe, Several Roads Lead to International Norms, but Few Via International Socialization: A Case Study of the European Commission.   There have been numerous claims regarding the power of the European Commission—that "engine of Europe"—to socialize individuals. Yet in a striking finding, Hooghe finds little evidence of such dynamics at work. Based on two surveys of senior Commission officials and controlling for a host of possible confounding factors, her central conclusion is unambiguous. While support for the European project is extraordinarily

---

[90] Zürn and Checkel, this volume.

high in the Commission, this has little, if anything, to do with preference shifts or the internalization of new values in it. Instead, top officials sustain Commission norms because national experiences motivate them to do so.

Jan Beyers, Multiple Embeddedness and Socialization in Europe: The Case of Council Officials. Early neofunctional, as well as contemporary, studies argue that social interaction and contact crosscutting national borders should lead to a shift of allegiance toward the European level. Yet most studies have ignored the multiple embeddedness of the actors involved and have failed to control for recruitment bias and presocialization in the domestic political sphere. Addressing these gaps, Beyers argues that this so-called contact hypothesis for socialization is in fact seriously underspecified, and must be supplemented with additional national-level factors. Utilizing quantitative interview data and factor analysis, he investigates the particular conditions under which new supranational role conceptions are adopted and internalized in working groups of the EU Council.

Jeffrey Lewis, The Janus Face of Brussels: Socialization and Everyday Decision Making in the European Union. Lewis examines the Committee of Permanent Representatives, or COREPER, a grouping composed of the EU permanent representatives. At the heart of everyday decision making, COREPER is thus a key laboratory to test whether and how national officials become socialized into the Brussels-based collective culture. Based on extensive interview data and a case study of negotiations for a controversial EU citizenship directive, Lewis documents a process in COREPER that includes elements of all three socialization mechanisms—strategic calculation, role enactment, and normative suasion. Equally importantly, he advances scope conditions—focusing on high issue density/intensity and insulation from domestic politics—for disentangling them.

Alexandra Gheciu, Security Institutions as Agents of Socialization? NATO and the 'New Europe.' Gheciu examines the dynamics and implications of NATO's socialization of Czech and Romanian actors after the end of the Cold War, arguing that the organization's involvement in Central/Eastern Europe has been more complex than rationalist analyses might lead one to expect. In addition to instrumental incentives, NATO has relied extensively on mechanisms of normative suasion. A close empirical study of the Czech and Romanian cases reveals that international socialization—under certain conditions theorized by the author—affected not just the socializees' strategies, but also their definitions of identity and interests.

Theoretical/Methodological Critiques and Regional Extensions

The following are descriptions of each critique.

Alastair Iain Johnston, Conclusions and Extensions: Toward Mid-Range Theorizing and Beyond Europe. In the first of two concluding essays, Johnston reflects on four issues. First, he summarizes and critiques the core analytic claims and main socialization scope conditions advanced by various authors. Second, and consistent with the volume's "both/and," bridge-building aspirations, Johnston explores how a critical socialization micro-process—persuasion—fits with a thin rationalist argument. Third, he critically assesses the volume's understanding of identity change, arguing that the latter needs further specification if we are to more fully explore the relation between it and socialization. Finally, Johnston looks at how the findings in the European case might be extended to, and compared with, empirical evidence from other parts of the world—in particular, Asia.

Michael Zürn and Jeffrey T. Checkel, Getting Socialized to Build Bridges: Constructivism and Rationalism, Europe and the Nation-State. In this concluding essay, Michael Zürn and Jeffrey Checkel advance three arguments, all captured by a "both/and" logic. For one, the volume's emphasis on mechanisms and scope conditions reveals that both rational choice and constructivism have much to contribute to the study of international socialization. Furthermore, they argue that theories of European integration and socialization will advance only if scholars systematically move to combine the supranational and the national in their frameworks. Finally, future research on socialization should supplement empirical theorizing—the focus here—with normative and critical perspectives. This matters—and all the more so in a Europe marked by supranational constitution- and polity building.

References

Acharya, Amitav, and Alastair Iain Johnston. 2007. Crafting Cooperation: The Design and Effect of Regional Institutions in Comparative Perspective. In *(Regional International Institution in Global Politics)*, edited by Amitav Acharya and Alastair Iain Johnston, chapter 1. Cambridge: Cambridge University Press.

Adler, Emanuel. 1997. Seizing the Middle Ground: Constructivism in World Politics. *European Journal of International Relations* 3 (3):319–63.

———. 2002. Constructivism and International Relations. In *Handbook of International Relations*, edited by Walter Carlsnaes, Thomas Risse, and Beth Simmons, 95–118. London: Sage Publications.

Adler, Emanuel, and Michael Barnett, eds. 1998. *Security Communities*. Cambridge: Cambridge University Press.

Alderson, Kai. 2001. Making Sense of State Socialization. *Review of International Studies* 27 (3):415–33.

Banchoff, Thomas. 1999. German Identity and European Integration. *European Journal of International Relations* 5 (3):259–90.

Barnett, Michael. 1993. Institutions, Roles and Disorder: The Case of the Arab States System. *International Studies Quarterly* 37 (3):271–96.

Barnett, Michael, and Martha Finnemore. 1999. The Politics, Power and Pathologies of International Organizations. *International Organization* 53 (4):699–732.

———. 2004. *Rules for the World: International Organizations in Global Politics*. Ithaca, N.Y.: Cor nell University Press.

Bennett, Andrew, and Alexander George. 2005. *Case Studies and Theory Development in the Social Sciences*. Cambridge, Mass.: MIT Press.

Bernauer, Thomas, and Ronald Mitchell. 1998. Empirical Research on International Environmental Policy: Designing Qualitative Case Studies. *Journal of Environment and Development* 1 (1):4–31.

Beyers, Jan. 1998. Where Does Supranationalism Come from? The Ideas Floating through the Working Groups of the Council of the European Union. Paper Presented at the Third Pan-European Conference on International Relations, September, Vienna.

Beyers, Jan, and Guido Dierickx. 1997. Nationality and European Negotiations: The Working Groups of the Council of Ministers. *European Journal of International Relations* 3 (4):435–72.

———. 1998. The Working Groups of the Council of the European Union: Supranational or Intergovernmental Negotiations? *Journal of Common Market Studies* 36 (3):289–317.

Brody, Richard, Diana Mutz, and Paul Sniderman, eds. 1996. *Political Persuasion and Attitude Change.* Ann Arbor: University of Michigan Press.

Bull, Hedley. 1977. *The Anarchical Society.* New York: Columbia University Press.

Caporaso, James. 1998. Regional Integration Theory: Understanding Our Past and Anticipating Our Future. *Journal of European Public Policy* 5 (1):1–16.

Caporaso, James, and Joseph Jupille. 1999. Institutionalism and the European Union: Beyond International Relations and Comparative Politics. *Annual Review of Political Science* 2:429–44.

Caporaso, James, Jeffrey T. Checkel, and Joseph Jupille, eds. 2003a. Integrating Institutions: Rationalism, Constructivism and the Study of the European Union. Special issue of *Comparative Political Studies* 36 (1–2):5–231.

———. 2003b. Integrating Institutions: Rationalism, Constructivism and the Study of the European Union—Introduction. *Comparative Political Studies* 36 (1–2):7–41.

Chayes, Abram, and Antonia Handler Chayes. 1995. *The New Sovereignty: Compliance with International Regulatory Agreements.* Cambridge, Mass.: Harvard University Press.

Checkel, Jeffrey T. 2000a. Compliance and Conditionality. Working Paper Series 00/18. Oslo, Norway: ARENA Centre for European Studies, University of Oslo.

———. 2000b. Review of The Power of Human Rights: International Norms and Domestic Change. *Comparative Political Studies* 33 (10):1337–41.

———. 2001. Why Comply? Social Learning and European Identity Change. *International Organization* 55 (3):553–88.

———. 2003. 'Going Native' in Europe? Theorizing Social Interaction in European Institutions. *Comparative Political Studies* 36 (1–2):209–31.

———. 2004. Social Constructivisms in Global and European Politics. A Review Essay. *Review of International Studies* 30 (2):229–44.

Checkel, Jeffrey T., and Andrew Moravcsik. 2001. A Constructivist Research Program in EU Studies? (Forum Debate). *European Union Politics* 2 (2):219–49.

Dawson, Richard, and Kenneth Prewitt. 1969. *Political Socialization.* Boston: Little, Brown.

Egeberg, Morten. 1999. Transcending Intergovernmentalism? Identity and Role Perceptions of National Officials in EU Decision-Making. *Journal of European Public Policy* 6 (3):456–74.

———. 2004. An Organizational Approach to European Integration: Outline of a Complementary Perspective. *European Journal of Political Research* 43 (2):199–219.

Elster, Jon, ed. 1998. *Deliberative Democracy.* New York: Cambridge University Press.

Farrell, Henry, and Gregory Flynn. 1999. Piecing Together the Democratic Peace: The CSCE and the 'Construction' of Security in Post–Cold War Europe. *International Organization* 53 (3): 505–36.

Fearon, James. 1998. Deliberation as Discussion. In *Deliberative Democracy*, edited by Jon Elster, 44–68. New York: Cambridge University Press.

Fearon, James, and Alexander Wendt. 2002. Rationalism v. Constructivism: A Skeptical View. In *Handbook of International Relations*, edited by Walter Carlsnaes, Thomas Risse, and Beth Simmons, 52–72. London: Sage Publications.

Finnemore, Martha, and Kathryn Sikkink. 1998. International Norm Dynamics and Political Change. *International Organization* 52 (3):887–917.

Grabbe, Heather. 1999. A Partnership for Accession? The Implications of EU Conditionality for the Central and East European Applicants. Robert Schuman Centre Working Paper 99/12. Florence, Italy: European University Institute.

———. 2001. How Does Europeanization Affect CEE Governance? Conditionality, Diffusion and Diversity. *Journal of European Public Policy* 8 (6):1013–31.

Haas, Ernst. 1990. *"When Knowledge is Power: Three Models of Change in International Organizations.* Berkeley: University of California Press.

Hedstroem, Peter, and Richard Swedberg, eds. 1998. *Social Mechanisms: An Analytical Approach to Social Theory.* Cambridge: Cambridge University Press.

Hemmer, Christopher, and Peter Katzenstein. 2002. Why Is There No NATO in Asia? Collective Identity, Regionalism and the Origins of Multilateralism. *International Organization* 56 (2):575–608.

Hooghe, Liesbet. 1999. Supranational Activists or Intergovernmental Agents? Explaining the Orientations of Senior Commission Officials Toward European Integration. *Comparative Political Studies* 32 (4):435–63.

———. 2001a. Top Commission Officials on Capitalism: An Institutionalist Understanding of Preferences. In *The Rules of Integration: Institutionalist Approaches to the Study of Europe*, edited by Mark Aspinwall and Gerald Schneider, 152–73. Manchester, England: Manchester University Press.

———. 2001b. *The European Commission and the Integration of Europe: Images of Governance.* Cambridge: Cambridge University Press.

Hovi, Jon. 2004. Causal Mechanisms and the Study of International Environmental Regimes. In *Regime Consequences: Methodological Challenges and Research Strategies*, edited by Arild Underdal and Oran Young, 71–86. Boston: Kluwer Academic.

Hurd, Ian. 1999. Legitimacy and Authority in International Politics. *International Organization* 53 (2):379–408.

Ikenberry, G. John, and Charles Kupchan. 1990. Socialization and Hegemonic Power. *International Organization* 44 (3):283–315.

Joerges, Christian, and Juergen Neyer. 1997a. From Intergovernmental Bargaining to Deliberative Political Processes: The Constitutionalisation of Comitology. *European Law Journal* 3 (3):273–99.

———. 1997b. Transforming Strategic Interaction into Deliberative Problem-Solving: European Comitology in the Foodstuffs Sector. *Journal of European Public Policy* 4 (4):609–25.

Johnson, James. 2002. How Conceptual Problems Migrate: Rational Choice, Interpretation and the Hazards of Pluralism. *Annual Review of Political Science* 5:223–48.

Johnston, Alastair Iain. 2001. Treating International Institutions as Social Environments. *International Studies Quarterly* 45 (4):487–516.

———. Forthcoming. *Social States: China in International Institutions.* Princeton, N.J.: Princeton University Press.

Katzenstein, Peter, ed. 1997. *Tamed Power: Germany in Europe.* Ithaca, N.Y.: Cornell University Press.

Katzenstein, Peter, Robert Keohane, and Stephen Krasner, eds. 1998. *International Organization* at Fifty: Exploration and Contestation in the Study of World Politics. *International Organization* 52 (3):645–1061.

Kelley, Judith. 2004. *Ethnic Politics in Europe: The Power of Norms and Incentives*. Princeton, N.J.: Princeton University Press.

Keohane, Robert, Gary King, and Sidney Verba. 1994. *Designing Social Inquiry: Scientific Inference in Qualitative Research*. Princeton, N.J.: Princeton University Press.

Keohane, Robert, Joseph Nye, and Stanley Hoffmann, eds. 1993. *After the Cold War: International Institutions and State Strategies in Europe, 1989–1991*. Cambridge, Mass.: Harvard University Press.

Kopstein, Jeffrey, and David Reilly. 2000. Geographic Diffusion and the Transformation of the Post-communist World. *World Politics* 53 (1):1–37.

Laffan, Brigid. 1998. The European Union: A Distinctive Model of Internationalization. *Journal of European Public Policy* 5 (2):235–53.

Lebow, Richard Ned. 2001. Thucydides the Constructivist. *American Political Science Review* 95 (3):547–60.

Lepgold, Joseph, and Alan Lamborn. 2001. Locating Bridges: Connecting Research Agendas on Cognition and Strategic Choice. *International Studies Review* 3 (3):3–30.

Lewis, Jeffrey. 1998. Is the 'Hard Bargaining' Image of the Council Misleading? The Committee of Permanent Representatives and the Local Elections Directive. *Journal of Common Market Studies* 36 (4):479–504.

Lynch, Marc. 1999. *State Interests and Public Spheres: The International Politics of Jordan's Identity*. New York: Columbia University Press.

———. 2002. Why Engage? China and the Logic of Communicative Engagement. *European Journal of International Relations* 8 (2): 187–230.

March, James, and Johan P. Olsen. Forthcoming. The Logic of Appropriateness. In *Handbook of Public Policy*, edited by Robert Goodin, Michael Moran and Martin Rein. Oxford, England: Oxford University Press.

March, James, and Herbert Simon. 1981. Decision-Making Theory. In *The Sociology of Organizations. Basic Studies*, 2d ed., edited by O. Grusky and G. A. Miller. New York: Free Press.

Martin, Lisa, and Beth Simmons. 1998. Theories and Empirical Studies of International Institutions. *International Organization* 52 (3):729–58.

Mayntz, Renate. 2003. Mechanisms in the Analysis of Macro-Social Phenomena. MPIfG Working Paper 03/3. Cologne, Germany: Max Planck Institute for the Study of Societies.

Merton, Robert. 1968 [1949]. *Social Theory and Social Structure*. New York: Free Press.

Meyer, John, and David Strang. 1993. Institutional Conditions for Diffusion. *Theory and Society* 22:487–511.

Moravcsik, Andrew. 1995. Explaining International Human Rights Regimes: Liberal Theory and Western Europe. *European Journal of International Relations* 1 (2):157–89.

———. 2000. The Origins of Human Rights Regimes: Democratic Delegation in Postwar Europe. *International Organization* 54 (2):217–52.

———. 2001. Constructivism and European Integration: A Critique. In *The Social Construction of Europe*, edited by Thomas Christiansen, Knud Erik Joergensen, and Antje Wiener, 176–88. London: Sage Publications.

Odell, John. 2000. *Negotiating the World Economy*. Ithaca, N.Y.: Cornell University Press.

Olsen, Johan P. 2001. Garbage Cans, New Institutionalism and the Study of Politics. *American Political Science Review* 95 (1):191–98.

———. 2002. The Many Faces of Europeanization. *Journal of Common Market Studies* 40 (5):921–52.

Orbell, John, Robyn Dawes and Alphons Van de Kragt. 1988. Explaining Discussion-Induced Cooperation. *Journal of Personality and Social Psychology* 54 (5):811–19.

Pevehouse, Jon. 2002. Democracy from the Outside-In? International Organizations and Democratization. *International Organization* 56 (3):515–50.

Pollack, Mark. 1998. Constructivism, Social Psychology and Elite Attitude Change: Lessons from an Exhausted Research Program. Paper Presented at the llth International Conference of Europeanists, February, Baltimore.

_____. 2003. Deliberative Democracy or Member-State Control Mechanism? Two Images of Comitology. *Comparative Political Studies* 36 (1–2):125–55.

Price, Richard. 1998. Reversing the Gun Sights: Transnational Civil Society Targets Land Mines. *International Organization* 52 (3):613–44.

Risse, Thomas. 2000. 'Let's Argue!': Communicative Action in World Politics. *International Organization* 54 (1):1–39.

Risse, Thomas, Stephen Ropp, and Kathryn Sikkink, eds. 1999. *The Power of Human Rights: International Norms and Domestic Change.* Cambridge: Cambridge University Press.

Risse-Kappen, Thomas. 1995a. *Cooperation among Democracies: The European Influence on US Foreign Policy.* Princeton, N.J.: Princeton University Press.

Risse-Kappen, Thomas, ed. 1995b. *Bringing Transnational Relations Back In: Non-State Actors, Domestic Structures and International Institutions.* New York: Cambridge University Press.

Ruggie, John Gerard. 1998. What Makes the World Hang Together? Neo-Utilitarianism and the Social Constructivist Challenge. *International Organization* 52 (4):855–85.

Schimmelfennig, Frank. 2003. *The EU, NATO and the Integration of Europe: Rules and Rhetoric.* Cambridge: Cambridge University Press.

Schimmelfennig, Frank, and Ulrich Sedelmeier. 2002. Theorizing EU Enlargement: Research Focus, Hypotheses and the State of Research. *Journal of European Public Policy* 9 (4):500–28.

Siegel, R. 1965. Assumptions about the Learning of Political Values. *Annals of the American Academy of Political and Social Sciences* 361.

Smith, Michael. 2004. Institutionalization, Policy Adaptation and European Foreign Policy Cooperation. *European Journal of International Relations* 10 (1):95–136.

Snyder, Jack. 2002. Anarchy and Culture: Insights from the Anthropology of War. *International Organization* 56 (1):7–46.

Soysal, Yasemin. 1994. *Limits of Citizenship: Migrants and Postnational Membership in Europe.* Chicago: University of Chicago Press.

Sterling-Folker, Jennifer. 2000. Competing Paradigms or Birds of a Feather? Constructivism and Neo-liberal Institutionalism Compared. *International Studies Quarterly* 44 (1):97–120.

Stryker, Sheldon. 1980. *Symbolic Interactionism: A Social Structural Perspective.* Reading, Mass.: Benjamin-Cummings.

Tallberg, Jonas. 2002. Paths to Compliance: Enforcement, Management and the European Union. *International Organization* 56 (3):609–44.

Tilly, Charles. 2001. Mechanisms in Political Processes. *Annual Review of Political Science* 4:21–41.

Wallander, Celeste. 1999. *Mortal Friends, Best Enemies: German-Russian Cooperation after the Cold War.* Ithaca, N.Y.: Cornell University Press.

_____. 2000a. What NATO Is and How It Can Cooperate with Russia. Policy Memo, No. 127. Washington, D.C.: Program on New Approaches to Russian Security, Center for Strategic and International Studies.

_____. 2000b. Institutional Assets and Adaptability: NATO after the Cold War. *International Organization* 54 (4):705–36.

Waltz, Kenneth. 1979. *Theory of International Politics.* New York: McGraw Hill.

Weber, Steven. 1994. Origins of the European Bank for Reconstruction and Development. *International Organization* 48 (1):1–38.

Wendt, Alexander. 1999. *Social Theory of International Politics.* Cambridge: Cambridge University Press.

————. 2001. Driving with the Rearview Mirror: On the Rational Science of Institutional Design. *International Organization* 55 (4):1019–50.

Wessels, Wolfgang. 1998. Comitology: Fusion in Action—Politico-Administrative Trends in the EU System. *Journal of European Public Policy* 5 (2):209–34.

Wight, Colin. 2002. Philosophy of Social Science and International Relations. In *Handbook of International Relations,* edited by Walter Carlsnaes, Thomas Risse, and Beth Simmons, 23–51. London: Sage Publications.

Zimbardo, Philip, and Michael Leippe. 1991. *The Psychology of Attitude Change and Social Influence.* New York: McGraw Hill.

Part II

The Socializing Power of
European Institutions

2

Strategic Calculation and International Socialization

Membership Incentives, Party Constellations, and Sustained Compliance in Central and Eastern Europe

Frank Schimmelfennig

After the end of the Cold War, European regional organizations proclaimed liberal democracy as the new standard of legitimacy for the states of the emerging pan-European international community. These organizations defined the international socialization of the ex-communist Central and East European countries (CEECs) to this standard as a new core task for themselves, and devised a diversified set of instruments—reaching from the provision of expertise to membership conditionally—to promote and support the democratic consolidation of the region.[1]

Fifteen years later, it is obvious that the results have been highly divergent. Whereas one group of countries, mainly the central European and Baltic countries, quickly and smoothly adopted fundamental liberal norms of state organization and conduct, other CEECs—most notably Belarus and Serbia—have long defied "Westernization." Still others have displayed inconsistent patterns characterized by stop-and-go processes or fluctuation between progress and reversals. The aim of this article is to explore the causal mechanism and conditions that have produced the uneven outcomes and pathways of democratic international socialization in the CEECs.

My argument is based on a rationalist approach to international socialization. It conceives of socialization as a process of reinforcement that has three major components. First, whereas European regional organizations have used a variety of strategies and instruments, only the high material and political rewards of membership in the European Union (EU) and the North Atlantic Treaty Organization (NATO) have triggered sustained domestic change in those CEECs that initially violated the liberal-democratic community norms. In contrast, normative suasion or social influence alone have not been effective. The accession conditionality of the EU and NATO consists in a positive strategy of reinforcement by reward. Both organizations offer the CEECs support and membership under the condition of conformance with the community

---

[1] See, for example, the 1990 "Charter of Paris for a New Europe" of the Conference on Security and Cooperation in Europe (CSCE), or the "Declaration on Central and Eastern Europe" by the Strasbourg summit of the European Community in December 1989.

norms and rules. If a country does not conform, the EU and NATO withhold the reward but do not engage in coercive enforcement.

Second, the main channel of international reinforcement in the CEECs is intergovernmental, because societies are too weak vis-à-vis the states, and electorates are too volatile, to serve as effective agents of socialization. Under a policy of intergovernmental reinforcement by reward, the outcome depends on the political cost-benefit calculations of governments. The higher the domestic political costs of adaptation to international human rights and democratic norms, the less likely target governments will conform with them. Thus, the high and tangible rewards of EU and NATO membership are only effective in combination with low adaptation costs in the target countries.

Third, the long-term prospects of international socialization not only depend on the incumbent government, but also on the calculations of their major competitors. As a consequence, the most important factor for successful international reinforcement is the constellation of parties. In countries in which all major parties are pro-Western and reform-minded (liberal party constellation), international socialization has been smooth and has produced stable, consolidated democracies. In these countries, the political costs of adaptation were low, and elections have led to an alternation between reform-friendly forces. In contrast, in states dominated by nationalist, populist, and/or authoritarian political forces (antiliberal constellation), international socialization has failed. In these countries, the governments' political costs of adaptation have been higher than the rewards of membership. Finally, countries with a mixed constellation, in which major parties are split between reform-oriented and nationalist-authoritarian parties, show a stop-and-go or up-and-down pattern of norm conformance. Thanks to lock-in effects, however, which led the nationalist-authoritarian parties to adapt to the requirements of Western integration, reinforcement by reward has eventually been successful. What is more, it is in the mixed-constellation countries that European organizations have had the most discernible effect on democratic consolidation.

In sum, the uneven outcomes and pathways of democratic international socialization in the CEECs can be explained by the mechanism of strategic calculation. The relevant conditions for sustained compliance have been the nature of international incentives and domestic political constellations. EU and NATO membership incentives have been effective in countries with liberal or mixed party constellations, but not in authoritarian systems.

The causal links between reinforcement activities, internalization, and sustained compliance are not straightforward in these cases. In most countries with a liberal party constellation, the internalization of a liberal identity and liberal norms preceded sustained compliance, and norm conformance preceded the reinforcement activities of the regional organizations. For the mixed-constellation countries, however, the causal pathway seems to be exactly the reverse: membership conditionality resulted in compliance, and behavioral compliance might eventually give way to internalization. However, because membership conditionality has been in place throughout the entire period of examination, it is currently impossible to tell whether internalization has progressed to the point at which norm-conforming behavior will be assured in the absence of external sanctions.

The design of this article is as follows. In the theory section, I develop a rationalist approach to international socialization based on strategic calculation. I describe the reinforcement mechanism and specify the conditions under which it is expected to lead to effective international socialization. In the remainder of the article, I explore the empirical plausibility of these conditions. Following a brief section on data and methods, I analyze the correlation between party constellations and conformance patterns and conduct a process-tracing analysis of the international socialization of Slovakia and Latvia. I conclude with a discussion of the prospects of internalization.

Theory: Reinforcement, Party Constellations, and Socialization

In this section, I specify the core mechanism and conditions of international socialization in Central and Eastern Europe. I claim that the generation of sustained compliance in the CEECs has been dependent on a socialization strategy of intergovernmental reinforcement by tangible membership rewards in combination with a liberal or mixed party constellation in the target countries.

Mechanism: Socialization by Reinforcement

I propose a rationalist approach to the study of international socialization based on strategic calculation.[2] This approach assumes a process characterized by exogenous, self-interested political preferences and instrumental action. Such an approach entails several conceptual and theoretical consequences.

1. The actors do not necessarily take the norms and rules of the international community for granted. They generally confront them as external institutional facts that work as a resource of support for norm-conforming behavior and as a constraint that imposes costs on norm-violating behavior. At any rate, their behavior in the socialization process is initially motivated extrinsically by self-defined political preferences. I assume these political preferences to be material and power-oriented. They consist in security and welfare benefits as well as the desire to attain and maintain political power.

2. Socialization works through reinforcement.[3] International organizations reward norm-conforming behavior and punish norm-violating behavior; target states conform with the norms and rules in order to avoid punishment and gain rewards. The relevant rewards and punishments are those that affect the security and welfare of a state and increase the chance of political actors to come to, and stay in, power.

---

[2] See Schimmelfennig 2000.

[3] Note that I do not use "reinforcement" as a "mechanical," nonrational mechanism as described, for example, by Elster 1989, 82–88.

3. The actors weigh up the costs and benefits of reinforcement and compliance in light of their goals. Target states conform with international norms if it increases their political utility, and on the condition that the costs of adaptation are smaller than the benefits of external rewards or the costs of external punishment.

4. In addition, actors manipulate the norms strategically to avoid or reduce the costs of socialization. They use and interpret international norms to justify their self-interested claims, and frame their preferences and actions as norm-consistent. In other words, they act rhetorically.[4]

Socialization by reinforcement differs from the alternative mechanism of normative suasion with regard to actor motivation, process, and outcome.[5] Actors calculate the consequences of norm conformance rather than reflecting on its appropriateness; they engage in bargaining and rhetorical action rather than consensus-oriented arguing; and they adapt their behavior rather than changing their views, interests, or identities. In the end, socialization by reinforcement does not exclude "sustained compliance based on the internalization of these new norms."[6] However, behavioral change will typically precede internalization, and behavioral conformance will persist for an extended period of time without internalization. There are two ways in which the switch from a logic of consequences to a logic of appropriateness may be conceived to occur at the end of a sustained and successful reinforcement process: routinization and rationalization. These correspond to the two types of internalization outlined by Checkel.[7] In the first case, the socializees come to follow the community norms and rules habitually, without being persuaded and changing their desires; in the second, they adapt their desires to the reinforced behavior in order to reduce cognitive dissonance.[8] In both cases, specific rewards and punishments are not necessary anymore to elicit norm-conforming behavior, although a stable "shadow of reinforcement" probably helps to sustain the belief that nothing is to be gained by reverting to a calculation of the costs and benefits of compliance.

Reinforcement mechanisms can be distinguished along three dimensions: first, reinforcement can be based on rewards or punishments; second, it can use tangible (material or political) or intangible (social or symbolic) rewards and punishments; finally, it can proceed through an intergovernmental or a transnational channel.

In intergovernmental reinforcement by tangible rewards, the socialization agency offers the governments of the target states positive incentives, which would improve their security, welfare, or political power and autonomy. The target governments are promised rewards, such as aid or membership, on the condition that they conform with the community norms and rules. If a target government rejects them or fails to comply, the socialization agency simply withholds these rewards but does not pressure

---

[4] See Schimmelfennig 2001 and 2003, 194–225.
[5] Risse 2000, 1–9.
[6] Checkel, this volume.
[7] Ibid. See also Johnston 2001.
[8] See Elster 1983; Ikenberry and Kupchan 1990, 291; and Zürn and Checkel, this volume.

the target state into norm-conforming behavior.[9] To be effective, this mechanism requires that the target government expect the promised rewards to be higher than the costs of adaptation.

In contrast, intergovernmental reinforcement by punishment consists in the coercive enforcement of international norms. The socialization agency threatens to punish the socializees in case of noncompliance (beyond merely withholding the rewards). To be effective, reinforcement by punishment requires that the costs of external punishment be higher for the target government than the costs of adaptation. Moreover, the rewards and punishments may be social rather than material (social influence). Such rewards include international recognition, public praise, and invitations to intergovernmental meetings; the corresponding punishments include exclusion, shaming, and shunning.[10]

Material and social, positive and negative, reinforcement mechanisms can also be used indirectly, via the transnational channel. In transnational reinforcement, the socialization agency uses rewards and punishments to mobilize groups and corporate actors in the society of the target state to apply pressure on their government to change its policy. Transnational reinforcement is effective if the costs of putting pressure on the government are lower for the societal actors than the expected community rewards, and if they are strong enough to force the government to adapt to the community norms and rules.

Conditions of Effective Socialization I: Membership Incentives

Which of these reinforcement strategies are used in the international socialization of Central and Eastern Europe? Which are most likely to be effective—that is, to produce sustained compliance and, eventually, internalization in the target countries—in light of the theoretical assumptions of the rationalist approach and the empirical conditions of socialization in the region? I argue that, while European regional organizations have pursued all of these strategies in different combinations at various points in time,[11] intergovernmental reinforcement using the tangible rewards of EU and NATO membership is likely to be most effective.[12]

All European regional organizations use social influence in both its positive and its negative form. These organizations monitor the development of democracy and human rights in the CEECs and regularly assess the state of democratic consolidation in official reports, intergovernmental meetings, and debates of their parliamentary assemblies. By drawing attention to violations of human rights and democratic norms,

---

[9] See the discussion of positive sanctions combined with "assurances" not to punish the target actor for noncompliance in Baldwin 1971, 25–27; and Davis 2000, 12.

[10] Johnston 2001, 499–500. Tangible and social rewards are sometimes hard to distinguish. For instance, membership in international organizations often enhances the status of states and gives them access to material resources at the same time, or social punishments by the international community might deter foreign investment and weaken the domestic power of governments in the future. Here I treat social rewards and punishments as those that are not directly linked to, or combined with, tangible ones by the same actor (socialization agency).

[11] In addition to teaching and persuasion; see Checkel 2001; and Gheciu, this volume.

[12] See also Kelley 2004; and Kubicek 2003.

or by expressing their satisfaction with the consolidation of democracy, European organizations distribute praise and disapproval by the international community. In addition, the graded integration process of most organizations—the differentiated promotion of states to "special guests" (Council of Europe), "partners for peace" (NATO), or "associates" (EU), then to candidates for membership and, finally, to full members—provides a system of status markers and confers different degrees of international legitimacy upon the CEECs.

In contrast, reinforcement by tangible punishments and rewards has been limited to the two organizations capable of providing material incentives and disincentives in the areas of security and welfare: the EU and NATO. Whereas reinforcement by tangible punishments—the use of coercion to stop the violation of community norms and to enforce change—has been the exception, and generally limited to situations of massive "ethnic cleansing" (above all in Bosnia-Herzegovina and Kosovo), both organizations have consistently used reinforcement by tangible rewards to promote human rights and democracy in the CEECs. Both organizations have set the consolidation of democracy and the rule of law, respect for human rights, and minority protection as political conditions for membership and the benefits that come with it: military protection by NATO, full access to the EU's internal market and economic subsidies, and full participation in the decision making of the most powerful organizations of the region. In both organizations, fulfillment of the political conditions has been a necessary, and most important, condition for being admitted to accession negotiations.[13] However, states that fail to meet the political conditions are not coerced to introduce political reforms, nor do they receive special assistance or support. They are simply left behind in the "regatta" to membership with an open invitation to join once the political conditions are in place.

In light of the theoretical assumptions of the rationalist approach, and leaving aside the exceptional use of coercive punishment by European organizations, I suggest that only intergovernmental reinforcement by tangible rewards has had an effective impact in favor of norm-conforming domestic change in those postcommunist CEECs that initially violated liberal norms, and that, among those rewards, the incentives of EU and NATO membership have been the most effective in promoting international socialization.

The predominance of intergovernmental reinforcement can be attributed to the state-centric domestic structure and the electoral volatility in the CEECs. As a broad rule, the domestic structure of the CEECs is characterized by the weakness of society vis-à-vis the state. This is obvious in the presidential systems of government that prevail in the former Soviet republics, but also applies to the advanced parliamentary democracies of Central Europe. Even here, political parties have been organized top-down, have no or only weak roots in society and social organizations, and depend on the state for their resources. A powerful civil society has failed to emerge despite promising beginnings in the revolutions of 1989. Rather, levels of political

---

[13] On the enlargement decision-making processes in the EU and NATO, see, for example, Goldgeier 1999; Sedelmeier 2000; and Schimmelfennig 2003.

participation have declined. This domestic structure gives both governments and parties ample space for discretionary decision making and strongly limits the influence of societal actors on day-to-day policymaking.[14] Thus, because societal strength is a necessary condition of transnational reinforcement, this mechanism is unlikely to be effective in the international socialization of Central and Eastern Europe.

To be sure, Central and Eastern European governments are generally subject to the most powerful sanctioning mechanism of society: electoral confirmation and defeat. "Electoral democracies" have come into being early in the transition process, and have persisted even though many CEECs have failed to institutionalize consolidated "liberal democracies."[15] Even the most illiberal Central and Eastern European governments have not prohibited independent opposition parties or abolished elections altogether; and even unfair elections can hold unpleasant surprises for the incumbents.[16] However, if elections are to serve as an effective instrument of reinforcement, a majority of the electorate must consistently reward norm-conforming—and punish norm-violating—state actors and programs.

It seems, however, that actual voting behavior is more strongly shaped by immediate concerns with personal security and welfare than by concerns about the government's conformance with Western norms. Most often, changes in government have been caused by societal dissatisfaction with the hardships of economic shock therapy, economic mismanagement by the incumbent government, and corruption scandals, and this dissatisfaction has turned against reform-friendly and reform-adverse governments alike.[17] The ascendance of centrist political forces in the Romanian and Bulgarian elections of 1996–97, the Slovak elections of 1998, and the Croatian and Serbian elections of 2000 certainly strengthened the reform orientation of these countries, but it was predominantly the economic situation that brought about the change. As the subsequent election outcomes (2000–2001 in Bulgaria and Romania and 2003–2004 in Croatia and Serbia) show, voters may again shift their allegiance away from the most Western-oriented political forces if these fail to provide for effective governance and an improvement of the economic situation. Thus, I suggest that elections in Central and Eastern Europe be best treated as a "random factor" that sometimes happens to provide an opening for improved norm conformance, but does not work consistently in favor of socialization.[18]

The primacy of tangible rewards follows from the assumption of material and power-oriented political preferences and from the nature of the community norms and rules. In general, adopting the liberal political norms of the European international community means a loss in autonomy and power for the target governments. These governments have to respect the outcome of free and fair elections, the competences

[14] See, for example, Ágh 1998a, 52, 106; Birch 2000, 15–16; Kaldor and Vejvoda 1999, 11, 19–22; Lewis 2001, 546, 556; and Sitter 2001, 75–76, 87.

[15] Diamond 1996, 23–25.

[16] See the Yugoslav elections in 2000 or the Ukrainian elections in 2004. See Jasiewicz 1998, 166.

[17] See Jasiewicz 1998, 186; and Pravda 2001, 26–27.

[18] This qualification distinguishes my argument from the more positive assessment of transnational reinforcement by Vachudova 2001.

of courts and parliaments, the rights of the opposition and national minorities, and the freedom of the media. These political disincentives need to be balanced in kind by incentives such as military protection or economic assistance to improve the security and the welfare of the state—and the reelection prospects of the government.[19] Moreover, only the highest international rewards—those associated with EU and NATO membership—can be expected to balance substantial domestic power costs.

Under a policy of intergovernmental reinforcement by reward, it is up to the target government to decide whether it accepts the costs of adaptation in exchange for the promised benefits. Whatever choice it makes, it will not be punished or coerced by the international organization. For two reasons, I suggest that these decisions will depend on the size of the domestic political costs rather than variation in international rewards. First, the EU and NATO have generally pursued an open and meritocratic policy of enlargement; that is, both organizations have invited all European countries to enter into accession negotiations on the same political preconditions. They have not discriminated against individual nonmember countries because of their strategic, economic, or cultural characteristics. Second, the material incentives of EU and NATO membership are high for all CEECs. CEECs have generally sought protection against a potential Russian threat and the ethnic wars in the region, and they depend on the EU market and investments. Thus if EU and NATO membership incentives are high and accessible to all CEECs, in principle, they can be treated as a constant. It also follows that any explanation of the divergence of reinforcement outcomes must be based on different domestic conditions and costs.

Conditions of Effective Socialization II: Party Constellations

Under the condition of electoral volatility and random election effects, the long-term prospects for socialization will not only depend on the cost-benefit calculations of the government currently in power, but of potential future governments as well. All major parties—that is, all parties that are able to form a government or will be dominant in any feasible coalition government—must therefore make the same basic cost-benefit assessment in favor of norm conformance. In other words, I claim that the effectiveness of international socialization will depend on the party constellations in the target countries.[20]

I distinguish three basic types of party constellations: liberal, antiliberal, and mixed.[21] If all major parties base their legitimacy claims and programs on liberal reform and integration into the Western organizations (liberal party constellation), the conditions of intergovernmental reinforcement by reward are favorable, because

---

[19] See Mattli 1999 for a similar argument on the incentives of nonmember states to join regional integration schemes.

[20] To be sure, this variable only qualifies as a proximate cause: the party constellation depends in turn on deeper factors such as ethnic cleavages, political culture, socioeconomic structures, or transition trajectories.

[21] See McFaul 2002 for a similar three-way categorization of transition countries and explanation of transition outcomes based on the domestic balance of power between democratic parties and supporters of the *ancien régime*.

the perceived costs of adaptation will be low and will not change after a change of government. If, however, the major parties base their legitimacy claims and pro- grams on nationalism, communism, populism, and/or authoritarianism (antiliberal party constellation), the political costs of adaptation to liberal norms will be high. As a consequence, the conditions for successful reinforcement will be unfavorable. In mixed party constellations with major liberal and antiliberal parties, the conditions of successful reinforcement are moderately positive.

As with the other countries of the region, the CEECs with a liberal party constel- lation had to go through the economic trough of transformation. Although they pur- sued different strategies of economic reform (for instance, gradualism in the Czech Republic and shock therapy in Poland), the population has had to suffer from the hardships of economic adjustment sooner or later, and has used the ballot to oust the incumbent parties from government. Moreover, political scandals have taken their toll. Whereas some of these countries have shown a remarkable stability of governments and parties (such as the Czech Republic and Slovenia), in others, governments have been highly fluctuating and short-lived (such as in Poland and the Baltic countries). What distinguishes these countries from the other CEECs, however, is a general ori- entation of the major parties toward liberal democracy and Western integration. Thus, whenever a government was dismissed or voted out of office, its successors followed the same basic parameters of political change. This not only applies to the parties of the center and the moderate right, but also to the reconstructed postcommunist parties that came to power through democratic elections only a few years after the communist breakdown in Hungary, Lithuania, and Poland.

The expectation for this group of countries is a quick and smooth socialization process resulting in high and stable conformance with Western democratic standards. This is because, given the political programs and predominant legitimation strategies of the major parties, the political benefits of Western integration are high and the costs of adaptation are comparatively low. Under these domestic conditions, how- ever, transformation countries are likely to engage in "anticipatory adaptation" in the first place; that is, they conform with liberal norms even in the absence of external reinforcement.[22] Thus, whereas socialization is highly successful, the independent contribution of international institutions to this outcome is limited.

The community organizations can have two kinds of impact on countries with a liberal party constellation. First, they reinforce and stabilize existing norm confor- mance and create a virtuous circle. They reward initial reform steps with material assistance and a strengthening of institutional ties. These rewards strengthen the norm-conforming government domestically, create incentives for further adaptation, and raise its stakes in integration: the costs of deviant behavior become increasingly high. Second, the community organizations may have an impact on compliance with particular rules that are not generally shared by liberal parties. In Central and Eastern Europe, this has mainly been the case with minority protection. It is only in these cases that intergovernmental reinforcement is expected to be a necessary condition of compliance in CEECs with a liberal party constellation. Just as in norm-violating

---

[22] Haggard et al. 1993.

CEECs with less favorable party constellations, however, it is still EU and NATO membership incentives, rather than less tangible rewards, that bring about domestic change.

In the mixed party constellation, there is no elite consensus on liberal-democratic reform and Western integration. Liberal parties or coalitions have been able to come to power in these systems, but did not exclusively shape their postcommunist development. Either superficially reconstructed communist parties initiated (but also slowed down and distorted) democratic transition from above (such as in Romania), or reform-adverse nationalists and populists benefited from the failure of reform-oriented parties to provide for economic recovery or efficient governance. In the former cases, norm conformance should have been slow and weak in the beginning. In the latter case, the level of conformance should have stagnated. In some of these countries (Bulgaria, Croatia, Romania, Slovakia), governmental authority has shifted more than once between the two camps. In these cases, I expect the level of conformance to change in a stop-and-go or up-and-down pattern.

Over time, however, these countries are still likely to be socialized effectively, although not as quickly and smoothly as the ones with a liberal party constellation.[23] When liberal parties control the government, the liberal domestic changes they institutionalize and the progress they make in Western integration raise the stakes in democratic consolidation and increase the costs of any future reversal. Populist parties therefore adapt their political goals to preserve the achieved benefits of integration. After the major nationalist-authoritarian parties of Croatia (Croatian Democratic Union or HDZ), Romania (Party of Social Democracy in Romania or PDSR), and Slovakia (Movement for a Democratic Slovakia or HZDS) had been voted out of government, Romania and Slovakia started accession negotiations with the EU, and Croatia became an EU associate and applied for membership. During the same time, these parties modified their programs and presented themselves as unequivocally pro-integration. When the PDSR and the HDZ were back in power in 2000 and 2003, they stayed the course of reform and integration. Thus, the lock-in effects of Western integration create path-dependency across changes in government and may, eventually, change the party constellation from mixed to liberal.

Finally, in the last group of countries, governments base their legitimacy on antiliberal (nationalist, populist, or communist) ideologies and/or rely on authoritarian practices for the preservation of power. Whereas governments may agree to cosmetic changes or tactical concessions to reap the political benefits of Western rewards, adaptation to liberal norms would undermine the basis of their rule. In these CEECs, socialization has little impact; autocracy, rather than democracy, is consolidated. Under reinforcement by reward, these countries are excluded from the benefits of assistance and membership. In contrast to states with mixed and liberal constellations, the stakes in reform therefore do not grow in countries with antiliberal regimes, and lock-in effects are absent. As a result, the conformance gap between these

[23] See McFaul 2002, 241–42.

countries and the rest of the CEECs widens. Only a domestic revolution (such as in Serbia in 2000) can reverse this trend.

In sum, assuming a socialization process characterized by strategic calculation and reinforcement, the following set of hypothetical expectations results from the discussion of domestic and international conditions of international socialization in the transformation countries of Central and Eastern Europe:

1. In norm-violating CEECs, only intergovernmental reinforcement offering the reward of EU and NATO membership can generate sustained compliance with liberal-democratic norms.

   Membership conditionality, however, is a necessary, but not a sufficient, condition of compliance.

2. The effects of EU and NATO membership incentives on sustained compliance with liberal-democratic norms will further depend on the party constellation of the target countries.

   a. In countries with a liberal party constellation, intergovernmental reinforcement by reward will not only be effective, but also quick and smooth.

   b. In countries with a mixed party constellation, intergovernmental reinforcement by reward will also be effective, but will take longer and proceed via stop-and-go or up-and-down processes.

   c. In countries with an antiliberal party constellation, intergovernmental reinforcement by reward will not be effective.[24]

In other words, EU or NATO membership incentives and a liberal or mixed party constellation are both necessary and jointly sufficient conditions for effective intergovernmental reinforcement in norm-violating target countries.

Data and Methods

To explore the empirical plausibility of my theoretical analysis and hypotheses, I proceed in two steps: correlation and process tracing. In the first step, I examine the hypotheses for individual countries in a simple bivariate correlation (between party constellations and compliance with Western liberal norms) based on graphical inspection. In order to capture as much variation as possible and to detect patterns of outcomes, I analyze a large number of CEECs: all ten new NATO members as well as the largest European successor states of the Soviet Union (Belarus, Russia, and Ukraine) and of Yugoslavia (Croatia and Serbia-Montenegro). To measure sustained compliance, I use the Freedom Index, the summary rating provided annually

[24] See Table 1 for country-specific predictions based on these hypotheses.

by Freedom House for civil liberties and political rights.[25] According to Diamond,[26] Freedom House ratings are "the best available empirical indicator[s] of 'liberal democracy.'" The Freedom House ratings allow me to measure overall conformance with the liberal-democratic community norms and rules in a large number of countries over an extended period of time. Consistently good ratings for a longer time period are a useful indicator of the sustained compliance that is used here as a proxy for effective socialization. They do not, however, give one information on compliance (and, possibly, variation in compliance) with specific rules and demands of Western organizations, nor do they tell one whether or not compliance resulted from internalization. In addition, even though the correlation provides a general plausibility probe for the hypothesized covariation, it cannot conclusively establish that intergovernmental reinforcement is a necessary condition of sustained compliance, nor does it tell one whether it was intergovernmental reinforcement that produced the observed behavior.

For these reasons, I turn to process-tracing analysis in the second empirical section. It serves a positive and a negative purpose. The positive purpose is to show that the international socialization of CEECs and their outcomes can be plausibly reconstructed as a process of intergovernmental reinforcement by reward, the results of which vary with the political costs of adaptation for the target governments. The negative purpose is to demonstrate that the process and the outcomes cannot be explained either by social influence or by normative suasion. Since process analysis is too resource-intensive for a large number of cases, and its output cannot be condensed as much as that of correlation, I examine only two cases representing different party constellations: Latvia (liberal party constellation) and Slovakia (mixed party constellation). Both cases are useful to analyze the impact of accession conditionality and domestic costs of adaptation, and to show the limits of alternative explanations. In order to obtain a detailed reconstruction of the process, I mainly use sources that provide day-to-day coverage of events: specialized news agencies and press reports.

Party Constellations and Conformance Patterns

In this section, I explore the hypothesized correlation between membership incentives, party constellations, and conformance patterns. Table 1 shows a classification of CEECs according to the independent variable "party constellations" and the expectations on socialization that follow from this classification.[27] As indicated in the theory section, I identified "liberal parties" on the basis of their general programmatic

---

[25] The Freedom Index combines the ratings for "civil liberties" and "political rights" and ranges from 1 (best) to 7 (worst). See ⟨http://www.freedomhouse.org⟩. I cross-checked the Freedom House ratings with Polity scores. Generally, correlation between Polity and Freedom House data is high—see Jaggers and Gurr 1995, 474—and the general patterns of scores for the CEECs largely coincide. (However, Ukraine is evaluated significantly better by Polity than by Freedom House; the opposite is true for the Baltic countries.) Moreover, there is less variation in Polity scores over time.

[26] Diamond 1996, 24.

[27] Note that the classification of CEECs is based on the 1990–2000 evidence.

Table 1. *Party Constellations and Predicted Socialization Patterns (1990–2002)*

Party constellation	Country	Major parties	Changes in major government party	Predicted socialization	Observed conformance pattern
Liberal	Czech Republic	ODS, CSSD	1998	Quick and smooth socialization; high and stable conformance	Quick, high, and stable conformance ahead of membership conditionality
	Hungary	MSzP, MDF, Fidesz	1990, 1994, 1998, 2002		
	Lithuania	Sajudis, LDDP, TS	1992, 1996, 2000		
	Poland	Post-Solidarity parties, SLD	1989, 1993, 1997, 2001		
	Slovenia	LDS, SLS	1992, 2000, 2000		
	Estonia	Pro Patria, Coalition Party	1992, 1994, 1995, 1999		High and stable conformance after membership conditionality
	Latvia	Latvia Way, TB/LNNK	1993, 1995, 1998, 2002		
Mixed	Bulgaria	BSP—UDF	1990, 1992, 1997, 2001	Slow and difficult socialization; medium and fluctuating levels of conformance	High conformance after slow and fluctuating process of improvement
	Croatia	HDZ—SDP	2000		
	Romania	PDSR—CDR	1996, 2000		
	Slovakia	HZDS—SDK	1994, 1994, 1998		
Antiliberal	Belarus	Lukashenka regime	Since 1994	No socialization; low and stable or deteriorating conformance	Stabilization of low conformance after small initial improvements
	Russia	Yeltsin/Putin presidential regime	Since 1991		
	Serbia-Montenegro	SPS, Milošević regime	Until 2000		
	Ukraine	Kuchma regime	Since 1994		

Source: Based on Ágh 1998b; Berglund, Hellén, and Aarebrot 1998; Blondel and Müller-Rommel 2001; and Ismayr 2002.

Note: BSP = Bulgarian Socialist Party; CDR = Democratic Convention of Romania; CSSD = Czech Social Democratic Party; Fidesz = Hungarian Civic Alliance; HDZ = Croatian Democratic Union; HZDS = Movement for a Democratic Slovakia; LDDP = Lithuanian Democratic Labor Party; LDS = Liberal Democracy of Slovenia; MDF = Hungarian Democratic Forum; MSzP = Hungarian Socialist Party; ODS = Civic Democratic Party; PDSR = Party of Social Democracy in Romania; SDK = Slovak Democratic Coalition; SDP = Social Democratic Party of Croatia; SLD = Democratic Left Alliance; SLS = Slovenian People's Party; SPS = Serbian Socialist Party; TB/LNNK = Union for the Fatherland and Freedom; TS = Homeland Union/Conservatives; UDF = Union of Democratic Forces.

Year

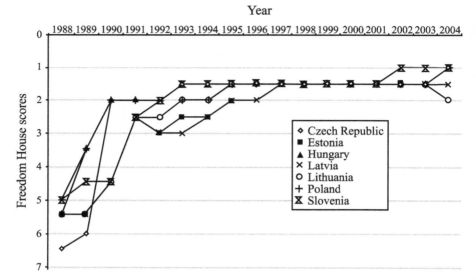

Figure 1. *Liberal party constellations and compliance*

orientation toward the Western, liberal international community and its values and norms. I mainly consulted the country-specific expert literature to do so. Because in some cases, liberal parties have violated, and nonliberal parties have conformed with, liberal norms, the relation between party orientation and compliance is not tautological.

EU and NATO offered the CEECs a general membership perspective in July 1993 (Copenhagen European Council) and January 1994 (Brussels NATO summit), but both organizations only began to select countries for accession talks in 1996 and 1997. Thus if membership incentives were a necessary and sufficient condition of sustained compliance, one should observe a marked improvement in Freedom House ratings in or immediately after this period. However, according to the hypotheses, the effect of external rewards is mediated by party constellations. Thus one should see prior norm conformance in the liberal countries and neither prior nor subsequent conformance in the antiliberal countries. In contrast, membership incentives should matter most in the mixed-constellation countries.

Figure 1 shows the Freedom House ratings for CEECs with a liberal party constellation between 1988 and 2004. The figure has three noticeable features. First, it illustrates a sharp rise in Freedom House ratings between 1988 and 1991. That is, the major improvements in democracy and human rights took place before the offer of EU and NATO membership and, indeed, before any European regional organization embarked on specific support activities for democracy in Central and Eastern Europe.

Second, many CEECs with a liberal party constellation also reached a high, Western level of conformance—the rating of 1.5 matches that of most Western countries—before the EU and NATO decided to admit CEECs. In 1993, the Czech Republic, Hungary, and Slovenia had a rating of 1.5; Poland and Lithuania were rated only

Year

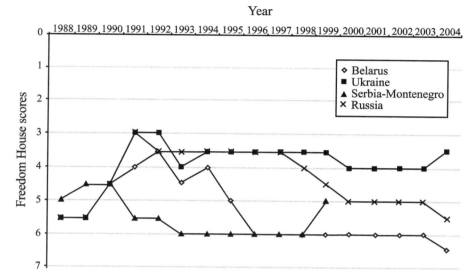

Figure 2. *Antiliberal party constellations and compliance*

slightly worse with a rating of 2.0. From 1995 onwards, these five countries have usually had a stable rating of 1.5 or better. Obviously, these are cases of domestically driven norm conformance or "self-socialization." In addition, high and sustained compliance in the absence of external incentives is an indication of internalization. However, this internalization cannot be attributed to specific activities of international institutions. As expected, international organizations appear to have had a stabilizing role at best.

Third, the two countries in this group that needed until 1996–97 to attain a rating of 1.5 were Estonia and Latvia. The reason for this slightly worse performance involved problems with the treatment and the rights of the large Russian-speaking minorities in both Baltic countries. The fact that the attainment of a high level of norm conformance coincided with the preparations of the EU and NATO for the first round of accession negotiations suggests a possible causal link between membership incentives and norm conformance. Moreover, it appears to confirm an independent role for international institutions when specific norms (such as minority protection) are contested among liberal parties (see the case study on Latvia, below).

In contrast, CEECs with antiliberal party constellations (see Figure 2) have generally scored badly throughout the postcommunist period.[28] None of them has been rated a "free country" even temporarily; conformance has been absent altogether or has remained at a low level. Following short periods of initial democratization immediately after the breakdown of communism, authoritarian or autocratic rule was consolidated (as indicated by stable ratings of 4.0 or worse after 1999). As expected,

---

[28] The line for Serbia-Montenegro ends in 1999. After the regime change of 2000, the country switched from "antiliberal" to "mixed."

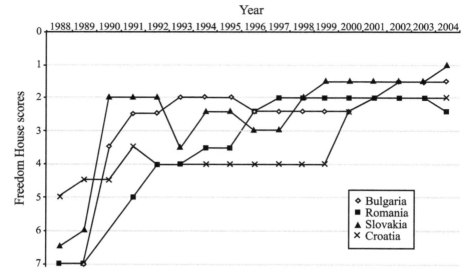

Figure 3. *Mixed party constellations and compliance*

EU and NATO accession conditionality did not have any discernible impact on democratization or democratic consolidation in these countries. Rather, conformance has deteriorated since the mid-1990s.

Figure 3 shows the development of norm conformance in the countries with a mixed constellation of major political forces. Again, I wish to emphasize three observations. First, as in the case of the liberal-constellation countries, big improvements in democracy and human rights took place between 1988 and 1991 and, thus, in the absence of specific socialization efforts by European regional organizations. In contrast with the liberal-constellation countries, however, these improvements did not attain high, Western levels of norm compliance before membership incentives became effective.

Second, the performance of mixed-constellation countries follows individual patterns, mostly reflecting changes in government. The up-and-down pattern of norm conformance in Slovakia mirrors the alternation between the populist and authoritarian-style Mečiar governments (1993 and 1994–98) and the reform coalitions of 1994 and since 1998. The ratings for Croatia worsened with the consolidation of the nationalist Tudjman regime at the beginning of the Yugoslav succession wars, and improved markedly after his death and the switch to a liberal coalition in 2000. Romania shows a slow but overall successful, stop-and-go process of compliance. During the first, postcommunist, Iliescu regime (1991–96), compliance improved slowly but the ratings did not get better than 3.5. The reform coalition (1996–2000) achieved a rating of 2.0. Only the Bulgarian case does not provide evidence for the conformance effect of mixed party constellations. According to Freedom House, the ratings were even better during the government of the Socialist Party than under the reformist Union of Democratic Forces between 1997 and 2001.

Finally, Figure 3 shows the expected long-term convergence toward high levels of norm conformance. Since 2000, the ratings for the four countries vary between 1.5 and 2.5, which mirrors the state of compliance in the liberal-constellation countries between 1994 and 1996. The clearest indicator for a lock-in effect of EU and NATO integration is Romania, where the rating of 2.0 was maintained after the return to power of the PDSR and Iliescu in 2000. A similar effect can already be observed for Croatia after the return of the HZS in 2003.

Generally, on graphical inspection, the results of the exploratory correlation analysis broadly corroborate the hypothetical expectations of the effects of party constellations on long-term norm conformance under a policy of intergovernmental reinforcement by reward. They are, however, too vague to demonstrate the impact of EU and NATO membership incentives or to exclude alternative mechanisms of socialization.

Process-Tracing Analysis: The International Socialization of Slovakia and Latvia

I selected Slovakia (under Vladimír Mečiar) and Latvia for the process-tracing analysis because they represent extreme cases in their category of countries and are best suited to demonstrate the causal relevance of intergovernmental reinforcement by rewards and domestic adaptation costs. Among the mixed-constellation countries, Slovakia has been the most likely case of effective socialization. It quickly established institutional ties with the Western organizations and has been a serious candidate for early membership; it has a vibrant and Western-oriented civil society with relatively strong transnational ties. The case study will show, however, that the governmental-power costs of adaptation prevented compliance during the Meciar government in spite of these favorable conditions.

Latvia is special because it represents a country with a liberal party constellation and a record of sustained noncompliance in the area of minority rights. The case study shows that a liberal party constellation is neither a sufficient condition of automatic compliance nor of effective persuasion or social influence. It demonstrates that even in a socialization-friendly domestic environment, intergovernmental reinforcement by tangible rewards has been a necessary condition of overcoming norm violation. Thus, whereas the Slovak study serves to establish the causal relevance of domestic adaptation costs (under otherwise favorable international and transnational conditions), the Latvian study emphasizes the crucial impact of external incentives (under otherwise favorable domestic conditions).

Slovakia under Mečiar

In September 1994, Mečiar and his party, the HZDS, won the parliamentary elections and formed a coalition with the Slovak National Party (SNS) and the Association of the Workers of Slovakia (ZRS). Immediately after the elections, the coalition embarked on an authoritarian path. Above all, it sought to concentrate political power in the hands of the prime minister: it curbed the rights of the opposition in parliament and harassed its members; it defamed, ignored, and tried to force out of office President Michal Kováč; it ignored decisions by independent courts; and it brought public administration at all levels under the control of its followers. Moreover, it expanded governmental control of the audiovisual media, applied financial pressure on the private media, and restricted the freedom of the press. Finally, it was hostile toward any autonomous rights of the Hungarian minority, which makes up around 12 percent of the population. In sum, the political style of the Mečiar government between 1994–98 is well-characterized as a "tyranny of the majority."[29]

Western Policy. In reaction to the authoritarian turn in Slovak politics, Western organizations used a variety of instruments. In line with a policy of reinforcement by reward, EU and NATO held out the carrot of membership but did not threaten to suspend existing agreements on EU association or NATO partnership. This policy was accompanied by an intensive shaming and shunning campaign against the Mečiar government.

Almost immediately after the 1994 elections, the EU began to criticize the political development in Slovakia.[30] After the session of the Slovak parliament in November 1994, in which the new majority replaced all major positions in parliament and the state media with their followers, the EU issued a first *démarche.* Unmistakably pointing at its accession conditionality, the EU expressed "concern at some political developments since the election," declared that a strengthening of relations with Brussels "involves not only benefits, but also obligations on Slovakia's side and will depend on the sort of policies which the new Slovak government pursues," and hoped that Slovakia would "thoroughly evaluate its own interests and will continue pursuing the course of democratic reforms."[31] In October 1995, the growing tension between the government and President Kovác triggered two further, separate *démarches* by the EU and the United States. The EU *démarche* clearly reminded the Mečiar government of "the EU's common democratic practices" and of the fact that "Slovakia is an associated country in a pre-accession period and . . . the criteria of approval at the Copenhagen Summit are applicable to it."[32]

In 1996, the Slovak government received increasingly concrete signals that its chances of joining the EU or NATO had diminished sharply. The EU ambassador, at a meeting near Bratislava, said that for Slovakia there still was "much work to be done and in this task there can be no delay." He added that "it is only through its own efforts in the field of democracy, as in the economy, that Slovakia can hope to join the EU."[33] The U.S. ambassador issued a similar warning with regard to NATO. When the U.S. Congress appropriated funds for the preparation of NATO enlargement in 1996, Slovakia was not on the list of beneficiaries. Finally, in 1997, Slovakia was not invited either to open accession negotiations with the EU or to join NATO. Even after

[29] See Bútora and Bútorová 1999, 84; and Schneider 1997.
[30] See Henderson 2002, 88–93; Krause 2003, 66–70; and Malová and Rybář 2003, 104–107.
[31] *BBC Summary of World Broadcasts,* 30 November 1994, Part 2, Cental Europe and the Balkans; EE/2166/A; *Financial Times,* 9 August 1995, 2.
[32] *Agence Europe,* 27 October 1995.
[33] Quoted according to Goldman 1999, 155. See also *Agence Europe,* 25 October 1996.

it had been decided that Slovakia would not be among the first-round candidates, the Western organizations continued to assure Slovakia that it was eligible to become a member in principle. Representatives of EU organizations and member states offered Slovakia a last chance to demonstrate its commitment to European integration and liberal democracy by quickly introducing a few changes in parliament.[34] However, the Western organizations were increasingly calling for a change in government as a prerequisite of membership. For instance, in October 1997, U.S. Deputy Secretary of State Strobe Talbott told a delegation of Slovak opposition leaders that "NATO's door is still open to Slovakia with the right democratic changes."[35] These calls for a change through elections were paralleled by transnational advice and financial support to NGOs and opposition parties from Western foundations, parties, and European party federations.[36]

In sum, the international conditions of effective reinforcement were extremely positive. Both the EU and NATO articulated their conditional promise of accession early, clearly, and consistently. However, domestic cost-benefit calculations frustrated the efforts of the regional organizations.

Target State Response.   In spite of the unambiguous Western warnings and the high stakes that EU and NATO membership involved, Western policy had no major or lasting impact on the compliance record of the Mečiar government. The most frequent discursive responses were denial and accusations of inconsistency: the Slovak government reproached the West for lacking information or misperceiving the situation in the country, for interfering with its domestic affairs, and for using double standards. Government representatives described the state of democracy in Slovakia as at least as good as in the other Central European countries, or emphasized the positive economic situation. Or they simply blamed the opposition or international media for the "distorted image" of Slovakia abroad.[37] Thus, the Mečiar government did not openly contest or reject Western norms, but sought to manipulate them rhetorically to avoid their practical implications.

At the behavioral level, Western criticism did little to change the authoritarian style of the government. Even the single most important success of Western policy, the signing of the Basic Treaty between Slovakia and Hungary, committing Slovakia to the Council of Europe (CE) guidelines for the treatment of national minorities, was compromised and rendered ineffective by domestic measures. Signed by Slovakia at the Stability Pact conference in March 1995, the treaty met with fierce resistance from Mečiar's nationalist coalition partners at home. Slovakia finally ratified the treaty in March 1996, but only after the government had planned several laws to dilute the treaty provisions.[38] First, the Language Law prescribed the exclusive use of the Slovak language for all public and official acts. Second, a territorial reform

---

[34] Krause 2003, 68.
[35] Goldman 1999, 166.
[36] See, for example, Bútora and Bútorová 1999, 89–90; and Pridham 1999, 1237.
[37] See, for instance, Goldman 1999, 159–64; Schneider 1997, 33–34; and *RFE/RL Newsline,* 13 February 1998.
[38] See, for example, Leff 1997, 250; and Schneider 1997, 20–24.

redefined administrative districts so that the share of Hungarians would remain low enough to deny them self-government without violating international norms. Third, the government passed a "Law on the Protection of the Republic," an amendment to the Penal Code, that was primarily, but not exclusively, directed against the Hungarian minority by threatening anyone allegedly undermining the state with criticism. Fourth, the Slovak government unilaterally added an appendix to the treaty rejecting the granting of collective minority rights. Finally, it flatly declined to pass a new language law according to the recommendations of the OSCE High Commissioner on National Minorities (HCNM).[39]

The failure of reinforcement by reward in the Slovak case can be attributed mainly to the preponderance of antiliberal parties and domestic political concerns of power preservation. Both the right-wing nationalist SNS and the left-wing ZRS favored neutralism and close collaboration with Russia, were staunchly anti-Western parties, and welcomed rather than deplored Slovakia's exclusion from EU and NATO membership.[40] The HZDS and Mečiar are more difficult to judge. The HZDS started out as a broad, ideologically diverse movement under the charismatic leadership of Mečiar. Although successive secessions and splits, on the whole, made the party more authoritarian and nationalist in the course of time, it remained without a specific ideological foundation or orientation. The HZDS program is best described as populist; the party "predominantly represented the older, less educated, rural, and less reform-minded part of the population."[41] The party was neither anti-Western, nor antiliberal, nor anti-Hungarian in principle. Nor, however, was it intrinsically committed to Western integration, liberal values and norms, or minority protection.

Mečiar's attitude toward Western integration and conditionality is best described as instrumental. He had allied himself with the SNS and the ZRS in order to return to government in 1994, and because the other parties in parliament refused to enter into a coalition with him, he needed to accommodate their nationalist and anti-Western preferences to remain in power. The primacy of domestic power preservation led to a dualistic policy. Externally, Mečiar and his foreign ministers ceremonially upheld Slovakia's bid to join the Western organizations and rhetorically vowed to fulfill the prerequisites of membership eventually. In its program, the Mečiar government accorded EU and NATO membership the first priority among its foreign policy goals, and when the new prime minister met EP President Klaus Haensch in January 1995, he assured him "that Slovakia would respect all the obligations incumbent upon countries which are applicants for admission to the EU," in particular with regard to the Hungarian minority and the privatization of the economy.[42] This promise was constantly reiterated and culminated in a series of last-minute rhetorical moves to secure participation in EU accession negotiations in 1997.[43] Internally, however, these promises were never implemented because Mečiar wanted to keep both his coalition partners and his authoritarian control of Slovak politics. Exposing the inconsistency

---

[39] *RFE/RL Newsline,* 5 October 1997.
[40] See Goldman 1999, 153, 157–58; Leff 1997, 243; and Samson 1997, 9.
[41] Bútora and Bútorová 1999, 81.
[42] *Agence Europe,* 26 January 1995.
[43] See *Agence Europe,* 26 February 1997; 28 June 1997; 14 October 1997; and 23 October 1997.

of this dualistic policy, Slovak foreign minister Pavol Hamzík resigned in May 1997, arguing that "Slovakia's vital international interests" were being subordinated to the domestic power struggle.[44]

Alternative Mechanisms. Could one explain the lack of compliance by the Mečiar government otherwise? First, it is true that core conditions for the effectiveness of social learning or social influence (norm resonance and identification with the Western aspiration group) were not particularly favorable. However, this applies mainly to Mečiar's coalition partners, and less to the HZDS or Mečiar himself (who had embraced Slovak nationalism for instrumental reasons and wanted to lead Slovakia into the Western organizations). Thus, the overriding concern with the preservation of domestic power is an indispensable element in explaining why both persuasive appeals and reward-based reinforcement had such a small impact. Even rhetorical entrapment did not work as an opening on the way to behavioral change and internalization.[45]

Despite comparatively favorable conditions, transnational reinforcement did not prove effective either. First, support for democracy in Slovakia was as strong as in the more consolidated democracies of the Czech Republic, Hungary, and Poland.[46] In addition, Slovak society was highly concerned about the deterioration of the human rights situation in their country. Of all the EU candidate countries, Slovakia saw their political development (between 1993 and 1997) most negatively.[47] Second, Slovakia has one of the most strongly developed (in terms of number of NGOs) and active civil societies in Central and Eastern Europe.[48] Third, Slovak opposition parties were linked transnationally with, and supported by, European party organizations. Nevertheless, transnational influences failed to change Slovak policy while Mečiar was in power, and were largely redundant in bringing about change in the parliamentary elections of 1998.[49]

The case study of Slovakia during the Mečiar government of 1994–98 confirms the postulated mechanisms and conditions of international socialization in Central and Eastern Europe. The process was primarily characterized by accession conditionality and by the self-serving manipulation of international norms ("rhetorical action") on the part of the Slovak government. However, in spite of the highest external incentives the European international community can offer, the power costs of Slovakia's nationalist-authoritarian government undermined their allure. Despite societal conditions that were highly favorable by regional standards, transnational reinforcement did not have a decisive impact either.

However, the Slovak case does not sufficiently discriminate between alternative socialization mechanisms. Conditions of successful reinforcement by reward were as bad as those of successful social influence or normative suasion; EU and NATO

---

[44] *RFE/RL Newsline,* 27 May 1997.
[45] Risse and Sikkink 1999, 16.
[46] See Stankovsky, Plasser, and Ulram 1998, 80. Some figures were even better than in the Central European neighboring countries. Ibid., 81, 83.
[47] Stankovsky, Plasser, and Ulram 1998, 78.
[48] See Kaldor and Vejvoda 1999, 16, 19.
[49] Ki-ause 2003, 78–81.

failed as much as the OSCE and the CE to produce compliance. I therefore analyze a second case—the promotion of minority rights in Latvia.

Latvia

Latvia is the Baltic state with the highest proportion of so-called "Russian-speakers." When it became independent from the Soviet Union in 1991, citizenship of the new state was granted only to the citizens of the interwar Latvian Republic and their descendants. This left 30 percent of the population stateless and deprived of political rights. Moreover, the government set prohibitively high conditions for their naturalization and enacted discriminating laws on the use of the Latvian language, education, and economic rights.

Western Policy.   Since 1993, the promotion of minority rights in Latvia had been mainly entrusted to Max van der Stoel, the OSCE's HCNM. In his frequent visits and subsequent recommendations to the Latvian government, van der Stoel used a mixture of expert advice, persuasion, and social influence to make Latvia comply with Western demands on minority policy. In order to induce Latvia to amend its laws, van der Stoel referred to Latvia's prior commitments, its international legal obligations, its obligations as a democratic country seeking membership in Western organizations, and to the example of other member countries of the Western community.[50]

For instance, in his April 1993 letter to Foreign Minister Georgs Andrejevs, in which he urged Latvia to pass a citizenship law with a naturalization requirement of only five years of residence, van der Stoel justified his suggestions as being "inspired . . . by the various CSCE [Conference on Security and Cooperation in Europe] documents to which Latvia . . . has subscribed" and recommended that Latvia should "restrict itself to requirements for citizenship which . . . would not go beyond those used by most CSCE states."[51] When he responded to the draft citizenship law in December of the same year, he conveyed his "impression that, within the community of CSCE states, the solution of citizenship issues is seen as being closely connected with democratic principles" so that, as a consequence of the denial of political rights to a large part of the population, "the character of the democratic system in Latvia might even be put into question. In this connection I refer to the 1990 CSCE Copenhagen Document which states that the basis of the authority and legitimacy of all governments is the will of the people."[52]

The CE, the EU, and NATO went beyond persuasion and shaming and linked compliance with membership. In December 1993, the CE stated clearly that Latvia would not be admitted as a member if it did not change the citizenship law according to the HCNM's recommendations. In July 1997, in its Opinions on the applicant countries, the European Commission judged Latvia to fulfill the political criteria for admission in general, but mirrored the concerns of the HCNM by demanding that "Latvia needs to

---

[50] See Zaagman 1999 and the documents cited there.
[51] van der Stoel 1993a.
[52] van der Stoel 1993b.

take measures to accelerate naturalisation procedures to enable the Russian-speaking noncitizens to become better integrated into Latvian society." Finally, in the run-up to NATO's Prague summit of 2002, NATO and U.S. representatives urged Latvia to abolish its language proficiency requirements for people standing in elections. "The NATO nations will be watching very carefully what you do this year in relation to the election laws so that they conform to standards throughout NATO countries and the wider international community," Secretary General George Robertson said in February 2002 in a speech to Latvia's parliament.[53]

Target State Response. In general, the major demands of the HCNM and his efforts to generate compliance by combining teaching and shaming were not effective alone. Only when they were linked to Latvia's accession to Western organizations did the Latvian government and parliament reluctantly give in. This process repeated itself several times on different issues.

In response to the April 1993 letter of van der Stoel, Foreign Minister Andrejevs argued defensively and evasively. He pointed out that the Supreme Council had no legal mandate to change the body of Latvia's citizenship law, so that a new law would have to await the election of a new parliament (the Saeima) in June 1993;[54] and in response to the December 1993 letter, he explained that the Latvian government would wait for further recommendations by other international organizations before expressing any views on van der Stoel's suggestions.[55] The Latvian parliament initially ignored the HCNM's suggestions altogether. Instead of granting citizenship to all persons with five years of residence in Latvia, the draft law of November 1993 made naturalization dependent on an annual quota to be determined by the government and parliament according to economic and demographic considerations. Although van der Stoel, in response to the quota system, had suggested that it be replaced by a gradual but legally determined naturalization system, the citizenship law of June 1994 modified the draft law only slightly. However, Latvian President Guntis Ulmanis, who had been consulting intensively with representatives of the CE (which had made accession conditional on a change of the law), sent the law back to the Saeima for revision. He justified his veto by citing international repercussions that would spell the danger of Latvia's isolation in Europe and damage its international reputation.[56] One month later, the Saeima passed a revised law, which envisaged widening windows of naturalization for different age cohorts until 2003. Although the time frame was longer than suggested by the HCNM, the law basically followed the principle of gradual naturalization and met with international approval. Having cleared this crucial hurdle, Latvia was admitted to the CE in early 1995.[57]

---

[53] See *NATO Enlargement Daily Brief,* 21 February 2002; and "U.S. NATO Team in Latvia," *NATO Enlargement Daily Brief,* 26 February 2002.

[54] Andrejevs 1993.

[55] Andrejevs 1994.

[56] Although the CE does not offer tangible rewards, it is generally seen as an antechamber to the EU and NATO.

[57] See Jubulis 1996.

Yet the implementation of the citizenship law did not meet expectations, because only a minor proportion of those eligible used and successfully completed the naturalization procedures. In his letters of October 1996 and May 1997 to Foreign Minister Valdis Birkavs, van der Stoel therefore made several recommendations to overcome the "stagnation of the naturalization process": the reduction of naturalization fees, the simplification of the tests required of new citizens, and, above all, the granting of citizenship to stateless children and the abolishment of the naturalization windows.[58] The response was again evasive and defensive. Birkavs pointed to "political difficulties" and an "ongoing discussion," defended Latvian practice as compatible with international law, and declared that a change in the law had to be decided by the Saeima, not the government.[59]

After the European Commission had published its Opinion on Latvia mirroring the HCNM's demands, the Latvian government drew up a package of laws in line with the OSCE recommendations. At the same time, however, the Saeima's working group drafted amendments that, according to van der Stoel, did not "comply in any way with my original Recommendations."[60] In May 1998, the lawmakers approved an amendment that would allow stateless children to become citizens only at the age of sixteen and only if they could prove sufficient knowledge of the Latvian language.[61] On 1 June, Foreign Minister Birkavs urged the parliament to comply with OSCE recommendations because Latvia would otherwise risk losing allies in Europe and the United States.[62] Later in June, the amendments as proposed by the government were approved by a center-left majority in the Saeima and hailed by both the U.S. administration and the EU as furthering Latvia's integration into European and transatlantic structures.[63]

Still, the party of Prime Minister Guntars Krasts (LNNK) called for a referendum. Ahead of the referendum, Western representatives stepped up their efforts to influence the electorate. Van der Stoel assured Latvians, on the one hand, that the amendments were "not dangerous"; on the other hand, he made it clear that the outcome of the referendum would have significant influence on Latvia's international position: U.S. President Bill Clinton had stressed that the amendments were essential for the country's integration into Euro-Atlantic institutions.[64] In the domestic debate, President Ulmanis pleaded: "Let those who have decided to vote for a rejection [of the amendments] think as to whether they are giving Latvia positive impetus or whether their vote will isolate Latvia from the rest of the world."[65] On 3 October 1998, 53 percent of the voters approved the amendments.

A further case is the Latvian state language bill. In 1998, the Saeima drafted a law that was criticized by the OSCE and the CE because it not only required the use of the

---

[58] van der Stoel 1996 and 1997.
[59] Birkavs 1996 and 1997.
[60] van der Stoel 1998.
[61] *RFE/RL Newsline*, 21 May 1998.
[62] *RFE/RL Newsline*, 2 June 1998.
[63] *RFE/RL Newsline*, 23 June 1998; and 24 June 1998.
[64] *RFE/RL Newsline*, 26 August 1998; and 6 September 1998.
[65] *RFE/RL Newsline*, 23 September 1998; and 29 September 1998.

state language in the public sector but also obligated private bodies and enterprises to conduct their activities in Latvian.[66] In April 1999, van der Stoel warned that passage of the bill in its current form might impair Riga's chances of integration into the EU. One day later, he was joined by Prime Minister Vilis Kriš-topāns, who stressed that the legislation must be compatible with Latvia's international obligations.[67] The Finnish EU presidency warned that the language law could damage Latvia's chances of joining the EU, but a large majority of the Saeima voted in favor nevertheless. At that point, the new president Vaira Vīķe-Freiberga refused to sign the law and asked the parliament to revise it to conform with EU legislation—a decision "warmly welcome" by van der Stoel.[68] On 9 December 1999, the Saeima passed a revised law that was "essentially in conformity" with international norms according to the HCNM. A few days later, Latvia was invited to begin accession negotiations with the EU.

A final case concerns the language proficiency requirements for candidates in local and national elections. Copying the linkage established by van der Stoel, Peter Semneby, the head of the OSCE mission to Latvia, called for an abolition of these requirements that "might prove an obstacle to EU and NATO accession."[69] In December 2001, a few days before the OSCE Permanent Council discussed the closure of the OSCE mission in Latvia, which the Latvian government regarded as an important step toward EU and NATO membership, President Vīķe-Freiberga announced an initiative to heed Semneby's call.[70] In May 2002, the Latvian parliament amended the election law to clear this last political hurdle before the EU's and NATO's upcoming enlargement decisions. According to Nils Muiznieks, the director of the Latvian Center for Human Rights and Ethnic Studies, these were the main incentives for legal change:

It was in the guidelines for closing the OSCE mission [in Latvia], and Latvia just had a case [against the language law] brought before the UN [Human Rights Committee] and another case before the European Court of Human Rights. But the only thing that really pushed the Latvian government to move in this direction was the fact that a number of NATO countries, especially America, said, "You must change this law!"[71]

In a parallel move to appease Latvian nationalists, the constitution was amended to strengthen the role of the Latvian language in parliament and local elected bodies.

Just as the in Slovak case, the Latvian case can be explained by the interaction of external incentives and domestic costs. Whereas weak incentives and high domestic costs blocked compliance initially, reduced costs of adaptation together with EU and NATO membership incentives produced norm-conforming behavior in the second half of the 1990s. Initially, the center-right governments that dominated Latvian politics in the 1990s perceived the naturalization of the large non-Latvian population as a grave political threat. In 1990 and 1991, a great majority of the "Russian-speakers" had

---

[66] For the CE, see Parliamentary Assembly 1999.
[67] *RFE/RL Newsline,* 19 April 1999; and 20 April 1999.
[68] Süddeutsche Zeitung, 16 July 1999; *RFE/RL Newsline, 7* July 1999; 9 July 1999; 15 July 1999; 1 September 1999; and van der Stoel 1999.
[69] *RFE/RL Newsline,* 15 November 2001.
[70] *RFE/RL Newsline, 7* December 2001; and 19 December 2001; Nick Coleman, "OSCE Mission Closures Boost EU and NATO Hopes for Estonia and Latvia," *Agence France Presse,* 19 December 2001.
[71] Quoted in Mite 2002.

voted against independence from the Soviet Union. Moreover, they favored parties on the left of the political spectrum. As a result, in a situation in which Russian troops were still stationed on Latvian territory and the Russian foreign policy doctrine put Latvia in its sphere of influence, the Latvian governments feared that large-scale naturalization would threaten Latvian independence and culture and strengthen the influence of Russia and the political left. Finally, the lack of a credible perspective of EU and NATO membership increased the sense of vulnerability. In the second half of the 1990s, however, the EU and NATO not only offered Latvia concrete prospects of accession. But, in addition, Russia had withdrawn its troops, the minority increasingly accepted Latvia as an independent state, and gradual naturalization did not upset the composition of the electorate in favor of the left.[72]

The process-tracing analysis reveals the crucial importance of membership incentives by Western organizations to turn around—usually at the last moment—the procrastinating behavior and evasive rhetorical action of a widely unconvinced Latvian body politic. Counterfactually speaking, it is safe to conclude that without these Western incentives and deadlines, Latvian laws relating to the treatment of national minorities would not have been changed. At least, the timing of the changes could not be explained otherwise.

Alternative Mechanisms.   The conditions of social influence and social learning were more favorable in Latvia than in the Slovak case. Whereas Latvian ethnic nationalism and anti-Russian sentiments represent "ingrained beliefs that are inconsistent with the persuader's message,"[73] Latvia's governments shared liberal norms in general and regarded the Western organizations as authoritative organizations of the international community to which they sought to belong.[74] Moreover, the initial efforts of the HCNM were of a deliberative and nonpoliticized kind.

Yet persuasion and social influence failed to change Latvian policy when domestic political costs were high, and even when domestic costs decreased, they did not trigger compliance unless they were explicitly linked to the membership decisions of Western organizations. On the other hand, the lack of resonance for minority rights among the Latvian parties in government did not prevent behavioral compliance when the cost-benefit calculation was positive. Furthermore, the fact that conditionality had to be used time and again during the past decade to overcome the defiance of Latvian governments and lawmakers, and to bring Latvian legislation in line with Western demands, shows that change has not resulted from persuasion and has not led to internalization or habitualization. Finally, the Latvian case demonstrates that the positive effects of a liberal party constellation on sustained compliance cannot be fully explained as identity-driven behavior. If liberal socializees perceive adapting to individual community norms as costly, there is no compliance without reinforcement and net benefits.

[72] Knobel 2004.
[73] Checkel 2001, 563.
[74] See Jubulis 1996, 69; Plakans 1997, 285; and Smith et al. 1998, 108.

In sum, the Latvian case study confirms that membership incentives and low domestic political costs are both necessary and jointly sufficient conditions of effective reinforcement and behavioral adaptation—even if the rule-breaking country has a liberal party constellation. With a view to discriminating between alternative socialization mechanisms, the case study clearly demonstrates that only intergovernmental reinforcement by rewards—the linking of the HCNM's demands with membership in the Western organizations—produced compliance—even though the conditions of social influence and learning were favorable, and shaming and persuasion were dominant in the initial socialization process conducted by the HCNM.

Conclusion

The international socialization of Central and Eastern Europe is work in progress. At the beginning of the 1990s, European regional community organizations set out to induct the transition countries into their core liberal norms and rules. When and how have their efforts been successful?

In this chapter, I have made two core arguments. First, whereas European regional organizations have used a wide array of instruments and channels to promote their rules and norms, only intergovernmental reinforcement offering the high and tangible reward of EU and NATO membership had the potential to produce norm-conforming domestic change in norm-violating countries. Second, however, EU and NATO membership incentives only worked in favor of sustained compliance when the domestic costs of adaptation for the target governments were low. This has most clearly been the case in countries in which all major parties are liberal-democratic and oriented toward Western integration (liberal party constellation). But membership incentives have also been effective, thanks to path-dependency, in CEECs with alternating liberal and nationalist-authoritarian governments, although the process has taken longer to succeed. Correspondingly, one can observe high levels of norm conformance in CEECs with a liberal party constellation since the mid-1990s, and after 2000 in those with mixed party constellations. In contrast, the authoritarian systems of Eastern Europe have not been positively affected by EU or NATO membership incentives at all.

The international socialization of Central and Eastern Europe thus provides evidence for socialization by reinforcement based on strategic calculation. Both the relevant processes and their divergent outcomes demonstrate the predominant role of conditional incentives by international organizations and of cost-benefit calculations and rhetorical action by their targets. Compliance with community norms was set as a condition for reaping the political and material benefits of membership in the community organizations, and nonmember governments weighed these benefits against the domestic political costs that adaptation would involve.

Whereas there is rather conclusive and cumulative evidence from a number of recent multicase comparative studies on the causal relevance and effectiveness of membership incentives and domestic constellations in the promotion of democracy and human rights in Central and Eastern Europe,[75] the central question in the context of this volume is whether there is also evidence for internalization. Has the switch from a logic of consequences to one of appropriateness occurred? If so, have international institutions been the relevant promoters of internalization? The findings of this analysis suggest that both questions cannot be answered jointly in the affirmative.

On the one hand, the sustained compliance with liberal norms in most of the CEECs with a liberal party constellation is strongly indicative of internalization. These countries have attained high conformance levels ahead of EU or NATO accession conditionality and have maintained them across numerous elections and changes in government. This observation suggests, however, that the contribution of international institutions to internalization has been small. At best, they have helped to reinforce and stabilize a preexisting domestic consensus (which may well have formed by diffuse transnational influences during the Cold War). It is highly probable that these countries would have embarked and continued on the path of democratic consolidation in the absence of any norm promotion by international organizations, be it in the form of persuasion, social influence, or membership incentives.

On the other hand, the reinforcement-driven changes in many other Central and Eastern European candidates for EU and NATO membership provide strong evidence for the causal relevance of international institutions as promoters of norms and rules. The case of minority rights in Latvia shows that this kind of promotion was in some instances even necessary in countries with a liberal party constellation. However, international organizations were most important in the mixed-constellation countries. Membership incentives and progress in European and transatlantic integration led nationalist-authoritarian opposition parties to "rebrand" themselves as pro-Western and to vow conformance with liberal norms. In these cases of clear external impact, however, the switch to internalization is not sufficiently evident yet. First of all, EU and NATO membership conditionality was in place until the end of the period of examination (2003). Thus, it cannot be excluded that norm conformance was driven by external incentives rather than internalization. The Latvian case study suggests that, even in this otherwise well-consolidated democracy, compliance with Western demands for minority rights has been purely instrumental to the very end. Likewise, it is too early to conclude that the nationalist-authoritarian parties of Romania, Slovakia, or Croatia have transformed themselves reliably into liberal parties. Whereas one can safely infer from the evidence that intergovernmental reinforcement has produced major norm-conforming behavioral change in the region, one cannot know, at the time of writing, whether this change has been internalized as a result of cognitive dissonance or habitualization.

The true test comes after EU and NATO accession. Although both organizations will continue to monitor political developments in the new member states, and also possess informal and formal instruments for sanctioning noncompliant behavior,[76]

---

[75] See Kelley 2004; Kubicek 2003; Schimmelfennig forthcoming; and Vachudova 2001.

[76] The most formal instrument is Article 7 of the Treaty on European Union. It empowers EU institutions to suspend the rights of a member state in case of a serious and persistent breach of the core community norms.

the strongest weapon will be not available anymore. If norm conformance in the pre-accession period has indeed been based on strategic calculation alone, there should be a strong incentive for governments to disregard minority rights, and for the nationalist and populist parties to exploit discontent with liberal reform and European integration and to revert to authoritarian programs and practices. Only if they forgo this opportunity in the absence of external sanctions will one have strong evidence of internalization. Only then will one know whether international socialization by reinforcement has been complete.

References

Ágh, Attila. 1998a. *Emerging Democracies in East Central Europe and the Balkans.* Cheltenham, England: Edward Elgar.

———. 1998b. *The Politics of Central Europe.* London: Sage.

Andrejevs, Georgs. 1993. Latvian Minister of Foreign Affairs' Reply to the OSCE High Commissioner to the National Minorities of April 18, 1993. Available at ⟨http://www.arts.uwaterloo.ca/MINELRES/osce/counrec.htm⟩. Accessed 22 June 2005.

———. 1994. Latvian Minister of Foreign Affairs' Reply to the OSCE High Commissioner to the National Minorities of January 25, 1994. OSCE Ref. Com. No. 8. Available at ⟨http://www.arts.uwaterloo.ca/MINELRES/osce/counrec.htm⟩. Accessed 22 June 2005.

Baldwin, David. 1971. The Power of Positive Sanctions. *World Politics* 24 (1):19–38.

Berglund, Sten, Thomas Hellén, and Frank H. Aarebrot, eds. 1998. *The Handbook of Political Change in Eastern Europe.* Cheltenham, England: Edward Elgar.

Birch, Sarah. 2000. Elections and Representation in Post-Communist Eastern Europe. In *Elections in Central and Eastern Europe: The First Wave*, edited by Hans-Dieter Klingemann, Ekkehard Mochmann, and Kenneth Newton, 13–35. Berlin: Sigma.

Birkavs, Valdis. 1996. Latvian Minister of Foreign Affairs' Reply of December 24, 1996, to the OSCE High Commissioner on National Minorities. No. 31/1003-7767. Available at ⟨http://www.arts.uwaterloo.ca/MINELRES/osce/counrec.htm⟩. Accessed 22 June 2005.

———. 1997. Latvian Minister of Foreign Affairs' Reply of September 11, 1997, to the OSCE High Commissioner on National Minorities. No. 31/666-5680. Available at ⟨http://www.arts.uwaterloo.ca/MINELRES/osce/counrec.htm⟩. Accessed 22 June 2005.

Blondel, Jean, and Ferdinand Müller-Rommel. 2001. *Cabinets in Eastern Europe.* Basingstoke, England: Palgrave.

Bútora, Martin, and Zora Bútorová. 1999. Slovakia's Democratic Awakening. *Journal of Democracy* 10 (1):80–95.

Checkel, Jeffrey T. 2001. Why Comply? Social Learning and European Identity Change. *International Organization* 55 (3):553–88.

Davis, James W., Jr. 2000. *Threats and Promises: The Pursuit of International Influence.* Baltimore, Md.: Johns Hopkins University Press.

Diamond, Larry. 1996. Is the Third Wave Over? *Journal of Democracy* 7 (3):20–37.

Elster, Jon. 1983. *Sour Grapes: Studies in the Subversion of Rationality.* Cambridge: Cambridge University Press.

———. 1989. *Nuts and Bolts for the Social Sciences.* Cambridge: Cambridge University Press.

Goldgeier, James M. 1999. *Not Whether But When: The US Decision to Enlarge NATO.* Washington, D.C.: Brookings Institution.

Goldman, Minton F. 1999. *Slovakia since Independence: A Struggle for Democracy.* Westport, Conn.: Praeger.

Haggard, Stephan, Marc A. Levy, Andrew Moravcsik, and Kalypso Nicolaidis. 1993. Integrating the Two Halves of Europe: Theories of Interests, Bargaining, and Institutions. In *After the Cold War: International Institutions and State Strategies in Europe, 1989–1991*, edited by Robert O. Keohane, Joseph S. Nye, and Stanley Hoffmann, 173–95. Cambridge, Mass.: Harvard University Press.

Henderson, Karen. 2002. *Slovakia: The Escape from Invisibility.* London: Routledge.

Ikenberry, G. John, and Charles A. Kupchan. 1990. Socialization and Hegemonic Power. *International Organization* 44 (3):283–315.

Ismayr, Wolfgang, ed. 2002. *Die politischen Systeme Osteuropas.* Opladen, Germany: Leske and Budrich.

Jaggers, Keith, and Ted Robert Gurr. 1995. Tracking Democracy's Third Wave with the Polity III Data. *Journal of Peace Research* 32 (4):469–82.

Jasiewicz, Krzysztof. 1998. Elections and Voting Behaviour. In *Developments in Central and East European Politics.* Vol. 2, edited by Stephen White, Judy Batt, and Paul Lewis, 166–87. Basingstoke, England: Macmillan.

Johnston, Alastair Iain. 2001. Treating International Institutions as Social Environments. *International Studies Quarterly* 45 (4):487–515.

Jubulis, Mark A. 1996. The External Dimension of Democratization in Latvia: The Impact of European Institutions. *International Relations* 13 (3):59–73.

Kaldor, Mary, and Ivan Vejvoda. 1999. Democratization in Central and Eastern European Countries: An Overview. In *Democratization in Central and Eastern Europe*, edited by Mary Kaldor and Ivan Vejvoda, 1–24. London: Pinter.

Kelley, Judith. 2004: International Actors on the Domestic Scene: Membership Conditionality and International Socialization by International Institutions. *International Organization* 58 (3):425–57.

Knobel, Heiko. 2004. Latvia. Unpublished manuscript, University of Mannheim, Germany.

Krause, Kevin Deegan. 2003. The Ambivalent Influence of the European Union on Democratization in Slovakia. In *The European Union and Democratization*, edited by Paul J. Kubicek, 56–86. London: Routledge.

Kubicek, Paul J., ed. 2003. *The European Union and Democratization.* London: Routledge.

Leff, Carol Skalnik. 1997. *The Czech and Slovak Republics: Nation versus State.* Boulder, Colo.: Westview.

Lewis, Paul G. 2001. The "Third Wave" of Democracy in Eastern Europe: Comparative Perspectives on Party Roles and Political Development. *Party Politics* 7 (5):543–65.

Malová, Darina, and Marek Rybář. 2003. The European Union's Policies Towards Slovakia: Carrots and Sticks of Political Conditionality. In *The Road to the European Union.* Vol. 1, *The Czech and Slovak Republics*, edited by Jacques Rupnik and Jan Zielonka, 98–112. Manchester, England: Manchester University Press.

Mattli, Walter. 1999. *The Logic of Regional Integration: Europe and Beyond.* Cambridge: Cambridge University Press.

McFaul, Michael. 2002. The Fourth Wave of Democracy and Dictatorship: Noncooperative Transitions in the Postcommunist World. *World Politics* 54 (2):212–44.

Mite, Valentinas. 2002. Latvia: Language Laws Amended, but Issue Remains Divisive. *RFE/RL Features*, 15 May 2002. Available at ⟨http://www.rferl.org/features/2002/05/15052002082221.asp⟩. Accessed 22 June 2005.

Parliamentary Assembly of the Council of Europe. 1999. *Honouring of Obligations and Commitments by Latvia.* Doc. 8426, 24 May 1999.

Plakans, Andrejs. 1997. Democratization and Political Participation in Postcommunist Societies: The Case of Latvia. In *The Consolidation of Democracy in East-Central Europe*, edited by Karen Dawisha and Bruce Parrott, 245–89. Cambridge: Cambridge University Press.

Pravda, Alex. 2001. Introduction. In *Democratic Consolidation in Eastern Europe*. Vol. 2, *International and Transnational Factors*, edited by Jan Zielonka and Alex Pravda, 1–27. Oxford: Oxford University Press.

Pridham, Geoffrey. 1999. Complying with the European Union's Democratic Conditionality: Transnational Party Linkages and Regime Change in Slovakia, 1993–1998. *Europe-Asia Studies* 51 (7):1221–44.

Risse, Thomas. 2000. "Let's Argue!": Communicative Action in World Politics. *International Organization* 54 (1):1–39.

Risse, Thomas, and Sikkink, Kathryn. 1999. The Socialization of International Human Rights Norms into Domestic Practices: Introduction. In *The Power of Human Rights: International Norms and Domestic Change*, edited by Thomas Risse, Stephen Ropp, and Kathryn Sikkink, 1–38. Cambridge: Cambridge University Press.

Samson, Ivo. 1997. *Die Slowakei zwischen Annäherung an Moskau und Streben nach "Westintegration* (Bericht 2/1997). Cologne, Germany: Bundesinstitut für ostwissenschaftliche und Internationale Studien.

Schimmelfennig, Frank. 2000. International Socialization in the New Europe: Rational Action in an Institutional Environment. *European Journal of International Relations* 6 (1):109–39.

———. 2001. The Community Trap: Liberal Norms, Rhetorical Action, and the Eastern Enlargement of the European Union. *International Organization* 55 (1):47–80.

———. 2003. *The EU, NATO, and the Integration of Europe: Rules and Rhetoric*. Cambridge: Cambridge University Press.

———. Forthcoming. International Norm Promotion in Eastern Europe: A Qualitative Comparative Analysis. In *EU Membership and Consolidation of Democracy in East Central Europe*, edited by Grzegorz Ekiert and Jan Zielonka. Baltimore, Md.: Johns Hopkins University Press.

Schneider, Eleonora. 1997. *Quo vadis, Slowakei? Von der eingeleiteten Demokratie zum Autoritarismus?* (Bericht 36). Cologne, Germany: Bundesinstitut für ostwissenschaftliche und Internationale Studien.

Sedelmeier, Ulrich. 2000. Eastern Enlargement: Risk, Rationality, and Role-Compliance. In *The State of the European Union: Risks, Reform, Resistance and Revival*, edited by Maria Green Cowles and Michael Smith, 164–85. Oxford: Oxford University Press.

Sitter, Nick. 2001. Beyond Class vs. Nation? Cleavage Structures and Party Competition in Central Europe. *Central European Political Science Review* 2 (3):67–91.

Smith, Graham, Vivien Law, Andrew Wilson, Annette Bohr, and Edward Allworth. 1998. *Nation-Building in the Post-Soviet Borderlands: The Politics of National Identities*. Cambridge: Cambridge University Press.

Stankovsky, Jan, Fritz Plasser, and Peter A. Ulram. 1998. *On the Eve of EU Enlargement: Economic Developments and Democratic Attitudes in East Central Europe*. Schriftenreihe des Zentrums für Angewandte Politikforschung 16. Vienna: Signum Verlag.

Vachudova, Milada Anna. 2001. The Leverage of International Institutions on Democratizing States: Eastern Europe and the European Union. RSC Working Paper No. 2001/33. San Domenico, Italy: European University Institute (EUI), Robert Schuman Centre of Advanced Studies (RSCAS).

Van Der Stoel, Max. 1993a. Letter of April 6, 1993, to Georgs Andrejevs, Latvian Minister of Foreign Affairs. Ref. No. 238/93/L/Rev. Available at ⟨http://www.arts.uwaterloo.ca/MINELRES/osce/counrec.htm⟩. Accessed 22 June 2005.

———. 1993b. Letter of December 10, 1993, to Georgs Andrejevs, Latvian Minister of Foreign Affairs. Ref. No. 1463/93/L. Available at ⟨http://www.arts.uwaterloo.ca/MINELRES/osce/counrec.htm⟩. Accessed 22 June 2005.

———. 1996. Letter of October 28, 1996, to Valdis Birkavs, Latvian Minister of Foreign Affairs. Ref. No. 1085/96/L. Available at ⟨http://www.arts.uwaterloo.ca/MINELRES/osce/counrec.htm⟩. Accessed 22 June 2005.

———. 1997. Letter of May 23, 1997 to Valdis Birkavs, Latvian Minister of Foreign Affairs. Available at ⟨http://www.arts.uwaterloo.ca/MINELRES/osce/counrec.htm⟩. Accessed 22 June 2005.

———. 1998. On the Proposals of the Working Group Concerning the Amendments to the Citizenship Law. Letter to Mr. Guntars Krasts, Prime Minister of Latvia. Ref. No. 984/98/L. Available at ⟨http://www.osce.org/documents/hcnm/1998/04/2734_en.pdf⟩. Accessed 22 June 2005.

———. 1999. Statement on Latvian Language Law by OSCE High Commissioner on National Minorities, 15 July. Vienna: OSCE Secretariat, Press and Public Information Section. Available at ⟨http:// www.osce.org/press_rel/ 1999/07/820-hcnm.html⟩. Accessed 3 January 2005.

Zaagman, Rob. 1999. Conflict Prevention in the Baltic States: The OSCE High Commissioner on National Minorities in Estonia, Latvia, and Lithuania. ECMI Monograph 1. Flensburg, Germany: European Centre for Minority Issues.

3

Several Roads Lead to International Norms, But Few Via International Socialization

A Case Study of the European Commission

Liesbet Hooghe

To what extent can an international organization socialize those who work within it? In order for international institutions in Europe to socialize states and state agents into international norms, they must themselves emanate these norms. But can one simply presume that the people who work within international organizations share international norms, and if so, what are the causal mechanisms?

The Commission of the European Union (hereafter the European Commission) is a crucial case for examining socialization within an international organization. Crucial cases "offer valuable tests because they are strongly expected to confirm or disconfirm prior hypotheses."[1] Compared with other international organizations in Europe, such as the North Atlantic Treaty Organization (NATO) or the Council of Europe, the European Commission is extraordinarily autonomous and powerful, and this, socialization theory predicts, should make it the most likely site for socialization. The European Commission is the steering body of the world's most encompassing supranational regime. It has a vocation to identify and defend the European interest over and above—and if need be, against—particular national interests. It is the agenda setter in the European Union (EU). It also has the authority to select and groom its employees with minimal national interference. So there are strong reasons to expect international socialization to be effective in the European Commission. If this powerful body cannot shape its employees' preferences, which international organization can?

How can one make sense of top Commission officials' support for, or opposition to, the European Commission's core norms? Support in itself does not, of course, mean that officials have been socialized in the Commission. What are the scope conditions for international socialization? When does international socialization work, and when does it not? When do alternative processes of preference formation predominate? Can international officials learn international norms outside the international organization?

In this article, I set out a theory of preference formation in international organizations. I frame expectations concerning when international socialization may work,

[1] See McKeown 2004, 141; and Eckstein 1975.

what shape it may take, and when it may be trumped by other processes or contexts. In the language of this volume, I am concerned with specifying the scope conditions of international socialization. I build primarily on work in comparative and U.S. politics and political psychology, as well as recent work on socialization in international organizations, to develop a theory applicable in international contexts. The first section describes the European Commission and the norms it embodies. I then lay out hypotheses about when, how, where, and to what extent international socialization works. Finally, I evaluate the validity of these hypotheses against evidence from two surveys of senior Commission officials.

My conclusion is that, while support for international norms is high, this is not primarily because of socialization in the European Commission. Top officials sustain Commission norms when national experiences motivate them to do so—when national political socialization predisposes them to embrace supranationalism, or when supranationalism appears to benefit their country. Like Beyers' national bureaucrats in EU Council working groups,[2] these quintessentially European bureaucrats take their cues primarily from their national environment. Several roads lead to Commission norms, but few run through international socialization.

The Engine of Europe

The role of the European Commission is described precisely in the Treaty of the European Union and is reinforced by the Commission's house rules. The Commission has a constitutional obligation to set the legislative agenda in the European Union (EU).[3] Unique among international institutions and unparalleled among executives in national democracies, the Commission has exclusive formal competence to initiate and draft EU legislation.[4] It decides when regulation is necessary and how it should be devised. The Council of Ministers, which represents national governments, and the European Parliament, which is directly elected, may request the Commission to draft an initiative, but the Commission can, and sometimes does, refuse. The Treaty also instructs the Commission to serve the European interest.[5] It also requires the Commission to be independent from any national government.[6] These Treaty rules apply to the two levels of the European Commission: the political College, composed of the twenty-five commissioners appointed jointly for five years by member states and the European Parliament to give the Commission political guidance; and the Commission bureaucracy, consisting of approximately 24,000 permanent career civil servants selected through central exams to take care of daily business.

---

[2] Beyers, this volume.

[3] Article 211, Treaty of the European Union.

[4] This monopoly has grown with the steady expansion of the Treaty's so-called pillar I from primarily internal market issues to political regulation, and the transfer of some pillar II and III issues, including aspects of asylum, immigration, and foreign policy, to pillar I. At the same time, the Commission's monopoly has been eroded by informal rules that give the European Parliament and the European Council certain rights to table initiatives.

[5] Article 213.2, Treaty of the European Union.

[6] Ibid.

It is with the career civil servants, and more precisely the most senior officials among them, that I am concerned. They are the men and women who soldier on as political Colleges—led by Delors, Santer, Prodi, or Barroso—come and go. In addition to being bound by the Treaty, they are expected to adhere to the European Commission's internal staff regulations, which instruct that "an official shall carry out his duties and conduct himself solely with the interests of the Communities in mind; he shall neither seek nor take instructions from any government, authority, organisation or person outside his institution. . . . He shall carry out the duties assigned to him objectively, impartially and in keeping with his duty of loyalty to the Communities."[7]

Constitutional rules and house rules create clear expectations—norms—that are expressly designed to guide Commission officials, whether as political appointees or as permanent career officials. They prescribe the Commission and its employees to (1) put the Union interest first (supranationalism),[8] (2) construe what this means proactively (agenda setting), and (3) promote the Union interest independently from national pressures (impartiality and autonomy).[9]

These norms have deep roots. The Commission's founding father, Jean Monnet, saw the Commission as a small, organizationally flexible and adaptive, multinational nucleus of individuals at the European level, akin to the Planning Commission *(Commissariat de plan)* he had set up after World War II in France to devise the first five-year national economic plan. Liberated from national interests, its role was to develop ideas freely, to stimulate and persuade. The Commission's autonomy, pro-European bias, and exclusive power of initiative were crucial to this conception, and Monnet persuaded national leaders to anchor these principles in the Treaty. The notion that the European Commission is, and should be, the engine of Europe was born.[10] This notion is a direct challenge to Westphalian state-centric norms in international relations.[11] No other national or international organization, with the exception of the European Court of Justice, represents so patently the view that supranational interest is not reducible to national interests.

---

[7] Article 11, Staff regulations of Officials of the European Communities (May 2004). Available from http://europe.eu.int/comm/dgs/personnel_administration, accessed on 23 August 2005.

[8] As Haas points out, supranationality is an elusive concept. He defines supranationality as a hybrid between federalism and intergovernmentalism, whereby more power is given to the central agency than is customary for conventional international organizations, but less than to a federal government. See Haas 1958, 34; see also Lindberg and Scheingold 1970, 14–21. The defining feature of supranationalism is that decisions are binding on member states. Supranationalism approaches federalism when decisions are made by independent European organizations, such as the European Court, European Parliament, or the European Commission.

[9] The draft constitutional treaty of the European Union, signed on 29 October 2004 by the members of the European Council in Rome, restates these norms: (1) Supranationalism: Article 25.1: "The European Commission shall promote the general European interest and take appropriate initiatives to that end." (2) Agenda setting: Article 25.2: "Except where the Constitution provides otherwise, Union legislative acts can be adopted only on the basis of a Commission proposal." (3) Impartiality and autonomy: Article 25.4: "In carrying out its responsibilities, the Commission shall be completely independent. In the discharge of their duties, the European Commissioners and the Commissioners shall neither seek nor take instructions from any government or other body." The treaty is available at ⟨http://europa.eu.int/futurum/constitution/⟩. Accessed 22 June 2005.

[10] See Duchěne 1994; and Pollack 2003.

[11] Caporaso 2000.

How widespread is support for these pro-European norms in the Commission itself? Do the people who work in the Commission support supranationalism, Commission agenda setting, and autonomy? Does this support arise because the Commission socializes those who work in it?

Shaping Preferences in International Organizations

Most research on international socialization examines states or state governments rather than individuals.[12] In this analysis, I focus on individuals within an international organization.[13]

Socialization refers to the process of inducting individuals into the norms and rules of a given community.[14] The mechanisms by which this occurs may range from the self-conscious (for example, normative suasion) to the subconscious (for example, social mimicking or role playing), and from the instrumental (for example, shaming) to the noninstrumental (for example, communication).[15]

Socialization demands that individuals change their preferences in accordance with organizational norms. This poses a challenge for analysis because preferences cannot be observed from behavior. Preferences need to be researched directly, for example in structured interviews, to yield information that is independent from behavior. This research strategy is time-consuming, and even then, uncertainty lingers about the veracity of stated preferences. Respondents may lie, or they may not be able to express their true preferences.[16] That is perhaps why social scientists treat preferences as exogenous.[17]

International socialization is present to the degree that individuals in an international organization support its mission as a result of experiences in the organization. One must diagnose a change in a person's mental state to show that norms have been internalized—Type II socialization, in Checkel's terms.[18] What questions should one ask to uncover the scope conditions of international socialization?

---

[12] See Finnemore 1996; Hemmer and Katzenstein 2002; Linden 2002; and Risse, Ropp, and Sikkink 1999.

[13] See Checkel 2003; Checkel, this volume; and Johnston 2001.

[14] See Checkel, this volume; Conover 1991; and Hooghe 2002.

[15] See Beck and Jennings 1991; Johnston 2001; Risse 2000; and Sears and Valentino 1997.

[16] Deception and attitude softness can be problematic among ordinary citizens, as public opinion research has demonstrated. Zaller 1992. Attitude softness, however, is rarely an issue for elites whose views tend to be more crystallized on political objects. Jennings 1992. There is no fire-proof method for distinguishing true from deceptive preferences. I cannot discount the possibility that some respondents concealed their true preferences, though the circumstances of the interview (anonymity, voluntary participation, nonsensitive character of the questions), and the senior status of the respondents (considerable discretion, weak peer control) are reassuring.

[17] In international relations, rationalists tend to take preferences as exogenous, while constructivists endogenize them. However, as Fearon and Wendt remind us, it is unwise to exaggerate the difference. Whether one endogenizes preferences is an analytical choice dictated by one's research question. See Fearon and Wendt 2002, 64. Preferences are the first step, and behavior the second step, in the two-step dance that is international cooperation. Legro 1996.

[18] Checkel, this volume.

- *How do organizational experiences shape preferences over time?* Is induction into organizational norms easier and faster for newcomers than for longtime members? Are younger recruits more likely to be socialized than older ones? How, in other words, does the rate of socialization vary over time?

- *How does organizational fragmentation affect socialization?* Socialization theory predicts that cohesive organizations are better at socializing agents than fragmented organizations.

- *How does international socialization interact with national socialization?* Individuals in international organizations usually come from diverse national backgrounds. When do national backgrounds reinforce, and when do they weaken, international socialization?

- *Can one splice the effects of socialization from alternative processes that induce support for organizational norms?* To accurately assess whether support is due to socialization, one must control for self-selection, selective recruitment, and utility maximization.

- *Does the effectiveness of socialization vary across beliefs?* An organization's mission usually consists of multiple norms. Are some norms more open to socialization than others?

How Do Organizational Experiences Shape Preferences over Time?

Inculcating values is a gradual process: the longer one's involvement in an organization, the more one's beliefs can be expected to approximate that organization's norms.[19] While socialization usually requires long-term exposure, some individuals need less time than others. Thus the rate at which individuals internalize individual norms varies.

Effect of Novelty. Initial experiences are more influential than subsequent ones. People in a new situation (that is, newcomers) are likely to be disoriented and eager to conform. They are more susceptible to efforts of persuasion, and more disposed to copy what others do.[20] As time goes by, views crystallize, that is, they become more consistent and stable.[21] The marginal effect of time spent in an organization is illustrated in Figure 1, where the slope of the line AA' flattens as it approaches t_1.

Primacy. Socialization varies inversely with a person's age and experience. This is the primacy effect. Psychologists theorize that new experiences stick best when a person has few relevant prior experiences.[22] There is debate about the optimal age for socialization and the extent to which older people become impervious to

---

[19] Searing 1986.
[20] See Johnston 2001; also Checkel 2003.
[21] Sears and Funk 1999.
[22] See Sears and Levy 2003; and Searing, Wright, and Rabinowitz 1976.

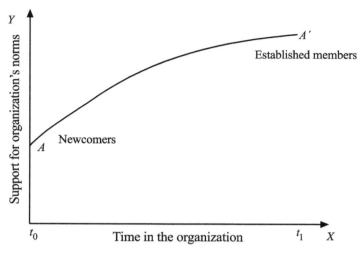

Figure 1. *Mapping socialization*

socialization. But even those who argue that core predispositions continue to crystallize well past adolescence accept that change takes place ever more slowly with age.[23] One should therefore find that young recruits and people with minimal relevant prior experience—blank slates, or "baby generals" as Gheciu calls them—are more susceptible to socialization than seasoned members.[24] Young recruits and "blank slates" are represented in Figure 2 by the steep curve AA'', while older recruits/experienced individuals are represented by the flatter curve AA'''.

These considerations temper one's expectations about the strength of socialization in international organizations. Few officials join international organizations as young adults, top functions are often filled through lateral appointments of national diplomats or experts, and personnel turnover tends to be high. To the extent that recruits are older, experienced, or mobile, I hypothesize that the socialization curve will be flattened or truncated.

How Does Organizational Fragmentation Affect Socialization?

Organizations are rarely unitary. Compartmentalization multiplies opportunities for socialization, but it also produces diversity within an organization. Compartmentalization intensifies ties within organizational subunits while loosening those among them. Because members' experiences are usually more intense in organizational subunits, socialization is likely to be more effective there.

However, different subunits within an organization may socialize different norms, some of which may reinforce the international organization's mission, and others not.

---

[23] Sears and Funk 1999.

[24] Gheciu, this volume. Novice and primacy effects are sometimes conflated, but they are analytically different. While the primacy effect is a function of age, the novice effect is a function of time spent in an organization.

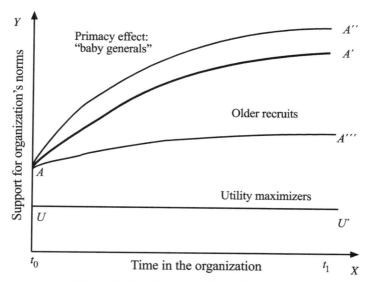

Figure 2. *Socialization, utility, self-selection*

The socialization curve will be steeper when socialization in the unit reinforces the norms of the organization as a whole, and flatter when it does not.

Fragmentation is a trademark of many organizations, both international and national, especially when political leadership is weak or divided. In his seminal article on the Cuban Missile Crisis, Allison emphasizes how weak presidential leadership fostered bureaucratic fragmentation. When a bureaucracy is divided, he argues, bureaucrats are inclined to identify with their department's interest over and above that of the administration as a whole.[25]

How Does International Socialization Interact with National Socialization?

Most individuals are members of several organizations and are therefore exposed to competing norms, but the extent to which exposure leads to socialization depends on the boundedness of the organization. An organization is bounded to the extent that it controls its members,[26] and in the last analysis, its members' life chances. Boundedness requires authority—over the mission of the organization, how it is to be pursued, and who should pursue it.

The relative boundedness of international organizations is usually constrained by national institutions. National institutions tend to have deeper historical roots, a more coherent mission, more extensive resources, and more cohesive membership than international organizations. The institutions of one's country of birth also tend to be most influential in pre-adulthood.[27] Children know whether they are American,

[25] Allison 1971.
[26] Nordlinger 1981.
[27] See Jennings and Stoker 2001; and Sears and Levy 2003.

German, or French by the age of six or seven[28]; they acquire basic beliefs about democracy, freedom, community, race, and rudimentary political allegiance and partisanship during adolescence. These political beliefs are cued by schools, parents, churches, media, associations, and peer groups in a particular national environment. Even in the age of globalization, nearly all individuals in Western societies grow up in one or, at most, two national states. So an international official's nationality comes with distinctive cultural baggage.

One should not assume that national institutions always dilute international norms. National institutions may actually deepen multilateral or supranational values. National and international socialization may produce the same outcome, and only an analysis sensitive to alternative contexts can disentangle these.

How might national context predispose individuals in one direction or another with respect to international norms? Countries vary widely in the degree to which they centralize or decentralize authority. Notwithstanding the United States and Switzerland, citizens of federal societies may have fewer inhibitions concerning supranationalism and multilevel governance.

Political parties constitute a second context for political socialization, and this is especially so with respect to the EU. European integration has become an issue that divides political parties and electorates.[29] To the extent that international officials identify with a political party ideology, one would expect this to influence their views on international norms. Finally, I expect an individual's prior work experiences to matter. I anticipate that those whose career has led them abroad are more sympathetic to international norms. In contrast, individuals who have worked exclusively in their national civil service have been socialized to place the highest value on public service to their nation.

Can One Distinguish Socialization from Self-Selection and Selective Recruitment?

Socialization is only one of several processes that connect individuals to groups. Even if those who work in an organization support its norms, this may not be because of socialization. The alternatives are threefold. Members may share an organization's norms because those who choose to join the organization are already supportive (self-selection), because the organization screens recruits for their views (selective recruitment), or because self-interest induces employees to share the organization's norms (utility maximization).

Self-selection and selective recruitment precede socialization; they do not say anything about whether people are socialized once they join the organization. Hence, they do not affect the shape of the socialization curve, but they do affect the point of departure—in Figure 2, they shift the intercept of the socialization curve north along the y axis.[30]

[28] Druckman 1994.
[29] See Evans 2002; and Marks and Steenbergen 2004.
[30] The distinction between self-selection and selective recruitment, on the one hand, and socialization, on the other, is hard to pin down empirically. What would be useful is data that allow *a)* comparison of the

Can One Distinguish Socialization from Utility Maximization?

Socialization theory states that individuals acquire preferences by internalizing norms embodied in the groups or institutions in which they live or work, or which are otherwise important to them. This view emphasizes affective group ties (identities) and long-standing personal dispositions. What motivates individuals is, in March and Olsen's words, "a logic of appropriateness."[31] Utility theory, in contrast, maintains that preferences reflect self-interest, usually conceived in materialistic terms. Individuals have particular preferences because this is rational in light of costs and benefits. March and Olsen describe this as a "logic of consequentiality."[32]

In many activities, individuals are motivated by some combination of identity and utility.[33] But the extent to which each is present varies from issue to issue, and from context to context. The question is not simply whether socialization or utility maximization determines the preferences of members of international organizations, but under what conditions members tend to be more influenced by one or the other.

Splicing socialization from utility maximization demands careful surgery. Socialization, in contrast to utility maximization, is all about the temporal effects of group influence. The socialization curves in Figure 2 are time-sensitive in that they tap cumulative experience in an organization. Utility maximization is time-*insensitive*: what matters are the incentives and disincentives that confront a person at a given moment (*UU'* in Figure 2).[34]

Socialization theory hypothesizes that individuals have a psychological need to minimize inconsistent beliefs. Cognitive dissonance reduction, the psychological mechanism whereby individuals seek to reduce dissonance among various beliefs, decreases information costs and thus preempts rational calculation.[35] An individual is more capable of reducing dissonance when the norm concerns diffuse values, and when the material stakes are low. I take a look at these in turn.

Large and Diffuse Norms. Socialization is more likely for norms that concern large or diffuse values in life.[36] Rational choice, on the other hand, "is more powerful when applied to medium-sized problems like the purchase of a car or of a house." But "large problems, in which the choice can be expected to have wide-ranging consequences . . . tend to fall outside the scope of the theory. Preference rankings over

---

preferences of self-selected individuals with those of potential candidates who chose not to apply, and *b)* comparison of the preferences of selected applicants with those of rejected applicants.

[31] March and Olsen 1989, 160.

[32] Ibid.

[33] See Chong 2000; Hooghe 2002; and Searing 1994.

[34] Over the long haul, it is often a combination of utility and socialization that brings an individual to support organizational norms. Initially, when a person joins an organization, incentives, persuasion, and mimicking may all nudge them toward particular preferences, so that it is impossible to distinguish socialization from utility. In the long run, individuals may internalize norms. The litmus test is whether preferences change in tandem with changing material incentives. If they do, utility maximization guides preference formation; if they do not, it is socialization. I thank Don Searing for raising the issue of changing processes of preference formation over time. See also Johnston, this volume.

[35] See Chong 2000; and Simon 1985.

[36] See Goren 2001; Huddy 2003; and Taber 2003.

big chunks of life tend to be incomplete, and subjective probabilities over events in the distant future tend to be unreliable."[37]

Material Stakes.   Utility maximization prevails when norms are perceived to have material consequences that can be estimated with some accuracy, are large enough to matter, and when a person's choice will probably affect the outcome.[38] Materialist content, transparency, large stakes, and personal impact correspond to central assumptions of rational choice concerning self-interest, information, and motivation. Utility maximization, then, is most likely to trump socialization when an individual's career chances are at stake.[39]

International norms that affect career chances or material outcomes, such as norms concerning tasks, work practices, and constituency relations, are more open to utility maximization. International norms that concern diffuse values, such as norms on international cooperation, multilateralism, supranationalism and inter-governmentalism, are more readily socialized.

I have theorized how individual characteristics, organizational variables, and type of norm affect socialization. Table 1 summarizes these. I now examine whether and how the European Commission socializes those who work in it.

Socialization in the European Commission

I draw on two surveys of senior permanent civil servants in the European Commission: director-generals, deputy director-generals, directors, senior advisors, and heads of cabinet. The first survey consists of semi-structured personal interviews averaging eighty minutes in length, which I conducted between July 1995 and February 1997. The same individuals answered thirty-six questions concerning their attitudes on EU and Commission-related topics. From September 2001 through February 2002, I mailed to all senior Commission officials a structured questionnaire replicating most of the 1995–97 questions. I also conducted short personal interviews with fifteen respondents in February 2002. Here I analyze responses to the two sets of closed-ended mail questionnaires, illustrated with direct quotations from transcribed interviews.[40]

---

[37] Elster 1990, 40.
[38] See Elster 1990; Sears and Funk 1991; and Young et al. 1991.
[39] See Chong 2000; Crano 1997; Sears 1993; and Taber 2003, 447–48.
[40] The value of closed-ended mail questionnaires for elite research is debated. Politically sophisticated actors tend to dislike closed-ended questions because it forces them to condense complex beliefs into blunt agree/disagree statements, while an interview allows them to be more subtle. In his elite study, Putnam reprints a letter from a British parliamentarian who makes this point. See Putnam 1973, 19. Likewise, I received a questionnaire from one official on which he had scribbled dense critical comments next to virtually every question but refused to take position on a single item! In their study of foreign policy makers, Hollis and Smith argue for taking accounts by elite actors seriously: "Our actors *interpret* information, *monitor* their performance, *reassess* their goals. The leading idea is that of reasoned judgment, not of manipulation" (emphasis in the original). See Hollis and Smith 1986, 283, quoted in Searing 1991, fn. 17. How can one make closed-ended questionnaires serve this purpose? A first step is to draw heavily on previous research. Where feasible, I replicated content and format from Searing's study of British parliamentarians and Putnam's study of political elites. See Searing 1994; and Putnam

Table 1. *Scope and Mechanisms of Socialization*

Independent variable	Hypothesis
Individual characteristics	
TIME IN ORGANIZATION	Socialization is most intense for newcomers and decreases over time.
PRIMACY (*age when joining*)	Inexperienced recruits are more rapidly socialized.
SELF-SELECTION	Self-selected recruits are more likely to support organizational norms.
Organizational variables	
ORGANIZATIONAL FRAGMENTATION	Fragmentation inhibits unitary socialization.
ORGANIZATIONAL BOUNDEDNESS	The more bounded the organization, the more effectively it socializes.
CONTROL OVER RECRUITMENT	Organizationally selected recruits are more likely to support organizational norms.
INCENTIVES (*sanctions and rewards*)	Incentives may induce support for organizational norms through utility maximization.
Type of norm	
SUBSTANTIVE SCOPE OF ISSUE	Large/diffuse issues facilitate socialization.
SIZE OF MATERIAL STAKES	Transparent/sizeable material stakes facilitate utility maximization.
STABILITY OF NORM	Unstable norms discourage preference structuring: socialization and utility maximization are weakened.

Of a population of 204 and 230 senior Commission officials at the respective time points, 105 responded in 1996 and 93 in 2002.[41] When question wording is consistent across surveys, I pool data, and this brings the sample to 198.

1973, respectively. This has the added value of comparability. Furthermore, I systematically pretested the questionnaire. Finally, I triangulated statistical analysis of the closed-ended elite questionnaires with qualitative reading of in-depth interviews. Personal interviews with 137 senior Commission officials produced 180 hours of taped interviews, so respondents had plenty of time to explicate their views (in French or English). Closed-ended questionnaires were handed out after the interview. The idea is to maximize the distinctive advantage of closed-ended questionnaires—an objective, quantifiable basis for systematic comparison—while minimizing their disadvantages.

[41] The higher response rate for the first survey (51 percent against 40 percent) reflects the fact that the personal interview had allowed me to establish rapport with the respondent. When necessary, I followed up by phone, e-mail, or fax. In 2001–2002, the procedure was more distant. A research assistant mailed questionnaires (in French and English) to 230 officials, but struggled to meet our target response rate. I wound up traveling to Brussels to set up fifteen short appointments, in which I asked respondents to fill out the questionnaire in my presence. I took care not to influence the process to ensure comparability with the mailed-in responses. The flying visit provided me with an opportunity for brief personal interviews. Facts and figures on response rate, sample bias, and interview strategy for the first survey are available in Hooghe 2002, and from my Web site ⟨http://www.unc.edu/~hooghe/⟩.

It is useful to establish a baseline for comparison. How do the views of top Commission officials on European integration compare with those of other actors? One knows an increasing amount about preferences by EU actors, including the Council of Ministers,[42] permanent representations,[43] European parliamentarians,[44] Commission officials, national civil servants,[45] national governments,[46] national political parties,[47] interest groups,[48] and public opinion.[49] But surveys often ask different questions.

Fortunately, there are some common points for comparison. An oft-repeated Eurobarometer question asks citizens how they want to distribute authority between the EU and national governments on thirteen individual policies. The same question was included in the 1996 national elite survey on attitudes concerning European integration, the only systematic survey of national elites to date in the fifteen pre-enlargement EU member states.[50] I also used the question in my 2002 survey of top Commission officials.[51]

Top Commission officials appear significantly more pro-European than either national elites or public opinion across the thirteen policies for which we have comparable data.[52] Average support among Commission officials is 65 percent, against 56 percent for national elites, and 53 percent for the public.

This pro-European bias is reflected in perceptions of identity (see Table 2). When Eurobarometer asks citizens to signal how much they are attached to their country and how much to Europe, European attachment is no match for national attachment, as the averages in the last column show. National attachment has a significantly smaller lead among top Commission officials. Top Commission officials are also much less likely to characterize their identity as exclusively national than are ordinary citizens.

---

[42] Beyers, this volume.

[43] Lewis, this volume.

[44] Thomassen, Noury, and Voeten 2004.

[45] Egeberg 1999.

[46] Hug and König 2002.

[47] Marks, Hooghe, Nelson, and Edwards forthcoming.

[48] Wessels 2004.

[49] See Gabel and Anderson 2002; and Van der Eijk and Franklin 2004.

[50] The public opinion data are from Eurobarometer 54.1 of fall 2000. Hartung 2001. The national elite data were collected in 1996 by EOS Gallup-Europe, which drew a representative sample from a database of 22,000 individuals from five elite sectors: elected politicians (national and European parliamentarians), senior national civil servants, business and trade union leaders, media leaders (including heads of broadcast and print media), and cultural elites (persons playing a leading role in the academic, cultural, or religious life). The survey was conducted by telephone $(N = 3778)$. See Spence 1996.

[51] Question 30 in Eurobarometer 54.1 reads: "For each of the following areas, do you think that decisions should be made by the [nationality] government, or made jointly within the European Union? 1 = nationality, 2 = jointly within the European Union, 3 = don't know." Hartung 2001. The question formulation for national elites and Commission officials differs somewhat from that for public opinion, in that it allows respondents to indicate support or opposition on a scale from 1 to 10. For comparability, elite data must therefore be transformed into a dichotomous variable. See Hooghe 2003.

[52] Hooghe 2003. The thirteen policies are currency, humanitarian aid/Third World, foreign policy, immigration and asylum, environment, agriculture, defense, research and development, regional policy, employment, social inclusion, health policy, and education. Of the twenty-six one-way analysis-of-variance means tests for group differences—thirteen are between Commission officials and public opinion, and thirteen are between Commission officials and national elites—twenty are significant at the .001 level, one at the .01 level, one at the .05 level, and only four are insignificant $(p > .05)$. The results are robust across the Bonferroni and Tukey methods.

Table 2. *National and European Identity among Commission Officials and the Public*

	National attachment					
	Not at all attached	*Not very attached*	*Fairly attached*	*Very attached*	*Don't know*	*Average on 4-point scale*
Public	1.4%	8.0%	38.1%	51.7%	0.7%	3.4*
Commission	3.3%	10.9%	46.7%	39.1%	0%	3.2*

	European attachment					
	Not at all attached	*Not very attached*	*Fairly attached*	*Very attached*	*Don't know*	*Average on 4-point scale*
Public	9.4%	27.4%	41.7%	18.1%	3.4%	2.7**
Commission	2.2%	19.4%	50.5%	24.7%	1.1%	3.0**

	European or national identity					
	European only	*European and national*	*National and European*	*National only*	*Don't know/ refuse*	*Average on 4-point scale*
Public	3.4%	5.8%	45.3%	42.4%	3.1%	3.3**
Commission	2.2%	43.0%	38.7%	0%	16.1%	2.4**

Note: Scales range from 1 (not at all attached: European only) to 4 (very attached; national only). The last column reports difference of means tests, whereby ** $p < .001$; * $p < .05$. The public opinion data are from Hating 2001, $N = 16,061$: data for Commission officials are from the author's survey in 2002, $N = 93$.

Forty-three percent of citizens describe themselves as "national only," but not a single official in the sample is so inclined.[53]

To summarize, Commission officials are more likely to identify with Europe and are more in favor of shifting policy to the European level than national elites or citizens. There is, then, considerable support among top Commission officials for the Commission norm of supranationalism. Is this because the Commission has socialized its officials, or for other reasons?

What Explains Commission Officials' Views on Supranationalism?

Table 3 presents a multivariate ordinary least squares (OLS) regression explaining top officials' preferences on supranationalism, which is measured by two items tapping

[53] The question is: "In the near future, do you see yourself as (1) [nationality] only, (2) [nationality] and European, (3) European and [nationality], or (4) European only?" Note that 16 percent of top officials (against 3.1 percent of the public) refused to choose one or the other option. Follow-up questions show that some officials object to having to rank European and national identity.

Table 3. *Explaining Supranationalism*

	All officials	*Primacy group*
Constant	4.381 (.655)**	4.313 (1.253)**
International socialization		
LENGTH OF SERVICE IN COMISSION	0.014 (.014)	0.077 (.032)*
INTERNATIONAL EDUCATION	0.156 (.121)	0.262 (.193)
Socialization outside Commission		
STATE STRUCTURE (DISPERSED VS. UNITARY):		
FEDERALISM	0.187 (.042)**	0.077 (.083)
SIZE OF COUNTRY	−0.012 (.005)*	−0.013 (.009)
IDEOLOGY	−0.110 (.075)°	−0.345 (.139)*
YEARS IN NATIONAL ADMINISTRATION	−0.031 (.019)°	0.070 (.103)
Utility factors		
POWER-DG UTILITY	0.033 (.058)	0.003 (.098)
NATIONAL ECONOMIC BENEFIT	0.180 (.121)°	0.300 (.363)
R^2	0.226	0.240
Adjusted R^2	0.182	0.111
N	198	78

Note: Ordinary least squares (OLS) are used in models for all officials and for the primacy group. The dependent variable (preferences on supranationalism) and the independent variables are detailed in Table A1 of Appendix 1. Coefficients are unstandardized. Standard errors are in parentheses. OLS regression analyses with pairwise deletion. Significance at ** $p < .01$; * $p < .05$: ° $p < .15$.

whether member states or supranational institutions should be central pillars of EU governance (see Appendix 1 for wording and statistics).

To estimate accurately the effect of international and Commission socialization, one must control for socialization outside the Commission and for utility. Table 3 reports that Commission socialization (measured as length of service in the Commission) and international socialization (measured as having studied abroad) are not significant.[54] In contrast, variables that capture socialization outside the Commission (that is, experience in a federal vs. unitary political system, ideology, and prior experience in a national administration) are highly significant. Utility maximization (that is, national economic benefit) also has a significant effect. Officials from countries that are net beneficiaries from EU policies are more likely to be supranationalist.

Figure 3 illustrates the relative effect of these variables. The solid boxes encompass the interquartile range and the whiskers indicate the 5th to the 95th percentiles, holding all other independent and control variables at their means. For example, an individual

---

[54] The argument for including international education is that it reinforces transnational norms, as students abroad are exposed to different ways of thinking and living. This happens during young adulthood when the primacy effect is powerful. Foreign students also experience firsthand that expatriates have limited citizenship rights compared to nationals at home, and I expect this to strengthen support for supranational institutions that could create overarching rights.

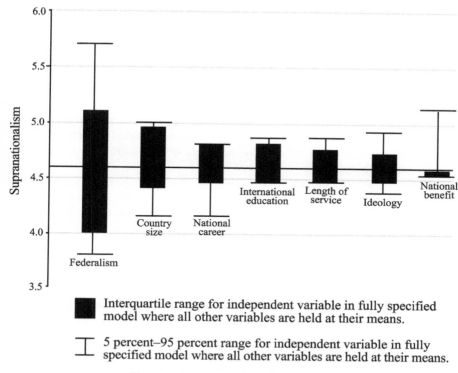

Interquartile range for independent variable in fully specified model where all other variables are held at their means.

5 percent–95 percent range for independent variable in fully specified model where all other variables are held at their means.

Figure 3. *Effects of independent variables*

at the 5th percentile on FEDERALISM has a score of 3.8 on SUPRANATIONALISM on a 1–7 scale, and an individual at the 95th percentile scores 5.7. The variables toward the left of Figure 3 have the largest effect across their interquartile range. The three most powerful variables relate to socialization outside, rather than within, the Commission. International education and length of service in the Commission are considerably weaker, as is utility maximization. I now take a closer look.

How Do Commission Experiences Shape Preferences over Time?

The effect of Commission socialization is modest: an additional year of service increases supranational support by 0.014 on a seven-point scale. At this rate, and controlling for the factors in Table 3, it would take seventy-one years to see someone who begins to work in the Commission as a neutral (four on our seven-point scale) change into a mild supranationalist at five.

But this conclusion does not hold for all Commission officials. The effect of Commission socialization is considerably stronger for the seventy-eight officials who joined the organization before their thirtieth birthday—the primacy group (see Table 3, second column).[55] The relative weight of international and national socialization is reversed. The effect of length of service is outweighed only by party ideology, and it is considerably stronger than federalism, national career, and country size. Each additional year of Commission service increases support by 0.077 on a seven-point scale. So "baby generals" need some thirteen years to change from a neutral four on the supranationalism scale to a mild prosupranationalist position of five. Commission socialization is concentrated among this group.

There is no support for the hypothesis that newcomers are more susceptible to socialization, or that the rate of socialization decreases with years of exposure.[56] The marginal effect of an additional year in the Commission is more or less linear with respect to time served.

Newcomers in the European Commission try hard to understand the rules and norms in their new organization. However, understanding rules is one thing, being persuaded by them is another. As one recently appointed Italian top official put it: "This is a huge organization, and when you arrive the first thing you do is to try to understand what is going on in the house. Of course, I do have, let's say, my own prejudices in this area and I did give some messages, but in the beginning most of the effort is in understanding." An Austrian top civil servant, six months on the job, echoed this. When asked whether she had the sense, in the first few weeks, that she would be able to pursue her goals, she replied: "My main interest was to fully capture what was going on and how it functioned—taking stock of things and how things were done." The prevailing attitude among newcomers appears to be to wait and see, and not, as one might expect, mimicking behavioral norms of the group.

Socialization is not helped by the fact that Commission rules and norms are often difficult to grasp. Several Commission officials whom I interviewed vividly recalled their bewilderment in coming to grips with the complex interplay between multicultural attitudes and national particularities, the charged politicking in an apparent bureaucratic organization, the paper bureaucracy which all condone but few take seriously, and the paradox of widespread informal networking in a formalistic hierarchy. This complexity undercuts normative transparency and inhibits socialization. Learning to circumvent formal norms is essential to survival. An official who worked his way up in the Commission to the absolute top summarizes the duplicitous character of work norms:

The Commission only works when hierarchy is put aside. While we respect the hierarchy in formal terms, we know that, to get this job done, we need to ask the question: "Who do we need to do it?"... We are task-oriented, person oriented. That requires a great deal of flexibility and adaptability. It's not possible to operate, except through an at best token acceptance of procedures and hierarchies. The only way to make this thing work effectively within the deadlines set by politics is by relying on key people committed to the same goal.

---

[55] Severe multicollinearity precludes testing the primacy effect in a single equation with overall Commission socialization (length of service).

[56] I tested this in several ways. I defined newcomers as those with up to two, up to three, up to five or up to seven years of service. Under no conditions is the difference between their rate of socialization and that of seasoned officials significant. I also tested several nonlinear permutations of length of service; none is superior to linearity.

In a private organization, you have blanket indoctrination of everyone concerned into the goals of whatever you are producing, whether it is a production program or the launching of a new product or a new financial exercise, every single person goes through something akin to a propaganda exercise. This does not happen in the Commission. You have to form informal coalitions . . . allies in the cause of a particular advancement of the policy from here to there."

Does Organizational Fragmentation Affect Socialization?

It is conventional wisdom that bureaucratic fragmentation in the Commission encourages local cultures,[57] and one would expect this to influence Commission socialization. Coombes, an early student of the Commission, described the Commission as a collection of feudal fiefdoms.[58] Cram conceives of the European Commission as a multi-organization, where subunits have their own goals and operational style.[59] Since the late 1980s, the Commission bureaucracy has also been scattered over some thirty-five buildings across Brussels, while in the old days many worked within walking distance of the Commission headquarters in the Berlaymont building on Schuman square. Spatial separation is said to have reinforced a culture of fiefdoms.

If the Commission is as fragmented as many observers and some policymakers claim it is, directorates with extensive supranational competences and discretionary budgets should be more effective in instilling supranational norms. This is not the case.[60]

The explanation appears to be mobility. Mobility hinders identification with a particular unit. In the mid- to late 1990s, the average time a top official spent in a particular top position was less than five years. Consider these statistics: of the people I interviewed in 1996, more than half had left the European Commission by September 2001, and 25 percent had changed departments. With a turnover rate among top officials of 75 percent over five years, there is not much time to mold individual preferences according to particular departmental cultures. After the Santer Commission resigned in 1999 over allegations of fraud, mismanagement, and nepotism, the newly appointed commissioner for personnel, Neil Kinnock, required top officials to change posts every five to seven years.[61] Contrary to common beliefs, only a small group of top officials is entrenched in a departmental world. Kinnock's mobility rules merely formalized common practice.

---

[57] See Page 1997; and Shore 2000.
[58] Coombes 1970.
[59] Cram 1994.
[60] For the 1996 sample, I calculate for each official the number of years he spent in departments with extensive legal competences or a significant discretionary budget, and I call this variable POWERDG/SOCIALIZATION. I also calculate the alternative utility hypothesis, i.e., officials who happen to work in a supranational department have career reasons to favor supranationalism, which is labeled POWER-DG UTILITY. As the OLS regression in Table A in Appendix 2 illustrates, neither hypothesis bites.
[61] Kinnock made these measures public in a press statement on 29 September 1999. Strictly speaking, the new rules make rotation mandatory only for director-generals, but in practice, directors have also been forced to rotate. Author's interview with a member of the Kinnock cabinet, February 2002.

High rates of interdepartmental mobility should privilege overarching Commission norms. Interdepartmental coordination, which compels top officials to clear their departmental policies with other departments, should reinforce this. The apex of this elaborate coordination network consists of weekly meetings of director-generals, where interdepartmental Commission business is settled.

Limits to the Commission's Boundedness: National Socialization

Table 3 strongly supports the contention that national socialization may be more effective than international socialization in shaping international officials' preferences. National socialization appears double-edged, as noted by authors in this volume. On the one hand, national socialization depresses support for supranationalism among former national civil servants. On the other, national socialization engenders support for international norms. The best predictor of top officials' support for supranationalism is whether they come from a federal country. Core beliefs about national governance shape preferences on European governance. Federalism divides sovereignty, and this notion underpins multilevel governance.[62] Thus, controlling for other factors, a Commission official who grew up in Belgium or Germany is more favorably disposed to supranationalism than one raised in Britain or France.

Contexts outside the Commission are powerful. The European Commission cannot afford to be a bounded institution. Shared authority is a vital feature of EU decision making. In few, if any, policy areas can one institution, national or European, take authoritative decisions unilaterally.[63] The European system of multilevel governance plugs top Commission officials into diverse institutional contexts. It is necessary and natural for Commission officials to be attuned to national governments, political parties, public opinion, and other EU institutions, as well as to their international organization.

The pull of national contexts is consistent with the socialization literature. Unlike international organizations, national institutions—from families to schools to governments—draw full advantage from the primacy effect. European children grow up in national contexts, and such contexts leave imprints that are hard to dislodge later in life.

It is instructive to compare national civil servants with European Commission officials. National civil servants work for powerful national governments that represent imagined communities having concrete expression in national systems of welfare or education, as well as bloc votes in the EU Council of Ministers. The notion of national public interest has a tangible core.[64] European public interest is shallower. While the EU has acquired some trappings of nationhood—an anthem, a flag, a public holiday, a European driver's license, a European passport, a European currency, membership of international organizations—these symbols register weakly in people's minds. Few outside the European institutions know that 9 May is Europe's "Independence Day."

---

[62] See Hooghe and Marks 2003; Keohane 2002; and Risse 2001.
[63] See Hooghe and Marks 2001; and Pollack 2000.
[64] Page and Wright 1999.

The Euro is the single exception in terms of capturing public attention, but its virtue is contested.[65] National civil servants speak for deeply rooted national communities, while Commission officials speak for a potential community.[66] The "gravitational pull" of the national often overwhelms that of Europe, even for those who work in the Commission. A long-serving top official describes this astutely:

There is a clear difference between national administrations and the Commission. National administrations have a broad consensus on objectives. All civil servants are interested in pulling the same cart, and they know in which direction and when to pull the cart. They may disagree about marginal adjustments or speed, but they basically all agree on where they want to go and what the national interest is. To use the word "national interest" gives immediately away why this cannot be the case inside the Commission. Even though we are supposed to work for the common interest of the Community, nobody forgets his background, his nationality. Much of the conflict between national interests has been transferred to the Commission. Some [officials] are almost unashamed of it; they go straight for it and make it no secret. Others—and I think this is also a question of how long you have been in the Commission—work much more for the common benefit. They tend to take a rational-reasoned balanced Community approach, whereas others choose a national-interest approach. So, national tensions are transferred to the Commission, and that makes it impossible to have everybody agree *ex ante* on common objectives. There are no common objectives. . . . This is still a relatively young, expanding and maturing institution, which has not yet found its own identity.

What Is the Role of Self-Selection and Selective Recruitment?

Socialization is only one of several processes by which members of an organization may come to support organizational norms. In this section, I discuss how self-selection and selective recruitment shape supranational preferences. In the next section, I demonstrate that material incentives help account for the views of top Commission officials.

One knows that top Commission officials, including recent recruits, are more in favor of shifting powers to the EU than either national elites or public opinion. This may, in part, result from self-selection. As the so-called engine of European integration, it is likely that the Commission appeals to "believers."

Evidence from interviews suggests that self-selection plays a role, but the effect may be more limited than is often assumed. When top officials are asked why they joined the Commission, about one-quarter talk about European integration as an ideal, which guarantees, or partially guarantees, peace, democracy, order, or good governance. As an older Dutch official explains, "I am a child of the war. People of my generation would do anything to avoid a third world war. We did not have a sophisticated notion of an institutionalized Europe, but we were deeply European because we never wanted to repeat that experience." Officials from Spain, Portugal, and Greece often mention that European integration helped consolidate their young democracies.

---

[65] For many Europeans, it is associated with economic hardship, as its popular German nickname, *Euro-Teuro* (expensive Euro) illustrates.

[66] See Abélès and Bellier 1996; and Shore 2000.

However, most officials cite more pragmatic reasons for joining the Commission, including building a career (39 percent); national connections (21 percent, for example, their government asked them to apply); connections in the policy community (21 percent, for example, they were approached when serving as national experts in Council or Commission working groups); party-political connections (8 percent); or the desire for a policy challenge (11 percent).[67] Overall, then, most officials enter the Commission for other than idealistic reasons. Self-selection motivates only a minority.

There is also limited evidence of pro-European selective recruitment. Formal recruitment rules allow the Commission to select officials on the basis of their preferences if it so wishes. The most supranational Commission president over the past three decades, Delors, took these rules to heart: he searched for officials who would press forward his supranational agenda. According to Ross, "Delors, with Pascal's [Lamy, Delors' chef de cabinet] advice, had very carefully replaced a considerable number of high Commission officials, directors-general and division heads, in critical areas."[68] But there is no firm statistical support for this in the data. Although Delors recruits tended to be more supranational than those recruited into top positions before or after Delors, the difference falls short of significance. There is no effect at all for the Santer or Prodi Commissions.[69] The Commission could, if it so chooses, influence its normative intake. But it rarely does so.

Can One Distinguish Socialization from Utility Maximization?

I have theorized that the effect of socialization depends on what is being socialized. The more a Commission norm invokes diffuse or large values, the greater the scope for socialization. Utility maximization, by contrast, should be stronger for norms that regulate tasks, work practices, and constituency relations—norms, in other words, with immediate career implications.

In the introduction, I identified three norms that characterize the Commission's mission: supranationalism; Commission agenda setting; and autonomy from national influence. How do the effects of socialization and utility vary across these?

Supranationalism is a prime example of a diffuse norm. It is nearly impossible for top officials to anticipate how a more supranational European Union may affect them professionally. Supranationalism has ambiguous career implications. On the one hand, more supranationalism means more policy tasks and resources. But on the other, it implies upgrading the College of Commissioners to the government of Europe, and this would imply downgrading permanent officials to mere civil servants. So one would expect socialization to be strong, and personal career utility to be weak, in shaping officials' norms regarding supranationalism.

Contrast this with the norm prescribing autonomy from national pressures. This is a norm with transparent implications for top officials' careers. Should the Commission's

---

[67] The percentages add up to more than 100 percent, because some officials mentioned two reasons.
[68] Ross 1995, 67.
[69] I seek to capture the effect of selective recruitment by respective Commission presidents by means of three dummies—one each for individuals appointed to top positions under Jacques Delors (1986–94), Jacques Santer (1995–98), and Romano Prodi (1999–2002). The OLS regression in Table A5 in Appendix 2 shows that none of these effects is significant.

personnel system be strictly Weberian and reward merit over and above nationality, or should it reflect national quotas? National quotas punish qualified candidates having the "wrong" nationality. That is to say, officials from smaller countries are disadvantaged because small countries have relatively few top slots to fill, and so are officials who have not cultivated strong national connections that could catapult them into national slots. Contrast the fate of two respected directors, one Dane and one Greek, interviewed in 1996. The Dane's ambition to reach the summit—director-general— was dashed when a younger compatriot with better political connections was promoted to the top slot reserved for Denmark. The Greek director rated his chances for promotion as virtually nil because the two Greek top-rank posts had recently been taken up. Fast-forward to 2002, when the Danish official had taken early retirement, while his Greek colleague was just promoted. What had happened? The Commission resignation crisis in 1999 changed the prospects for the Greek director when one of the two top Greeks was sacked under a cloud of negligence and alleged fraud. So, unexpectedly, a window of opportunity opened briefly and then closed again. A merit-based promotion system, on the other hand, disadvantages candidates from recent member states, who usually have less experience with the Commission's way of working. One would therefore expect support for the norm of Commission autonomy to vary in tune with utility considerations, such as the strength of national or political connections, the size of a country's quota, or the timing of a country's membership, while socialization is expected to be weak.

Finally, one would expect support for the norm of Commission agenda setting to be influenced by both socialization and utility. This norm is diffuse in that it embodies Monnet's vision of the Commission as the engine of Europe; consequently, it should be amenable to socialization. But the norm also has calculable implications for officials' careers, in that it privileges a particular type of Commission activity (creating new policies) above another (administering existing policies); therefore, one would expect that utility calculations, informed by whether they are vested in one or the other kind of activity, to matter as well.

Tables 4a, 4b, and 4c allow one to evaluate the relative effects of socialization and utility on these norms. Table 4a presents OLS models explaining variation among Commission officials on the norm of supranationalism; Table 4b provides the same for Commission agenda setting; and Table 4c presents models explaining variation on the norm of autonomy from national influence. Each table reports three explanatory models for two time points, 1996 and 2002.[70] The first two columns in each table represent socialization variables; the following two columns represent utility variables; the final two columns combine socialization and utility variables.

The coefficients of determination (R^2) at the bottom of each table estimate the proportion of variance explained by each model. Socialization has the greatest causal weight for supranationalism (Table 4a); socialization is about evenly balanced with utility maximization for Commission agenda setting (Table 4b); and in Table 4c, socialization is dwarfed by utility maximization for the norm of autonomy from national influences. These results are consistent across time points, with the exception of 2002 for the autonomy norm.

---

[70] Appendix 3 hypothesizes causal effects and operationalizes variables.

Table 4a. *Explaining Supranationalism: Socialization versus Utility*

	Socialization model		Utility maximization model		Full model	
	1996	*2002*	*1996*	*2002*	*1996*	*2002*
Constant	5.050	4.860	5.204	5.961	3.804	5.344
	(1.388)**	(.801)**	(.952)**	(.743)**	(1.879)*	(1.045)**
Commission socialization						
LENGTH OF SERVICE	0.027	−0.007			0.042	−0.007
	(.026)	(.015)			(.033)	(.016)
INTERNATIONAL	0.226	0.105			0.176	0.038
EDUCATION	(.256)	(.120)			(.275)	(.136)
Socialization outside Commission						
STATE STRUCTURE						
(DISPERSED VS.						
UNITARY:)						
FEDERALISM	0.176	0.141			0.182	0.150
	(.078)*	(.047)**			(.081)*	(.050)**
SIZE OF COUNTRY	−0.022	−0.004			−0.018	−0.002
	(.010)*	(.006)			(.011)°	(.007)
IDEOLOGY	−0.150	−0.062			−0.120	−0.042
	(.151)	(.083)			(.154)	(.085)
YEARS IN NATIONAL	−0.032	−0.023			−0.032	−0.024
ADMINISTRATION	(.036)	(.020)			(.038)	(.021)
Utility factors						
POWER-DG UTILITY			0.089	−0.075	0.122	−0.092
			(.079)	(.071)	(.102)	(.071)
NATIONAL ECONOMIC			0.117	−0.041	0.225	0.086
BENEFIT			(.161)	(.131)	(.228)	(.136)
NATIONAL CLUBNESS			−0.510	−0.265	−0.125	−0.141
			(.199)*	(.160)°	(.300)	(.194)
PARACHUTAGE			−0.285	−0.056	0.367	0.026
			(.328)	(.262)	(.633)	(.316)
Control factor: gender	−0.099	0.012	−0.085	−0.009	−0.032	0.041
	(.822)	(.417)	(.644)	(.419)	(.837)	(.423)
R^2	0.234	0.150	0.091	0.038	0.276	0.182

Note: Ordinary least squares (OLS) regression analyses with pairwise deletion. The N is 105 for 1996 and 93 for 2002. Dependent and independent variables are detailed in Appendix 3. All models in this and the following tables control for gender. Significance at $**p < .01$; $*p < .05$; $°p < .15$.

Table 4b. *Explaining Views on Commission Agenda Setting: Socialization versus Utility*

	Socialization model		Utility maximization model		Full model	
	1996	2002	1996	2002	1996	2002
Constant	4.446	3.438	6.795	1.586	8.178**	2.313**
	(1.633)**	(1.038)**	(2.426)**	(1.699)**	(3.414)	(1.941)
Commission socialization						
LENGTH OF SERVICE	0.021	0.020			0.024	0.007
	(.025)	(.017)			(.031)	(.022)
INTERNATIONAL	−0.076	0.136			−0.118	0.202
EDUCATION	(.323)	(.164)			(.325)	(.170)
Socialization outside Commission						
IDEOLOGY	−0.363	−0.204			−0.346	−0.203
	(.200)°	(.119)°			(.204)°	(.124)°
NATIONAL						
ADMINISTRATIVE						
TRADITION	−1.156	0.507			−0.865	0.245
WEAK WEBERIAN	(.945)	(.630)			(.973)	(.705)
	−0.272	−0.412			−0.462	−0.245
STRONG WEBERIAN	(.747)	(.510)			(.780)	(.528)
PRIVATE-SECTOR	−0.177	−0.280			−0.358	−0.222
EXPERIENCE	(.656)	(.466)			(.661)	(.476)
Utility factors						
NATIONAL ECONOMIC			0.001	−0.181	0.114	−0.204
BENEFIT			(.196)	(.160)	(.269)	(.166)
ADMINISTRATIVE/MANA-			−0.381	0.373	−0.317	0.347
GERIAL-DG UTILITY			(.405)	(.344)	(.552)	(.367)
SOFT-DG UTILITY			−0.406	0.771	−0.447	0.425
			(.489)	(.503)°	(.694)	(.573)
DELORS RECRUIT			−0.925	−0.110	−0.910	−0.052
			(.398)*	(.379)	(.542)°	(.387)
AGE			−0.054	0.024	−0.054	0.023
			(.037)	(.029)	(.058)	(.035)
Control factor: gender	1.096	0.841	0.605	0.765	0.920	0.848
	(1.066)	(.593)	(.815)	(.562)	(1.116)	(.612)
R^2	0.143	0.117	0.103	0.089	0.232	0.155

Note: Ordinary least squares (OLS) regression analyses with pairwise deletion. The N is 105 for 1996 and 93 for 2002. Dependent and independent variables are detailed in Appendix 3. Significance at ** $p < .01$; * $p < .05$; ° $p < .15$.

Table 4c. *Explaining Views on Commission Autonomy: Socialization versus Utility*

	Socialization model		Utility maximization model		Full model	
	1996	*2002*	*1996*	*2002*	*1996*	*2002*
Constant	4.245	5.308	6.119	5.869	6.453	5.105
	(.854)**	(.559)	(.880)**	(.618)**	(1.062)**	(.804)**
Commission socialization						
LENGTH OF SERVICE	−0.020	0.008			−0.020	0.022
	(.017)	(.012)			(.024)	(.015)
INTERNATIONAL	0.089	0.035			−0.109	0.111
EDUCATION	(.206)	(.112)			(.190)	(.124)
Socialization outside Commission						
NATIONAL						
ADMINISTRATIVE						
TRADITION	1.316	0.726			0.586	0.561
WEAK WEBERIAN	(.607)*	(.417)°			(.595)	(.494)
	−0.953	0.687			−0.659	0.651
STRONG WEBERIAN	(.475)*	(.345)°			(.465)°	(.357)°
CABINET EXPERIENCE	−0.546	0.131			−0.503	0.086
	(.368)°	(.235)			(.327)°	(.239)
Utility factors						
PARACHUTAGE			0.498	−0.116	0.272	0.039
			(.321)°	(.250)	(.458)	(.283)
SOFT-DG UTILITY			−1.341	0.556	−1.500	0.448
			(.379)**	(.340)°	(.389)**	(.381)
NATIONAL CLUBNESS			−0.881	0.175	−0.816	0.226
			(.186)**	(.140)	(.221)**	(.171)
NATIONAL QUOTA			−0.137	−0.055	−0.075	−0.080
			(.058)**	(.044)	(.065)	(.048)°
Control factor: gender	−0.345	−0.404	0.393	−0.526	0.222	−0.450
	(.683)	(.392)	(.607)	(.385)	(.611)	(.394)
R^2	0.136	0.095	0.320	0.064	0.365	0.147

Note: Ordinary least squares (OLS) regression analyses with pairwise deletion. The N is 105 for 1996 and 93 for 2002. Dependent and independent variables are detailed in Appendix 3. Significance at ** $p < .01$; * $p < .05$; ° $p < .15$.

Furthermore, the results in Tables 4a, 4b, and 4c highlight a point made above: socialization requires stable norms; utility maximization requires transparent incentives. Commission norms became less stable and less transparent after the resignation of the Santer Commission in 1999, which happened in the face of allegations of fraud, mismanagement, and nepotism. The result is that top officials' views in 2002 are markedly less structured than in 1996. The 2002 data capture an organization in turmoil. The crisis shattered consensus in the Commission around the agenda-setting norm, which prescribes that the European Commission's primary role is to initiate, not administer, EU policies (see Table 4b). In 1999, a new Commission team under Romano Prodi began rewriting internal work practices to encourage "sound management," and thus shifted the focus from policy creation to management. The crisis also forced the organization to face up to a duplicitous personnel policy whereby the norm of autonomy from national influences (see Table 4c) was contradicted by the practice of national quotas in top appointments.[71] The Commission responded by overhauling its personnel policy. The new policy rejects national quotas, favors merit and seniority, privileges internal promotion over lateral appointments, lays down a code of impartial conduct, and imposes mobility on the higher echelons. The upshot is that, as long as the Commission's organizational mission is in flux, the Commission is in a weak position to shape—either through socialization or through career incentives—top officials' views on Commission norms.

Table 5 summarizes, then, how this empirical study of socialization in the Commission bears on the theory.

Conclusion

International socialization is hardly a panacea for those interested in diffusing international norms. The European Commission is surely among the most favorable sites for socialization of international norms. Yet the evidence suggests that Commission and international socialization is considerably weaker than socialization outside the Commission.

Why is international socialization weak? One reason is that international organizations rarely benefit from the primacy effect – the opportunity to influence members in their young adult years. The European Commission is an unusual international organization in that 35 percent of its top employees began to work in the Commission in their twenties. Commission socialization is almost exclusively concentrated in this group. It is extremely difficult—nigh impossible—for an international organization to substantially shift the views of mature recruits.

A second reason for the weakness of international socialization is that international organizations lack control over their members' life chances. Socialization flourishes in homogeneous, bounded environments; it is suppressed when an organization is fragmented and vulnerable to external influences. The European Commission is unusual in that it has more control over its members than all but a few international organizations. It has formal autonomy in recruiting and promoting its personnel. It has the authority to impose mobility on its officials to discourage divergent bureaucratic subcultures. It has extensive supranational powers and the constitutional writ to insulate its work from national and other influences. This is fertile ground for instilling Commission norms. However, the European Commission coexists with national institutions. The Commission sets the agenda, but it must engage the Council of Ministers, individual governments, and the European Parliament in order to legislate. Openness comes at a price: it diminishes the Commission's control over its officials, and induces these people to tap additional loyalties. Hence, even in an international organization as

---

[71] See Peterson 1999; and Ross 1995.

Table 5. *Scope and Mechanisms of Socialization: Evidence*

Hypothesis	Evidence
Socialization is most intense for newcomers and decreases over time.	Weak support
Inexperienced recruits are more rapidly socialized.	Strong support
Self-selected recruits are more likely to support organizational norms.	Moderate support
Fragmentation inhibits unitary socialization.	Weak support
The more bounded the organization, the more effective in socializing.	Strong support
Organizationally selected recruits are more likely to support organizational norms.	Weak support
Explicit sanctions/rewards induce utility maximization, not socialization.	Strong support
Large or diffuse issues facilitate socialization.	Strong support
Transparent, sizeable material stakes facilitate utility maximization.	Strong support
Unstable norms discourage preference structuring: socialization and utility maximization are weakened.	Strong support

powerful as the Commission, one finds that national norms, originating in prior experiences in national ministries, loyalty to national political parties, or diffuse national political socialization, decisively shape top officials' views on European norms.

One might turn the question around: Why is support for international norms so strong? One conclusion of this study is that there is no intrinsic contradiction between national and international norms. The most powerful influences on pro-European support among top officials are national or subnational. National and subnational socialization can, and do, produce support for international norms.

Supranationalism can also be generated by utilitarian incentives. One knows that material incentives can nudge state actors toward, or away from, international norms,[72] and I discern a similar logic at the micro level in the Commission itself. But the causal power of material utility is limited. Views about general principles of international governance are influenced more by ideological predispositions and conceptions of identity than by cost-benefit calculations. This is explicable within the paradigm of rational choice itself: When general governance norms are at issue, the immediate material impact on individual lives tends to be obscure or, to the extent it can be calculated, small.

Finally, there is some circumstantial evidence that self-selection nudges up support for Commission norms. Indeed, individuals who choose to work in an international organization are likely to be favorably disposed to the organization's norms.

There are, then, multiple paths through which preferences may be molded to reflect international norms. International socialization, in the sense of inducting international norms within the organization itself, is one of them. But in the crucial case of the European Commission, international socialization is by no means the most powerful.

---

[72] See Schimmelfennig, this volume; and Kelley 2004.

Appendix 1

Table A1. *Explaining Supranationalism*

Dependent variable	
SUPRANATIONALISM	Index of two equally weighted items ranging from 1 (strongly opposed) to 7 (strongly in favor): (1) member states should be the central pillars of the EU (item reversed); and (2) Commission should be the government of the European Union.

Independent variables	
Socialization variables	
LENGTH OF COMMISSION SERVICE (COMMISSION SOCIALIZATION) PRIMACY EFFECT	Years in Commission service. *Source:* Biographical data from *The European Companion* 1992, 1994; *Euro's Who's Who* 1991; Commission press communications; and interviews by the author. An interaction term of years in Commission service and (age 65 − age at time of entry).
INTERNATIONAL EDUCATION	4-category variable whereby no international education = 0, studied in other European country = 1, studied outside Europe = 2, and studied in other European country and outside Europe = 3. *Source:* Biographical data and interviews.
FEDERALISM	Extent of regional governance combining measures for constitutional federalism, autonomy for special territories in the national state, the role of regions in central government, and presence or absence of direct regional elections. Values range from 0 to 12, and reflect situation in 1990. Values allocated to top officials according to home country. *Source:* Hooghe and Marks 2001, app. 2.
SIZE OF COUNTRY	Population size of home country of each senior Commission official. Values in millions.
IDEOLOGY	For 1996: self-reported partisan affiliation, recoded into ideological 11-point left/right scale. For 2002: self-reported 11-point left/right ideological positioning. *Source:* Hix and Lord 1997.
NATIONAL ADMINISTRATION	Years in national service. Only national state, not posting in Brussels. *Source:* Biographical data and interview data.
Utility maximization variables	
POWER-DG UTILITY	Composite index ranging from 0 to 9 of three measures: (1) DG discretion in regulation, measured as proportion of Commission regulatory output without Council approval; (2) DG discretion in adjudication, measured as the absolute number of Court cases initiated by a DG; and (3) DG reputation from interviews with top officials reporting three or four most powerful Commission DGs. *Source:* Hooghe 2002.
NATIONAL ECONOMIC BENEFIT	EU structural aid for 1994–99 as percentage of GDP for each member state. *Source:* European Commission 1996. Percentage of GDP per country. Extrapolated to 2002. Scores to officials by nationality.

Table A2. *Descriptive Statistics*

Name	N	Mean	Median	Min.	Max.	SD
SUPRANATIONALISM	198	4.61	4.75	1	7	1.49
LENGTH OF SERVICE	198	18.71	20.00	1	41	10.38
PRIMACY EFFECT	196	618.51	608.00	7	1722	438.15
INTERNATIONAL EDUCATION	196	0.73	0.00	0	3	0.97
FEDERALISM	198	4.30	4.00	0	10	3.08
SIZE OF COUNTRY	198	40.44	57.00	0.40	79.30	25.92
IDEOLOGY	152	5.24	5.00	1.50	9.30	1.50
YEARS IN NATIONAL ADMINISTRATION	198	5.48	1.00	0	29	7.23
POWER-DG UTILITY	198	4.64	4.00	1	9	1.94
NATIONAL ECONOMIC BENEFIT	198	0.68	0.25	0.11	3.98	1.04

Table A3. *Correlation Matrix*

	(1)	(2)	(3)	(4)	(5)	(6)	(7)	(8)	(9)
(1) SUPERNATIONALISM	1.00								
(2) LENGTH OF SERVICE	0.16*	1.00							
(3) PRIMACY EFFECT	0.13*	0.97**	1.00						
(4) INTERNATIONAL EDUCATION	0.22**	0.01	−0.00	1.00					
(5) FEDERALISM	0.33**	0.22**	0.20**	0.16*	1.00				
(6) SIZE OF COUNTRY	0.01	0.40**	0.41**	−0.04	0.44**	1.00			
(7) IDEOLOGY	−0.17*	−0.03	−0.07	−0.05	−0.16*	−0.14	1.00		
(8) YEARS IN NATIONAL ADMINISTRATION	−0.22**	−0.50**	−0.57**	−0.18*	−0.11	−0.26**	0.11	1.00	
(9) POWER-DG UTILITY	0.04	−0.00	−0.00	−0.05	0.06	0.00	0.02	0.02	1.00
(10) NATIONAL ECONOMIC BENEFIT	0.08	−0.26**	−0.23**	0.17*	−0.28**	−0.39**	0.01	0.04	−0.14*

Note: ** $p < .01$; * $p < .05$.

Appendix 2

Table A4. *The Effect of Socialization in Selective DGs (Power DG)*

Constant	3.849 (1.369)**
International socialization	
LENGTH OF SERVICE IN COMMISSION	0.033 (.027)
INTERNATIONAL EDUCATION	0.215 (.259)
POWER-DG SOCIALIZATION	− 0.003 (.036)
Socialization outside Commission	
STATE STRUCTURE (POOLED/UNITARY SOVEREIGNTY):	
FEDERALISM	0.188 (.80)*
SIZE	− 0.020 (.010)°
IDEOLOGY	− 0.132 (.151)
YEARS IN NATIONAL ADMINISTRATION	− 0.030 (.036)
Utility factors	
POWER-DG UTILITY	0.132 (.116)
NATIONAL ECONOMIC BENEFIT	− 0.030 (.036)
R^2	0.268
Adjusted R^2	0.139
N	105

Note: Ordinary least squares (OLS) regression for 1996 sample. Coefficients are unstandardized. Standard errors are in parentheses. OLS regression analysis with pairwise deletion. ** $p < .01$; * $p < .05$; ° $p < 15$.

Table A5. *The Effect of Selective Recruitment by Commission Presidents*

Constant	4.141 (.748)**
International socialization	
LENGTH OF SERVICE IN COMMISSION	0.017 (.014)
INTERNATIONAL EDUCATION	0.156 (.122)
Socialization outside Commission	
STATE STRUCTURE (POOLED/UNITARY SOVEREIGNTY):	
FEDERALISM	0.181 (.043)**
SIZE	−0.012 (.006)*
IDEOLOGY	−0.112 (.078)°
YEARS IN NATIONAL ADMINISTRATION	−0.028 (.019)°
Utility factors	
POWER-DG UTILITY	0.033 (.059)
NATIONAL ECONOMIC BENEFIT	0.184 (.123)°
Selective recruitment	
DELORS RECRUIT	0.287 (.345)
SANTER RECRUIT	0.168 (.371)
PRODI RECRUIT	0.322 (.463)
R^2	0.230
Adjusted R^2	0.169
N	198

Note: Ordinary least squares (OLS) regression for pooled sample. Coefficients are unstandardized. Standard errors are in parentheses. OLS regression analysis with pairwise deletion. ** $p < .01$; * $p < .05$; ° $p < .15$.

Appendix 3

Table A6. *Views on Supranationalism*

Dependent variable

SUPRANATIONALISM	Index of two equally weighted items ranging from 1 (strongly opposed) to 7 (strongly in favor): (1) member states should be the central pillars of the EU (item reversed); and (2) Commission should be the government of the European Union.

Independent variables

Socialization variables: See Table A1.
Utility maximization variables: See Table A1 and the following.

NATIONAL CLUBNESS	*H:* The better one's nationality is organized in Brussels, the more an official has career incentives to support intergovernmentalism and oppose supranationalism. *O:* Index measuring degree of cohesion, organizational resources, national government's policy toward compatriots, and Commission cabinet resources of nationalities in Brussels; the degree of organization determines the effectiveness of nationalities in pushing career interests of their compatriots. Values are $1 =$ low, $2 =$ medium, $3 =$ strong. *Source:* Hooghe 2002. Values allocated to officials by nationality.
PARACHUTAGE	*H:* A parachuted official is likely to support intergovernmentalism to pay back the government that helped appoint him. *O:* Dummy for official who was externally appointed into a senior position.

Note: H = Hypothesis; *O =* Operationalization.

Table A7. *Views on Commission Agenda Setting*

Dependent variable

AGENDA SETTING	Item: "Administration, management should be Commission priority (item reversed)." Ranges from 1 (strongly opposed) to 7 (strongly in favor).

Independent variables

Socialization variables

COMMISSION SOCIALIZATION	*H:* The longer an official has served in the Commission, the more likely he internalizes support for Commission agenda setting. *O:* See Table A1.
INTERNATIONAL EDUCATION	*H:* An internationally educated official is more likely to be socialized into wanting maximal Commission agenda setting. *O:* See Table A1.
IDEOLOGY	*H:* A left-oriented official is more likely to prefer Commission agenda setting because it increases political regulation of the single market. *O:* See Table A1.

Table A7. *(Continued)*

PRIVATE-SECTOR EXPERIENCE	*H:* An official with private-sector managerial experience is more likely to prefer a managerial Commission. *O:* Dummy with value of 1 if official had experience in industry or banking. *Source:* Biographical data and interviews.
NATIONAL ADMINISTRATIVE TRADITION	*H:* An official socialized in Weberian administrative tradition is more likely to prefer an agenda-setting Commission than an official from a weak Weberian administration. *O:* Dummies for weak-Weberian, medium-Weberian, strong-Weberian. Values allocated by nationality to officials with national administrative experience. *Source:* Page 1995; and Page and Wright 1999.

Utility maximization variables

NATIONAL ECONOMIC BENEFIT	*H:* An official from a country that draws net benefits from the EU has material incentives to prefer Commission agenda setting because an active Commission is likely to deepen positive integration. *O:* See Table A1.
DELORS RECRUIT	*H:* An official appointed under Delors to run the internal market program has career incentives to emphasize Commission management. *O:* Dummy with value of 1 if official was recruited to top position under Commission president Jacques Delors. *Source:* Biographical data.
AGE	*H:* A younger official has career incentives to emphasize Commission agenda setting. *O:* Age of official at time of interview.
ADMINISTRATIVE/ MANAGERIAL-DG UTILITY	*H:* An official from an administrative-managerial DG has career incentives to oppose Commission agenda setting. *O:* Dummy taking a value of 1 for officials in DGs with tasks that are primarily routine administration, implementation or adjudication; consistent with the definition of managerial roles by Page 1997.
SOFT-DG UTILITY	*H:* Officials from DGs with soft nonbudgetary power have career incentives to prefer Commission agenda setting. *O:* Danny taking a value of 1 for officials working in a DG concerned with policy areas that use most frequently benchmarking, soft law, peer group pressure, technical reporting, and other soft policy instruments. *Source:* Interview data.

Note: H = Hypothesis; *O =* Operationalization.

Table A8. *Views on Commission Autonomy from National Influence*

Dependent variable	
COMMISSION AUTONOMY	Index of two equally weighted items tapping into views on national quota, and on national dossiers. The index ranges from 1 (strongly opposed) to 7 (strongly in favor). Wording differs between 1996 and 2002.
	Items in 1996: (1) "It hurts Commission legitimacy that certain DGs tend to be dominated by particular nationalities," and (2) "Too many Commission officials let their nationality interfere with professional judgments."
	Items in 2002: (1) "Some argue that positions in the Commission should be distributed across nationalities proportionate to respective populations (item reversed)," and (2) "Some think that it is preferable to have dossiers of special interest to particular nationalities managed by officials of those nationalities (item reversed)."

Independent variables	
Socialization variables	
COMMISSION SOCIALIZATION	*H:* The louder an official has served the Commission, the more be is likely to have internalized the norm of Commission autonomy. *O:* See Table A1.
INTERNATIONAL EDUCATION	*H:* An internationally educated official is more likely to be socialized into wanting autonomy from national influence. *O:* See Table Al.
CABINET EXPERIENCE	H: An official with cabinet experience is likely to appreciate the need to work closely with nationals. *O:* A dummy with the value of 1 if an official has served in a Commission cabinet.
NATIONAL ADMINISTRATIVE TRADITION	*H:* An official who worked previously in a Weberian administration prefers a Commission autonomous from national interest. *O:* See Table A7.

Utility maximization variables	
PARACHUTAGE	*H:* A parachuted official has career incentives to oppose Commission autonomy from national influence. *O:* See Table A6.
SOFT-DG UTILITY	*H:* An official from a soft DG has career incentives to cooperate with national stakeholders, which leads to opposition of the Commission norm. *O:* See Table A7.

Table A8. *(Continued)*

NATIONAL CLUBNESS	*H:* The better one's nationality is organized in Brussels, the more an official has career incentives to oppose Commission autonomy from national influence. *O:* See Table A6.
NATIONAL QUOTA	*H:* An official from a country with a small quota has career incentives to support Commission autonomy from national influence. *O:* Number of votes in the Council of Ministers, which is used in the Commission as a proxy for determining national quota of Commission jobs. Variable ranges between 2 and 10. Scores allocated to officials by nationality.

Note: H = Hypothesis; *O* = Operationalization.

References

Abélès, Marc, and Irène Bellier. 1996. La Commission européenne: du compromis culturel à la culture politique du compromis. *Revue Française de Science Politique* 46 (3):431–56.

Allison, Graham T. 1971. *Essence of Decision: Explaining the Cuban Missile Crisis.* Boston: Little, Brown.

Beck, Paul, and M. Kent Jennings. 1991. Family Traditions, Political Periods, and the Development of Partisan Orientation. *Journal of Politics* 53 (3):742–63.

Caporaso, James. 2000. Changes in the Westphalian Order: Territory, Public Authority, and Sovereignty. *International Studies Review* 2 (2):1–28.

Checkel, Jeffrey. 2003. 'Going Native' in Europe? Theorizing Social Interaction in European Institutions. *Comparative Political Studies* 36 (1):209–31.

Chong, Dennis. 2000. *Rational Lives: Norms and Values in Politics and Society.* Chicago: University of Chicago Press.

Citrin, Jack, Donald P. Green, Christopher Muste, and Cara Wong. 1997. Public Opinion Toward Immigration Reform: The Role of Economic Motivations. *Journal of Politics* 59 (3):858–81.

Conover, Pamela Johnston. 1991. Political Socialization: Where's the Politics? In *Political Science: Looking to the Future*, Vol. 3, edited by William Crotty, 125–52. Evanston, Ill.: Northwestern University Press.

Coombes, David. 1970. *Politics and Bureaucracy of the European Community: A Portrait of the Commission of the E.E.C.* London: Allen and Unwin.

Cram, Laura. 1994. The European Commission as a Multi-Organization: Social Policy and IT Policy in the EU. *Journal of European Public Policy* 1 (2):195–217.

Crano, William D. 1997. Vested Interest, Symbolic Politics, and Attitude-Behavior Consistency. *Journal of Personality and Social Psychology* 72 (3):485–91.

Dod's European Companion. 1992, 1994. London: Dod's Politial Publishing.

Druckman, Daniel. 1994. Nationalism, Patriotism, and Group Loyalty: A Social Psychological Perspective. *Mershon International Studies Review* 38 (1):43–68.

Duchéne, François. 1994. *Jean Monnet: The First Statesman of Interdependence.* New York: Norton.

Eckstein, Harry. 1975. Case Study and Theory in Political Science. In *Handbook of Political Science*, Vol. 7, edited by Fred I. Greenstein and Nelson W. Polsby, 79–137. Reading, Mass.: Addison-Wesley.

Egeberg, Morten. 1999. Transcending Intergovernmentalism? Identity and Role Perceptions of National Officials in EU Decision-Making. *Journal of European Public Policy* 6 (3):456–74.

Elster, Jon. 1990. When Rationality Fails. In *The Limits of Rationality*, edited by Karen Schweers Cook and Margaret Levi, 19–51. Chicago: University of Chicago Press.

Evans, Geoffrey. 2002. European Integration, Party Politics and Voting in the 2001 Election. *British Elections and Parties Review* 12:95–110.

European Commission. 1996. *First Report on Economic and Social Cohesion 1996*. DG XVI, 144, Table 24. Brussels: European Commission.

European Convention. 2003. *Draft Treaty Establishing a Constitution for Europe*. CONV 850/03. Brussels: European Parliament.

Euro's Who's Who: Who's Who in the European Communities and in the Other European Organizations. 1991. Brussels: Editions Delta.

Fearon, James, and Alexander Wendt. 2002. Rationalism versus Constructivism: A Skeptical View. In *Handbook of International Relations*, edited by Walter Carlsnaes, Thomas Risse, and Beth A. Simmons, 52–72. London: Sage.

Finnemore, Martha. 1996. *National Interests in International Society.* Ithaca, N.Y.: Cornell University Press.

Gabel, Matthew, and Chris Anderson. 2002. The Structure of Citizen Attitudes and the European Political Space. *Comparative Political Studies* 35 (8):893–913.

Goren, Paul. 2001. Core Principles and Policy Reasoning in Mass Publics: A Test of Two Theories. *British Journal of Political Science* 31 (1):159–77.

Haas, Ernst. 1958. *The Uniting of Europe: Political, Social and Economic Forces, 1950–1957.* Stanford, Calif.: Stanford University Press.

Hartung, Harald. 2001. Eurobarometer 54.1: Building Europe and the European Union: The European Parliament, Public Safety, and Defense Policy, November–December 2000. Brussels: European Opinion Research Group EEIG.

Hemmer, Christopher, and Peter Katzenstein. 2002. Why Is There No NATO in Asia? Collective Identity, Regionalism, and the Origins of Multilateralism. *International Organization* 56 (3):575–607.

Hix, Simon, and Christopher Lord. 1997. *Political Parties in the European Union.* London: MacMillan.

Hooghe, Liesbet, and Gary Marks. 2001. *Multi-Level Governance and European Integration.* Lanham, Md.: Rowman & Littlefield.

———. 2002. *The European Commission and the Integration of Europe: Images of Governance.* Cambridge: Cambridge University Press.

———. 2003. Europe Divided? Elites vs. Public Opinion on European Integration. *European Union Politics* 4 (3):281–305.

———. 2003. Unraveling the Central State, but How? Types of Multi-Level Governance. *American Political Science Review* 97 (2):233–43.

Huddy, Leonie. 2003. Group Identity and Political Cohesion. In *Oxford Handbook of Political Psychology*, edited by David O. Sears, Leonie Huddy, and Robert Jervis, 511–58. Oxford: Oxford University Press.

Hug, Simon, and Thomas König. 2002. In View of Ratification: Governmental Preferences and Domestic Constraints at the Amsterdam Intergovernmental Conference. *International Organization* 56 (4):447–76.

Jennings, M. Kent. 1992. Ideological Thinking among Mass Publics and Political Elites. *Public Opinion Quarterly* 56 (4):419–41.

Jennings, M. Kent, and Laura Stoker. 2001. *The Persistence of the Past: The Class of 1965 Turns Fifty.* Berkeley: Institute of Governmental Studies, University of California at Berkeley.

Johnston, Alastair Iain. 2001. Treating International Institutions as Social Environments. *International Studies Quarterly* 45 (4):487–515.

Kelly, Judith. 2004. International Actors on the Domestic Scene: Membership Conditionality and Socialization by International Institutions. *International Organization* 58 (3):425–57.

Keohane, Robert O. 2002. Ironies of Sovereignty: The European Union and the United States. *Journal of Common Market Studies* 40 (4):743–65.

Legro, Jeffrey. 1996. Culture and Preferences in the International Cooperation Two-Step. *American Political Science Review* 90 (1):118–37.

Lindberg, Leon N., and Stuart A. Scheingold. 1970. *Europe's Would-Be Polity: Patterns of Change in the European Community.* Englewood Cliffs, N.J.: Prentice-Hall.

Linden, Ronald H., ed. 2002. *Norms and Nannies: The Impact of International Organizations on the Central and East European States.* Lanham, Md.: Rowman & Littlefield.

March, James G., and Johan P. Olsen. 1989. *Rediscovering Institutions: The Organizational Basis of Politics.* New York: Free Press.

Marks, Gary, and Marco Steenbergen, eds. 2004. *European Integration and Political Conflict.* Cambridge: Cambridge University Press.

Marks, Gary, Liesbet Hooghe, Moira Nelson, and Erica Edwards. 2006. Party Competition and European Integration in East and West: Different Structure, Same Causality. *Comparative Political Studies* 39.

McKeown, Timothy. 2004. Case Studies and the Limits of the Quantitative Worldview. In *Rethinking Social Inquiry: Diverse Tools, Shared Standards*, edited by Henry E. Brady and David Collier, 139–67. Lanham, Md.: Rowman & Littlefield.

Nordlinger, Eric. 1981. *On the Autonomy of the Democratic State.* Cambridge: Cambridge University Press.

Page, Edward. 1995. Administering Europe. In *Governing the New Europe*, edited by Jack Hayward and Edward Page, 257–85. Durham, N.C.: Duke University Press.

———. 1997. *People Who Run Europe.* Oxford: Clarendon/Oxford University Press.

Page, Edward C., and Vincent Wright, eds. 1999. *Bureaucratic Elites in Western European States: A Comparative Analysis of Top Officials.* Oxford: Oxford University Press.

Peterson, John. 1999. The Santer Era: The European Commission in Normative, Historical and Theoretical Perspective. *Journal of European Public Policy* 6 (1):46–55.

Pollack, Mark. 2000. The End of Creeping Competence? EU Policy-Making Since Maastricht. *Journal of Common Market Studies* 38 (3):519–38.

———. 2003. *The Engines of European Integration: Delegation, Agency, and Agenda Setting in the EU.* Oxford: Oxford University Press.

Putnam, Robert. 1973. *The Beliefs of Politicians: Ideology, Conflict and Democracy in Britain and Italy.* New Haven, Conn.: Yale University Press.

Risse, Thomas. 2000. 'Let's Argue!': Communicative Action in World Politics. *International Organisation* 54 (1):1–39.

———. 2001. A European Identity? Europeanization and the Evolution of Nation-State Identities. In *Transforming Europe: Europeanization and Domestic Change*, edited by Maria Green Cowles, James Caporaso, and Thomas Risse, 198–216. Ithaca, N.Y.: Cornell University Press.

Risse, Thomas, Stephen Ropp, and Kathryn Sikkink, eds. 1999. *The Power of Human Rights: International Norms and Domestic Change.* Cambridge: Cambridge University Press.

Ross, George. 1995. *Jacques Delors and European Integration.* New York: Oxford University Press.

Searing, Donald. 1986. A Theory of Political Socialization: Institutional Support and Deradicalization in Britain. *British Journal of Political Science* 16 (3):341–76.

———. 1991. Roles, Rules and Rationality in the New Institutionalism. *American Political Science Review* 32 (l):47–68.

———. 1994. *Westminster's World: Understanding Political Roles.* Cambridge: Cambridge University Press.

Searing, Donald, Gerald Wright, and George Rabinowitz. 1976. The Primacy Principle: Attitude Change and Political Socialization. *British Journal of Political Science* 6 (1):83–113.

Sears, David O. 1993. Symbolic Politics: A Socio-Psychological Theory. In *Explorations in Political Psychology*, edited by Shanto Iyengar and William J. McGuire, 113–49. Durham, N.C.: Duke University Press.

Sears, David O., and Carolyn Funk. 1991. The Role of Self-Interest in Social and Political Attitudes. *Advances in Experimental Social Psychology* 24 (1):1–91.

———. 1999. Evidence of the Long-Term Persistence of Adults' Political Predispositions. *Journal of Politics* 61 (l):1–28.

Sears, David O., and Sheri Levy. 2003. Childhood and Adult Political Development. In *Oxford Handbook of Political Psychology*, edited by David O. Sears, Leonie Huddy, and Robert Jervis, 60–109. Oxford: Oxford University Press.

Sears, David O., and Nicholas A. Valentino. 1997. Politics Matters: Political Events as Catalysts for Preadult Socialization. *American Political Science Review* 91 (l):45–65.

Shore, Cris. 2000. *Building Europe: The Cultural Politics of European Integration.* London: Routledge.

Simon, Herbert A. 1985. Human Nature in Politics: The Dialogue of Psychology with Political Science. *American Political Science Review* 79 (2):293–304.

Spence, Jacqueline M. 1996. The European Union 'A View from the Top': Top Decision Makers and the European Union. Prepared for EOS Gallup Europe's European Omnibus Survey. Brussels: EOS Gallup Europe. Available at: ⟨http://europa.eu.int/comm/public_opinion/archives/top/top_en.htm⟩. Accessed 22 June 2005.

Taber, Charles S. 2003. Information Processing and Public Opinion. In *Oxford Handbook of Political Psychology*, edited by David O. Sears, Leonie Huddy, and Robert Jervis, 433–76. Oxford: Oxford University Press.

Thomassen, Jacques, Abdul Noury, and Erik Voeten. 2004. Political Competition in the European Parliament: Evidence from Roll Call and Survey Analyses. In *European Integration and Political Conflict*, edited by Gary Marks and Marco Steenbergen, 141–64. Cambridge: Cambridge University Press.

Van Der Eijk, Cees, and Mark N. Franklin. 2004. Potential for Contestation on European Matters at National Elections in Europe. In *European Integration and Political Conflict*, edited by Gary Marks and Marco Steenbergen, 32–50. Cambridge: Cambridge University Press.

Wessels, Bemhard. 2004. Contestation Potential of Interest Groups in the EU: Emergence, Structure, and Political Alliances. In *European Integration and Political Conflict*, edited by Gary Marks and Marco Steenbergen, 195–215. Cambridge: Cambridge University Press.

Young, Jason, Cynthia J. Thomsen, Eugene Borgida, John L. Sullivan, and John H. Aldrich. 1991. When Self-Interest Makes a Difference: The Role of Construct Accessibility in Political Reasoning. *Journal of Experimental Social Psychology* 27:271–96.

Zaller, John. 1992. *The Nature and Origins of Mass Opinion.* Cambridge: Cambridge University Press.

4

Multiple Embeddedness and Socialization in Europe

The Case of Council Officials

Jan Beyers

Socialization is an important theme in much research about European integration. Since Haas' seminal study, crucial questions have been to what extent, under which conditions, and through which processes political elites and the broader public within the member states shift their allegiance toward the European Union (EU).[1] This connection between European integration and change among domestic actors and institutions is also characteristic of contemporary "Europeanization" studies, and the socialization theme has recently regained attention within the ranks of empirically oriented constructivists.[2] The basic idea behind socialization is as follows: the organization of social interactions (that is, institutional conditions and informal/formal rules that structure social life) and/or the logic of these interactions (that is, instrumental bargaining, role playing, or suasion) affect which behavioral practices, norms about appropriateness, and preferences about outcomes are internalized by individual actors. More importantly, these practices, norms, and preferences are not only internalized by individual actors, but, because they are shared by many, also characterize and shape the identity of larger social aggregates (that is, a bureaucratic agency, a political party, a country, and so on). Socialization thus refers to both individuals (that is, when and how they socialize) and groups (that is, the social aggregate's features and how interactions among individuals shape these aggregates).

Because regional integration in Europe can be considered as a process that transforms the organization of the European political space, it is no surprise that early and contemporary scholars consider "socialization" a key feature of regional integration. This article focuses on one specific set of domestic actors, national bureaucrats representing their country in the working groups of the Council of the European Union (Council working groups or CWGs hereafter) and investigates the extent to which their experiences with the EU's institutions, and more specifically the Council, shape

---

[1] Haas 1958.

[2] For an overview of the Europeanization literature, see Cowles, Caporaso, and Risse 2001; Vink 2003; and Mair 2004. For reviews of the constructivist socialization literature, see Checkel 1999; and Johnston 2001.

their role conceptions. Role conceptions are norms held by state representatives on what constitutes appropriate behavior in the CWGs. Do bureaucrats who are regularly and intensively involved in policymaking arenas that transcend national borders adopt supranational norms of appropriate behavior as a result of these experiences (compared to those that are only occasionally involved)? Are bureaucrats who are closely connected to their domestic environment more inclined to view their occasional participation in the CWGs as an act of exchanging and balancing member-state interests instead of finding solutions in the interest of a common, European, good? Which other arenas function as socialization sites if European arenas, such as the CWGs, are not consequential for actor socialization?

As Zürn and Checkel point out, these questions are not trivial: they relate to the political legitimacy of the EU's multilevel institutional framework.[3] Although I do not address this normative issue explicitly, the empirical observations are relevant in the sense that they demonstrate the extent to which national bureaucrats operating at the European level can still be considered "national" representatives. The current populist wave in Europe includes the idea that the more policymaking and policymakers become Europeanized, the more distant the EU will become from domestic values and norms. In the EU, the populist argument goes, policies are made in "hidden committees" staffed by bureaucrats and diplomats who enjoy great autonomy vis-à-vis their domestic polity. The extent to which state representatives enhance the autonomy of international organizations (IOs) and less formal transnational networks—such as epistemic communities—by developing norms and values that are distinct from domestic norms and values is an important question in the study of foreign policymaking and IOs.[4] This concern is also visible in day-to-day diplomatic practice. In general, after three to four years at a diplomatic post, most states rotate their diplomats to another diplomatic location, and after several years abroad diplomats return to their home country for a period of three to four years. This practice of rotation is designed to avoid narrow specialization resulting from prolonged attention to the affairs of one country or a particular series of problems. Although frequent rotation would not allow diplomats to familiarize themselves with specific problems and conditions, prolonged exposure may lead to the gradual adoption of norms, customs, and values typical of the country where diplomats are stationed. Rotation allows diplomats to stay in touch with their state or, to put it in the terminology of this volume, to constrain the potential consequences of international socialization.

This example suggests that in studying international socialization at least two sets of factors need to be distinguished: factors connected with the international socialization site, on the one hand, and factors related to potential socialization that takes place outside the international site, on the other hand. Phrased differently, role enactment is considerably shaped by actors' embeddedness in multiple international, European, and domestic contexts. This article qualifies, specifies, and tests the strong socialization hypothesis, which states that social interactions cutting across national borders stimulate individuals to shift their allegiances and basic orientations toward the

---

[3] See Zürn and Checkel, this volume.
[4] See, for instance, Keohane 1969, 862; and Haas 1992, 24, 32.

European level. This hypothesis assumes that the EU is a site that has a substantial socializing impact. It presumes that, as a result of prolonged and intensive exposure to EU affairs, individuals adopt role conceptions that promote a sense of "we-ness," and that fit into a view of the EU as an autonomous level primarily designed for finding policy solutions in the interest of a common, European, good.

The next section further defines and explicates the dependent variable, role conceptions. In the second section, I take a brief look at the Council of the European Union, and I argue that the formal and informal rules that apply in the CWGs may lead to actor behavior governed by notions of appropriateness. Building on this argument, the third section presents several scope conditions as independent variables shaping the adoption of role conceptions. After listing the hypotheses that are tested, I present the research design and the data set. Based on quantitative interview data, I demonstrate that extensive exposure to the European level does not necessarily lead to supranational role playing. By controlling for socialization that potentially takes place before an actor enters the European socialization site, I conclude that especially domestic scope conditions, not European conditions, positively affect the adoption of supranational role conceptions.

Role Conceptions

The standard sociological definition of "role" is "the behavior expected of an actor in a specific social position."[5] This definition consists of two key components—a specific social position and the behavior expected—which I clarify below.

First, "role" refers to a more or less systematic pattern of relations between actors and specific positions. For instance, civil servants from the EU's member-state ministries deliberate in small bureaucratic EU committees (that is, their position) and prepare decisions to be taken by the Council of Ministers. Role playing includes the act whereby these officials define themselves and other actors (that is, the politicians, the other member-state officials, and so on) in relation to the specific position in which they are situated (that is, the bureaucratic committee). Role playing is the act wherein information is transmitted about how, in such positions, interests are defined, which resources are useful, and how disputes should be resolved. Thus actors form their social context by playing roles; that is, they transmit information on how things should be done. Although roles are properties of individual actors, they also provide information about how groups, networks, or larger social aggregates function. In sum, a study of role playing should focus on the individual without losing sight of the broader context in which this individual is embedded.

Second, roles are norms that include expectations about what constitutes appropriate behavior given the actors' position. The way actors conceive their role—their "role conception"—is not actual behavior that directly leads to specific policy outcomes. Role playing contrasts with what March and Olsen have labeled the "logic of consequences," which implies political events understood as a consequence of strategic

---

[5] See Homans 1961, 11; and Sealing 1991, 1239, 1245.

choices in which a logical connection is made between individual interests, prefer-ences, and outcomes.[6] When making choices, actors will consider which course of action will be most effective and efficient in reaching the desired outcome. However, choices, March and Olsen argue, are characterized by ambiguities, uncertainties, lim-ited computational abilities, and restricted access to information. Moreover, choices are not only made with future consequences (and how these affect specific interests) in mind, but they are also informed by normative concerns about how choices should be made. National bureaucrats will ask "what is the proper role I am expected to play in Council working groups?" To put it differently, political events may be evaluated and understood according to a "logic of appropriateness;" that is, instead of considering potential political outcomes, actors also care about the informal norms and rules that structure the policy process. Therefore, it is difficult to establish the impact of appro-priate behavior on specific policy outcomes in a straightforward manner.[7] Indeed, rule and role conceptions are formed, designed, and used as cues in situations wherein goals, potential outcomes, and formal rules of interaction are imprecise, more fluid, and less well-known.

"Role" is not only a theoretical concept invented by sociologists. It is used exten-sively by scholars evaluating different actors within the EU multilevel system. This use is apparent in statements such as, "The duality of the Presidency [of the Council of Ministers] as being both supranational and national is exemplified by the different roles played by the member-state officials or ministers, on the one hand, and the Presidency representatives, on the other."[8] In this chapter, I investigate whether state representatives have adopted systematic conceptions of their role and which scope conditions (as will be discussed in section three) stimulate them to adopt a specific role. Broadly speaking, two roles may be distinguished among state representatives—intergovernmental and supranational—and the literature offers numerous exam-ples of both role conceptions. Moreover, authors often disagree whether events should be understood as the result of intergovernmental or supranational prac-tices (author x explains event a as an example of intergovernmental role playing, while author y considers the same event as an illustration of supranational role playing).

First, when state representatives adopt a supranational role, they view Europe as an autonomous level primarily designed for finding policy solutions in the interest of a common, European, good. This role implies a desire to promote the project of European common policymaking, and includes a disposition to view oneself as an autonomous actor responsible for crafting an EU-wide policy consensus. One of the major events in recent European history, the emergence of the Economic and Monetary Union (EMU), is often explained as the outcome of such appropri-ate behavior. The delegation of monetary policies to "institutionalized transnational actors" via the creation of the Delors Committee of central bankers provided Europe

---

[6] March and Olsen 1989.
[7] March and Olsen forthcoming.
[8] Christiansen 2002, 35.

with a forum in which transnational elites were able to disconnect from domestic politics and to internalize the belief that monetary unification was a sensible next step in the process of European integration.[9] Moreover, the relative autonomy to speak as bankers, and not as government representatives, enabled them to persuade politicians.

Second, when assuming the role of intergovernmental state representative, officials conceive European policymaking as an act of exchanging and balancing member-state interests: officials define themselves as national representatives, and they confine their task to defending national positions. The same event, the EMU, is understood by other scholars as the outcome of deliberate intergovernmental behavior. Moravcsik, for instance, argues that national preferences were largely a result of domestic processes, and these preferences diverged from the beginning of the negotiation process.[10] The process, including the establishment of the Delors Committee, was designed by governments to bolster their position vis-à-vis domestic constituencies (for example, the German government and the Bundesbank). This intergovernmental bargaining process resulted in an outcome that can be characterized as a balance of give and take among key governmental representatives.

European socialization concerns the extent to which European scope conditions, such as extensive experiences with the CWGs, stimulate state representatives to adopt a specific role. Socialization could imply a change from one role to another; that is, instead of playing an intergovernmental role, actors adopt a supranational role. However, socialization does not necessarily concern the adoption of supranational views at the expense of intergovernmental views or the mere shift from one category to another; it might also imply a reconceptualization of existing intergovernmental dispositions or the playing of multiple roles that are not considered to be in conflict. For instance, officials continue to define themselves as national representatives while at the same time they increasingly consider national perspectives as overlapping and compatible with a common European perspective. In this situation, actors systematically play both roles. They adopt layers of multiple roles in the sense that an intergovernmental role is supplemented with a supranational role. When supranational roles correlate positively with intergovernmental roles, as in this situation, actors do not experience so-called role conflicts.[11] Rather, such conflicts emerge when representing and defending national perspectives is considered incompatible with promoting a common European interest. Actors with an outspoken supranational view reject intergovernmental roles, and vice versa; they view both roles as incompatible and not reconcilable. Such a negative relation between roles suggests that Council negotiations are characterized by a dominant cleavage between those adopting supranational roles and those adopting intergovernmental roles. Thus a situation exists in which cooperative norms and practices are less deeply internalized by individuals and their immediate surrounding.

[9] Cameron 1995, 74.
[10] Moravscik 1999, 379–471.
[11] Stryker 1980.

The Council of Ministers' Working Groups

Decision making in the EU's Council of Ministers is organized into three stages. First, the CWGs composed of member-state representatives specialize in obtaining information about particular policies and try to negotiate a first compromise. Second, high-profile committees such as the Committee of Permanent Representatives (COREPER) or, for the Common Agricultural Policy, the Special Committee on Agriculture (SCA), further refine the legislative proposals made by the European Commission and prepare the meeting of the ministers. Finally, the ministers representing the member states decide by taking a vote, but often consensus reached in the earlier stages is rubber-stamped by unanimity. This structure portrays Council decision making as divided into a bureaucratic level (the CWGs, on the one hand, and COREPER or SCA on the other hand) and a political level (the ministers). Little exact information exists on the amount and the nature of issues that are resolved at the bureaucratic level, but experienced observers estimate that about 70 percent to 80 percent of all issues are settled there.[12]

It may sound somewhat surprising to consider supranational role playing as a mechanism at work in the EU's Council of Ministers and its working groups. Is not the European Commission expected to be the mainstay of supranational policy-making, while the Council is expected to act as a countervailing, intergovernmental body?[13] Should intergovernmental role playing not prevail in such a situation? In contrast to a perspective that depicts the Council as an arena where only specific national interests are represented and defended, I argue that the Council is a fertile laboratory for studying actor behavior that is governed by role playing and rules of appropriateness.

Although the Council is conceived as an intergovernmental body, there are few formal rules that shape Council officials' role conceptions.[14] True, some formal rules may have an effect. For instance, the European Commission is responsible for drafting legislative proposals and has the right to withdraw proposals as long as the Council has not come to a decision. More importantly, the participation of the European Commission in all stages of the Council negotiations means that, at least formally, cooperation with the European Commission is crucial to get things done. Additionally, the dual role played by the presidency—that is, the member state chairing the Council, as both a member state and an actor facilitating consensus-building—tempers the Council's intergovernmental nature. With respect to political objectives, Article 202 (of the EU Treaty) vaguely stipulates that the Council must ensure that the objectives set out in the Treaty are attained. "The Rules of Procedure of the Council" basically concern organizational and procedural issues (Articles 19 and 21 briefly mention that working groups may be set up to carry out preparatory work).[15] Although these stipulations could be understood and read as "The Council should promote European integration and the common European interest," this is still an ad hoc interpretation.

---

[12] Hayes-Renshaw and Wallace 1997.
[13] Wessels 1991, 138.
[14] Article 203, Treaty of the European Union.
[15] See Council decision 2004/338/EC.

To conclude, in stark contrast to the Commission,[16] no compelling formal rules are formulated that explicitly require state representatives to restrict their role to purely defending the national interest (or the opposite, that is, to act with the interest of the Community in mind).

Rationalist analyses of the Council strongly emphasize the importance of formal rules, that is, voting rules and legislative procedures, as the strategic context shaping the optimizing behavior of state agents.[17] The rational perspective does not consider the potential socializing effect informal rules have on dispositions, norms, identities, and preferences. On the contrary, ideas are shaped outside the EU context; many assume ideas to be exogenous to the formal and informal institutional environment. One general result from these studies is that, assuming that ministers vote sincerely, unanimity is not likely and there will always be a minority of one or more states voting against EC proposals. However, as Mattila and Lane have shown, irrespective of the legislative procedure used, it appears that between 75 percent and 80 percent of Council of Ministers' decisions are taken unanimously, including decisions that can be taken by qualified majority vote (QMV).[18] Thus vetoes and negative votes are unlikely to occur. One explanation for the frequency of unanimity is vote trading or "log-rolling." In contrast to other international organizations, the EU makes hundreds of decisions each year, and these decisions concern a large set of policy areas ranging from agricultural prices, regional policies, mergers, and acquisitions, to the enforcement of trade policies. In such circumstances, actors may gain from linking different issues by voting strategically instead of voting sincerely. Instead of vetoing a less preferred, but less salient proposal, actors accept less salient issues in exchange for support on other issues. Thus voting decisions are not guided entirely by how member states conceive their utility to one specific policy issue. However, high issue density makes cooperation through the exchange of votes in the Council difficult to structure through a set of formal binding agreements. Mattila and Lane, for instance, argue that although one can interpret the frequency of unanimity as the strategic behavior of vote trading, such exchanges are more likely to occur in circumstances in which actors have developed an atmosphere of mutual understanding and trust.[19]

In sum, one should not attach too much explanatory power to formal rules. Indeed, some formal rules with respect to the Council (for instance, the entrepreneurial role Commission officials play in it) may promote a spirit of supranational cooperation in addition to intergovernmental bargaining. But formal rules may differ considerably from an organization's actual operations. Often, formal rules are inadequate, weakly specified, or not consistent with all relations, attitudes, and behavior that exist in an organization.[20] Lindberg already pointed out that the degree of integration does not only depend on formal rules, but also, to a significant extent, on how actors define

---

[16] See Hooghe, this volume.
[17] See, for instance, Garrett and Tsebelis 1996; Crombez 1996; and Steunenberg 2000.
[18] See Mattila and Lane 2001, 37–38; and also Elgström, Bjurulf, Johansson, and Sannerstedt 2001, 114–15.
[19] Mattila and Lane 2001, 45–48.
[20] Sealing 1991, 1241–43.

their roles within the constraints imposed by the formal rules.[21] For understanding when and how a culture of compromise arises in the Council, strategic decision-making models may overestimate the importance of formal rules and underestimate the impact of informal rules of appropriateness that shape the actor's environment and their propensity to compromise.[22]

This focus on informal rules of appropriateness is typical for the more qualitative literature on Council decision making. Several authors stress that officials involved in EU policymaking are exposed to a spirit of cooperation.[23] In addition, some scholars claim that territorial role identifications lose importance and are replaced or supplemented by functional, expertise-based role perceptions. State representatives are more than diplomats in the traditional sense. Most of them are technical experts within a specialized field of competence.[24] In addition, the functional, fragmented character of the Council, especially at the level of the working groups, decreases the relevance of territorially bounded practices and views. Expertise-based and functional role conceptions are becoming much more important. Meetings of such specialists create an atmosphere of mutual understanding as a setting for the deliberations, which makes the difference between national and European definitions of interests likely to blur. It is also important to note that deliberations take place in a patchwork of working groups and committees that ensures the extensive discussion of issues among bureaucrats and the negotiation of successive amendments until the final decision is taken by the Council of Ministers.

Explaining Role Conceptions of State Representatives

Major disagreement exists on the role of state representatives. I begin by briefly reviewing a set of arguments drawn from neofunctional and supranationalist approaches, which view European experiences as conducive to the adoption of supranational roles. In contrast to this, I present intergovernmentalism as an approach that is quite skeptical vis-à-vis the strong socialization hypothesis (and socialization as such). Next, and more importantly, I advance my institutionalist perspective, which is informed in key ways by political psychology and organization theory. Finally, I identify a set of scope conditions that form the basis of several hypotheses related to the adoption of supranational roles.

Strong Socialization versus No Socialization

Socialization is a crucial component in all neofunctional definitions of regional integration; all include the notion that interactions cutting across national borders gradually socialize actors, supranational and domestic elites, into adopting pro-European

---

[21] Lindberg 1998 [1963], 105.
[22] Lewis 2003, 106–7.
[23] See Hayes-Renshaw and Wallace 1997; Wessels 1991; Westlake 1995; and Lewis 1998.
[24] Westlake 1995, 318–20.

norms and practices.[25] This hypothesis, "as more and more people come to participate directly in these decisions and to perceive them as mutually rewarding, these people will develop more favorable attitudes toward integration," [26] led to numerous systematic surveys of national and international policy elites during the 1970s.[27] Although this research program is somewhat forgotten nowadays, it is important to note that it has not produced conclusive insights into the effects of European/international institutions on political attitudes.[28] One of the reasons was that controls for presocialization or recruitment, especially domestic socialization and recruitment, were not fully considered.[29]

Nonetheless, the strong socialization hypothesis is still important for three "schools" on European politics. As Checkel discusses constructivism and the Habermasian approaches in his introductory chapter, I confine myself to a brief summary of contemporary "supranationalism," which draws, to a large extent, upon its neofunctionalist predecessors. In contrast to constructivist, Habermasian, and early neofunctionalist approaches, which expect identity change (Checkel's Type II socialization),[30] supranationalists leave open the extent to which European experiences lead to an identity change and a shift of loyalties to the European level.[31] However, this does not exclude actor socialization, as "many of the rules governing EC policymaking are behavioral, that is, they have resulted from many years of constant interaction between state and supranational officials in a myriad of settings."[32] By this logic, EU politics also affects the context in which actor strategies and roles take shape (Checkel's Type I socialization). Maybe the EU is still viewed as an organization through which national interests are promoted, but—through European experiences— domestic actors get a better sense of other member states' interests, the salience of specific issues for other actors, and the willingness to compromise. This not only has consequences for individual actor opportunities; it also leads to an *esprit de corps* and mutual understanding.[33] At minimum, it leads to a substantial redefinition of existing intergovernmental roles, in the sense that these are supplemented by supranational roles.

In contrast to neofunctionalists and supranationalists, intergovernmentalists do not consider the EU to be an important socialization site. Although Hoffman, an intergovernmentalist, had no explicit theory on socialization, he was outspoken with respect to the remaining stickiness of national institutions. For instance, he argued that cross-border interactions sustain territorial allegiances and that several institutional features of the EU reinforce this.[34] Diversity, in contrast to convergence emphasized by neofunctionalists, constrains a shift of allegiances. In this perspective, the Council, which

---

[25] See Haas 1958, 16; and Lindberg 1963, 4–7.
[26] Kerr 1973, 47.
[27] See Peck 1979; Scheinman and Feld 1972; Smith 1973; and Wolf 1973.
[28] For an overview, see Pollack 1998.
[29] Martin and Simmons 1998, 95–96.
[30] Checkel, this volume.
[31] Stone Sweet and Sandholtz 1997, 301.
[32] Ibid., 305.
[33] See Kerremans 1996, 232; and Christiansen 2002, 50–51.
[34] See Hoffmann 1966 and 1982.

should be viewed as the body *par excellence* through which national politics interacts with the European level, imposes a nationality label on domestic officials participating in it. State representatives are delegated negotiators; they represent national views and their roles are predominantly intergovernmental. Recent versions of intergovernmentalism are even more silent about the potential European socialization of state representatives.[35] Domestic politics is considered a key arena for aggregating domestic preferences, while little or no endogenous preference formation or political spillover takes place at the European level. Role playing by state representatives is not shaped by European experiences, but should be seen as an outcome of domestic processes and fitting into the national government's position on particular issues. Norms and ideas represented by state agents are considered to be epiphenomena of underlying issue-specific preferences, not as rules of appropriateness shaping the institutional context in which state representatives interact. Therefore, intergovernmentalism has been more successful in explaining "the delegation and pooling of specific and precise powers," but "it leaves unexplained patterns of support for more general institutional commitments."[36]

The Conditional Emergence of Supranational Role Playing

EU studies remain inconclusive with respect to the socialization of state representatives. Some argue that state representatives are resocialized, while others argue that a loyalty transfer does not take place. The institutionalist perspective I propose in this section includes the notions that roles are affected by institutional affiliations and that they are endogenously shaped, but also that endogeneity may be related to embeddedness in multiple international, European, and domestic contexts. To some extent, European experiences may affect role enactment, but controls for the potential effect of other institutional affiliations are needed.

Let me elaborate on this point by referring to the ambiguous nature of political representation. Representation, the activity of state representatives in the Council, means the paradox of "making present *in some sense* of something which is nevertheless *not* present literally or in fact."[37] One of the long-standing controversies in the study of representation concerns, on the one hand, the extent to which representatives ought to be delegates instructed by constituencies or principals and, on the other hand, the extent to which representatives should follow their own judgment, unbiased by mobilized constituencies or uninformed principals.[38] When applied to the Council, this means that representatives could act on the basis of the member state's interests, but also that they may enjoy discretion to promote constructive deliberations in the Council. However, representatives who act solely on the basis of instructions, without taking care of other member-state perceptions and preferences, could be considered a tool through which the instructor acts. Likewise, those who act autonomously, but are constantly ignoring domestic preferences, cannot be considered true representatives.

---

[35] See Moravcsik 1993 and 1999.
[36] See Moravcsik 1999, 488; and also Pollack 2003, 256–59.
[37] Pitkin 1972, 8–9 (emphasis in original).
[38] See Pitkin 1972, chap. 7; and Beyers and Trondal 2004.

Moreover, state representatives' constituencies or principals do not always behave as unitary actors with defined and fixed preferences on all issues. Or, the member state's subunits—the national government, the parliament, the subnational government, the minister, the head of the department—may have several conflicting preferences.[39] The differentiated nature of the state representatives' environment means that the content of representation cannot a priori be assumed to be well-defined or unambiguous. On the contrary, representation implies dilemmas regarding the interests to be represented and defended. For instance, bureaucrats are expected to be loyal to their member state, to take care of the functional domain or the epistemic community to which they belong, and to consider the views expressed by other state representatives.[40]

Thus "multiple embeddedness" means actors identify with different rules and expectations related to the multiple contexts in which they are embedded. Although representatives may have similar preferences on specific issues and experience the same European socialization stimuli, they do not necessarily act in the same way; some consider their representational role as defender of the national interests, while others see themselves as being responsible for the governing of Europe. Much depends on presocialization and the primary institutional affiliation of officials. Committee work is one of the many duties of state representatives whose domestic ministry or agency remains an important point of reference.[41] Or as Bulmer notes, "their interaction with the domestic level is important. Institutional traditions and their cultural dimension are more embedded at that level than at the EU-level."[42] In more general terms, variation in domestic conditions constrains a general pattern of European socialization.[43] Socialization, if it occurs, is mediated through institutional, political, and cultural factors varying among the member states.[44] Some domestic experiences are consistent, or fit well with supranational role conceptions, so that actors shift their allegiances faster. Or, actors can have negative experiences with the domestic realm (for example, interorganizational conflicts, mismanagement, or weak coordination devices), try to escape from this, and start to defend supranational solutions. The less representatives are tied by specific domestic institutions or desired outcomes (because their principals have not yet defined their preferences), the more likely they will deviate from self-perceptions as intergovernmental bargainers.

Hypotheses to Be Tested

The strong socialization hypothesis states that contact with the EU will lead to the emergence of supranational roles. Yet "contact" is a slippery concept.[45] Usually the *duration* of contact, for instance length of attendance in CWGs, is assumed to be

---

[39] Mayntz 1999.
[40] State representatives may be perceived by themselves, but also by their superiors, as representatives of the EU in their member state. Their role may be one of explaining, even "selling," compromises to a domestic audience. Because of their inside knowledge about EU policymaking, they may play a huge part in the design of their instructions.
[41] Egeberg 1999.
[42] Bulmer 1994, 373.
[43] Harmsen 1999, 85–87.
[44] Sealing 1969, 490–95, and 1986, 363–72.
[45] See Checkel, this volume.

a proxy for involvement in processes that are presumed to socialize agents. But duration as a variable does not say much about the quality of involvement or the social mechanism that leads to socialization. It does not trace the interaction process between t_0 (entering the organization) and t_{0+1} (working for a while or leaving). Nevertheless, contact with the European level is a necessary condition; without this, little European socialization takes place. However, duration of contact is not a sufficient condition. In addition to duration, I expect that especially time-demanding (or *intense*) and long-lasting (or *dense*) interactions contribute to the adoption of supranational roles.

H1–H3: Strong European socialization implies that the more frequently the interactions occur (H1), the more intense these interactions are (H2); and the longer the duration (H3), the more state representatives internalize supranational roles.

In addition to involvement in CWGs, I explore the effect of QMV. While formal voting is not allowed at this level of the Council, knowledge about voting weights and member-state positions allows state representatives to estimate the extent to which a majority has been reached. If QMV is the informal rule, the centrality of supranational actors such as the presidency and the Commission should increase. The latter may adapt its initial proposal in order to reach the required majority; the former can threaten to call a vote, and by doing this, may intensify the interaction process. Research has shown that QMV triggers state representatives to build more extensive communication networks in order to find compromises.[46] In this respect, QMV can be seen as a proxy for the above-mentioned density contact-variable, or for the frequency of CWG-meetings.

H4: According to a supranational socialization logic, state representatives that are active in CWGs where QMV applies for the issues on the agenda are more likely to adopt supranational roles.

However, there are two reasons to question this hypothesis. First, for intergovern-mentalists, formal rules such as QMV do not shape roles; the views stated by state representatives are to be seen as expressions of national governments' preferences on specific issues. Second, supranationalists argue that the decreasing number of issues for which unanimity applies excludes the exit option of the veto—vetoing that is generally seen as noncooperative and intergovernmental behavior. However, Johnston also shows that in situations where unanimity applies, actors may be cautious about defection and noncooperation.[47] Building a reputation of being cooperative may be rewarding and important for the creation of trust among partners that have regular contact with each other. Especially in multilateral settings such as the EU, concerns about image and status are important; systematic defection from cooperation might be a costly strategy. As mentioned above, many observers report that in daily practice, state representatives search for consensus and avoid formal voting. Thus formal rules may be important, but should not be considered the most important explanatory

[46] See Beyers and Dierickx 1998, 308; and Trondal 2001, 11.
[47] Johnston 2001, 502–6.

factor, because their effect depends considerably on the informal rule of consensus that applies in multilateral settings such as the EU.

In recruiting representatives, member-state governments are likely to juggle several criteria. On the one hand, officials with extensive European or international professional experiences are likely candidates because they already know the codes of conduct in European/international policymaking settings and, therefore, adapt more easily. Although a correlation between this experience and supranational role playing could be seen as evidence to support the strong socialization hypothesis, it is not direct evidence of socialization through involvement in the EU. Rather, it means that those representatives who are already supportive are likely to be recruited.[48] On the other hand, an intergovernmental logic implies that CWGs basically aim to preserve national control over EU policymaking. Therefore, officials are needed who have a profound knowledge of domestic sensitivities, and an extensive domestic socialization record may contribute to this. Thus domestic socialization is conducive to intergovernmental roles and constrains supranational roles. This leads to the following two hypotheses:

H5: The likelihood of European socialization depends on domestic politics. In recruiting their representatives, member-state governments look for candidates with extensive European or international experiences. Such experiences have a positive impact on supranational role playing.

H6: The likelihood of European socialization depends on domestic politics. In recruiting their representatives, member-state governments look for candidates with an extensive domestic socialization record, and this stimulates intergovernmental role playing.

With respect to domestic socialization, I add two further specifications. First, some representatives are only occasionally exposed to the CWGs. These so-called part-timers are often bureaucrats from sectoral ministries in the member states. They combine their task as state representatives with other, mainly domestic, tasks, and CWGs are secondary institutional affiliations. In contrast, bureaucrats attached to the Permanent Representations and professional diplomats are more exposed to the peculiarities of European policymaking than the part-timers. This leads to my seventh hypothesis:

H7: The strong European socialization hypothesis implies that full-timers should develop more supranational roles than part-timers, since the European arena is more a point of reference for them.

Second, as already suggested, the position officials are supposed to represent may be less well-conceived because of weak domestic coordination structures, unclear instructions, or information shortages. If this is the case, representatives are less tied by specific outcomes, and this allows them to use the CWGs not for defending

---

[48] Another factor leading to the recruitment of representatives with strong European/international experiences may be self-selection; the eagerness of those with European/international experiences to become part of the Council infrastructure is great because they are already favorable to the norms and values. Such individuals spend more effort soliciting EU-related tasks and, therefore, are more likely to become selected. See also Hooghe, this volume.

preestablished national guidelines, but for searching for European solutions to problems for which they have no "national" answer.[49] Those who perceive deficiencies and shortcomings in their political administrative setting develop supranational roles more easily. They experience less inconsistency between, on the one hand, their role as a state representative—which is ambiguous because the "national interest" is ill-defined—and, on the other hand, someone who actively promotes a European interest. A similar expectation is put forward by Marks and Hooghe, who write that "those who already rely on effective national networks have an interest in intergovernmentalism. Officials from weak national networks have an interest in supporting supranationalism."[50] Hypothesis 8 is as follows:

H8: The likelihood of European socialization is conditioned by how state representatives are tied to their domestic environments. State representatives that are less tied by detailed instructions and perceive deficiencies in their domestic coordination system develop supranational roles more easily.

Finally, I consider two conditions measured at the level of the member state. First, consistent with the strong socialization hypothesis, older member states' representatives should be more supranational. This factor has a similar effect as *duration,* or length of attendance, in the sense that length of membership implies more experiences. However, length of membership is collinear to some specific nation-state, or non–European-level, factors. The founding member states—the Benelux countries, France, Germany, and Italy—started European integration during an era characterized by a permissive consensus; their political elites laid the basis for the current institutional infrastructure; and they had more time to learn the peculiarities of European policymaking. If duration plays a role, then countries that are part of the first enlargement, or "first wave" (the United Kingdom, Ireland, and Denmark) should adopt supranational roles more easily than second-wave countries (Spain, Portugal, and Greece). However, countries belonging to the first wave were, at the moment of their entrance, reluctant about supranationalism, and it is therefore plausible to assume that these governments did not appoint their most supranationalist bureaucrats as state representatives. Although these representatives had more time to become socialized than those entering the EU at a later stage, they started off as more intergovernmental.[51] If this is correct, the evidence should point to a curvilinear pattern; the founding members (Benelux, France, Italy and Germany) and the second-wave states (Greece, Spain, Portugal) should be more supranationalist and less intergovernmentalist, while first-wave states (UK, Denmark, Ireland) should be intergovernmental and less supranational.

H9: The strong European socialization hypothesis implies that the longer a state has been an EU member, the more likely that officials who represent this state adopt supranational roles.

---

[49] Beyers and Trondal 2004.
[50] Hooghe and Marks 2001, 158.
[51] See Hooghe, fig. 2, this volume.

Second, state representatives receive a substantial part of their training and political education within national political systems. It is there that they learn the values and orientations of the national political and administrative elite to which they belong. From this perspective, European factors only slightly affect the adoption of supranational roles, and the roles adopted by domestic officials are basically a reflection of values shared by the respective national elites to which they belong.[52] Hypothesis ten thus also views national officials as weakly socialized by European factors:

H10: The ideas represented by state representatives are formed at the domestic level. Domestic bureaucrats represent norms and values in accordance with national elite orientations and, consequently, the more the domestic elite favor supranationalism (intergovernmentalism), the more state representatives adopt supranational (intergovernmental) roles.

Table 1 situates these ten hypotheses within the three theoretical perspectives on socialization—strong socialization, no socialization, and conditional socialization—that were presented in the previous section. It also summarizes disagreement and inconclusiveness with respect to the socialization of state representatives.

Methodological Issues and Data Set

The evidence for testing the hypotheses comes from a quantitative quasi-experimental design that includes explicit controls for scope conditions at both the European and the domestic level. Data is drawn from a survey among state representatives, who were, to a varying degree, involved in the CWGs. It was decided that, given the large number of working groups (approximately 170 at the time of the fieldwork), it would not be valid to rely on a small number of respondents to establish the facts. However, at the time the research project started (1993), detailed and systematic information regarding state representatives and their involvement in the CWGs was not available. Therefore, I started with a list of 170 working groups (provided by the Belgian Permanent Representation) and collected information regarding the officials who were active in these 170 groups. On the basis of twenty-eight in-depth, qualitative interviews, most CWGs were coded according to density of meetings (ranging from "never" to "several times a week"), policy area (based on the items discussed), type (cross-cutting policy fields, technical regulation in an existing policy field, and so on), composition (traveling part-timers or Brussels-based full-timers), and the applicable voting procedure for the issues on its agenda (QMV or unanimity).

In sampling state representatives, two sources of variation were considered as crucial: first, variation with respect to the member state represented by the official; and second, variation according to the level of involvement in the CWGs—that is, part-timers and full-timers (see Hypothesis 7). Part-timers are officials from sectoral ministries who only occasionally take part in CWGs and combine this with other, mainly domestic, tasks. Full-timers are involved in CWGs on a more regular basis and include diplomats at the Foreign Office or the Permanent Representation (PR) and

---

[52] See Hooghe 1999; and Hooghe, this volume.

Table 1. *Expected Relation between Independent Variables and the Adoption of Supranational Roles or Role Supplementation*

	Conditional socialization depending on multiple institutional embeddedness (institutionalism)	*No European socialization (intergovernmentalism)*	*Strong European socialization (neofunctionalism, supranationalism, constructivism)*
Hypotheses on EU-level factors			
H1. Prolonged duration of involvement	Can lead to supranational roles, but controls for alternative socialization sites are needed.		
H2. High intensity of involvement			
H3. High density of involvement			Leads to supranational roles.
		Does not lead to supranational roles.	
H4. QMV in CWG	Not the single explanatory variable, as informal rules are equally important.		
Hypothesis on European/international experiences			
H5. Intense European/international professional experiences	Can lead to supranational roles, but controls for alternative socialization sites are needed.	Does not lead to supranational roles	Positive relation (but no direct evidence of EU socialization).

Hypotheses on domestic experiences

H6. Long domestic professional experiences	Leads to intergovernmental role playing.	Likely to be recruited, but socialization effect is not investigated in this literature.	.... Usually not investigated in this literature.
H7. Part-time at the EU-level, full-time domestic level	Part-time exposure to the EU weakens the socialization impact of EU-level factors.	.... Usually not investigated in this literature	
H8. Low level of organizational self-esteem	Poor domestic coordination structures lead to ill-defined domestic interests and increase likelihood of supranational role playing.		

Hypotheses on the features of the represented member states

H9. Prolonged length of membership	Can lead to supranational roles, but controls for alternative socialization sites are needed	Nonlinear, depending on individual member-state features.	Positive, longer membership leads to supranationality.
H10. Euro-skeptic elite opinion within member state	No explicit hypothesis.	State representatives play intergovernmental roles.	No relation.

Note: CWGs = Council working groups; QMV = qualified majority vote.

officials of sectoral ministries attached to the PR.[53] For comparative reasons, the ideal data set should include full-timers and part-timers in each member state, but neither the personnel nor the funds were available for the required interviews with part-timers located in all national capitals. Therefore it was decided to construct two subsamples, one subsample including full-time (that is, based in Brussels) state representatives of each member state and one subsample including full-timers and part-timers of one member state, namely Belgium.[54]

From the set of 170 CWGs, thirteen groups were selected. Only groups that were situated in different first-pillar policy domains and were staffed, as much as possible by representatives from the PRs in Brussels, were included.[55] Respondents in the group of so-called full-timers, both Belgian and non-Belgian, were mostly involved in one of these thirteen CWGs. In 1993, before the accession of Austria, Finland, and Sweden, each CWG was composed of at least fourteen members, twelve member-state representatives, one representative from the European Commission, and one from the Council Secretariat. My intention was to interview all the national representatives in each of these thirteen CWGs. In this, I was moderately successful as 123 respondents (and not $12 \times 13 = 156$ respondents) were interviewed. In addition, eighteen Belgian full-timers, officials belonging to the Foreign Office or the PR, were interviewed regarding their involvement in other working groups. Adding these to the twelve Belgian full-timers interviewed regarding the thirteen CWGs, brings the total of Belgian full-timers to thirty. The subgroup of Belgian part-timers was interviewed regarding their involvement in another set of CWGs. With respect to this group, sixty-five Belgian state representatives—that is, officials attached to national sectoral ministries and only sporadically exposed to the CWGs—were interviewed.

A final comment concerns some limitations of the data.[56] Socialization means that actors do not adopt new roles the first moment they interact in a new environment; some experience and time are needed before new roles are adopted. It is exactly this notion of "time" that troubles the construction of an "ideal" data set. In my research, the change of role playing over time is implicitly, not explicitly, incorporated. Qualitative process tracing or carrying out some in-depth case studies would be more suitable for examining socialization as a process unfolding over time. Another research strategy would be a panel design: interviewing state representatives before they enter the

---

[53] On the composition of the PR, see Hayes-Renshaw and Wallace 1997.

[54] The choice of Belgium was driven mainly by practical considerations; the location of the Belgian government institutions in Brussels facilitated the fieldwork. One could argue that this biases the research outcomes in the sense that it is easier for Belgian part-timers to develop contacts with the European institutions and to adopt supranational norms. Unfortunately, as the data set does not include part-timers from other member states, I cannot substantiate this claim from a comparative perspective. However, there are two reasons why this bias is not necessarily large or problematic. First, research on Belgium's relation with the EU shows the irrelevance of proximity when it comes to the Europeanization of the Belgian system. It appears that the networks of Belgian bureaucrats remain largely separate from EU policy networks. On this aspect, see Dierickx and Beyers 1999; Bursens 2002; see also fns. 60 and 61. Second, within a sample including Belgian full-timers and Belgian part-timers, proximity remains constant and will not cause biased research outcomes within this sample.

[55] The first pillar of the Treaty on the European Union consists of policy domains that belong to the three original treaties: European Community for Coal and Steel (ECCS), European Atomic Energy Community (Euratom), and the European Economic Community (EEC).

[56] See also Hooghe, this volume.

Council, followed by an interview when the representative is active in the Council and, finally, if possible, an interview after the representative leaves the organization (for example, returns to a domestic governmental agency). However, such designs are complicated and rather difficult to implement in international organizations.

Measuring the Dependent Variable, Role Conceptions

One of the first questions to be answered is whether state representatives have adopted systematic conceptions of their role and to what extent their roles correspond to two more or less distinguishable conceptions, namely a supranational and an intergovernmental role. During the interviews, the interviewees were given nine statements designed to measure how they believed they should act, that is, their role, or how they conceived the policy process (the situation in which they were placed), specifying their view on a scale ranging from 1 (disagree) to 6 (agree). The higher the score, the more convinced the interviewees were that they should act according to the role conception outlined in a particular statement.

The first column of Table 2 shows all nine items. These nine observed variables do not measure nine separate roles. By factor analyzing the nine items, I explore the extent to which these observations can be explained by a set of hypothetical factors that correspond to the two role conceptions I outlined in the first section. The major aim of factor analysis is to represent a set of observed variables, which are answers to different questions, by a smaller set of factors. In order to interpret the outcome, I inspected the matrix with factor loadings; factor loadings are to be considered as correlations between latent factors and observed variables. The higher the factor loadings, the more an observed variable is associated with an underlying latent factor or the more an unobserved latent concept explains variation in the set of observed and measured variables.[57] In using factor analysis to analyze a set of variables, one may assume that the common factors are orthogonal (the Pearson correlation between the factors explaining variation in a set of variables is zero), or, one may relax the restriction that the factors be uncorrelated (the Pearson correlation between the factors might be larger/smaller than zero). Because I do not consider European socialization to be the adoption of supranational roles at the expense of intergovernmental roles or the mere shift from one category to another, I can imagine instances in which both role conceptions correlate positively. For this reason, I have chosen an oblique rotation instead of imposing an orthogonal structure. In this way I explore whether and to what extent it is realistic to assume complete independence between the two conceptions.

The factor loadings in Table 2 show that state representatives distinguish two roles. Columns (2) and (3) ("All respondents") present the matrix of factor loadings, that is, correlations between the latent factor and the observed variables, for all respondents. In order to check the similarity of the outcome, I show in the other columns two additional analyses, one for all Belgian respondents and another for the

[57] See Kim and Mueller 1978; and Tacq 1997.

Table 2. *Supranational and Intergovernmental Role Conceptions (Matrix of Factor Loadings, Procrustean Oblique Rotation)*

	All respondents (N = 203)		All Belgian respondents, full-timers and part-timers (n = 95)		Multinational sample of full-timers (including Belgian full-timers in thirteen CWGs) (n = 123)	
	Supran.	Interg.	Supran.	Interg.	Supran.	Interg.
1. In the working groups the European Commission and the national representatives should take an active part in drawing up guidelines for member states' policies.	**.70**	.03	**.74**	.26	**.64**	–.07
2. In the working groups the representatives should develop a strong common policy and lay down clear directions for the national governments.	**.72**	–.14	**.55**	.01	**.78**	–.08
3. The main task of the working groups is to look for common objectives and a common policy in collaboration with the different member states and with the European Commission.	**.61**	.06	**.58**	.27	**.57**	–.04
4. In my opinion, in the working groups the European Commission has to arbitrate between the diverse national interests in order to make a common policy possible.	**.44**	.04	**.55**	.01	**.43**	–.01
5. In my opinion, in the working groups we should work toward a strongly united policy which strengthens the executive role of the European Institutions.	**.70**	.03	**.54**	.13	**.78**	11
6. In my opinion, the exchange of information on positions in working groups helps avoiding open differences of opinion that might stand in the way of an agreement at the level of the COREPER, the SCA, or the Council.	–.07	**.38**	**.33**	**.33**	.00	**.41**
7. Information on national positions in working groups is useful in order to be able to take into account interests of the other member states when setting out our national policy.	.07	**.40**	.24	**.33**	–.01	**.47**
8. In my opinion, in a working group we have to inform and defend our national position.	–.14	**.40**	.04	**.59**	–**.34**	.22
9. According to me, we should inform the representatives of the other member states and the European Commission about our national points of view in order to facilitate higher-level consultations.	–.02	**.63**	.15	**.74**	–.18	**.48**
Explained variance	33%		33%		33%	
Interfactor correlations			r = .28, p = .0059		r = .08, p = .3707	

Note: Interfactor correlations are Pearson product-moment correlations between additive indices. COREPER = Committee of Permanent Representatives; CWGs = Council working groups; Interg. = factor referring to intergovernmental roles; SCA = Special Committee on Agriculture; Supran. = factor referring to supranational roles. In order to make the contrast, factor loadings higher than .30 are put in bold.

multinational sample (including Belgian full-timers). The first five items clearly correspond to a supranational role conception (that is, they strongly correlate with one common factor): officials should "draw up guidelines for the member states," "play an active part," "develop a common policy," "collaborate and look for common objectives," and "strengthen the role of European institutions." The next four items fit more into an intergovernmental role conception. Key phrases are "taking into account interests of other member states," "defend national positions," and "exchange and balance national viewpoints." Two other features are typical for these intergovernmental items. First, "the national position" is a key ingredient of someone's evaluation of the process in the CWGs and, second, bureaucrats do not view themselves as autonomous consensus-builders. On the contrary, they exchange information to facilitate decision making at the higher levels.

The pattern of correlations between observed variables and the two underlying factors suggests that state representatives have consistently adopted two more or less distinct roles, a supranational role and an intergovernmental role. What about the possibility that actors, to some extent, combine roles? Or, do officials separate one role from the other and thus keep each role distinct? To reiterate briefly, different patterns in the data would indicate different ways of combining role conceptions. First, a positive correlation would suggest that actors combine both roles in the sense that evoking an intergovernmental role is combined with a supranational role, a situation in which role conflict is unlikely. Second, in the case of a negative correlation, outspoken supranational roles would imply a rejection of intergovernmental roles. This outcome would suggest the existence of role conflict. Finally, the absence of a substantial correlation means that, on average, both the positive combination of roles and role conflict are not taking place, but it does not rule out blurring role conceptions or role conflict under some specific scope conditions. For example, compared to less experienced state representatives, more experienced state representatives find it easier to combine both roles; they do not necessarily see a difference between defending a national and a European interest (see below).

The evidence shows that some state representatives tend to combine different role conceptions. A closer inspection of the factor pattern in Table 2 suggests that both conceptions are quite, but not perfectly distinguishable. The positive inter-factor correlation for Belgian respondents (full-timers and part-timers) shows that on average, Belgian officials tend to combine intergovernmental roles with supranational roles ($r = .28$, $p = .0059$); that is, in the Belgian case it is difficult to assume that both role conceptions are completely distinct from each other. Some positive and rather substantial cross-loadings—that is, factor loadings or correlations of one variable with two factors—also point in this direction. The outcome is less straightforward when I consider the multinational sample of full-timers. The interfactor correlation is low and insignificant ($r = .08$, $p = .3707$), but some cross-loadings suggest role conflict instead of a positive role combination. For instance, it is noteworthy that an "intergovernmental" statement referring to the defense "of our national position" points to conflict with a supranational role conception (negative loading of $-.34$). Thus there are some indications of role conflict among full-timers, but the overall pattern remains too weak and unsystematic to make firm conclusions.

Recruitment and Professional Experiences

Role playing may be affected by scope conditions at multiple levels of governance, namely the European and the domestic level. As suggested earlier, member-state governments juggle several criteria. They may prefer to appoint those with extensive European/international professional experience, or prefer officials with profound insight into domestic sensitivities and an extensive domestic socialization record (Hypotheses 5 and 6). The importance of socialization experiences at both the domestic and European levels is apparent from my quantitative data as well as from the various in-depth interviews that I carried out. It also appears that many EU diplomats combine a strong 'European' curriculum with extensive domestic experiences.

First, although diplomats are supposed to rotate every four years to another post, the traditional four-year rule does not apply to the Belgian EU Permanent Representative.[58] Often, EU Permanent Representatives serve much longer periods at the PR than one would expect of an average professional diplomat. Second, diplomats at the highest position in the PR had previous, sometimes extensive, experiences with the EU and its member states. Third, these "European" experiences correspond with extensive experience and involvement in various domestic political networks. Being part of the PR is not just an ordinary thing, and the prestige of the job has political consequences. Domestic party political considerations are unambiguously and openly taken into account when making appointments.[59] In the act of balancing different prestigious diplomatic functions among the different political parties and—important for Belgium—between the two language groups, the PR is considered to be one of the most prized positions. In all cases, diplomats, attachés at the PR, and Foreign Office officials involved in European matters are high-ranking officials. In contrast, the recruitment of part-timers is more decentralized, takes place in an ad hoc manner, and depends largely on the ministry that sends a representative to the CWGs. Neither the Permanent Representative, nor the Foreign Office is systematically involved in the selection of part-timers; and my interviews suggest that ministers and interdepartmental coordination processes play limited roles in this recruitment process.

Do these observations from the in-depth interviews correspond with the available quantitative evidence? What about the European embeddedness of officials, their current involvement in policymaking processes at the European level in general, and their participation in CWGs in particular?

Above I suggested that the distinction between part-timers and full-timers relates to their embeddedness in CWGs (Hypothesis 7). However, what is the nature of this embeddedness? As Table 3 shows, the distinction between part-timers and full-timers is not significantly related to the duration—in years—of involvement in various CWGs, but it corresponds with the intensity of contact and the density of CWG gatherings in which officials were involved. Within the group of Belgian respondents, the duration of involvement is slightly higher for the full-timers (twelve years) than for the part-timers (eleven years), and the non-Belgian respondents had, on average, spent nine years in CWGs. Yet the differences are small and statistically irrelevant

---

[58] Kerremans and Beyers 2001.
[59] Dierickx and Beyers 1999, 200–3.

Table 3. *Comparison of European Involvement of Part-timers and Full-timers*

	Non-Belgian full-timers (n = 108)	Belgian full-timers (n = 30)	Belgian part-timers (n = 65)
1. Duration of involvement: the average number of years bureaucrats are involved in European policymaking	9	12	11
2. Intensity of involvement: percentage of bureaucrats who devote half of their time or more to meetings with CWGs	89%	80%	42%
3. Density of involvement: percentage of bureaucrats involved in CWGs that met more than once per month	87%	70%	29%

Note: CWGs = Council working groups.

(F = 1.69, df = 2, p = .1872). It is more the intensity of involvement and the density of CWG meetings that differentiates part-timers from full-timers. Among the full-timers, 80 percent of the Belgian officials and 89 percent of the non-Belgian officials devoted more than half of their time to meetings with CWGs. Only 42 percent of the Belgian part-timers spent more than half of their time in meetings with CWGs.[60] The density of CWG-meetings is substantially higher for the CWGs in which full-timers were involved (compared to part-time CWG-officials). Of the Belgian part-timers, only 29 percent were involved in CWGs that met more than once per month. The proportion of Belgian full-timers and European full-timers involved in these densely meeting CWGs was 70 percent and 87 percent, respectively.[61] To conclude, full-timers are more intensively involved in CWGs, and they meet more frequently with officials from other member states. Further analysis (see below) shows the extent to which supranational role playing is more prevalent among full-timers (Hypothesis 7).

Tables 4 and 5 show results concerning previous professional experiences. In general, the extensiveness of European/international and domestic professional

---

[60] Time devoted to CWGs, *intensity* of involvement, is measured by an ordinal five-point scale ranging from one (less than 25 percent) to five (100 percent). Note that the data concern a period during which Belgium held the Presidency of the Council (1993) and that the time devoted in CWG meetings might be somewhat overestimated. Nevertheless, the observed difference between Belgian and non-Belgian full-timers is relatively small and statistically insignificant ($\chi^2 = 5.958$, df $= 4$, $p = .202$), while the difference between Belgian full-timers, non-Belgian full-timers and Belgian part-timers is strongly significant ($\chi^2 = 61.332$, df $= 8$, $p = .001$).

[61] Each CWG was coded on the basis of twenty-eight in-depth expert-interviews. The *density* of meetings for each CWG ranges on an ordinal six-point scale from zero (CWG did not meet) to 5 (CWG met several times a week). The observed difference between Belgian full-timers and non-Belgian full-timers might be attributable to the fact that the group of Belgian full-timers included more diplomats and Foreign Office staff. Notably, the difference between Belgian and non-Belgian full-timers is relatively small ($\chi^2 = 7.386$, df $= 4$, $p = .117$) compared to the difference between Belgian full-timers, non-Belgian full-timers and Belgian part-timers ($\chi = 78.748$, df $= 10$, $p = .001$). By adding Belgian part-timers, the heterogeneity of the evidence substantially and significantly increases ($d\chi^2 = 71.362$, ddf $= 6$, $p = .000$).

Table 4. *Comparison of Part-timers and Full-timers Regarding Previous European/international Professional Experiences*

	Non-Belgian full-timers (n = 108)		Belgian full-timers (n = 30)		Belgian part-timers (n = 65)	
	% with this experience	Years (average)	% with this experience	Years (average)	% with this experience	Years (average)
1. Having worked as a civil servant in an international organization	7	.67	3	.08	3	1.42
2. Having been attached to an embassy in another EU member state	10	1.15	17	3.63	0	.00
3. Having been attached to an embassy in a non-EU state	15	2.21	23	3.92	5	4.67
4. Having been attached to a diplomatic mission toward an international organization	6	.65	17	1.31	0	.00
5. Having worked as a bureaucrat for the European Commission	3	.10	3	.23	3	.29
Overall European/ international professional experiences	36	4.78	43	9.17	9	6.38

Note: The average number of years (columns) refers to only those officials with the professional experience mentioned.

experiences correlates substantially with the distinction between part-timers and full-timers. As qualitative evidence has already illustrated, full-timers follow a professional trajectory that has a pronounced European/international character; they spend more of their professional career in other member states, an indication of extensive "European" socialization opportunities. The Belgian full-timers in particular are characterized by extensive European/international and domestic professional experiences.[62] When comparing the domestic and European/international social

---

[62] We have to be somewhat careful in distinguishing "international" from "European" professional experiences. For instance, if a respondent had been attached to an embassy in a non-EU state, this might imply a post in another European state before it entered the EU.

Table 5. *Part-Timers and Full-Timers Compared Regarding Previous Domestic Professional Experiences*

	Non-Belgian full-timers (n = 108)		Belgian full-timers (n = 30)		Belgian part-timers (n = 65)	
	% with this experience	*Years (average)*	*% with this experience*	*Years (average)*	*% with this experience*	*Years (average)*
1. Having been attached to the personal staff or the cabinet of a minister	33	2.57	50	2.70	18	2.35
2. Having worked for local authorities	3	.66	3	.05	6	.27
3. Having worked for regional authorities	5	.35	3	.35	8	2.07
4. Having worked for a domestic political party	2	.12	13	1.90	3	.18
5. Having worked for an interest group; trade union	1	.02	7	.30	2	.36
6. Having worked for an interest group; farmer's union	2	.24	7	.13	2	.23
7. Having worked for an interest group; employer's union	2	.12	3	.25	2	.05
8. Having worked for an interest group; small and medium enterprises (SMEs)	1	.05	0	.00	0	.00
Overall domestic professional experiences	38	4.14	67	5.68	34	5.50

Note: The average number of years (columns) refers to only those officials with the professional experience mentioned.

environments, it also appears that among Belgian full-timers domestic professional experiences are quite relevant. That Belgian full-timers, had more experiences with ministerial cabinets and more affinities (as previous staff members) with domestic political parties, confirms the importance of domestic political factors in the recruitment of Belgian full-timers (as compared to Belgian part-timers and non-Belgian full-timers). Although the data set is too small to reach firm conclusions regarding experiences with interest groups, the quantitative evidence and in-depth interviews suggest that several sector-specialists at the PR have strong ties with the domestic interest groups of their sector.

Table 6. *Average Supranational and Intergovernmental Role Conceptions and Interfactor Correlations, by Scope Conditions*

	Average supranationalism		Average intergovernmentalism		Interfactor correlation	
	BS-FPT (n = 95)	*MNS-FT* (n = 123)	*BS-FPT* (n = 95)	*MNS-FT* (n = 123)	*BS-FPT* (n = 95)	*MNS-FT* (n = 123)
Hypotheses on European-level factors						
H1. Duration of involvement; state representatives who						
–were already involved in CWGs before 1986	.08	–.06	**–.15**	.22	.26	ns
–became involved in CWGs after 1986	–.04	.03	**.26**	–.14	ns	ns
H2. Intensity of involvement; state representatives who spend						
–more than 50 percent of their time in CWGs	.06	–.02	.00	–.02	ns	ns
–less than 50 percent of their time in CWGs	–.07	.11	–.00	.11	.48	ns
H3. Density of involvement; state representatives who attend						
–more dense CWGs (more than one meeting per month)	.07	–.02	.03	–.00	ns	ns
–less dense CWGs (less than one meeting per month)	–.05	.17	–.02	.03	.47	ns
H4. Applicable voting procedure; state representatives who attend CWGs						
–with QMV (including mixed groups)	.10	–.02	–.07	–.09	ns	ns
–with unanimity	–.17	.03	.12	.13	.39	ns
Hypothesis on European/international experiences						
H5. Previous European/international professional experiences; state representatives						
–without European/international professional experience	.05	.07	.03	**.19**	.28	ns
–with European/international professional experience	–.22	–.12	–.11	**–.30**	ns	ns

Hypotheses on domestic experiences

H6. Previous domestic professional experiences; state representatives

–with no previous domestic professional experience	.04	–.01	.10	.03	ns	ns
–with previous domestic professional experience	–.05	.01	–.12	–.04	ns	ns

H7. Full-timers versus part-timers (only Belgian sample)

–part-timers; officials attached to domestic ministries	.09	—	–.05	—	.36	—
–full-timers; officials attached to the permanent representation and diplomats	–.20	—	.02	—	ns	—

H8. Organizational self-esteem[1]; state representative has a

–high organizational self-esteem	**–.97**	–.12	.25	–.12	ns	ns
–moderate organizational self-esteem	**–.27**	–.02	–.11	–.00	.39	ns
–low organizational self-esteem	**.29**	.35	.08	.05	ns	ns

Hypotheses on the features of the represented member states (only multinational sample)

H9. Length of membership; official represents

–original member states (Benelux, France, Germany, Italy)	—	**.17**	—	**–.17**	—	.25
–first-wave enlargement countries (United Kingdom, Denmark, Ireland)	—	**–.46**	—	**.43**	—	ns
–second-wave enlargement countries (Greece, Spain, Portugal)	—	**.13**	—	**–.10**	—	ns

H10. How pro-European are national elites[2]; national elite represented by state representative is

–very pro-European (Belgium, Greece, Germany, Italy)	—	**.26**	—	**–.18**	—	ns
–moderately pro-European (Netherlands, Luxembourg, France, Spain)	—	**–.03**	—	**–.12**	—	ns
–the least pro-European (Ireland, Denmark, Portugal, United Kingdom)	—	**–.26**	—	**.30**	—	ns

Note: The higher the averages, the more the roles assumed are supranational or intergovernmental; averages that differ significantly (according to an F test, $p < .05$) from each other are put in bold. Only interfactor correlations for which $p < .05$ are reported. BS-FPT = Belgian sample of full-timers and part-timers ($n = 95$); CWGs = Council working groups; MNS-FT = Multinational sample of Belgian and non-Belgian full-timers ($n = 123$); ns = correlations were not statistically significant; QMV = qualified majority vote.

[1] See Table 8 for details.

[2] Categorization based on the Eurobarometer elite survey of 1996. See Spence 1997.

125

It is clear that Belgian full-timers have strong domestic experiences and that Belgian part-timers have, compared to the Belgian full-timers, weak historical ties with their domestic environment. In the Belgian case, the full-timers' recruitment correlates strongly with both an extensive domestic socialization record and extensive European/international experiences. In the next section, I explore the extent to which these experiences affect the adoption of supranational role conceptions.

Role Conceptions and Multiple Embeddedness

As the factor analysis shows (see Table 2), state representatives adopt a consistent conception of their role and distinguish between two possible roles, a supranational role and an intergovernmental role. Within the Belgian sample, state representatives tend to see a supranational role as complementary to an intergovernmental role; that is, on average, Belgian bureaucrats do not experience role conflict. Although there are some minor indications of role conflict among full-timers, both roles were quite separable within this sample. The previous section showed that representatives are embedded in multiple contexts and that many of them, especially Belgian full-timers, have strong domestic ties in addition to their European responsibilities.

But to what extent are these variable socialization experiences associated with the adoption of supranational roles and a rejection of intergovernmental roles? I constructed two factor scales by making an additive index of the observed variables belonging to the factors supranational and intergovernmental role conceptions, respectively. These scales are standardized and used in the analyses summarized in the tables and figures below. The first column of Table 6 introduces categorical distinctions related to the various socialization experiences that were identified as potential scope conditions explaining role playing (Hypotheses 1–10). The next four columns show the average scores for supranational and intergovernmental role playing—first for the Belgian sample of full-timers and part-timers (BS-FTP), and then for the multinational sample of full-timers (MNS-FT). The higher the mean, the more supranational or intergovernmental state representatives are.

I demonstrated above that on average, multinational full-timers do not combine both roles (see interfactor correlations in Table 2). However, this does not rule out blurring role conceptions under some specific circumstances. For instance, especially extensively involved officials may be able to combine both roles. In general, if European socialization takes place, then the combination of role conceptions—substantiated by a significant correlation between the two factor scales—and the adoption of supranational roles should occur among the extensively involved state representatives. The last two columns of Table 6 show interfactor correlations within different categories; these correlations indicate whether and to what extent roles are combined under specific scope conditions.

One of the limitations of the results shown in Table 6 is the use of categorical distinctions that may be criticized for their crudeness. Therefore, I show in Table 7 the Pearson product-moment correlations of the two role conceptions with the original

Table 7. *Bivariate Correlations of Scope Conditions with Supranational and Intergovernmental Role Conceptions*

	Correlation with suprantionalism		Correlation with intergovernmentalism	
	BS-FPT $(n = 95)$	MNS-FT $(n = 123)$	BS-FPT $(n = 95)$	MNS-FT $(n = 123)$
European-level factors				
H1. Duration of involvement (number of years)	ns	ns	ns	ns
H2. Intensity of involvement (5-point scale)	ns	ns	ns	ns
H3. Density of involvement (6-point scale)	ns	ns	ns	ns
H4. Qualified majority voting in CWG (dichotomous)	ns	ns	ns	ns
European/international experiences				
H5. Previous European/international professional experiences (number of years)	ns	ns	ns	ns
Domestic experiences				
H6. Previous domestic professional experiences (number of years)	ns	ns	ns	ns
H7. Full-timers versus part-timers (only Belgian sample) (dichotomous)	ns	ns	ns	ns
H8. Organizational self-esteem (additive index)[1]	.32	.23	ns	ns
Features of the member states				
H9. Length of membership (three waves)	—	−.24	—	.23
H10. Member states with pro-European elites[2]	—	.31	—	−.19

Note: BS-FPT = Belgian sample of full-timers and part-timers ($N = 95$); MNS-FT = Multinational sample of Belgian and non-Belgian full-timers ($N = 123$); ns = correlations were not statistically significant. Only correlations for which $p < .05$ are reported.
[1] See Table 8 for details.
[2] Categorization based on the Eurobarometer elite survey of 1996. See Spence 1997.

noncategorized independent variables. For instance, instead of making a rough dichotomous distinction about whether or not previous European professional experiences occurred, I look at the number of years these experiences lasted.

The discussion of the results starts with the interfactor correlations in Table 6 (see the last two columns). Given the absence of negative correlations, it can be concluded that role conflict is not the usual pattern within different subgroups. Moreover, the predominance of role combination (that is, defining oneself as playing both intergovernmental and supranational roles), in contrast to role conflict, is further confirmed.

Table 8. *Organizational Self-Esteem (Five-Point Likert Scales, Factor Loadings)*

	Belgians (n = 95)	Multinational sample (n = 123)
1. The internal coordination of the viewpoints of the different ministries in our country is chaotic.	0.68	0.76
2. In the administration of my country there is not sufficient training for officials who have to take part in negotiations at a European level.	0.59	0.48
3. It often happens that I am not quite certain what point of view I should put forward in the working groups.	0.68	0.71
4. For officials it is very important that the preparation of a policy is easily surveyable. The structure of the administration in our country does not always add to this effect.	0.69	0.60
5. Most member states prepare themselves more thoroughly for the negotiations in Brussels than we do.	0.52	0.56
6. I only learned how I had to deal with complicated European dossiers as I went along.	0.49	0.56
7. I always get very clear instructions from my ministry or my department as to what position I should take up.	0.59	0.61
Explained variance	37%	38%

Especially among representatives of the larger member states (not in the table) and within CWGs where unanimity applies for the issues on the agenda, both role conceptions are combined.[63] These observations are not irrelevant, as they clearly refute the conception of European politics as characterized by hard bargaining and noncooperative intergovernmental negotiation behavior among the big member states.[64] It is also important to observe that (for the CWGs to which Belgian full-timers and part-timers belong), especially under conditions of unanimity, representatives combine both role conceptions ($r = .39, p = .0254$). To put it differently, a formal rule such as unanimity does not necessarily exclude supranational role playing (Hypothesis 4).

Does intensive, dense, and prolonged participation in CWGs lead to supranational and less intergovernmental role conceptions (Hypotheses 1–3, 7)? To some extent, European/international experiences seem to mitigate intergovernmental role conceptions. Among Belgian respondents, those officials that became involved in the CWGs before 1986 have a less intergovernmental role conception ($F = 4.00$, df = 1, $p = .0484$). In the group of full-timers, having previous European/international professional experiences decreases intergovernmentalism ($F = 7.25$, df = 1, $p = .0081$). However, the latter observation is not direct confirmation of EU socialization (see

[63] When isolating the four member states with the biggest voting power (Italy, France, Germany, and the United Kingdom), a significant correlation is observed ($r = .43, p = .0026$) between the adoption of an intergovernmental and a supranational role.
[64] See Lewis 1998; and Lewis, this volume.

Hypothesis 5). Moreover, in general, these are rather weak and unsystematic associations. Neither the bivariate correlations in Table 7, nor the categorical distinctions in Table 6, provide strong and systematic confirmation of the strong European socialization hypothesis. The only evidence suggesting European socialization concerns duration of involvement. Belgian officials that were involved in CWGs before 1986 are slightly more disposed to combine intergovernmental roles with supranational role conceptions ($r = .26, p = .0438$). The strong socialization hypothesis that especially extensive and intense experiences with CWGs lead to a combination of roles receives no strong support. On the contrary, in the Belgian sample there is considerable evidence for role combination among part-timers ($r = .36, p = .0033$), among those without previous transnational experiences ($r = .28, p = .0127$), among those involved in less dense CWGs ($r = .47, p = .0003$) and among those who spent less than 50 percent of their time in CWGs ($r = .48, p = .0010$). These observations suggest the opposite of the strong socialization hypothesis, namely that weak and casual, not strong, European ties lead actors to adopt supranational roles in combination with intergovernmental roles.

The data also indicate that ties with the domestic arena affect role playing. Hypothesis 8 (see Table 1) suggests that the less frequently and extensively representatives are instructed by domestic institutions with respect to desired outcomes, the more supranational role playing may emerge. To measure the nature of ties with the domestic politico-administrative system, seven Likert items were combined in a scale labeled "organizational self-esteem" (see Table 8). In general, low organizational self-esteem is positively associated with the adoption of supranational role conceptions. In the Belgian case in particular, the perceived weaknesses of domestic networks contribute to supranationalism (see results in Tables 6 and 7).

I illustrate this finding in a more succinct manner. The distinction between part-timers and full-timers corresponds to embeddedness in CWGs and may be used as a proxy for involvement. In general, average organizational self-esteem is somewhat higher among Belgian full-timers than among Belgian part-timers; that is, full-timers feel that they get more detailed instructions and guidelines, but this difference is statistically insignificant ($F = 1.61, \mathrm{df} = 1, p = .2076$). A covariance analysis with one interaction term (involvement × organizational self-esteem) reveals that in particular, a low domestic organizational self-esteem stimulates supranational roles ($F = 5.29$, $\mathrm{df} = 2, p = .0067$). Figure 1 displays the average supranational role conception according to self-esteem and involvement. Again, it is not an extensive or intensive involvement in the CWGs that makes the most substantial difference. Rather, the evidence suggests that the less frequent and intensive the involvement in Europe (as is so for part-timers), the more a low organizational self-esteem (that is, a perception of weak instructions, poor domestic coordination and policy preparation) leads to the adoption of supranational role conceptions.

Much of my qualitative data also points in this direction. From the in-depth interviews, I learned that, among Belgian officials, complaints about the complexity of the domestic political system prevailed.[65] The interplay between different agencies

---

[65] See also Bursens 2002.

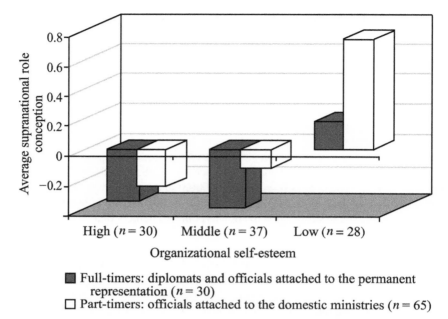

Figure 1. *Average supranational role conception among Belgian officials, by organizational self-esteem and domestic experience (Hypothesis 8)*

was considered to be inefficient or absent, the involvement of a large number of ministries "increases the probability of bad instructions." One respondent said that most of the time, Belgian negotiators work without detailed instructions, but that they have adopted one big instruction: "Do what you think is appropriate, but try to improve European decision making, do not make enemies and ensure that you have a positive working relation with everyone." Almost all stressed that the appropriate way to deal with Europe was "to comply with the views of the Commission" or "to follow the Commission's ideas, because these usually fit what is good for Belgium." In general, domestic political control was considered to be weak or even completely absent.

Tests of hypothesis nine, which refers to length of member-state EU membership, systematically confirm the importance of domestic socialization. First, as expected, older member-state representatives develop more supranational roles ($r = -.24$, $p = .0074$) and fewer intergovernmental roles ($r = .23$, $p = .0094$) than the newer member states (see Table 6). However, the distinctions in Table 6 nuance this general conclusion considerably. The covariation is curvilinear instead of linear.[66] Founding member states' representatives—the Benelux countries, France, Italy, and Germany—are most supranationalist and the least intergovernmentalist. These are followed by the supranationalist (less intergovernmentalist) representatives of the

---

[66] *F* test for supranational roles and intergovernmental roles are, respectively, $F = 4.67$, df $= 2, p = .0112$, and $F = 4.09$, df $= 2, p = .0192$.

second wave (that is, Spain, Portugal, and Greece). State representatives belonging to the first enlargement (that is, the United Kingdom, Denmark, and Ireland) are the most intergovernmentalist and the least supranationalist. Although states that were part of the first enlargement had more time to socialize, they are still more intergovernmentalist than those who belong to the second enlargement. This suggests that the adoption of supranational roles is moderated by member-state features and not by the duration of EU membership.

Finally, there is considerable support for Hypothesis 10, namely that adopted roles reflect the overall elite attitude within a member state. In general, if an official represents a member state with a pro-European societal elite, the official tends to act according to a supranational role conception ($F = 6.36$, df $= 2$, $p = .0130$) and rejects intergovernmental roles ($F = 4,98$, df $= 2, p = .0276$). In contrast, if a CWG-official represents a member-state where the overall elite attitude is more Euro-skeptic, I observe the opposite. In this respect, domestic Council officials are quite "representative."

Conclusion

The Council of Ministers and its working groups are a fertile laboratory for studying actor behavior that is governed by role playing and rules of appropriateness. Few formal rules prescribe how state representatives at the lower levels of the Council are expected to behave, and the notion of representation implies that state representatives may face several dilemmas regarding the interests they are supposed to represent. In this case, representatives operate under the condition of bounded rationality; that is, their computational abilities are limited and their access to information is restricted. They adopt role conceptions—norms, rules, expectations, and prescriptions of appropriate behavior—enabling them to prioritize and respond to particular policy problems and interests (and to de-emphasize others).

This perspective fits Checkel's category of Type I socialization studies, focusing on scope conditions and with a view of actors as boundedly rational. My findings also demonstrate that state representatives adopt supranational role conceptions as norms of appropriate behavior. This observation, which contrasts with pure intergovernmental role playing or what Lewis labeled the "hard bargaining" image of the Council, confirms that joint problem solving is an important feature of the processes in the CWGs.[67] Although the possibility of normative suasion as a socialization mechanism has not been fully explored here, the evidence suggests that many processes in the Council are not only motivated by member-state interests. State representatives also puzzle over joint and deliberative problem solving, seek information, and try to learn about problems in other member states. Such role-driven behavior is reasonable because it enables state representatives to act under circumstances that are often ambiguous.

[67] Lewis 1998.

However, in contrast to the strong socialization hypothesis, one cannot conclude that it is especially those interactions cutting across national borders that lead to the adoption of supranational roles among state representatives. Nor are state representatives operating in a context that is largely disconnected from domestic values and norms. Recruitment and selection are significantly shaped by domestic networks, and state representatives' role perceptions are considerably consistent with the overall elite attitude in the member state they represent. Scope conditions that refer to European experiences—such as intensity, duration, and density of contact—showed no systematic relationship with the dependent variable. On the contrary, in the Belgian subsample, in which there is more variation regarding the level of involvement, I observed that weak and casual, not strong or regular, European ties correlate positively with supranational roles. Supranational role playing among state representatives that are only occasionally involved in the Council can be seen as a counterindication of strong EU socialization.

One possible explanation for this finding relates to specific organizational features of the domestic polity. My research strongly endorses the notion that a profound understanding of international socialization depends to a large extent on an in-depth exploration of how domestic politics is organized.[68] Domestic ties are crucial. However, the importance of domestic ties should not be interpreted as an example of strong domestic socialization contradicting European norms.[69] State representatives are not "structural idiots" or oversocialized individuals who are obedient to the dictates of domestically developed norms. On the contrary, it seems that supranational roles are likely to emerge among part-timers who have generally weak European and domestic ties (compared with full-timers). One might argue that weak domestic socialization contributes to supranational roles. When state representatives are less bound by specific and detailed domestic instructions over desired outcomes, they experience less contradiction between representing the national interest and supranational role playing.

More generally, my findings suggest that the variable ways in which domestic institutions are organized significantly affect the potential of system transformation at the EU level.[70] "Nonsocialization" may be highly conducive to cooperative role orientation. True, it is too early to generalize these research outcomes to other international organizations or, with regard to part-timers, to other EU member states. Neither should it be seen as proof of the impossibility of European socialization in other settings, such as COREPER or the Commission.[71] However, my research illustrates that bold claims regarding the transformative effects of European institutions on individual state agents should be viewed skeptically.[72] Domestic factors matter considerably and, indeed, in some cases they positively affect the adoption of supranational role conceptions.

---

[68] Checkel 2004, 237–38.
[69] See also Hooghe, this volume.
[70] See Egeberg 2004; and Beyers and Trondal 2004.
[71] See Lewis, this volume; and Hooghe, this volume.
[72] Goetz 2000.

References

Beyers, Jan, and Guido Dierickx. 1998. The Working Groups of the Council of the European Union: Supranational or Intergovernmental Negotiations? *Journal of Common Market Studies* 36 (3):289–317.

Beyers, Jan, and Jarle Trondal. 2004. How Nation-States 'Hit' Europe. Ambiguity and Representation in the European Union. *West European Politics* 27 (5):919–42.

Bulmer, Simon J. 1994. The Governance of the European Union: A New Institutionalist Approach. *Journal of Public Policy* 13 (4):351–80.

Bursens, Peter. 2002. Why Denmark and Belgium Have Different Implementation Records: On Transposition Laggards and Leaders in the EU. *Scandinavian Political Studies* 25 (2):173–95.

Cameron, David R. 1995. Transnational Relations and the Development of European and Monetary Union. In *Bringing Transnational Relations Back In: Non-State Actors, Domestic Structures and International Institutions*, edited by Thomas Risse-Kappen, 37–78. Cambridge: Cambridge University Press.

Checkel, Jeffrey. 1999. Social Construction and Integration. *Journal of European Public Policy* 6 (4):545–60.

———. 2004. Social Constructivism in Global and European Politics: A Review Essay. *Review of International Studies* 30 (2):229–44.

Christiansen, Thomas. 2002. The Role of Supranational Actors in EU Treaty Reform. *Journal of European Public Policy* 9 (1):33–53.

Cowles, Maria Green, James Caporaso and Thomas Risse. 2001. *Transforming Europe: Europeanization and Domestic Change*. Ithaca, N.Y.: Cornell University Press.

Crombez, Christophe. 1996. Legislative Procedures in the European Community. *British Journal of Political Science* 26 (2):199–228.

Dierickx, Guido, and Jan Beyers. 1999. Belgian Civil Servants in the European Union. A Tale of Two Cultures? *West European Politics* 22 (3):198–222.

Egeberg, Morten. 1999. Transcending Intergovernmentalism? Identity and Role Perceptions of National Officials in EU Decision-Making. *Journal of European Public Policy* 6 (3):456–74.

———. 2004. An Organizational Approach to European Integration: Outline of a Complementary Perspective. *European Journal of Political Research* 43 (2):199–219.

Elgstrom, Ole, Bo Bjurulf, Jonas Johansson, and Anders Sannerstedt. 2001. Coalitions in European Union Negotiations. *Scandinavian Political Studies* 24 (2):111–28.

Garrett, Geoffrey, and George Tsebelis. 1996. An Institutional Critique of Intergovernmentalism. *International Organization* 50 (2):269–99.

Goetz, Klaus. 2000. European Integration and National Executives: A Cause in Search of an Effect? *West European Politics* 23 (4):210–31.

Haas, Ernst B. 1958. *The Uniting of Europe: Political, Social, and Economical Forces 1950–1957*. Stanford, Calif.: Stanford University Press.

Haas, Peter M. 1992. Introduction: Epistemic Communities and International Policy Coordination. *International Organization* 46 (1): 1–35.

Harmsen, Robert. 1999. The Europeanization of National Administrations: A Comparative Study of France and the Netherlands. *Governance: An International Journal of Policy and Administration* 12 (1): 81–113.

Hayes-Renshaw, Fiona, and Helen Wallace. 1997. *The Council of Ministers*. London: MacMillan.

Hoffmann, Stanley. 1966. Ostinate or Obsolete? The Fate of the Nation State and the Case of Western Europe. *Daedalus* 95: 862–915.

———. 1982. Reflections on the Nation-State in Western Europe Today. *Journal of Common Market Studies* 21 (1-2): 21–38.

Homans, G. C.1961. *Social Behavior: Its Elementary Forms*. New York: Harcourt, Brace & World.

Hooghe, Liesbet. 1999. Supranational Activists or Intergovernmental Agents?: Explaining the Orientations of Senior Commission Officials Toward European Integration. *Comparative Political Studies* 32 (4): 435–63.

Hooghe, Liesbet, and Gary Marks. 2001. *Multi-Level Governance and European Integration*. Lanham, Md.: Rowman & Littlefield.

Johnston, Alastair Iain. 2001. Treating International Institutions as Social Environments. *International Studies Quarterly* 45 (4):487–515.

Keohane, Robert O. 1969. Institutionalization in the United Nations General Assembly. *International Organization* 23 (4):859–96.

Kerr, Henry H. 1973. Changing Attitudes Through International Participation: European Parliamentarians and Integration. *International Organization* 27 (1):45–83.

Kerremans, Bart. 1996. Do Institutions Make a Difference? Non-Institutionalism, Neo-Institutionalism, and the Logic of Common Decision-Making in the European Union. *Governance* 9 (2):217–40.

Kerremans, Bart, and Jan Beyers. 2001. The Belgian Permanent Representation to the European Union: Mail Box, Messenger, or Representative? In *The National Co-ordination of EU Policy*, edited by Hussein Kassim, Anand Menond, B. Guy Peters, and Vincent Wright, 1991–210. Oxford: Oxford University Press.

Kim, Jae-On and Charles W. Mueller. 1978. *Factor Analysis: Statistical Methods and Practical Issues*. London: Sage.

Lewis, Jeffrey. 1998. Is the 'Hard Bargaining' Image of the Council Misleading? The Committee of Permanent Representatives and the Local Elections Directive. *Journal of Common Market Studies* 36 (4):479–504.

———. 2003. Institutional Environments and Everyday EU Decision Making: Rationalist or Constructivist? *Comparative Political Studies* 36 (1/2):97–124.

Lindberg, Leon N. 1963. *The Political Dynamics of European Economic Integration*. London: Oxford University Press.

———. 1998 [1963]. Political Integration: Definitions and Hypotheses. In *The European Union: Readings on the Theory and Practice of European Integration*, edited by Brent Nelsen and Alexander Stubb, 145–56. London: Macmillan.

Mair, Peter. 2004. The Europeanization Dimension. *Journal of European Public Policy* 11 (2):337–48.

March, James G., and Johan P. Olsen. 1989. *Rediscovering Institutions: The Organizational Basis of Politics*. New York: Free Press.

———. Forthcoming. The Logic of Appropriateness. In *Handbook of Public Policy*, edited by Robert Goodin, Michael Moran, and Martin Rein. Oxford: Oxford University Press.

Martin, Lisa, and Beth A. Simmons. 1998. Theories and Empirical Studies of International Institutions. *International Organization* 52 (4):729–57.

Mattila, Mikko, and Jan-Erik Lane. 2001. Why Unanimity in the Council? A Roll Call Analysis of Council Voting. *European Union Politics* 2 (1):31–52.

Mayntz, Renate 1999. Organizations, Agents and Representatives. In *Organizing Political Institutions: Essays for Johan P. Olsen*, edited by Morten Egeberg and Per Laegreid, 81–91. Oslo, Norway: Scandinavian University Press.

Moravcsik, Andrew. 1993. Preferences and Power in the European Community: A Liberal Intergovern-mentalist Approach. *Journal of Common Market Studies* 31 (4):473–524.

———. 1999. *The Choice for Europe: Social Purpose and State Power From Messina to Maastricht.* London: UCL Press.

Peck, Richard. 1979. Socialization of Permanent Representatives in the United Nations: Some Evidence. *International Organization* 33 (3):365–90.

Pitkin, Hanna F. 1972. *The Concept of Representation.* Berkeley: University of California Press.

Pollack, Mark A. 1998. *Constructivism, Social Psychology and Elite Attitude Change: Lessons from an Exhausted Research Program.* Paper Presented at the 11th International Conference of Europeanists, February, Baltimore.

———. 2003. *The Engines of European Integration: Delegation, Agency, and Agenda Setting in the EU.* Oxford: Oxford University Press.

Scheinman, Lawrence, and Werner Feld. 1972. The European Economic Community and National Civil Servants of the Member States. *International Organization* 26 (1):121–35.

Searing, Donald D. 1969. The Comparative Study of Elite Socialization. *Comparative Political Studies* 1 (4):471–500.

——— 1986. A Theory of Political Socialization: Institutional Support and Deradicalization in Britain. *British Journal of Political Science* 16 (3):341–76.

———. 1991. Roles, Rules, and Rationality in the New Institutionalism. *American Political Science Review* 85 (4):1239–60.

Smith, Keith A. 1973. The European Economic Community and National Civil Servants of the Member States—A Comment. *International Organization* 27 (4):563–68.

Spence, Jacqueline M. 1997. *The European Union 'A View from the Top': Top Decision Makers and the European Union.* Prepared for EOS Gallup Europe's European Omnibus Survey. Brussels: EOS Gallup Europe. Available at ⟨http://europa.eu.int/comm/public_opinion/archives/top/top_en.htm⟩. Accessed 21 June 2005.

Steunenberg, Bernard. 2000. Seeing What You Want to See: the Limits of Current Modelling on the European Union. *European Union Politics* 1 (3):368–73.

Stone Sweet, Alec, and Wayne Sandholtz. 1997. European Integration and Supranational Governance. *Journal of European Public Policy* 4 (3):297–317.

Stryker, Sheldon. 1980. *Symbolic Interactionism: A Social Structural Perspective.* Reading, Mass.: Benjamin-Cummings.

Tacq, Jacques. 1997. *Multivariate Analysis Techniques in Social Science Research: From Problem to Analysis.* London: Sage.

Trondal, Jarle. 2001. Is There Any Social Constructivist-Institutionalist Divide? Unpacking Social Mechanisms Affecting Representational Roles among EU Decision-Makers. *Journal of European Public Policy* 8 (1):1–23.

Vink, Maarten. 2003. What Is Europeanisation? And Other Questions on a New Research Agenda. *European Political Science* 3 (1):63–74.

Wessels, Wolfgang. 1991. The EC Council: The Community's Decisionmaking Center. In *The New European Community: Decisionmaking and Institutional Change*, edited by Stanley Hoffmann and Robert O. Keohane, 133–54. Boulder, Colo.: Westview.

Westlake, Martin. 1995. *The Council of the European Union.* London: Catermill.

Wolf, Peter. 1973. International Organization and Attitude Change: A Re-Examination of the Functionalist Approach. *International Organization* 27 (3): 347–71.

5

The Janus Face of Brussels

Socialization and Everyday Decision Making in the European Union

Jeffrey Lewis

Not many international institutional environments can match the density or robustness of collective decision-making norms found in the European Union (EU).[1] But there are surprisingly few empirical studies of how these collective norms operate in the EU. There is an even greater shortfall of research on the effects of this institutional environment on the basic actor properties of the national officials who participate in this system.[2] How does the culture of decision making in the EU affect agents and their bargaining behavior? This article focuses on the Committee of Permanent Representatives (COREPER), a Brussels institution responsible for preparing upcoming ministerial meetings of the Council, and, as such, the heart of "everyday" EU decision making.[3] The members of COREPER, known as the EU permanent representatives, are exemplars of "state agents" given their prominence in articulating, arguing, and defending national interests across the gamut of EU affairs.[4] COREPER is thus a key laboratory to test whether and how state agents become socialized into a Brussels-based culture of EU decision making.

COREPER is the main preparatory body for the Council of the European Union, the legislative heart and unabashed defender of national interests in the EU. Composed of senior civil servants and career diplomats, COREPER members meet weekly and

---

[1] For a discussion of this point, see Kahler 1995, 82–89; and Wallace 1994, 41–50.

[2] Recent exceptions include Trondal 2001 and 2002; Egeberg 2004 and 1999; Egeberg, Schaefer, and Trondal 2003; and Joerges and Vos 1999.

[3] Since 1962, COREPER has met weekly in two formats: COREPER II is composed of the EU ambassadors and works primarily on the monthly meetings of the foreign ministers in the General Affairs Council (GAC); COREPER I is made up of the EU Deputies, and they preside over a wide range of so-called "technical" Councils such as the Environment, Fisheries, Employment and Social Policy, and so on. Thus, strictly speaking, COREPER consists of fifty members (twenty-five ambassadors, and twenty-five deputies) who are jointly referred to as the EU permanent representatives. For the more subtle differences in prestige and clout between COREPER I and II, see Lewis 2002; and Hayes-Renshaw and Wallace 1997.

[4] There are two substantive exceptions: the Agricultural Council (which is prepared by the Standing Committee on Agriculture [SCA]) and the Ecofin Council (prepared by the Economic and Finance Committee [EFC], which has its own vertical channels to the finance ministers, effectively bypassing COREPER).

137

have evolved a style of decision making that is rooted in a collective culture with its own informal norms, rules, and discourse.[5] Some permanent representatives even joke that this collective culture makes them unpopular with home ministries; for example, German Ambassador Dietrich von Kyaw claimed that back home he was known as the *ständiger Verräter* (permanent traitor) instead of the *ständiger Vertreter* (permanent representative).[6]

The central question of this article is whether and how the context and quality of interaction among national representatives in COREPER can have transformative effects on basic actor properties. Unlike traditional rationalist accounts, which begin from the premise that institutional environments primarily affect strategy,[7] this article seeks to test constructivist claims that institutional environments can also affect cognition, attitudes, and identity. Rather than posing this as an "either/ or" question, to competitively test rationalism "versus" constructivism, this article asks whether the constructivist line of questioning can add value to baseline rationalist accounts. Based on an original data set of interviews with participants and case-study research of negotiation histories, this article documents how COREPER offers an unambiguous example of interstate negotiation in which state actors' range of motivations include a blend of appropriateness and consequentialist logics.[8]

Following Checkel's definition of socialization as "a process of inducting actors into the norms and rules of a given community,"[9] this article tracks how COREPER participants exhibit a range of behavior and collectively legitimate arguments on the basis of a "reasoned consensus" that the logic of consequences by itself cannot explain. The outcome of socialization is the internalization of group-community standards by the EU permanent representatives (permreps), reflected in bargaining behavior and decision outcomes. Successful socialization, then, is evidenced by what Checkel calls "sustained compliance based on the internalization of . . . new norms and rules."[10] Furthermore, fine-grained analysis of the EU local elections negotiations (as will be discussed in the fourth section) will allow more nuanced discrimination between Type I (role playing) and Type II (normative suasion) patterns of internalization.[11]

Joining the COREPER "club" involves more than behaviorial adaptation to institutional norms that alter incentives and strategies. EU permreps also internalize group-community standards that become part of an expanded conception of the self. This internalization includes a distinct epistemic value in the collective decision-making process itself.[12] The standards of appropriateness found in COREPER include norms ruling out certain instrumental behavior (such as "pushing for a vote" under conditions

[5] See Lewis 2000; and Bostock 2002.
[6] Dietrich von Kyaw was Germany's EU Ambassador from 1993–99. For a discussion of his *Verräter* quip, see Lionel Barber, "The Men Who Run Europe," *The Financial Times,* 11 March 1995, Sec. 2, I–II. See also Hayes-Renshaw and Wallace 1997, 224–25; and Wallace 1973, 56.
[7] For examples, see Eising 2002, 87; and Bjurulf and Elgstrom 2004.
[8] March and Olsen 1998.
[9] Checkel, this volume.
[10] Ibid.
[11] Ibid.
[12] This is compatible with what Lax and Sebenius call the development of "process interests" or "intrinsic interests in the character of the negotiation process itself." Lax and Sebenius 1986, 72.

of qualified majority voting), obligations to practice mutual responsiveness and collectively legitimate arguments (including appropriateness standards for dropping arguments that fail to convince the group), and a duty to "find solutions" and keep the legislative agenda of the Council moving forward. However, this collective culture does not trigger shifts of loyalty or transfers of allegiance. Instead, one sees a more complex layering of national and European frames. The interview data consistently show that EU permreps do not perceive sharp tradeoffs between national and European allegiances. When discussing their job descriptions, permreps frequently refer to having dual personalities, performing multiple roles, wearing different hats, even having a "Janus face."[13] As former British Deputy Permanent Representative David Bostock explains:

Members of COREPER describe themselves as being bound by a "dual loyalty." It is their responsibility faithfully to represent their Member States; but it is also their responsibility to reach agreement. The Roman god Janus, facing in two directions, is thus COREPER's patron saint, mascot, or role model.[14]

Thus the identity configuration of EU permreps appears, even at first glance, more subtle and complex than zero-sum notions of loyalty and allegiance. In COREPER, what one sees instead is the cognitive blurring of sharp definitional boundaries between the "national" and "European" frames, and a shared sense of responsibility to deliver both at home and collectively. As this article will show, the pattern of socialization found in COREPER does not lead to the creation of a new overarching supranaational identity, but rather to a more complex configuration of identity than is typically acknowledged.

The remainder of this article is organized as follows. The next section provides a concise summary of the theoretical argument. The second section details the pathway of socialization found in COREPER, with an emphasis on the scope conditions and mechanisms at work. The necessary scope conditions are high issue density/intensity and insulation from domestic politics, both of which imply that the socialization process in COREPER is forged by the "quality" of the link. The mechanisms explaining how socialization occurs in this institutional environment include strategic calculation, role playing, and normative suasion. Following this, the third section discusses methods and the strategy of empirical triangulation. Section four contains the empirical story, which traces the negotiations of a controversial EU citizenship directive that was quietly resolved by COREPER and sent to the ministers for formal adoption. Specifically, the case covers the 1994 local elections directive granting all EU citizens the right to vote and run for office in the local elections of their current residence (that is, granting nonnational EU citizens local voting and participation rights). Finally, a brief concluding section summarizes how the identity configuration of permreps muddies conventional distinctions between "national" and "supranational" agency.

---

[13] Author's interview, 20 February 1996. All interviews were conducted in Brussels unless noted otherwise.
[14] Bostock 2002, 217.

Overview of the Theoretical Argument

For rationalists, identities and interests are taken as preset and given, and the empirical focus is on the role of formal decision rules, relative power, and instrumental rationality in explaining bargaining outcomes.[15] State agents are motivated more by a "logic of anticipated consequences and prior preferences"[16] than by notions of responsibility, obligation, or informal, "soft law" rules and norms. In the rationalists' strategic conception of rules, actors employ language and communication as rhetorical devices to pursue instrumental interests, manipulate incentive structures via social influence, and so on.[17] Normative compliance is the result of crafted, calculative reasoning and expected future benefits. While institutional environments have constraining and enabling effects on behavior by altering incentives, the impact of institutions on basic actor properties (attitudes, identities) is considered epiphenomenal.

Constructivism relaxes the assumption of preset, given interests and identities, allowing for the possibility that institutional environments may have transformative effects on basic actor properties. Relative power brokering and instrumental rationality are accorded less primacy than in rationalism, and supplemented with attention to the deliberative aspects of negotiation, such as the role of discourse, persuasion, and the collective legitimation of arguments. According to the constructivist approach, EU institutions are hypothesized to have "thick" socializing effects on actors, which go beyond instrumental adaptation and strategic calculation to include the internalization of norms and rules into self-conceptions. In other words, the densities of institutional and normative environments are considered causal variables that, under the right background conditions, can have transformative effects on basic actor properties, including how individuals see themselves (conceptions of the self) and how they conceptualize their interests. In the case of successful socialization, then, the constructivist expects to see interests that "have been conditioned by a community standard that delimits the acceptable."[18] As the case evidence will show, one can further distinguish the internalized norms argument into Type I cases, where agents follow "socially expected behavior in a given setting or community," and Type II cases of accepting community norms as "the right thing to do."[19]

The socialization story documented here does not disprove or contradict a rationalist reading,[20] but at the same time there is abundant support for a "soft" constructivist account that brings the collective culture and normative environment of Brussels-based decision making into the picture. Essentially, what one sees in the institutional environment of COREPER among the EU permreps is an expanded conception of the self that includes noninstrumental, pro-norm behavior without the threat of external sanctioning; it is based on the internalization of standards of appropriateness. This can be consistent with rationalism, but it is necessary to expand the baseline of

[15] Moravcsik 1998.
[16] March and Olsen 1998, 949.
[17] See Schimmelfennig 2000; and Schimmelfennig, this volume.
[18] Hurd 1999, 397.
[19] Checkel, this volume.
[20] See Zürn and Checkel, this volume, for a thoughtful "double interpretation."

"self-interest" beyond utility maximization to include a wider range of egoistic and other-regarding perspectives. As such, this study joins a growing number of researchers who see value in developing more nuanced models of rationality beyond the instrumental understanding embedded in nearly all forms of rational choice.[21]

Alternative Explanations: Internalized Norms or Diplomacy 101?

The alternative explanation for everyday EU decision making is standard negotiation theory and two-level games analysis.[22] The falsification test for the socialization story presented here is essentially: how does this differ from "diplomacy 101"? Using standard negotiation analysis, one would not be surprised to find, among the EU permreps, regularized practices of mutual understanding, moderating demands, and generalized reciprocity, especially given the scope conditions discussed in the next section. But according to this model, the motivations and incentive structures of the permreps would be firmly rooted in the consequentialist logic of an instrumental conception of the self and attendant interests. Against this default argument, I ask whether the empirical record shows an institutional context in which not just a logic of consequences is in play, but a distinct logic of appropriateness as well. Can one find evidence of an expanded conception of the self among national officials, and how would this differ from "normal" unsocialized bargaining in mixed-motive games?

To illustrate such differences, one can hypothesize four measures that would support the appropriateness logic and cut against the grain of conventional bargaining and two-level games analysis wedded to a logic of consequences.

1. *Noninstrumental self-restraint in demands and arguments.* Unlike the instrumental cost-benefit logic implicit in negotiation theory, self-restraint is now motivated by a sense of responsibility or obligation (especially to protect what Lax and Sebenius call "process" and "relationship" interests).[23] Consistent with standard negotiation theory would be evidence of EU officials with an altered "feasibility calculus"[24] for determining what strategies work, including when and how to make demands and to avoid being a *demandeur* too often. However, self-restraint as it is used here involves a noncalculative, noninstrumental rationale. Examples of self-restraint would include delegations who drop demands or reservations after failing to convince the group of an argument. Most relevant for the alternative-explanation test is whether one finds instances of self-restraint that do not follow from calculative reasoning (for example, "Do I have the

---

[21] For a discussion of different "models of theoretical dialogue" between rationalism and constructivism, including the tricky issues of "paradigmatic privileging" and "first mover" advantages, see Jupille et al. 2003, 19–28.

[22] The literature on negotiation theory is voluminous. Classic works include Lax and Sebenius 1986; Raiffa 1982; Iklé 1964; Rapoport 1960; Pruitt 1981; Strauss 1978; Zartman and Berman 1982; and Walton and McKersie 1965. See also Jones 1994; Kramer and Messick 1995; and Rubin and Sander 1988. On two-level games, see Putnam 1988; and Evans 1993.

[23] See fn. 12 for their definition of "process" interests. "Relationship" interests are those in which negotiators "stress the value of their relationships," which can sometimes (under iterative bargaining) take on "an almost transcendent status." Lax and Sebenius 1986, 72.

[24] Kerremans 1996, 232.

votes?") or, especially, self-restraint where the option of veto or threat thereof exists. To the extent that one finds evidence supporting acts of self-restraint under such conditions, this would lend support to the internalized norms argument.

2. *Self-enforcing adherence to informal decision-making norms without threats of external sanctioning.* If standard negotiation theories were on the mark, one would expect to see a utilitarian conception of rule-following behavior, supplemented by evidence of regularized cost-benefit analysis. The reason, as Kurd explains, is because "any loyalty by actors toward the system or its rules is contingent on the system providing a positive stream of benefits... actors do not value the relation itself, only the benefits accruing from it."[25] If the instrumental conception of rules fit here, one would also expect to see reliance on institutional enforcement mechanisms and formal rules governing acceptable bargaining behavior.[26] In contrast, "sustained compliance"[27] with informal norms in the absence of external sanctions and calculative reasoning would support the argument that state agents negotiate from shared understandings of appropriate community standards.[28]

COREPER norms are informal and self-enforcing[29] because adherence to them is considered the "right thing to do," as part of the permreps' principled commitment to collective decision making.[30] The reflex to make decisions by consensus is a classic example of this and a durable practice viewed by the EU permreps as the "right thing to do" regardless of the formal decision-rule. One ambassador claimed that the "consensus-seeking assumption... penetrates, in my mind, everything we do."[31] The mode of social control in COREPER is compatible with Hurd's legitimacy model, in which it is "noncompliance that requires of the individual special consideration and psychic costs," and in which "the internalization of external standards can... defuse Olsonian problems of collective action by causing actors to interpret the mutually cooperative option as also being the individually rational one."[32] Or as Wendt puts it, "external

---

[25] Hurd 1999, 387.

[26] For example, one would expect to see wide recourse to formal rules such as the 1994 Ioannina Compromise, which holds that under conditions of qualified majority voting when a clear blocking minority does not exist (but at least twenty-three to twenty-five votes oppose), the Council will still "do all within its power" to find a "satisfactory solution." Dinan argues that the Ioannina Compromise was a "face-saving device" for "anti-EU" back-benchers in the British parliament and has "had no practical impact on EU decisionmaking." Dinan 1998, 299. For a similar argument—that the impact of the infamous 1966 Luxembourg Compromise to protect "vital national interests" has been highly exaggerated and largely unimportant for bargaining outcomes—see Golub 1999.

[27] See Checkel, this volume.

[28] Although it should be added here that evidence of this measure may be compatible with either Type I or Type II internalization. Additional tests are needed to measure the degree of "taken-for-grantedness." A useful index to operationalize the distinction used here is the discussion in Hurd 1999 of "habitual" versus "holistic" internalization.

[29] See the "Socialization Mechanisms" section below.

[30] See also Gheciu, this volume, in which she codes successful socialization as cases where norms are accepted because they are considered normal and "the right thing to do" is to comply with them; norms are not accepted just because they are directly linked to instrumental rewards.

[31] Author's interview, 18 March 1997.

[32] Hurd 1999, 388–89.

constraints become internal constraints, so that social control is achieved primarily through self-control."[33] Evidence of self-enforced informal norms without the threat of external sanctions and constraints would support the noninstrumental appropriateness logic.

3. *Empathy and other-regarding behavior not linked to calculative reasoning.* The alternative explanation would expect to find empathic behavior linked to instrumental calculations, and in an issue-intensive, in-camera setting such as COREPER, this would be based on both longer time horizons (for example, "I may need help next week") and reputational concerns. But the internalized norms argument expects to see acts of empathy and other-regarding behavior based on a different kind of calculus. The difference from the consequentialist logic is that the internalized norms model expects such acts to be what Wendt calls "self-binding" or "unilateral initiatives with no expectation of specific reciprocity."[34] Evidence supporting the internalized norms argument would include examples of empathy not linked to an instrumentalist conception of interests but seen as "the right thing to do."

More specifically, evidence for Type II—internalized norms—socialization would include those cases in which national representatives worked to convince superiors back in the capitals to accept another delegation's plea or argument while dropping their own, even when veto options existed. This practice would be coded as normative suasion because actors who are persuaded by another's argument then defend the position to their authorities, seeking to convince those authorities to accept the reasoning while at the same time dropping their own unconvincing claim. In other words, these actors are successfully persuaded to change positions, and this carries potential costs to implement (that is, they risk the ire of the capital). Especially relevant for the collective community standards argument are those cases in which the group actively "plots" solutions to overcome domestic reserves, sometimes faking group outrage or artificially simulating a delegation's isolation on a position.[35]

But the empathy indicator is also clearly a case in which it is misleading to frame the question as "rationalism versus constructivism," as both schools offer similar predictions. Indeed, Keohane discusses several different ways that states can interpret self-interests "empathetically," some of which are consistent with standard bargaining (this would include other-regarding behavior he terms "instrumentally interdependent" and "situationally interdependent") and some of which are more akin to the internalized norm conception (for example, what he calls "empathetic interdependence").[36]

4. *Limits on instrumentalism through the collective legitimation of arguments.* Such acts would be especially relevant—and contrary to standard negotiation predictions—where delegations drop demands after failing to convince

[33] Wendt 1999, 361.
[34] Wendt 1999, 362.
[35] For a discussion of "plotting" practices in COREPER, see the "Mechanisms" section below.
[36] Keohane 1984, 120–25.

the group, despite a theoretical recourse to the threat or use of veto under the unanimity decision-rule. Evidence that standards of appropriateness exist can be seen in cases where group outrage is used to signal that certain things are just not acceptable. One can further contextualize the internalized norms argument into Type I cases in which agents follow "socially expected behavior in a given setting or community" and Type II cases of accepting community norms as "the right thing to do,"[37] a point returned to in the fourth section, below. But in general, both variants deviate from the alternative explanation of standard negotiation by their noninstrumental, noncalculative motivations.

The Pathway of Socialization in COREPER

COREPER is "responsible for preparing the work of the Council and for carrying out the tasks assigned to it by the Council."[38] From this austere legal basis, COREPER has evolved into a major player in the EU system. Among its "assigned tasks" is the remit to "coordinate the work of the various Council meetings and to endeavour to reach agreement at its level."[39] In essence, this means that COREPER holds responsibility for the performance of the Council as a whole. Permreps claim that this responsibility is an implicit part of the job description. As one ambassador put it, "there is a high collective interest in getting results and reaching solutions. This is in addition to representing the national interest."[40] Another claimed to have an unwritten, global, permanent instruction to "find solutions."[41] Whatever the case and as these quotes suggest, logics of appropriate behavior and socialization dynamics seem evident within COREPER. The analytic challenge is to establish their scope conditions and mechanisms of operation, tasks to which I now turn.

Scope Conditions

Issue Density/Intensity.   COREPER's structural placement imparts a coherence and continuity in the representation of interests that would otherwise be difficult to match. In terms of structural location, COREPER occupies a unique institutional vantage point in the EU system. Vertically placed between the experts and the ministers and horizontally situated with cross-sectoral policy responsibilities, the permreps have a general overview of the Council's work. Relative to the experts meeting in the working groups, they are political heavyweights; but compared to the ministers, they are both policy generalists and experts in the substantive questions of a file.

Since the Council's work is based on a concept of sectoral differentiation, pursuing the "national interest" across its sixteen or so formations requires national systems of

---

[37] Checkel, this volume.
[38] Art. 207, Treaty on European Union.
[39] Council of the European Union 1997, 39.
[40] Author's interview, 12 July 1996.
[41] Author's interview, 20 February 1996.

interest intermediation and interministerial coordination that are complex even for the smallest member states or those with the most centralized EU affairs machinery. It is here that the permreps in COREPER, with their cross-Council negotiating mandates and intersectoral policy responsibilities, practice an essential aggregation function. A central feature of COREPER's institutional environment is the density of issues and issue-areas that are covered in the agendas of the weekly meetings. No other site of everyday EU decision making approximates the intensity of weekly COREPER negotiations (measured in terms of the number of weekly agenda items and the horizontal nature of these agendas). Thus the agendas of COREPER meetings are qualitatively different than the type encountered at the Council working group level. Unlike the "contact thesis" then, which equates socialization with the amount of interaction,[42] the pattern discerned here is contingent on the density and quality of interactions.

Not only is COREPER distinguished by the intensity of negotiations, but the permreps' involvement across the different domains of EU decision making is pervasive as well. In addition to the regular cycle of weekly meetings, the permreps sit beside their ministers during Council sessions, briefing them and offering tactical suggestions. Permreps attend European Council summits and can serve as behind-the-scenes consultants. The growth of codecision (now considered the EU's "ordinary" legislative procedure) has also created an intense negotiation forum between members of the European Parliament (MEPs) and the deputy permreps who represent the Council.[43]

Reinforcing the intensity of interactions, the EU permreps also accumulate a great deal of experience through long periods of participation.[44] The average tenure is five years, slightly longer than the typical three- or four-year diplomatic rotation.[45] But some permreps remain in Brussels for much longer, upwards of a decade or beyond. Another reinforcement mechanism is the COREPER luncheon, held by COREPER II before the monthly General Affairs Council (GAC) and sometimes on a more topical, ad hoc basis. Lunches are frequently used to tackle the thorniest of problems, since attendance is heavily restricted, no notes are taken, and not even translators are present.[46] There are also informal COREPER trips, hosted by the presidency, that precede European Council summits.

In sum, the first scope condition is COREPER's unique structural position in everyday EU decision making, with a brand of intensity that is generated by the density and scope of agendas and widespread participation in nearly all aspects of the Council's work; this is reinforced by extensive periods of interaction and numerous informal venues for negotiation. This scope condition can also be restated in hypothesis form:

HI: The internalization of new role conceptions and conceptions of the self in line with group-community norms is more likely when individuals are in settings where contact is intense and sustained.

---

[42] See Checkel, this volume.
[43] Bostock 2002.
[44] See Checkel, this volume, for a discussion of the methodological problems in conflating the intensity and duration of interaction.
[45] Lewis 1998, 111–13.
[46] Butler 1986, 30.

Insulation.   One of the central features of COREPER diplomacy is a high degree of insulation from the normal currents of domestic constituent pressures. The meetings themselves are treated with an air of confidentiality, and many sensitive national positions are ironed out in restricted sessions in which the permreps clear the room and can speak frankly and in confidence that what is said will not be reported to the capitals or the media. This often includes group discussion on how an agreement will be packaged and sold to the authorities back home. "At our level, publicity does not exist," an ambassador explained, "Our body is absolutely black; we can do deals."[47] The norms of insulation are so developed that national experts from the capitals are not allowed to attend COREPER meetings at all (one official referred to them as "spies," another called them "the watchdogs" who "are not allowed in the room").[48] The role of insulation in COREPER diplomacy supports Checkel's hypothesis[49] that persuasion and socialization are more likely in "less politicized and more insulated, in-camera settings."

A structural feature of COREPER that often goes unnoticed is that insulation affords member states the capacity to reshape domestic constraints. As an ambassador put it, "COREPER is the only forum in the EU where representatives don't have a domestic turf to defend." Because of this, he went on to add, "it is often politically necessary to present a position knowing it is unrealistic. My minister of finance needs certain arguments to be presented. He has certain pressures from his constituencies. We have to make it look like we fought for this even though we both know it will lead nowhere. I will present it, and if it receives no support, I will drop it."[50] Along with insulation comes a high degree of input ("voice") in the instruction process, including how arguments/interests are articulated and defended. The degree of voice that the permreps can obtain stems from COREPER's basic mission to find solutions and keep the work of the Council moving forward. One intriguing argument as to why states would choose to create such a highly insulated body comes from recent work by Stasavage. Using a rational choice framework, he shows how "open-door bargaining" and greater levels of transparency can increase "posturing" by negotiators, since they have built-in incentives to present unyielding positions "in order to demonstrate to their constituents that they are effective or committed bargainers."[51]

Domestic insulation has enabled the permreps to develop de facto decision-making capabilities.[52] The best empirical indicator of the weight of COREPER's decision-making role is the prolific "A-point" procedure. A-points are "agreed points" (that is, issues agreed to within COREPER) that are passed *en bloc* and without discussion by the ministers at the beginning of each Council session.[53] Even for files marked

[47] Author's interview, 23 May 2000.
[48] Author's interviews, 23 May 2000; and 18 April 1997.
[49] See Checkel, this volume.
[50] Author's interview, 15 May 2000.
[51] Stasavage 2004, 673.
[52] The permanent representatives have no formal decision-making authority. Juridical decision-making authority is a power exclusively reserved for the ministers, and formal voting is expressly prohibited at any other level of the Council (compare Art. 7[1] of the Council's Rules of Procedure).
[53] Recent studies of the Council have documented the growth and importance of the A-point procedure in the EU legislative process. See, for example, van Schendelen 1996; and Gomez and Peterson 2001.

as B-points (that is, issues sent to the ministers that require further discussion), the input of COREPER should not be ruled out. In many cases, detailed negotiations have already taken place in COREPER (see the case study below for an example). It is remarkable, in fact, that COREPER's burgeoning de facto decision-making power has escaped every post-Maastricht "democratic deficit" revision unscathed, entirely on the rather thin reed that only ministers have juridical decisional authority.

To summarize, the second scope condition for COREPER socialization is insulated—from both domestic constituencies and domestic line ministries—negotiation, coupled with de facto (as opposed to juridical) decision-making authority. This can be restated as follows:

H2: The internalization of new role conceptions and conceptions of the self in line with group-community norms is more likely when individuals are in private, in-camera settings with a high degree of domestic insulation.

Having identified the key conditions under which to expect socialization, I turn now to the major factors that explain how this process occurs and how it can lead to shared understandings of appropriateness—understandings that produce behaviors different from those based on instrumental and utilitarian calculations alone.[54]

Socialization Mechanisms

Strategic Calculation and Role Playing: Adherence to Informal Norms. A distinctive feature of COREPER's institutional environment is a robust set of durable yet unwritten and purely informal decision-making norms. One of the most striking aspects of these informal norms is their seemingly "self-binding" nature (Wendt's term). Why do national representatives comply? The interview data strongly suggests that COREPER participants practice pro-norm behavior (in the absence of external sanctioning) because it leads to the acquisition of social influence and diffuse, intangible "social capital."[55] As a mechanism of socialization, behaviorial adaptation to acquire social influence is what this volume would code as strategic calculation.[56]

The explanation does not end there, however. To get what you want in COREPER, you must also subscribe to socially accepted standards of behavior. Evidence of this pattern would support what this volume calls Type I internalization or role-playing socialization. These informal norms act as cognitive markers for newcomers to adapt to the group's accepted standards. As I will show below in the case of Austria's "opt-out" argument, the group can reject arguments with exaggerated ferocity to shame capitals and pressure a change in national demands. Group outrage is used to signal that certain behavior and justification for demands is simply not done or is not acceptable.

Five informal norms stand out. First, there is a norm of diffuse reciprocity, or the diffuse balancing of concessions over an extended shadow of the future.[57] Diffuse

---

[54] I thank an anonymous reviewer for suggesting this language.
[55] For a discussion of "social capital," see Putnam 1993, 169–70.
[56] See Checkel, this volume.
[57] See Keohane 1986 for the classic treatise on "diffuse reciprocity."

reciprocity can take many forms, including concessions and derogations, or "going out on a limb" to persuade the capital for changes or a compromise. Dropping reserves or abstaining (rather than voting "no") are also political gestures that can be filed away and later returned in kind.

Second, there is a norm of thick trust and the ability to speak frankly, which is reinforced by weekly meetings, trips, and lunches. Thick trust is especially important during endgame negotiations or restricted sessions when the "real knives come out on the table."[58] Third, there is a norm of mutual responsiveness that is best described as a shared purpose to understand each other's problems. Knowing and understanding each other's interests and arguments is a key to "receiving understanding from the group."[59] Mutual responsiveness is a form of collective legitimation, wherein arguments or pleas for special consideration are collectively accepted or rejected by the group. The fourth norm is a consensus-reflex. This is what Hayes-Renshaw and Wallace refer to as "the instinctive recourse to behave consensually."[60] Although systematic empirical data is lacking because of the confidentiality of negotiations, participants claim that the overwhelming bulk of decisions are made consensually. Even under conditions of qualified majority voting (QMV), permreps often spend extra time to "bring everyone on board." Pushing for a vote is considered inappropriate in most cases, and the "consensus assumption" is a reflexive habit.[61]

Finally, there is a culture of compromise premised on a basic willingness to accommodate divergent interests and reinforced by the other norms listed above. This culture is facilitated by the "dynamic density" of COREPER's work and the horizontal nature of agendas. The normative effects of this culture include a self-restraint in the calculations and defense of interests, seen for example when delegations quietly drop reserves after failing to convince the others of their arguments.

Taken together, these informal norms are widely practiced and firmly institutionalized in COREPER's organizational culture.[62] As the case study of local elections negotiations will show, adherence to these norms cannot be explained by either a pure incentive-based (consequentialist) or normative (appropriateness) logic, but instead represents a subtle blending of the two. That is, pro-norm behavior is rooted in a complex combination of both strategic calculation and role-playing socialization. Which came first, and how these normative scripts became institutionalized into COREPER routines, remains largely to be told.

Normative Suasion.   COREPER has its own locution, with signals, key phrases, and unspoken meaning. There is also a certain element of theatricality, in manufacturing intrigue; how else could one sit through yet another round of fishing quotas, as one permrep alluded. All of this is the typical grammar of diplomats, to be expected in

---

[58] Author's interview, 14 March 1996. On the concept of thick trust, see Putnam 1993, 167–71.
[59] Author's interview, 17 February 1997.
[60] Hayes-Renshaw and Wallace 1995, 465.
[61] Author's interview, 18 March 1997.
[62] See Noël 1967; and Lewis 2003.

issue-intensive, insulated settings where negotiators develop long-term interpersonal relationships. Going further though, one also sees a wide range of discursive resources that permreps can use in presenting and collectively legitimating arguments. This real possibility for normative suasion is what separates COREPER from the alternative argument of "normal" interstate negotiation. For example, as the local election case study will show, COREPER is considered the EU's *locus classicus* for "opt-out" negotiations, since permreps use collective legitimation to determine who warrants special consideration backed by standards of fairness where persuasive justifications carry the day (rather than relative power, voting weights, or the decision-rule). Evidence of this pattern would tend to support Checkel's hypothesis[63] that socialization is more likely where agents do not "lecture or demand" but rather act on "principles of serious deliberative argument."

Learning the derogation discourse is an important tool of the trade in COREPER, and senior permreps develop idiosyncratic methods for signaling when they need special dispensations. For many, this includes having a sense of humor when isolated or when national political sensitivities are being discussed. Normative suasion is an important socialization mechanism in COREPER, and unlike the mechanism of strategic calculation, it is sustained over time without respect to the structure of incentives or the existence of external sanctions. But argumentative resources are intertwined by consequentialist and appropriateness logics, and it is often difficult to tear the two motivations apart.

Put differently, in COREPER, arguments matter. While a truism in almost any type of negotiation, there are no comparable sites within the Council where the persuasive power of one's arguments weighs on outcomes.[64] Representatives claim that they come prepared to convince and be convinced by others, and many of the weekly meetings are geared toward reaching a "reasoned consensus" rather than a vote.[65] Arguing and persuasion are also seen in how the permreps signal that something is particularly important or request mutual understanding from the group (irrespective of the formal decision-rule).

Participants claim that even in rare instances when they do vote, it is exceptional that this is done without the consent of the "no's."[66] In COREPER, the power of a good argument can be as compelling as a blocking minority or the shadow of the veto. The possibility of persuading others with a convincing argument and the norms of mutual responsiveness work as a great equalizer in COREPER negotiations. As a result, smaller member states who articulate sound arguments and/or clearly explain their positions can often punch above their weight. According to one participant, "If you convince others, it's with good arguments. Big or small makes no difference. In

[63] See Checkel, this volume.

[64] But see Puetter's 2003 analysis of the Eurogroup Council as a deliberative process based on a "shared normative framework."

[65] Although it is important to emphasize here that EU permreps, without exception, stress the importance of the decision-rule in contextualizing negotiations. It is a cliche in COREPER that qualified majority voting is the surest way to reach consensus.

[66] Author's interviews, 15 May 2000; and 12 July 1996.

fact, the big member states often have higher burdens of proof in order to convince the others."[67]

Another example of normative suasion is how permreps engage in the collective "plotting" of agreements.[68] Plotting is a negotiation pattern in COREPER that demonstrates how a collective rationality can reformulate individual, instrumental rationality. The basic function of plotting is using the group to redefine a national position or to reshape domestic constraints.[69] "To get new instructions we have to show [the capital] we have a black eye," an ambassador explained, "We can ask COREPER for help with this; it is one of our standard practices."[70] According to another, "Sometimes I will deal with impossible instructions by saying, 'Mr. Chairman, can I report back the fierce opposition to this by the fourteen others?' And sometimes fierceness is exaggerated for effect."[71] Exaggerating the fierceness of opposition is thus a group strategy to collectively legitimate or reject arguments. A clear illustration of this practice is seen below in the way the group handles Austria's claim for special treatment.

In general, as standard negotiation theory explains, plotting and underlining opposition are tools of the trade to deal with recalcitrant bargaining positions. But in COREPER, this takes on an additional layer of collective legitimation as a framework of shared meaning within the standards of appropriateness. As Risse argues, in a "collective communicative process" actors are engaged in determining "whether norms of appropriate behavior can be justified, and which norms apply under given circumstances."[72] This is a hallmark of COREPER's role in the EU system, and viewed from the process level of everyday decision making, the stamp of collectively negotiated standards of appropriateness is unmistakable. In the case of local elections (see below), this can be seen in how the permreps deliberate derogation requests against a principled commitment for maximal interpretation of "equal treatment" standards in EU voting rights.

Methods and Data

My research design follows a methodological strategy of "empirical triangulation" combining several qualitative and quantitative data sources: semi-structured interviews, archival documentation (Council documents such as the *travaux preparatoires,* press releases, agendas, and so on), and secondary sources. My primary data sources are semi-structured interviews with COREPER participants. To date, I have conducted 118 interviews at the permanent representations and with regular

---

[67] Author's interview, 29 May 2000. Based on survey data of 218 national officials in the EU, Egeberg, Schaefer, and Trondal find that influence on committees is considerably higher among those with demonstrable expertise than those from big states per se. Egeberg, Schaefer, and Trondal 2003, 28, tab. 11.
[68] See Lewis 2002, 292, for an example.
[69] Two-level games researchers call this "COG collusion." Evans 1993, 406–7.
[70] Author's interview, 15 May 2000.
[71] Author's interview, 26 May 2000.
[72] Risse 2000, 7.

COREPER participants from the Commission and the Council General Secretariat (COS).[73] Interviewing took place in four rounds over a seven-year period.[74]

Controlling for Prior Exposure and Self-Selection

Three methods were used to limit potential measurement problems, such as prior exposure to EU decision making. First, interview subjects were asked direct questions about their initial participation in COREPER negotiations, how they articulated their written instructions, and what, if any, changes occurred over time. Second, the interviews sampled "newcomers" at two levels: individual participants and new member states (both Nordic and Central/Eastern European newcomers are included in the sample). Third, I was able to re-interview some participants at a later date and compare their responses.

Several generalizable patterns emerged. The interviews track similar learning curves for newcomers, even those with different backgrounds and from different national administrative cultures. Participants typically claim that when they began attending the Committee, they learned that defending instructions alone had limited effectiveness.[75] This involves more than learning just strategy; effectiveness, according to participants, includes developing a sense of self-restraint and the ability to balance the specific instructions on a single file with more global instructions to keep the work of the Council moving forward.

Another pattern is that newcomers initially tend to view their counterparts as rivals. "I saw my colleagues as opponents at first," one deputy commented.[76] Another claimed, "Early in our membership we acted tough and we had these positions, 'Others don't like it, too bad.' But the politicians back home learned fast to be prepared to compromise. Now we are known as a country others can turn to for a compromise."[77] On balance, the evidence suggests that newcomers have relatively high levels of ingrained cognitive priors, which supports Checkel's hypothesis[78] that under such conditions there will be greater resistance to normative suasion. The COREPER novice who "treats colleagues as opponents" undergoes a period of social learning (and mimicry) during which they adopt new cognitive templates in order to operate in an unfamiliar environment. Some newcomers recall receiving extra patience and understanding from the group; a permrep from one of the newer EU member states commented, "They [COREPER] gave [us] and the new member states special patience, but now I think that's over."[79]

---

[73] The sample includes thirty-one permanent representatives (eighteen ambassadors and thirteen deputies), thirty-two top advisors to the permreps (known as the "Antici" [COREPER II] and "Mertens" [COREPER I] counselors), thirty policy specialists, nine legal advisors, ten officials in national capitals, and six others.

[74] Specifically, February–July 1996, February–April 1997, May 2000, and May–June 2003.

[75] One common response was that following written instructions alone (that is, just reading from them) was a sure way to be left out of the discussion.

[76] Author's interview, 17 March 1996.

[77] Author's interview, 14 March 1996.

[78] See Checkel, this volume.

[79] Author's interview, 14 March 1996.

In summary, while no guarantee against potential measurement bias, the built-in controls of triangulation, newcomer sampling, and re-interviewing help to minimize such effects. More importantly, they strengthen the case for the independent causal influence of socialization dynamics within COREPER. To directly test the four socialization measures spelled out in section two, the argument now shifts to an examination of the 1994 local elections directive, a controversial and politically unpopular extension of voting and participatory rights for EU citizens. With this directive, for the first time, the EU allowed citizens from any member state to vote and run for office in municipal elections based on wherever they resided in the EU.[80]

Socialization in COREPER: The Case of the 1994 Local Elections Directive

The EU foreign affairs ministers, meeting in the GAC, adopted a directive on the right to vote and run for municipal elections on 19 December 1994.[81] The substance of this directive had already been agreed upon twelve days earlier in COREPER. Negotiations were intentionally kept out of the GAC and the ambassadors were encouraged to reach an agreement in COREPER that could then be formally rubber-stamped by the ministers.

The local elections directive covered sensitive domestic political issues of electoral and citizenship laws, requiring the majority of member states to pass constitutional amendments to extend rights to "nonnational" EU citizens. The directive effectively established a principle of equal treatment between national and nonnational EU citizens. Moreover, the principle of equal treatment was agreed upon at a level of maximum coverage, with a minimalist interpretation of acceptable national "opt-outs." The principle of equal treatment agreed to in COREPER even went beyond earlier Commission proposals that considered minimum residency requirements a prerequisite for expanding local voting rights to Community nationals.[82]

During negotiations, several delegations (including Denmark, France, the Netherlands, and Sweden) initially voiced preferences for maintaining residency requirements that already existed in national law (see Table 1). However, the final terms of the directive allowed minimum residency rules in Luxembourg and, on an extremely limited basis, in Belgium. It was a shared understanding among the EU permreps that "opt-outs" would have to meet high standards for justification because of the potential for derogations to water down the scope and application of local voting rights. From the earliest discussions in COREPER, there was an informal and sometimes shifting

---

[80] Numerically, the directive enfranchised approximately 5.3 million EU citizens living in another EU-15 member state. Lewis 1998, tab. 5–2, 215.

[81] Council Directive 94/80/EC. The full title is the directive "[L]aying down detailed arrangements for the exercise of the right to vote and to stand as a candidate in municipal elections by citizens of the Union residing in a Member State of which they are not nationals." Official Journal L 368/38, 31 December 1994.

[82] The Commission's position was for minimum residence at least equal to the term of local office to vote, and double the term of office in order to stand for election. *European Communities Bulletin* 9–1986, 44. In effect, this would apply the Luxembourg derogation (see discussion below) to the entire EU.

Table 1. *National Legislation Governing Municipal Elections*

Member state	Basis for electoral rights	Existing national legislation before the 1994 local elections directive
Ireland	Residence	All nonnational residents eighteen years and older, who have lived in Ireland for at least six months can vote and run for office in local elections (1973 Electoral Act, right to vote; 1974 Electoral Act, right to run for office).
Denmark	Residence	Since 1977, the right to vote and run for local office has been extended to nationals of the Nordic Union (Finland, Sweden, Iceland, Norway) who are eighteen years or older and have met minimum residency requirements (Law of 18 May 1977). In 1981, these rights were extended to all nonnationals (Law No. 143 of 30 March 1981 Amending the Law Governing Municipal Elections and by Decree of the Minister of the Interior No. 196 of 22 April 1981).
Netherlands	Residence	In 1983, Article 130 of the Constitution was amended to allow all nonnationals the right to vote and run for office in local elections, subject to a minimum residency requirements.
Britain	Residence and nationality	The right to vote and run for office in local elections is extended to Irish nationals and Commonwealth citizens who are over the age of eighteen (to vote) or twenty-one (to stand as candidate) and have met minimum residency requirements.
Spain	Nationality	Since 1985, the right to vote in local elections (but not to stand as a candidate) can be extended to nonnational residents by treaty or law on a reciprocal basis (Article 3 of the General Electoral Law of 19 July 1985).
Portugal	Nationality	Since 1982, nationals of a Portuguese-speaking country may be given the right to vote in local elections by treaty or by law on a reciprocal basis. Only one such agreement was reached, with Brazil, extending the right for Brazilian nationals to vote in local Portuguese elections after having lived in Portugal for five years.
Finland	Nationality	Since 1977, the right to vote and run for local office has been extended to nationals of the Nordic Union (Denmark, Sweden, Iceland, Norway) who are eighteen years or older, and have met minimum residency requirements.
Sweden	Nationality	Since 1977, the right to vote and run for local office has been extended to nationals of the Nordic Union (Finland, Denmark, Iceland, Norway) who are eighteen years or older, and have met minimum residency requirements.

(continued)

Table 1. *(Continued)*

Member state	Basis for electoral rights	Existing national legislation before the 1994 local elections directive
France	Nationality	The rights to vote and run for office are constitutionally reserved for French nationals (Article 3).
Germany	Nationality	The rights to vote and run for office are constitutionally reserved for German nationals (Articles 20 and 28[1] of the Basic Law).
Italy	Nationality	The rights to vote and run for office are constitutionally reserved for Italian nationals (Articles 48 and 51).
Belgium	Nationality	The rights to vote and run for office are constitutionally reserved for Belgian nationals (Article 4).
Luxembourg	Nationality	The rights to vote and run for office are constitutionally reserved for Luxembourg nationals (Articles 52 and 107).
Greece	Nationality	The rights to vote and run for office are constitutionally reserved for Greek nationals (Article 51).
Austria	Nationality	The rights to vote and run for office are constitutionally reserved for Austrian nationals.

majority of members who defended the need for equal treatment between national and nonnational EU citizens. Counterfactually, the argument presented here is that minus socialization, the final outcome would have been very different—if agreement would have been reached at all.

Explaining the Local Elections Negotiations: Testing the Alternative Explanation

This article contends that everyday EU decision making is not all about relative power, formal decision-rules, and instrumental interest calculations. If it were, the alternative argument is that bargaining behavior and everyday outcomes can be explained with standard negotiation theory and two-level games analysis. However, if the alternative explanation was correct, one would expect to see a very different sequence of bargaining behavior leading to a different kind of outcome than what occurred in this case. First, although at least four delegations (Denmark, France, Greece, and Austria) were interested in derogations and could have credibly linked such claims to the "shadow of the veto", none did. Moreover, after failing to convince the group on the merits of their special circumstances, each reconsidered or dropped their demands. In the counterfactual "diplomacy 101" scenario, COREPER *sans* socialization, this behavior would remain anomalous.

Second, the alternative explanation would not hypothesize a maximalist interpretation of Article 8 (b) establishing the principle of equal treatment between national and nonnational EU citizens. Given the sensitive domestic political issues concerning electoral and citizenship laws,[83] as well as the unanimity decision-rule that applied here, one would expect a much wider acceptance of national derogation and exemption claims than resulted. In short, the "diplomacy 101" model would predict a tendency toward a least-common-denominator application of Article 8(b). But as I will show, explaining the bargaining behavior of the EU permreps as well as the (maximalist) outcome is not possible without reference to how standards of appropriateness and group-community norms to collectively legitimate arguments are an internalized part of COREPER's collective culture.

Relevance of Scope Conditions

The local elections case provides solid evidence for how scope conditions play a role in promoting socialization. The intensity dimension is seen in the complex linkages between local elections and the larger political stakes of implementing the necessary secondary legislation of the Maastricht Treaty on time. Specifically, the treaty set a 31 December 1994 deadline to reach agreement on the detailed implementation rules for local voting rights. There was a general perception of responsibility among the permreps to reach agreement on a directive that would become a key substantive component of the fledgling EU citizenship chapter agreed to at Maastricht. This sense of responsibility comes out clearly in content analysis of interviews with participants, who claimed there was a shared belief that if it was sent to the ministers they would either not reach agreement at all or would be unable to "contain" discussions for derogations. A protracted stalemate on local elections, a heated debate among the foreign ministers, or a substantively watered-down directive in the scope and terms of application were all scenarios that the EU permreps collectively wanted to avert. Within this context, negotiations were both intense and sustained, supporting Hypothesis 1 (that internalized group-community standards are more likely under such conditions).

The local elections case also illustrates the importance of the second background condition: insulation. In this instance, many of the permreps were instructed by their capital to keep negotiations at their level and avoid the GAC. One official claimed his ambassador's instructions clearly signaled the need to "keep it away from the press, where it would have been politicized quickly."[84] Another explained, "We all knew that if the discussion was put a certain way we never would reach agreement. Because of the press, pressure from national populations, the idea that 'We will be run by foreigners.'"[85] This supports Stasavage's findings that insulated negotiations

---

[83] In fact, Eurobarometer data from this era show no issue-area where EU citizens opposed EU action more. Eurobarometer, No. 39, EC, DG X, 1993. Cited in Eurostat 1996, 241. For example:

	% for	% against
Common foreign policy toward countries outside the EU	66	19
A single currency should replace all the national currencies in the EU by 1999	52	38
Each citizen of a country in the EU should have the right to vote in the municipal elections of the country in which he/she is resident	48	41

[84] Author's interview, 10 May 1996.
[85] Author's interview, 18 April 1997.

are a strategically rational institutional design where the risks of posturing run high.[86] The high degree of insulation manufactured to help COREPER "find solutions" also clearly supports Hypothesis 2 (that internalized norms are more likely under such conditions). Indeed, insulation proved critical to the process of normative suasion, seen below in the use of "restricted" sessions to sort out whose pleas for special consideration warranted attention. The restricted ambassadors-only setting provided a degree of insulation for principled debate and deliberative argumentation that other Council bodies, especially the GAC, simply did not possess.

Negotiating Derogations: Collective Legitimation and the Principle of Equal Treatment

The most critical stage of negotiations centered on who would receive derogations from the scope and application of the directive. The entire agreement hinged on this issue, because it would define how extensive coverage was and whether the principle of equal treatment would be interpreted in a maximal or minimal sense. When the ambassadors began derogation discussions in the fall of 1994, nearly half were under instruction to seek special consideration, although the presentation of these "special problems" would only be played out over the next seven weeks. In particular, six member states would claim serious domestic political difficulties: Luxembourg, Denmark, France, Greece, Austria, and Belgium. See Table 2.

Luxembourg received the earliest support for a derogation, and discussion reiterated why this was justified, given the high proportion of nonnational Community residents—nearly 30 percent of the total electorate.[87] There was also the precedent of the 1993 directive on the right to vote in European Parliament elections, where Luxembourg was allowed to set minimum residency requirements of five years for nonnational EU voters and ten years for candidates.[88] The agreed wording of the derogation covers a member state where nonnational EU citizens form more than 20 percent of the total electorate, effectively limiting the exemption to Luxembourg (that is, the 20-percent threshold is not applicable to individual municipalities within member states). But the Luxembourg exception did create a precedent that other delegations would try to extend to their own "special" problems in justifying a case for national derogations.

Denmark, for example, already allowed all foreign nationals the right to vote in local elections after a minimum residency of three years. They therefore wanted to extend this residency requirement to nonnational EU citizens as a special clause to the directive. But few supported a fixed residency requirement, under the logic that Danish nationals were not subject to the same restriction and, it was argued, this

---

[86] Stasavage 2004.

[87] In the other member states, the average proportion of nonnational EU residents to nationals varied from 0.1 percent (Finland) to 6 percent (Belgium) of the electorate. See Lewis 1998, tab. 5–3, 222.

[88] Council Directive 93/109/EC. Official Journal L 329/34, 30 December 1993. Following adoption of the EP voting directive, a number of researchers predicted the local elections directive would be more controversial. See, for example, Koslowski 1994, 389; and Oliver 1996, 475, 489.

Table 2. *Derogation Arguments for the 1994 Local Elections Directive*

Member state	Nature of the problem	Persuasive argument?	Collectively legitimated outcome
Luxembourg	30 percent of electorate are non-national EU citizens.	Yes	Article 12(1). May establish minimum residency requirements for nonnational EU citizens, not to exceed the term length of the local office in question (to vote) and twice the term length to stand as candidate.
Denmark	All foreign nationals can vote in local elections after meeting a residency requirement of three years; Community nationals should still be required to meet this requirement.	No	Danish nationals are not subject to this requirement; would violate the principle of equal treatment between all EU citizens.
France	Certain local offices participate in the *Collège des grands élercteurs sénaioriaux* and have powers to elect delegates to the parliamentary assembly.	Yes	Article 5(4). Allows additional restrictions on local offices designating delegates who vote in or elect members to the parliamentary assembly.
	In municipalities where more than 20 percent of voters are nonnational EU citizens, only 20 percent of the seats in the local assembly should be held by such nationals.	No	Violates the principle of equal treatment, and the restriction of posts to own nationals in Article 5(3).
Greece	Desired extension of the Luxembourg derogation to the local level.	No	Exemptions should be as restricted as possible and are not applicable to local government units; die Luxembourg derogation applies to the national level.
Austria	Desired extension of the Luxembourg derogation to the local level.	No	Exemptions should be as restricted as possible.
Belgium	Territorial division of electorate into linguistic communities.	Yes	Article 12(2). May restrict application of directive to certain communes, a list of which must be published one year before elections are held.

would violate the principle of equal treatment between national and nonnational EU citizens.[89]

Group discussion led to a consensus that equal treatment should not be enforced by sliding scale, whereas justification in the case of Luxembourg could be extended by varying degrees to other domestic contexts.[90] This argument carried considerable persuasive power, and there is no evidence that Denmark put up much of a struggle after failing to sell their case in COREPER. The Danish ambassador kept the reservation on the table until the 7 December session of COREPER, neither removing the request for a residency requirement nor pushing very hard for amendment. Unable to convince others, the Danish delegation dropped their reserve and accepted the directive as it stood. Standard bargaining theory would have expected something different here, either a tacit or explicit linkage to the "shadow of the veto," or at minimum, a more visible cost-benefit analysis weighing an agreement with no residency requirements against the political difficulty of reforming national electoral and citizenship legislation. "Diplomacy 101" would also expect to find an active campaign by Denmark to support other delegations with similar preferences (especially France, Belgium, and possibly Greece and Austria).

France requested a derogation because of special problems in municipalities where mayors had authority to elect Senate delegates. Specifically, the French wished to exclude municipal offices with independent powers in Senate elections from the scope of the directive. Based on this argument, they received support and understanding in COREPER. The group's rationale for accepting the derogation was that Article 8b(1) of the Maastricht Treaty clearly delimits the scope of voting and participatory rights to the municipal level.

In addition, the French made a second special request to restrict the directive's scope by limiting the number of local seats open to nonnational EU citizens in specific municipalities. In October, under pressure from Paris and the political signals being sent from the Senate, the French ambassador was instructed to argue for a clause limiting the number of seats open to other member states' citizens to 20 percent in municipalities where more than 20 percent of the electorate were nonnational EU citizens.[91] The new French proposal suggested the following restriction:

In the basic local government units where the number of voters within the scope of Article 3 represents more than 20% of national voters, the Member State of residence may limit to this proportion the number of elected representatives who are nationals of other Member States authorized to sit in the assemblies of such local authorities.[92]

In practical terms, this would have extended the Luxembourg derogation to the local level. Greece showed early support for the idea, but the German, Portuguese, Spanish, Italian, and British delegations placed the "gravest reservations" on the proposal as a violation of the principle of equal treatment.[93] In the course of discussing the

[89] Author's interview, 21 May 1996.
[90] Author's interviews, 21 May 1996; 18 April 1997; and 18 May 2000.
[91] Author's interview, 10 March 1997.
[92] Council Document 8810/94, 7 September 1994,
[93] Author's interviews, 4 and 18 March 1997.

"quota system" at several different meetings, a majority of ambassadors spoke in support of rejecting this argument, while others, including the French ambassador, remained silent. The ambassadors who found the French request unconvincing argued that the derogation would result in a patchy implementation of the directive and render the Treaty's objective of endowing EU citizenship with distinct rights a hollow shell. The French ambassador, under instruction, kept this reservation in place right up until the end, when it was dropped after the lunch session of COREPER on 7 December.[94]

Why the French would drop this reserve requires a two-part explanation, of which neither part fits the standard negotiation story. First, the French ambassador became convinced that a maximal interpretation of equal treatment was essential and the quota system was incompatible with this concept.[95] Second and more tellingly, the French ambassador then went "out on a limb" to convince foreign ministry superiors (who were well aware of the bellwether position of the Senate on nonnational citizenship rights) that the quota argument was unconvincing and lacked justification.[96] Going one step further, below I track how the change in French position and quiet removal of the quota proposal, coupled with acceptance of others' derogation claims, shows a clear instance of Type II normative suasion.

Greece and Austria both experienced difficulties generating understanding for their special problems. Both arguments were rejected in COREPER, and each shows a dynamic of collective legitimation that the alternative explanation would miss because of the irreducible quality of communicative rationality involved. Nor can standard negotiation theory explain why the rejectees made no recourse to the "shadow of the veto." One rejection came informally and was essentially unspoken, while the other required a more dramatic technique. Raised initially at the working-group level and during informal bilateral talks, the Greek delegation voiced what one group member described as "their hypothetical concern that they could have the future obligation to give Turkish citizens the right to vote" should Turkey ever become an EU member state.[97] But Greece never came out and made an argument for a derogation at the group level in COREPER. The Greeks, perhaps aware that their argument lacked persuasive power, quietly dropped their reserve.

A similar hypothetical concern was raised by Austria, but this time the group relied on a more explicit rejection from the presidency, then held by Germany, to delegitimize and even "shame" Austria's claim for special understanding. "They were afraid of how the directive would be accepted internally," a group representative recalled, "They are afraid of extreme Right movements and they have a high standard of living, so it was not easy to explain to them the advantage of the directive."[98] The Austrian ambassador pressed for a special derogation twice at the level of COREPER. The first time, no one said anything in reply. "We just sat there and listened," a participant recalled:

---

[94] See discussion below.
[95] Author's interviews, 10 March 1997; 18 May 2000; and 23 May 2000.
[96] Author's interview, 18 May 2000.
[97] Author's interview, 17 February 1997.
[98] Author's interview, 18 March 1997.

[German Ambassador] von Kyaw [as Chair] waited to see what would happen. But the second time Austria raised the issue, von Kyaw was very rough to the Austrian Permanent Representative. The Austrian Ambassador said in COREPER, "What is the logical argument why you cannot accept our case?" Von Kyaw replied very sharply, "We are here meeting very pragmatically, I don't have to explain the logical case to you." He said this very rough and it was the last we heard of the Austrian derogation."[99]

Interviews at Austria's permanent representation confirm that the group rejection was presented back in Vienna as a consensus among the other member states for a maximal interpretation of the directive's application, but that the group gave assurances that a review procedure would enable future revaluation.[100] Austria's "black eye" in this case is consistent with the delegation's reputation early in their membership for delivering rigid instructions and inflexible policy positions in Brussels.

It is plausible that differences between the Greek and Austrian appeals to the group were partly a function of the latter's noviceness (Austria joined the EU in January 1995). One large member state's ambassador with senior status among the group summarized Austria's behavior in this case as simply, "they were too new."[101] The pattern evidenced here also lends support to Checkel's hypothesis that socialization is more likely when agents have fewer ingrained cognitive priors and beliefs that are inconsistent with the socializing agency's message.[102] While it is important to avoid overstating the difference in tact by Greece and Austria, the internalized norms argument would account for the difference in argumentation by contrasting two delegations at very different stages of membership and degrees of internalization.[103]

The noviceness argument is also relevant for relating the differential behavior of Greece and Austria to what this volume calls role-playing (Type I) socialization. As Checkel explains, role-playing socialization involves a process whereby an agent learns new roles, acquiring the knowledge to act upon them.[104] In this instance, one can code Austrian bargaining behavior as too new to act the role, compared to Greece's more cautious and informal probing of group support for some form of limited exemption. A key question for Type I socialization is how does one know what is a socially expected role in a given community setting? Austria's bargaining approach shows how such a learning process among newcomers might work in COREPER, and it represents an important learning experience for them to acquire the knowledge to act on a new role.

Whatever the case, the interviews consistently confirm that the group rejection of Austria's demand was a key delimiter in derogation negotiations. Indeed, from this point on, a maximal interpretation of equal treatment prevailed. For those who still had outstanding derogation claims—including Denmark, France, and Belgium, as well as

---

[99] Author's interview, 10 March 1997.
[100] Author's interviews, 18 March 1996; and 10 May 1996.
[101] Author's interview, by telephone to national capital, 22 April 2003.
[102] See Checkel, this volume.
[103] An irony here is that few EU specialists would code Greece as an exemplar at internalizing EU norms. For an argument that Greece is a laggard in adopting EU norms, see Marks 1997.
[104] Checkel, this volume.

Greece's hypothetical and as-yet informal request—the Austrian rejection served as a marker for the standards by which derogation arguments would be measured.

The final "special" problem was raised by Belgium, which proved to be the endgame of derogation talks. Because of cleavages between the French, Dutch, and German language communities in Belgium, the directive had the potential to alter linguistic majorities within municipalities.[105] Strategically, the Belgian delegation waited to present their case until the others' arguments had been heard. One ambassador recalled that the issue was "How to accept the Belgium problem without opening the Pandora's box of Treaty revision?" "We were able to do it in COREPER," he added, "but it would have been difficult to do in a crowded, mediacized General Affairs Council."[106]

The Belgian ambassador requested a restricted session to clear the room and said, "We will need constitutional changes to transpose this directive and the Flemish Chamber will not accept it without a derogation." Unlike the other failed derogation arguments, the Belgian problem was justified with a persuasive argument, and one that genuinely convinced the others, even those who were initially skeptical. According to an ambassador from one of the large member states, "An example of persuasion and being convinced was the Belgian derogation on local elections. When I first read it, I thought, 'This is stupid.' But I became convinced they had a real problem there."[107]

The Belgian derogation was settled the following week over lunch (on 7 December), again in the restricted, ambassadors-only format. The terms of the derogation are included as an annex to the directive. Specifically:

Belgium states that if it were to make use of the derogation provided for in Article 12(2) that derogation would be applied to only some of the local government units in which the number of voters within the scope of Article 3 exceeded 20% of all voters where the Belgian government regarded the specific situation as justifying an exceptional derogation of that kind.[108]

The 7 December lunch included a group discussion of how to explain the Belgian derogation to their capitals. As one participant explained, "we had a discussion of the type of arguments we could use back to our capitals to explain why this derogation was necessary."[109] The ambassadors from France and Denmark agreed to drop their requests for exemption. The Greek and Austrian delegates remained quiet. Portugal's ambassador also expressed confidence that Lisbon would agree to abstain, despite instructions to reject any derogation. Before restarting COREPER after lunch, the ambassadors each telephoned their foreign ministers to explain the agreement reached.

The trickiest conversations were with Paris and Lisbon. The French ambassador used his considerable seniority to convince his foreign minister that the directive was acceptable. Likewise, the Portuguese ambassador sold the compromise reached in COREPER, but only after a lengthy conversation with his foreign minister. In this case, the minister and ambassador agreed that dissatisfaction with the extent of derogations did not warrant the use (or threat) of veto, but instead it was decided that

[105] de Wilde d' Estmael and Franck 1996, 40.
[106] Author's interview, 18 March 1997.
[107] Author's interview, 18 May 2000.
[108] Official Journal L 386/47, 31 December 1994.
[109] Ibid.

Portugal would abstain.[110] Portugal's abstention, rather than use (or threat) of the veto, shows how informal norms such as diffuse reciprocity operate in the context of COREPER's institutional environment and how they can promote pro-norm behavior. Portugal's carefully weighted decision to abstain following detailed communications between the ambassador and foreign minister also displays evidence of what this volume calls strategic calculation. Specifically, the abstention was a creative solution to signal a difference of view while conforming to normative standards and the reasoned consensus, and in the process generating potential "social capital" for the future. Abstaining, in this framework of meaning, is a "self-binding" form of restraint that can contribute to one's social influence.

Alternative Explanations Revisited: Internalized Norms or Diplomacy 101?

Critical to showing that this goes beyond simple negotiation theory, I found ample evidence of how group discussions collectively legitimated some arguments while rejecting others. The group actively persuaded delegations with derogation instructions to accept a strong interpretation of the principle of equal treatment. In some cases persuasion was informal and bilateral, in others it was via strategic interventions of the German presidency, and sometimes (as in the case of Austria), this persuasion was at the collective COREPER level.

As negotiations reached their final stages, the issue of how to handle the Belgian argument was contained within COREPER's institutionalized remit to find solutions. This differs from the standard logic of two-level games analysis (that is, Belgium shows they have "tied hands" to gain a dispensation) because of the socialization component involved. Without the collective legitimation of derogation claims by group-community standards, one would have expected the principled commitment to equal treatment of national and nonnational EU citizens to unravel at this stage because of recourse to the veto and the capacity of veto threats to become credibly linked to the Belgian exception. If this were all about instrumental rationality, relative power, and the formal decision-rule, one would have expected a style of brinkmanship by Denmark, France, Greece, and Austria as the Belgian issue lurked in the background and the 31 December deadline loomed. In short, one would have seen a different outcome. As the participants saw it, the Belgian problem lurked in the background even before the Belgian ambassador asked for a partial, flexible derogation; the issue was more how to justify the Belgian exception without opening the Pandora's box of special dispensations for any member with sensitive national concerns. Reaching a normative consensus on acceptable derogations was based on group-community standards of fairness, and included obligations of appropriate self-restraint for those delegations who lacked persuasive arguments (which helps account for the complete lack of veto threats, even among "exporter" states such as Portugal).

---

[110] As one of the largest "exporters" of EU citizens, Portugal preferred no derogations beyond the Luxembourg exception. As such, the Portuguese were skeptical of both the French concession regarding scope and the limited territorial application for Belgium. An official at Portugal's permrep explained that the abstention "was an elegant way to live with the text. It was a special way to avoid disagreement, but to make a political gesture." Author's interview, 10 March 1997.

In the case of Austria's argument, the instrumental rationale ("Why can't the group explain the logical case to us") not only failed, but group norms were used to shame the Austrian position and delegitimize the argument as unacceptable. The Belgian ambassador, widely considered the *doyen* of COREPER during the late 1980s and 1990s, used his considerable argumentative resources to convince the others that the derogation would be of a closed nature, and used as sparingly as possible. The Belgian derogation unambiguously demonstrates the power of persuasion and role of argumentative rationality in everyday EU decision making: a small state with a "good" argument convinced the others, some of whom were initially skeptical, to accept their claim and in a few cases "go out on a limb" to sell the agreed results back home to the capital.

The local elections example thus offers empirical support for the internalized norms argument, and the case evidence displays both Type I and Type II characteristics. Type I internalization—rule-following behavior based on socially expected standards[111]—can be seen in the way those with unconvincing derogation claims dropped their demands. This includes Denmark, Greece, Austria, and France on quotas. Evidence of Type I internalization can also be seen in the nonaction of "exporter" states such as Portugal, who logically preferred no derogations at all, but displayed none of the instrumental calculative reasoning (including any hint of recourse to veto rights) that would be expected in the standard bargaining explanation. Portugal's abstention is more consistent with the logic of appropriateness and socially accepted standards to avoid blockage of the group's "reasoned consensus" around partial, limited exemption for Belgium, France (on mayoral candidates), and Luxembourg.

Type II internalization—accepting group-community standards as "the right thing to do"[112]—is evidenced by the "reasoned consensus" legitimating Belgium's plea for special consideration. The strongest evidence of Type II normative suasion can be seen in the actions of the French ambassador. Carefully triangulated interview histories support a characterization that he was genuinely persuaded by his Belgian colleague's argument, after initial doubts, and then went on to convince his superiors in Paris to accept Belgium's partial exemption while at the same time dropping the French preference for a quota system. According to the key participants involved, this action was premised on becoming convinced that helping Belgium was the right thing to do. As one ambassador put it, "we found understanding in our capitals . . . in the end we persuaded our governments, we did it very much for Belgium."[113]

In summary, the local elections case offers evidence that COREPER socialization affects not only strategies, but also conceptions of the self. Evidence of an expanded conception of the self, in which permreps practice internalized group-community standards based on a noncalculative logic of appropriateness, can be seen in both the bargaining behavior and outcome of the local elections case. The interview and case-study data offer confirming evidence for the four socialization measures discussed in section two. First, I have shown noninstrumental self-restraint among several

---

[111] See Checkel, this volume.
[112] Ibid.
[113] Author's interview, by telephone to national capital, 22 April 2003.

delegations after they failed to convince the others of their argument (including Denmark, France, and Greece). Second, there were numerous examples of self-enforcing adherence to informal norms, such as the "self-control" of derogation claimants to not explicitly reference veto options or drop reserves based on favorable cost-benefit ratios. Third, evidence of empathy and other-regarding behavior not linked to calculative reasoning can be seen in the "reasoned consensus" to legitimate Belgium's derogation claim even though several ambassadors had to sell the validity of Belgium's case to their superiors while dropping their own claims. Fourth, and finally, this case illustrates the limits on instrumentalism through the collective legitimation of arguments. Restricted sessions were used to collectively accept and reject derogation claims (and "plot" ways to sell the Belgian derogation to ministers) around a shared understanding of maximal interpretation of equal treatment. As a result, the internalized norms argument can more fully account for the way in which Denmark, France, and Greece quietly dropped, or chose not to articulate, derogation claims than can "diplomacy 101." More dramatically, the group rejection of Austria's claim demonstrates how collective legitimation places limits on instrumental behavior by signaling that certain behavior is just not acceptable. In sum, the constructivist logic of internalized norms can better account for both the bargaining behavior and outcomes of the local elections case than the rationalist logic of consequences alone.

Conclusion: Blurring the National and the European

COREPER's institutional architecture challenges the conventional dichotomy that sharply demarcates the national and European levels. As a collectivity of member-state representatives, COREPER exemplifies the imagery of national and European levels of governance becoming amalgamated.[114] Accordingly, COREPER's Janus-like design is an anomaly for theorists who draw rigid distinctions between "national" and "supranational" agency. For example, in one prominent account of European integration, the corporate body of "supranational entrepreneurs" in the EU is effectively limited to European Commissioners.[115] But the EU permreps belie such a straightforward pigeonhole. As Wallace puts it, "It would be a caricature of this intricate policy process to counterpose national actors and supranational entrepreneurs as separate elites, promoting opposed interests."[116] The permreps who participate in weekly COREPER negotiations and share a collective responsibility to maintain the output of the Council as a whole, nicely illustrate how the logics of consequences and appropriateness can interface, which in turn suggests that national and supranational identifications can become complexly intertwined. According to March and Olsen, "Political actors ... calculate consequences and follow rules, and the relationship between the two is often subtle."[117]

---

[114] H. Wallace 2000, 7.
[115] Moravcsik 1998, 54–60, 479–85.
[116] W. Wallace 2000, 529–30.
[117] March and Olsen 1998, 952.

Perhaps surprisingly, permreps do not self-reflectively see these as competitive or contradictory role/identity sets. My findings are somewhat at odds with others in this volume, such as Beyers and Hooghe, who offer clear-cut evidence of ranked "primary" and "secondary" allegiances among EU officials.[118] A major difference, of course, is the point of reference: they are examining the administrative expert level of Council working groups and Commission officials, and both of these display qualitative differences from COREPER in scope conditions as well as what Egeberg refers to as "organizational characteristics."[119]

The testimonies of the permreps interviewed for this project suggest that identities and role conceptions are not so clearly juxtaposed at this level of the EU system. Overall, the evidence points to a pattern of symbiosis between national and collective identities.[120] The EU permreps have operationalized the concept of "double-hatting."[121] Instead of limited notions of shifts and transfers of identity, or clearly juxtaposed primary and secondary affiliations, what one sees in COREPER is a cognitive blurring of the sharp definitional boundaries between the national and the European. None of this implies national identities are becoming marginalized; rather, what stands out is the interpenetration of the national with the European and vice versa.[122] The identity configuration of the EU permreps is compatible with what Risse suggestively describes as a "marble cake" concept of multiple identities, in which "the various components of an individual's identity cannot be neatly separated on different levels."[123] On this reading, an actor's "identity components influence each other" and "mesh and blend."[124] Nor does this in any way imply that socialization effects are homogenous.[125] A more systematic study of socialization processes in COREPER would build controls into the model for variation caused by preexisting differences in member states' European policy, administrative culture, and policy styles.[126]

Finally, it is worth further consideration how the socialization effects identified in this article are potentially reversible. That is to say, the Brussels-based culture of decision making, endowed with dense informal norms and standards of appropriateness, could be undone. First, there is little, if any, evidence to support a "holistic" internalization thesis in which norm compliance becomes automatic.[127] Rather, COREPER socialization is a process of incremental, partial internalization. This point

---

[118] See Beyers, this volume; and Hooghe, this volume. See also Egeberg 1999; and Egeberg, Schaefer, and Trondal 2003.

[119] Egeberg 2004.

[120] The symbiosis analogy is a trademark of some of the subtler findings (now often overlooked) in the early neofunctionalist literature on the ECSC and EEC. See Haas 1958, 526; and Lindberg and Scheingold 1970, 94–95.

[121] See Laffan 2004, 90–94, for a conceptual discussion of "double hatting" among Council actors.

[122] For a conceptualization of how "the European dimension is included in national self-conceptions," see Waever 1995, 412, 430. For a detailed case study on Germany, see Katzenstein 1997.

[123] Risse 2004, 251.

[124] Ibid., 251–52.

[125] See Legro 1997 for a discussion of how pro-norm behavior may exist in "varying strengths" within a given community.

[126] For a detailed analysis of how socialization is affected by domestic organizational embeddedness, see Beyers, this volume.

[127] On "holistic" internalization, see Hurd 1999, 398.

is evidenced more clearly in my larger multiple-case-study project, where the British, for example, display a more *a la carte* adherence to informal norms when there are principled objections to EU policies (as in social policy).[128]

This study did find hard evidence of Type II internalization,[129] particularly in the way those with rejected derogation claims convinced their capitals and/or "went out on a limb" to secure the Belgian derogation once a "reasoned consensus" was reached in COREPER—contrary to what standard bargaining theory and instrumental cost-benefit predictions would have expected. But it does not necessarily follow that a switch from a logic of consequences is complete: just ask the British if they could find someone else's argument on fiscal federalism convincing, or the French if policy toward the Middle East is open to EU deliberation and collective legitimation norms. In other words, it would be inaccurate to characterize the internalization of group-community standards as "taken-for-granted" in a holistic sense, but the bargaining behavior and decisional outcomes documented in this article do consistently confirm instances of pro-norm behavior as the "right thing to do."

Second, it is possible to imagine scenarios in which the scope conditions for this socialization story were fundamentally altered: either the density of issue coverage (for example, due to the increased fragmentation of preparatory authority among rival committees) or insulation (for example, because of domestic political pressures to address the "democratic deficit" and increase transparency). Changing the scope conditions would likely alter what neofunctionalists called *l'engrenage* effects,[130] and it is quite possible that the standards of appropriateness would be altered as a result. Under altered background conditions or changes in the standards of appropri-ateness,[131] one would expect the identity configuration of EU permreps to revert to more egoistic and instrumental variants. Under such conditions, pro-norm behavior would become contingent on more explicit and regularized calculation, and agents might use voting weights and veto threats rather than appeals to fairness or principled debate that would, over time, affect the perceived legitimacy of the EU's collective decision-making culture.

References

Bjurulf, Bo, and Ole Elgström. 2004. Negotiating Transparency: The Role of Institutions. *Journal of Common Market Studies* 42 (2):249–69.

Bostock, David. 2002. COREPER Revisited. *Journal of Common Market Studies* 40 (2):215–34.

Butler, Michael. 1986. *Europe: More Than a Continent*. London: William Heinemann.

Council of the European Union. 1997. *Council Guide, Volume II: Comments on the Council's Rules of Procedure, Sept 1996*. Luxembourg: Office for Official Publications of the European Communities.

---

[128] Lewis 1998.

[129] See Checkel, this volume.

[130] Roughly translated, *l'engrenage* means "getting caught up in the gears." See Dinan 1998, 166.

[131] Could enlargement change expectations of collective legitimation and group-community norms? Many Brussels insiders see the EU-25 as a qualitative leap in heterogeneity that will have unintended conse-quences for the Council's everyday decision-making environment.

De Wilde d'Estmael, Tanguy, and Christian Franck. 1996. Belgium. In *The European Union and Member States: Towards Institutional Fusion?* edited by Dietrich Rometsch and Wolfgang Wessels, 37–60. Manchester, England: Manchester University Press.

Dinan, Desmond, ed. 1998. *Encyclopedia of the European Union.* Boulder, Colo.: Lynne Rienner.

Egeberg, Morten. 1999. Transcending Intergovernmentalism? Identity and Role Perceptions of National Officials in EU Decision Making. *Journal of European Public Policy* 6 (3):456–74.

———. 2004. An Organisational Approach to European Integration: Outline of a Complementary Perspective. *European Journal of Political Research* 43 (2):199–219.

Egeberg, Morten, Günther Schaefer, and Jarle Trondal. 2003. The Many Faces of EU Committee Governance. *West European Politics* 23 (3):19–40.

Eising, Rainer. 2002. Policy Learning in Embedded Negotiations: Explaining EU Electricity Liberalization. *International Organization* 56 (1):85–120.

Eurostat, Statistical Office of the European Communities. 1996. *Social Portrait of Europe.* Luxembourg: Office for Official Publications of the European Communities.

Evans, Peter. 1993. Building an Integrative Approach to International and Domestic Politics: Reflections and Projections. In *Double-Edged Diplomacy: International Bargaining and Domestic Politics,* edited by Peter Evans, Harold Jacobson, and Robert Putnam, 397–430. Berkeley: University of California Press.

Golub, Jonathan. 1999. In the Shadow of the Vote? Decision Making in the European Community. *International Organization* 53 (4):733–64.

Gomez, Ricardo, and John Peterson. 2001. The EU's Impossibly Busy Foreign Ministers: 'No One is in Control.' *European Foreign Affairs Review* 6 (1):53–74.

Haas, Ernst. 1958. *The Uniting of Europe: Political, Social, and Economic Forces, 1950–1957.* Stanford, Calif.: Stanford University Press.

Hayes-Renshaw, Fiona, and Helen Wallace. 1995. Executive Power in the European Union: The Functions and Limits of the Council of Ministers. *Journal of European Public Policy* 2 (4):559–82.

———. 1997. *The Council of Ministers.* New York: St. Martin's Press.

Hurd, Ian. 1999. Legitimacy and Authority in International Politics. *International Organization* 53 (2):379–408.

Ikle, Fred Charles. 1964. *How Nations Negotiate.* New York: Harper & Row.

Joerges, Christian, and Ellen Vos, eds. 1999. *EU Committees: Social Regulation, Law, and Politics.* Portland, Ore.: Hart.

Jones, Bernie. 1994. A Comparison of Consensus and Voting in Public Decision Making. *Negotiation Journal* 10 (2):161–72.

Jupille, Joseph, James Caporaso, and Jeffrey Checkel. 2003. Integrating Institutions: Rationalism, Constructivism, and the Study of the European Union. *Comparative Political Studies* 36 (1/2):7–41.

Kahler, Miles. 1995. *International Institutions and the Political Economy of Integration.* Washington, D.C.: Brookings Institution Press.

Katzenstein, Peter. 1997. United Germany in an Integrating Europe. In *Tamed Power: Germany in Europe,* edited by Peter Katzenstein, 1–48. Ithaca, N.Y.: Cornell University Press.

Keohane, Robert. 1984. *After Hegemony: Cooperation and Discord in the World Political Economy.* Princeton, N.J.: Princeton University Press.

———. 1986. Reciprocity in International Relations. *International Organization* 40 (1):1–27.

Kerremans, Bart. 1996. Do Institutions Make a Difference? Non-Institutionalism, Neo-Institutionalism, and the Logic of Common Decision-Making in the European Union. *Governance* 9 (2):217–40.

Koslowski, Rey. 1994. Intra-EU Migration, Citizenship and Political Union. *Journal of Common Market Studies* 32 (3):369–402.

Kramer, Roderick, and David Messick, eds. 1995. *Negotiation as a Social Process*. London: Sage.

Laffan, Brigid. 2004. The European Union and Its Institutions as "Identity Builders." In *Transnational Identities: Becoming European in the EU*, edited by Richard Herrmann, Thomas Risse, and Mari-lynn Brewer, 75–96. Lanham, Md.: Rowman and Littlefield.

Lax, David, and James Sebenius. 1986. *The Manager as Negotiator: Bargaining for Cooperation and Competitive Gain*. New York: Free Press.

Legro, Jeffrey. 1997. Which Norms Matter? Revisiting the Failure of Internationalism. *International Organization* 51 (1):31–63.

Lewis, Jeffrey. 1998. *Constructing Interests: The Committee of Permanent Representatives and Decision-Making in the European Union*. Ph.D. diss., University of Wisconsin-Madison.

———. 2000. The Methods of Community in EU Decision-Making and Administrative Rivalry in the Council's Infrastructure. *Journal of European Public Policy* 7 (2):261–89.

———. 2002. National Interests: COREPER. In *The Institutions of the European Union*, edited by John Peterson and Michael Shackleton, 277–98. Oxford: Oxford University Press.

———. 2003. Institutional Environments and Everyday EU Decision Making: Rationalist or Constructivist? *Comparative Political Studies* 36 (1/2):97–124.

Lindberg, Leon, and Stuart Scheingold. 1970. *Europe's Would-Be Polity: Patterns of Change in the European Community*. Englewood Cliffs, N.J.: Prentice-Hall.

March, James, and Johan Olsen. 1998. The Institutional Dynamics of International Political Orders. *International Organization* 52 (4):943–69.

Marks, Michael. 1997. Moving at Different Speeds: Spain and Greece in the European Union. In *Tamed Power: Germany in Europe*, edited by Peter Katzenstein, 142–66. Ithaca, N.Y.: Cornell University Press.

Moravcsik, Andrew. 1998. *The Choice for Europe: Social Purpose and State Power from Messina to Maastricht*. Ithaca, N.Y.: Cornell University Press.

Noël, Emile. 1967. The Committee of Permanent Representatives. *Journal of Common Market Studies* 5 (3):219–51.

Oliver, Peter. 1996. Electoral Rights Under Article 8B of the Treaty of Rome. *Common Market Law Review* 33 (3):473–98.

Pruitt, Dean. 1981. *Negotiation Behavior*. New York: Academic Press.

Puetter, Uwe. 2003. Informal Circles of Ministers: A Way Out of the EU's Institutional Dilemmas? *European Law Journal* 9 (1):109–24.

Putnam, Robert. 1988. Diplomacy and Domestic Politics: The Logic of Two-Level Games. *International Organization* 42 (3):427–60.

———. 1993. *Making Democracy Work: Civic Traditions in Modern Italy*. Princeton, N.J.: Princeton University Press.

Raiffa, Howard. 1982. *The Art and Science of Negotiation: How to Resolve Conflict and Get the Best Out of Bargaining*. Cambridge, Mass.: Harvard University Press.

Rapoport, Anatol. 1960. *Fights, Games, and Debates*. Ann Arbor: University of Michigan Press.

Risse, Thomas. 2000. 'Let's Argue!': Communicative Action in World Politics. *International Organization* 54 (1):1–39.

————. 2004. European Institutions and Identity Change: What Have We Learned? In *Transnational Identities: Becoming European in the EU*, edited by Richard Herrmann, Thomas Risse, and Mari-lynn Brewer, 247–71. Lanham, Md.: Rowman and Littlefield.

Rubin, Jeffrey, and Frank Sander. 1988. When Should We Use Agents?: Direct vs. Representative Negotiation. *Negotiation Journal* 4 (4):395–401.

Schimmelfennig, Frank. 2000. International Socialization in the New Europe: Rational Action in an Institutional Environment. *European Journal of International Relations* 6 (1):109–39.

Stasavage, David. 2004. Open-Door or Closed Door? Transparency in Domestic and International Bargaining. *International Organization* 58 (4):667–703.

Strauss, Anselm. 1978. *Negotiations: Varieties, Contexts, Processes, and Social Order*. San Francisco: Jossey-Bass.

Trondal, Jarle. 2001. Administrative Integration Across Levels of Governance: Integration Through Participation in EU Committees. ARENA Report No. 01/7. Oslo, Norway: ARENA Centre for European Studies, University of Oslo.

————. 2002. Beyond the EU Membership—Non-Membership Dichotomy? Supranational Identities among National EU Decision-Makers. *Journal of European Public Policy* 9 (3):468–87.

Van Schendelen, M. P. C. M.1996. 'The Council Decides' : Does the Council Decide? *Journal of Common Market Studies* 34 (4):531–48.

Waever, Ole. 1995. Identity, Integration and Security: Solving the Sovereignty Puzzle in EU Studies. *Journal of International Affairs* 48 (2):389–431.

Wallace, Helen. 1973. *National Governments and the European Communities*. London: Chatham House.

————. 2000. The Institutional Setting: Five Variations on a Theme. In *Policy-Making in the European Union*, 4th ed., edited by Helen Wallace and William Wallace, 3–37. Oxford: Oxford University Press.

Wallace, William. 1994. *Regional Integration: The West European Experience*. Washington, D.C.: Brookings Institution Press.

————. 2000. Collective Governance. In *Policy-Making in the European Union*, 4th ed., edited by Helen Wallace and William Wallace, 523–42. Oxford: Oxford University Press.

Walton, Richard, and Robert McKersie, eds. 1965. *A Behavioral Theory of Labor Negotiations: An Analysis of a Social Interaction System*. New York: McGraw-Hill.

Wendt, Alexander. 1999. *Social Theory of International Politics*. Cambridge: Cambridge University Press.

Zartman, William, and Maureen Berman. 1982. *The Practical Negotiator*. New Haven, Conn.: Yale University Press.

6

Security Institutions as Agents of Socialization? NATO and the 'New Europe'

Alexandra Gheciu

In recent years, the relationship between the North Atlantic Treaty Organization (NATO) and the former communist countries of Europe has been the focus of numerous analyses in the field of international relations. This article seeks to contribute to those analyses by arguing that, following the end of the Cold War, NATO became systematically engaged in the projection of a particular set of Western-based norms into Central and Eastern Europe. Conventional wisdom about international security portrays NATO as a military alliance, irrelevant to processes of constructing or reproducing domestic norms and institutions. Contrary to that view, I show that NATO played an important role in the reconstitution of postcommunist polities. The alliance relied especially on mechanisms of teaching and persuasion in an effort to socialize Central and East European actors into a particular, liberal-democratic vision of correct norms of governance.

NATO was especially heavily involved in the eastern projection of liberal-democratic norms in the field of security. These include accountability and transparency in the formulation of defense policies and budgets, the division of powers within the state in the area of security, government oversight of the military through civilian defense ministries, and accountability for the armed forces. In addition, NATO has sought to project into Central and East European countries Western-defined liberal norms and rules of international behavior, in particular involving peaceful settlement of disputes, multilateralism, and democracy and human rights promotion in the international arena.

This article examines the dynamics and implications of socialization conducted by NATO between 1994 and 2000, in interactions with actors from the Czech Republic and Romania.[1] The comparison between the Czech Republic and Romania is useful because, in the period covered in this study, only the former received the reward of NATO membership. Moreover, in light of the lessons learned in the process of

---

[1] 1994 marked the beginning of more systematic interactions between NATO and former communist states, particularly through the establishment of the Partnership for Peace. The end point of 2000 was chosen to cover the 1999 enlargement and the Kosovo conflict.

incorporating the first wave of newcomers, NATO changed its policy vis-à-vis second-wave candidates. In the case of the three countries admitted in 1999, the promise of membership preceded the completion of many of the reforms prescribed by the alliance. Subsequently, the allies established the Membership Action Plan, aimed at promoting change and assessing the candidates' records prior to inviting them to join NATO. Consequently, second-wave countries faced the dilemma of having to carry out comprehensive reforms, and having to adopt a series of costly courses of action (for example, support for NATO wars abroad), without any guarantee that they would receive the reward of membership. Nevertheless, NATO carried out similar socialization practices in the Czech Republic and Romania and, despite the differences in the structure of rewards, those practices did have a powerful impact on both countries.

The analysis proceeds as follows. In the next section, I briefly place my argument within a broader theoretical framework. In the second section, I provide an explanation of relevant mechanisms of socialization and anticipated scope conditions. I then turn, in the third section, to the empirical story—NATO's socialization of Czech and Romanian actors. Here I examine examples of teaching and persuasion that occurred in different contexts and targeted diverse sets of socializees. The fourth section analyzes the effects of socialization; and the fifth section revisits the question of scope conditions in light of the preceding empirical analysis.

Theoretical Framework

In recent years, several analysts have argued that NATO is more than just a military alliance. For instance, neoliberal institutionalists—most famously, Keohane and Wallander—have argued that there is a difference between alliances (defined as exclusive coalitions that respond to threats) and security management institutions (which are designed to address a variety of risks).[2] From this perspective, NATO is a security management institution, which has always sought to deal not only with external threats, but also with problems of mistrust and misunderstandings among its members. The institutionalist argument is that, in the context of the post-1989 shift in security priorities away from the containment of the Soviet threat, NATO was able to transfer risk management practices developed during the Cold War to the new situation. Institutionalists argue that, in the instability characteristic of the early post–Cold War environment, NATO's experience in cooperation, trust building, and integration among members was extended into Central and Eastern Europe via the process of NATO enlargement.[3] Institutionalists are right to argue that post–Cold War NATO has sought to address instability, but they do not explain the processes through which the alliance has acted to shape state identities around norms perceived as a source of peace and progress.

In analyzing NATO as a self-defined institutional expression of the Western liberal-democratic community, it is useful to start from Risse's account of the collective

---

[2] See Wallander and Keohane 1999; and Wallander 2000.
[3] Wallander 2000, 720–21.

identity on which the alliance is founded.[4] As Risse has argued, by virtue of the norms and sense of collective identity it embodied, NATO did not disappear following the end of the Cold War. Indeed, "[t]he end of the Cold War... not only does not terminate the Western community of values; it extends that community into Eastern Europe and, potentially, even into the successor states of the Soviet Union, creating a "pacific federation" of liberal democracies from Vladivostock to Berlin, San Francisco and Tokyo."[5] This article seeks to build on Risse's argument by examining the dynamics of change promoted by the organization in Central and Eastern Europe; in other words, by placing greater emphasis on the actual politics involved in the eastern projection of liberal-democratic norms.

More recently, a series of analysts have tried to establish, empirically, whether NATO spreads liberal-democratic norms in Central and Eastern Europe. Particularly influential has been Reiter's critique: according to him, to the extent that democratization occurs in certain ex-communist countries, this is the result of domestic, rather than international, factors.[6] In response, critics such as Waterman and Zagorcheva, among others, have argued that, through the Partnership for Peace, the Membership Action Plan, and various other programs, NATO has "co-opted" Central and East European actors into activities that are likely to affect the ways in which the latter think and behave. In other words, NATO has been involved in "socializing" Central and Eastern Europeans into the "Western ways."[7] The introduction of the concept of socialization is a significant step forward in explaining the relationship between NATO and Central and Eastern Europeans, but analyses such as those provided by Waterman and Zagorcheva need to be taken even further, to include an examination of the specific mechanisms used to socialize Central and Eastern Europeans into the Western ways of thinking and acting. That is precisely what this article seeks to achieve.

Following Checkel's definition, socialization is understood here as a process of inducting actors into the norms and rules of a given community.[8] To account for the complexity of NATO's involvement in Central and Eastern Europe, I adopt a constructivist approach, conceptualizing socialization as a process in which the socializer (NATO) has targeted—and sometimes affected—changes in the definitions of identity and interests held by the socializees. From a constructivist perspective, successful socialization results in the internalization of the prescribed norms and rules. The new norms come to be taken for granted—accepted because they are seen as normal, given "who we are."[9] In other words, successful socialization results in a situation in which compliance with the new norms occurs via a logic of appropriateness.[10]

---

[4] See Risse-Kappen 1995 and 1996.

[5] Risse-Kappen 1996, 396.

[6] Reiter 2001.

[7] Waterman, Zagorcheva, and Reiter 2002.

[8] See Checkel, this volume; and Lauer and Handel 1977. Also relevant are Berger and Luckmann 1967; and, within the field of international relations, especially Wendt 1999.

[9] Checkel, this volume.

[10] For analyses of different logics operating in international politics, see, for example, Katzenstein, Keohane, and Krasner 1998; March and Olsen 1998; and Ruggie 1998. Also relevant are March and Olsen 1989; and Powell and DiMaggio 1991.

It is interesting to examine NATO's involvement in Central and Eastern Europe within the framework of rationalist/constructivist debates about socialization.[11] It might be tempting to portray this case as a simple example of rationalist (self-) socialization of instrumental actors engaged in the pursuit of predefined interests. By this logic, in the post–Cold War context of asymmetric distribution of power between the West and the former Eastern bloc, the Central and Eastern Europeans adopted the norms prescribed by the Western world in order to reap the material benefits that the latter could provide. For instance, it could be that the Central and Eastern Europeans sought membership to obtain the alliance's protection from a potential military resurgence of Russia. Linked to this, it could be argued that NATO was important to Central and Eastern Europeans because it represented the key forum for organizing their relations to the only remaining superpower, the United States.[12] From this perspective, for the decision makers of former communist states, the question was simply one of strategically altering their behavior to join NATO and thus advance their objective, pregiven interest: security. Farrell succinctly captured this perspective when he argued that "[p]ower and interests, in the form of coercion and inducement, can play a particularly important role in international norm diffusion. A contemporary example of this is the adoption of Western norms of military professionalism by post-communist states desperate to join the North Atlantic Treaty Organization."[13] On this logic, the role of NATO as "socializer" was minimal, involving the use of instrumental incentives to preconstituted actors, and the provision of information regarding the conditions attached to those incentives.

I argue in this article that the logic of socialization of Central and Eastern Europeans into the norms prescribed by NATO departed in important ways from the rationalist logic of socialization.[14] Two dimensions of this process are relevant to this study: (1) the dynamics of the process (that is, the types of practices or mechanisms employed by NATO in the international diffusion of new norms, and the conditions that facilitated or inhibited the operation of these mechanisms); and (2) the outcome of the process of socialization (the internalization of new norms). Drawing on Jepperson, Wendt, and Katzenstein, I take state identities to mean the prevailing intersubjective ideas of collective distinctiveness and purpose.[15] By defining the key characteristics of a given polity, these ideas shape both its domestic politics (as they are tied to a particular set of norms of governance recognized as consistent with "who we are"), and its foreign

---

[11] For useful analyses, see Checkel and Moravcsik 2001; Checkel 2001 and 2003; and Schimmelfennig 2003.

[12] I would like to thank Thomas Risse and Lisa Martin for bringing to my attention the importance of discussing the role of the United States within NATO in the context of interactions between the alliance and Central and Eastern Europeans.

[13] Farrell 2002, 70–71.

[14] My argument here is similar to Adler's critique of neoliberal institutionalist analyses of the role of Western institutions in the former communist bloc. With particular reference to the Organization for Security and Cooperation in Europe (OSCE), Adler has demonstrated that international institutions have played an important role in former communist countries, not necessarily by increasing interstate coordination and reducing transaction costs, but by engaging in community-building socialization practices that have had the effect of changing intersubjective knowledge through which identities and interests are defined. See, in particular, Adler 1998.

[15] Jepperson, Wendt, and Katzenstein 1996, 59.

policy (through an identification of national distinctiveness in relation to other states, definitions of state identity position the national self in the international arena and enable decision makers to identify friends and enemies). Useful indicators of change in the definition of national identity include the emergence of new intersubjective ideas about the key characteristics of the given polity (a new understanding of the collective self, and of the nature of correct or appropriate norms of governance), and a new conception of the relationship between the national self and the outside world (such as a rearticulation of the self's particular position—identification with, similarity to, or difference from, even opposition to—various international others, and the purpose of the self in the context of interactions with those different others).

The rationalist argument that NATO was able to use the issue of membership as an efficient carrot and stick fails to take into account the constraints within which the alliance was operating in pursuing enlargement. For example, vis-à-vis the Czech Republic, NATO's ability to use membership as an effective carrot was undermined by the fact that, by the time the accession talks began, the carrot had already been promised. Already in 1997 there was a widespread belief both among allied decision makers and in Prague's political circles that, if they wished, the Czechs would be included in the first wave of enlargement.[16] Subsequently, although NATO representatives sometimes expressed concern and even dissatisfaction regarding particular Czech policies, there is no evidence that they linked those concerns to threats to withdraw the membership invitation. Conversely, Romania was excluded from the first wave of enlargement and the allies refused to promise NATO membership in the foreseeable future, even in the case of complete Romanian compliance with Western prescriptions. This placed Romanian decision makers in a difficult position in the domestic arena: they were running the risk of paying the domestic costs of reform and pro-NATO foreign policy (for example, supporting the controversial war in Kosovo) without even having the guarantee of a significant international reward for their efforts.

Under these circumstances, to understand the influence exercised by NATO in the ex-communist bloc, one needs to move beyond a narrow focus on material resources. Key here is a move away from an individualist perspective to an inter-subjective understanding of power as competence. According to the competence model, status and the power to act are not inherently attributed to the resources possessed by a given entity, but depend on their recognition in a given set of international interactions.[17] Here, intersubjective power refers to the ability of NATO to act as an authoritative agent providing "correct" interpretations of the world, including definitions of the self and others, and identifying reasonable actions in that world. At the same time, that social role entailed duties for NATO, and placed limitations on what the organization

---

[16] Author's interviews with senior NATO officials from the Political Affairs division, 12 October 1999 and 28 April 2000, Brussels; and with Czech foreign affairs officials, 10 April 2000, Prague. See also the Czech News Agency (CTK) press release on "NATO Membership," 10 October 1997. For a broader empirical analysis of NATO's post–Cold War enlargement, see, for example, Asmus 2002.

[17] On the competence model of power, see Guzzini 2000; Williams 1997; and Williams and Neumann 2000. Also relevant are Adler 1997; Adler and Barnett 1998; and Barnett and Finnemore 1999. For a recent analysis of the role of power in social relations of constitution, see also Barnett and Duvall 2005.

could legitimately do in Central and Eastern Europe (for example, it ruled out the use of force against democratically elected governments in the name of promoting reforms).

Of course, the post–Cold War world has been marked by substantial asymmetries in resources between East and West. It is also true that at least the centrist, proliberal political elites from the Czech Republic and Romania were, from the early 1990s, keen to see their countries integrated into the Euro-Atlantic structures, including NATO. But what was key to this relationship was not simply the material power yielded by the allies—either collectively, or by the United States within the framework of the alliance. Rather, key here was the Czechs' and Romanians' identification with the Western community, and, hence, their trust in NATO—as the main security institution of that community. This identification made the Czechs and Romanians regard the allied material capabilities as friendly, rather than a source of threat. Indeed, the material strength of NATO allies (particularly the United States) is not always seen as benign; many actors in the world assign a different interpretation to the Western community and to the United States as a perceived leader of that community, and, on this basis, regard the strength of this community as a source of threat. To appreciate the multitude of possible meanings that states can attach to the material capabilities of NATO allies, one need only consider the meaning that, say, some Middle Eastern countries would attach to NATO offers of guidance in the reform process, the presence of allied troops on their territory, or requests to participate in the wars waged by the alliance. By contrast, Romanian reformers continued to pursue their country's integration into NATO, to act as a de facto allied state (particularly in the Kosovo crisis), and to carry out the liberal-democratic reforms prescribed by the allies, even when it became clear that it was more likely for Romanian troops to die fighting NATO's wars abroad than it was for NATO troops to die defending Bucharest against an invasion by an enemy state (for example, Russia). After all, in Kosovo and Bosnia, and later in Afghanistan and Iraq, Romanian troops participated alongside the allies in wars that had nothing to do with the territorial defense of their country.

Mechanisms of Socialization

In interactions with Czech and Romanian actors, NATO relied heavily on teaching and persuasion. Recent constructivist analyses have shown that persuasion is more successful when the parties involved act within the framework of a Habermasian "common lifeworld," consisting of collective interpretations of the world and a common system of rules perceived as legitimate.[18] This is an important argument. But, particularly in situations when "novices" are involved, it is useful to start analyses of international socialization at an earlier stage—in which socializees are brought into a given cultural framework—and to examine the power that might be involved in this process. Teaching, from this perspective, can be seen as an attempt to project into

---

[18] Risse 2000, 10–11.

Central and Eastern Europe the common lifeworld of the Euro-Atlantic community, consisting of shared liberal ideas and norms.[19] A significant, although subtle, form of power is involved in this because, if the pedagogic work is effective, it effectively shapes subjects, leading them to regard the schemes of thought and action disseminated by the socializing agent not as a contingent cultural product, but as the normal way of thinking and doing things.[20]

Here, it is useful to draw on analyses provided by sociologists, anthropologists, and social psychologists who have argued that the establishment of shared inter-subjective interpretations of the world, and definitions of proper modes of behavior vis-à-vis particular subjects/objects in the world, is the result of socialization processes involving the dissemination of a particular set of conceptual categories and behavioral dispositions (in Bourdieu's terminology, a habitus), which shape the ways in which people think about—and act in—the world.[21] These meanings enable socializees to define subjects and objects that populate the world, and identify "normal" relations and attitudes vis-à-vis them. Such pedagogic processes are usually carried out by state-authorized agencies in the domestic arena. In our case, however, NATO was able to perform a similar pedagogic role by virtue of the authority it enjoyed *qua* the key security institution of the Western community with which Czech and Romanian pro-reform elites identified.

Again, it is useful to place this discussion within the framework of rationalist/ constructivist debates about socialization. Rationalists have argued that, in disseminating new norms into the former communist bloc, NATO sought to minimize its involvement in the socialization of Central and East European states.[22] In their view, NATO interacted only with decision makers from targeted states, and even then it adopted a reactive stance, relying, effectively, on "self-socialization" by those actors. In turn, Central and East European socializees engaged in attempts at manipulation (for example, rhetorical action), so as to secure the rewards provided by NATO with a minimum of domestic adaptation.[23] It is reasonable to expect that, if Central and East European socializees acted according to this rationalist logic, they would try to increase their ability to engage in rhetorical action by limiting the information that NATO had regarding the domestic situation of the reform process. Furthermore, actors defined by characteristics of methodological individualism would not redefine preferences/identity through social interaction.[24]

By contrast, the type of sociological teaching outlined above—involving the dissemination of new conceptual categories and new dispositions—would involve a deeper engagement by NATO in Central and Eastern Europe. How can one establish whether NATO has actually conducted this kind of teaching? If one were to find

---

[19] See Risse 2000, 15; and Adler and Barnett 1998.

[20] See Bourdieu and Passeron 1977, 31–39; and Douglas 1975 and 1986. For analyses of international institutions as teachers of norms, see Adler and Barnett 1998, particularly 39–41; and Barnett and Finnemore 1999, 699–732. For an earlier account of international socialization via institutions, see Finnemore 1996.

[21] See Bourdieu and Passeron 1977; and Bourdieu 1990 and 1991.

[22] Schimmelfennig 2000, 125–27.

[23] Ibid., 129.

[24] Checkel and Moravcsik 2001.

that, rather than simply informing Czech and Romanian decision makers about the conditions attached to NATO membership, NATO actually engaged in systematic efforts to teach diverse sections of Czech and Romanian societies, even actors with no decision-making power, and to teach them a whole "lifeworld," (a set of new meanings and dispositions for making sense of (and acting in) the world), then it would be reasonable to argue that this process of socialization conformed to the constructivist logic of teaching.

From a constructivist perspective, one would expect to find consistency in the activities carried out by various NATO representatives in diverse settings. Consistency refers to efforts to spread the same sets of norms in systematic interactions, to different sets of students, and even in situations that are not expected to generate specific changes in policies in targeted states. If, however, one were to find that different NATO representatives spread different norms, or that they changed their normative prescriptions depending on the context of interactions with Central and Eastern Europeans (for example, public versus private settings), then one could argue that NATO made rhetorical reference to norms to enhance its public image, but was not involved in the kind of deep sociological teaching outlined above. The constructivist position would be strengthened if one were to find that Czech and Romanian socializees relied on NATO for guidance in the process of identifying the goals of democratic reform in areas that involved significant ceding of sovereign power.

In addition to teaching, NATO also relied heavily on persuasion in the socialization of Central and Eastern Europeans. Persuasion typically occurs in social interactions between actors who have drawn different conclusions regarding the nature, merits, and/or implications of X action or policy, and in which one or more of those parties attempt, through arguments, to get their interlocutors to rethink their conclusions.[25] In the case of persuasion, socializees need not, and indeed often do not, accept their role as students in the process of learning, from an authoritative teacher, broad schemes for making sense of the world. They must, however, recognize the other parties as legitimate partners in a process of (international) communication.

As in the case of teaching, there are interesting differences between constructivist and rationalist accounts of persuasion. From a rationalist perspective, persuasion is closely related to the provision of instrumental incentives. For instance, rationalists suggest that the persuader is more likely to be successful when it can provide significant carrots or sticks to the persuadees.[26] This, then, would lead one to expect that NATO had an especially weak influence on the Czech Republic, and particularly after 1997, given that Czechs had reached the conclusion that they would be included in the first wave of enlargement. Moreover, attempts at persuasion would revolve around reminders of the sticks and carrots in NATO's arsenal (particularly the power to withhold or grant membership), and would involve establishing linkages between reforms and the likelihood of securing membership in NATO.

---

[25] I relied particularly on Cialdini 1993; Terry and Hogg 2000; and Zimbardo and Leippe 1991. See also, for political scientists' accounts, Checkel 2001; Gibson 1998; Johnston 2001; Mutz et al. 1996; Payne 2001; and Risse 2000.

[26] See Schimmelfennig, this volume; and Schimmelfennig 2003.

From a constructivist perspective, interactions governed by the logic of persuasion involve different dynamics. Actors that engage in persuasion do not mobilize coercion vis-à-vis their interlocutors. Similarly, they do not rely on the promise of direct instrumental benefits as a way of getting subjects to enact prescribed reforms. Rather, actors engaged in persuasion try to present a given course of action as "the right thing to do," even in the absence of direct international rewards for taking that action.[27] The lack of coercion, however, does not mean that no power is involved in interactions governed by the logic of persuasion. As I mentioned above, such interactions take place within a socially constructed framework of ideas, which reflect the power of particular actors to define the "common life-world" within which certain arguments are regarded as legitimate, while others (which violate the established collective interpretations of the world) are not.

Successful socialization would lead the socializees to internalize the new ideas about the nature and purpose of their polity. This internalization would, I suggest, be revealed by a series of indicators: the socializees would be consistent in their (re)definition of identity/interest in accordance with the new ideas, and they would uphold the new definitions vis-à-vis different audiences and in different circumstances (rather than invoke different definitions to different audiences, in an attempt to enhance their international gains and minimize domestic costs). In the case of political elites with decision-making power in the process of postcommunist reconstruction, it is also reasonable to expect that they would try to protect and promote the definitions they now take for granted, for instance by seeking to embed them in the institutions, legislation, and practices of their polity.

Anticipated Scope Conditions

Drawing on work developed by social psychologists and sociologists, I suggest that several interrelated conditions facilitated efforts by NATO to teach new sets of meanings to Central and Eastern Europeans. To begin with, a pedagogic agent is more likely to be successful when the parties involved recognize their respective roles as "teacher" and "students." Two subconditions are relevant in my case. Regarding the socializer, this involves NATO's definition of Central and Eastern Europeans as changeable and responsible—and thus teachable subjects.[28] Teaching would most likely not be a reasonable option vis-à-vis those actors if they were seen as, say, inherently nationalistic subjects with no significant capacity for change. At the same time, one can expect teaching to be facilitated by Central and Eastern Europeans' self-definition as "students" (or novices) engaged in the process of learning new norms of governance. The novice factor should be even more important when socializees recognize a given international socializer as representative of a given social group, or community, with which they identify.[29]

---

[27] See Risse 2000; Checkel 2001; and Checkel and Moravcsik 2001. Also relevant is Jupille, Caporaso, and Checkel 2003.

[28] I owe this point to Michael C. Williams.

[29] On identity in social communications, see Checkel 2001; and Checkel and Moravcsik 2001.

Another condition affecting international teaching involves systematic interactions with targeted subjects. As anthropologists and sociologists of culture have argued, to succeed in constructing the "common sense" of targeted subjects, educational practices must be carried out consistently, over a relatively long period of time.[30] Therefore, I suggest that NATO is likely to be particularly successful in teaching actors who are intensely and extensively exposed to the ideas promoted by the organization. An examination of educational practices using analytical tools developed by sociologists such as Bourdieu and Passeron enables one to nuance the time/contact hypothesis, which maintains that socialization is more likely to be effective if socializers and socializees meet repeatedly over a long period of time.[31] I expect to find that the extensive use of teaching made a difference, particularly when the nature of social interactions met certain additional conditions—in this case, mutual recognition of their social roles as teacher or students. In other words, what mattered was not just the amount of socialization that occurred, but also its characteristics.

In my view, persuasion can be facilitated by successful educational practices. The logic behind this is that, if the socializees were to adopt the worldview taught by the pedagogic institution, further social communication would occur within a shared normative framework. In this article's case, the emergence of such a shared normative framework would enable NATO to formulate arguments within a set of—Western-defined—interpretations of the world that its Czech and Romanian interlocutors also accept as correct.[32] Furthermore, that group of socializees would have already recognized NATO as a legitimate normative guide in the process of reconstruction of their polities. As a consequence, NATO representatives engaged in attempts at persuasion would probably be more easily recognized as trustworthy, knowledgeable participants in debates regarding the desirability of particular reforms/courses of action.[33]

However, one should not assume that prior teaching guarantees the success of particular attempts at persuasion. For instance, Czech and Romanian socializees might adopt the norms taught by NATO regarding transparency, accountability, and civil society empowerment in the area of defense and security. Yet they might also challenge NATO's specific prescriptions, arguing for a different interpretation regarding the correct application of the new norms in a particular case. I suggest that persuasion is especially likely to fail when persuadees perceive an inconsistency in the logic of their persuader's arguments (for example, in cases of apparent tension between the liberal-democratic norms to which NATO is explicitly committed, and particular courses of action prescribed by the alliance). More broadly, persuasion is likely to fail in cases of breakdown of trust: in our case, when either NATO per se, or particular representatives of the alliance, are not—or are no longer—regarded as trustworthy

---

[30] Bourdieu and Passeron 1977, 31–39.

[31] On the contact hypothesis, see also Beyers, this volume; and Hooghe, this volume.

[32] Risse 2000, 10–11, 14–16.

[33] A series of social psychologists have conducted extensive studies demonstrating that arguments put forward by actors recognized as members of the reference group (versus "other-group" messages) are far more likely to be persuasive. See, for example, Terry and Hogg 2000; see also Checkel's contribution to the debate with Moravcsik in Checkel and Moravcsik 2001.

participants in debates about domestic reform. A breakdown of trust can occur, for instance, if a given NATO representative (or team of representatives) appears insufficiently knowledgeable about the issue at stake, appears to pursue a hidden agenda, and/or departs from the norms of arguing (for example, if they dictate a course of action, rather than seek to convince their interlocutors of the merits of the prescribed solution).[34]

Data Sources and Methods

Given time and space constraints, this article relies on a limited set of cases of socialization carried out by NATO. To try and compensate for that limitation, I have selected my examples in such a way as to include variation on the parties involved, both within the socializer category (for example, different NATO representatives) and among the socializees, ranging from decision makers involved in individual accession dialogues, to "next-generation elites" involved in Partnership for Peace (PfP) programs. Regarding the category of socializees, because it was impossible to interview more than a handful of people out of the thousands being trained in the various NATO/PfP educational programs, I sought to compensate for this weakness in the data by also obtaining evidence from actors who had numerous opportunities to work with Czech and Romanian socializees, both before and after their socialization by NATO (for example, officials affiliated with the Czech and Romanian ministries of defense—both locals and Western advisers, as well as members of the armed forces who command PfP graduates). To minimize the problem of methodological biases, I adopted a strategy of triangulation, involving: in-depth, semi-structured interviews with NATO representatives and Czech and Romanian socializees; participant-observation in three different NATO/PfP educational activities (courses and workshops); and discourse analysis of relevant public and semi-confidential documents.[35] Discourse analysis was important in my study, as it helped to reveal background intersubjective assumptions regarding the nature of the world, the identity of subjects inhabiting that world, and relations among them.[36]

NATO and International Socialization: An Empirical Analysis

Following the collapse of communism, the old norms that had governed Central and East European states lost their legitimacy, communist definitions of state identity and interests were rejected, and the people from the former Eastern bloc began the process of reconstituting their polities and rearticulating their relationships with the outside world. From the point of view of many Central and Eastern Europeans, including many Czechs and Romanians, the West ceased to be seen as the enemy and became the *generalized other* by reference to which the new identity of their countries was

---

[34] On arguing as opposed to dictating, see Joergensen, Kock, and Roerbech 1998. On the importance of expertise, see Terry and Hogg 2000.
[35] See Checkel 2001; and Lewis, this volume.
[36] Milliken 1999.

to be defined. Thus the changes that occurred in Central and Eastern Europe in the late 1980s and early 1990s made possible a new kind of engagement with Western institutions, including NATO. Subsequently, through complex socialization practices, NATO came to play an important role in the reconstitution of former communist countries such as the Czech Republic and Romania.

Teaching

Given their political prominence in the Czech Republic and even Romania during the greater part of the period covered in this study, proliberal elites tended to represent both countries in interactions with NATO.[37] Those elites identified with the Western community, and, hence, recognized it as a source of expertise on—and key forum for recognition of—those new identities.[38] Following the electoral success of the pro-West coalition, the Democratic Convention, in Romania, Prime Minister Victor Ciorbea argued that, "historically and culturally, [Romania] belongs in the West."[39] Accordingly, by this logic, it was the duty of the new government to lead Romania in the process of (re)building a modern democracy and "returning to Europe." In private, the pro-West elites that had just been projected to power tended to recognize their position as actors who, in the process of rebuilding their polity, needed to learn from—and secure the recognition of—Western institutions, including NATO. In the words of a Romanian Foreign Affairs official, "as a people who grew up with the communist ideology, we needed to travel on a long journey of learning," and needed "help from the West" to successfully complete that journey.[40]

In a similar vein, in the Czech Republic shortly after the Velvet Revolution, Manfred Wörner, then Secretary General of NATO, reportedly asked President Vaclav Havel what was the most urgent problem of the postrevolutionary period. Havel allegedly replied: "I don't know how we are going to run this country. We have two options: we can rely on communists who do have some useful experience but are not politically reliable; or we can put former dissidents in key positions; these are reliable, but lack the knowledge necessary to run the country. If we opt for the second solution, we are going to need a lot of advice from Western experts." [41] As with their Romanian

---

[37] Between 1993–98, the Czech Republic was governed by center-right political forces, grouped in coalitions that included the Civic Democratic Alliance (ODA), the Civic Democratic Party (ODS), the Christian Democratic Union, and the Freedom Union. The 1998 elections led to the formation of the Opposition Agreement between the Social Democrats and the Civic Democrats. In Romania, between 1990–96, the most powerful political actors were of nationalist and socialist orientation. The ruling party between 1992–96 was the Party of Social Democracy of Romania (PDSR), which was seen by NATO as too communist to be socializable into Western ideas. Hence, vis-à-vis that party, NATO engaged in little teaching or persuasion. Gheciu 2005. But that situation changed following the 1996 elections, which brought to power a pro-West coalition centered around the Democratic Convention.

[38] This was acknowledged by several Czech and Romanian foreign affairs and defense officials, as well as NGO representatives in interviews with the author, March–April 2000, Bucharest and Prague.

[39] Rime Minister Ciorbea, in an interview given shortly after President Bill Clinton's visit to Bucharest. The interview was reproduced, in part, in the *Washington Post,* 12 July 1997, Al.

[40] Author's interview, 6 April 2000, Bucharest. This view was echoed by two members of the Romanian Delegation to NATO, 28 April 2000, Brussels.

[41] Author's interview with a senior NATO official, international staff, 12 October 1999. Brussels.

counterparts, Czech reformers regarded NATO as a key institutional expression of the Western community with which they identified. Thus, as Havel repeatedly explained to various Czech audiences, NATO should not be regarded just as a defensive alliance, but, more broadly, as the expression—and protector—of a "certain civilization circle with its cultural tradition and responsibility."[42] Revealingly, after the second round of accession dialogues with NATO, Deputy Defense Minister Jiri Payne acknowledged the Czechs' position as novices in the area of security, as he pointed out that they still had a lot to learn in the area of planning, programming, and budgeting for security. As Payne explained, "planning security is something we never really did. It used to be made in Moscow and we only received instructions."[43]

It is true that in the early 1990s Prague initiated a series of reforms in the area of defense. However, in important ways those reforms were inconsistent with the norms of liberal democracy, as defined by NATO.[44] At the start of the accession dialogues, the vision of state-society relations held by Czech and, later, Romanian reformers revolved around a rigid, highly hierarchical model.[45] From NATO's point of view, that was not what liberal democracy was all about. The prevailing idea in Prague and Bucharest was that the military ought to be governed in a top-down style, which left little if any room for transparency and democratic accountability of civilian leaders. For their part, not only were the armies of former communist countries top-heavy and inefficient; they were also indoctrinated with communist ideas. For instance, particularly in Romania, there was virtually no understanding of the concept of soldiers as citizens in uniform, entitled to basic rights and bound by a set of duties concerning the protection of the rights of citizens even in times of crisis.

From NATO's point of view, the prevailing Central and East European visions of a democratic polity were flawed, as they were based on a fundamental misconception of the proper relationship between the state and civil society, a misunderstanding of the proper roles of different branches of the state in the area of defense, and a lack of awareness of the domestic and international duties associated with the liberal-democratic identity.[46] In the words of a high-ranking NATO official: "after the end of the Cold War, we realized that while [Central and East European reformers] were anti-communist, they were not liberal democrats . . . their views of normal state-society relations [in the area of defense] were very different from those held by NATO members."[47]

In response to that situation, NATO took on the role of educator. On several occasions, senior NATO officials pointed to the education of Central and Eastern Europeans as a key process in the transformation of the former Eastern bloc, and the preparation of partner countries for greater integration into the Euro-Atlantic community.

---

[42] Havel, quoted by Hybner 2001, 50–52. This was confirmed by a senior member of the Czech Delegation to NATO, 11 April 2000.

[43] Payne, quoted by Simon 2004, 56.

[44] Author's interviews with NATO officials, including senior officials from the Political Affairs division, October–November 1999, Brussels.

[45] See also Sava 2002; Simon 2000; and Donnelly 1997a and 1997b.

[46] Author's interviews with NATO officials, including senior officials from the Political Affairs division and the Office of the Secretary General, October–November 1999, Brussels.

[47] Author's interviews with a senior NATO official, international staff, 28 April 2000, Brussels.

A key priority vis-à-vis relations with these countries was the transformation of the ideational framework within which the political elites and the armed forces, as well as the general publics, thought about the world, and—more specifically—about national and international security issues. The prevailing view within NATO was that only such an ideational change could ensure the evolution of former communist countries into stable, "like-minded" democracies. As Chris Donnelly, then Special Adviser to NATO's Secretary General, put it, what was particularly important to NATO was: "changing the way in which the armed forces [and their civilian leaders] think."[48] Shortly before he was appointed Secretary General of NATO, then British Defense Secretary George Robertson referred to the Czech Army as still having to do a lot of work to completely transcend old habits and communist attitudes.[49] According to a senior NATO official, the challenge was to turn people who had "lived under a highly repressive and rigidly hierarchical system into members of an alliance of free states, based on consensus, shared values and the norms of consultation."[50]

Evidence obtained through interviews confirmed the information contained in public records regarding the view that ideational change in Central and Eastern Europe was key to the process of reform in those countries. According to three NATO officials, the shared understanding within the alliance was that they would have to lead the latter "by the hand" in the process of building liberal-democratic polities. The idea was that NATO would have to teach people from the former Eastern bloc the proper relationships between state and society, particularly in the area of defense, to help change their communist mentalities and get them to understand that "it was not acceptable for civilian leaders to make decisions in isolation from, and without the knowledge of, their society."[51] There was also an effort to teach the Central and Eastern Europeans the "duties" of peaceful settlement of disputes and international promotion of human rights and democracy.

NATO's acceptance of this position of teacher was also reflected in the organization's actions—particularly the effort to organize hundreds of workshops and seminars, as well as formal and informal consultations targeting Central and Eastern Europeans. NATO teams that conducted collective briefings and individual accession dialogues, NATO experts who led workshops in Brussels, Prague, and Bucharest, and—since March 1999—Western advisers based at the Romanian Ministry of Defense, have all stressed the importance of educating pro-reform political elites to think about democracy within Western-defined categories. In other words, the condition of mutual recognition of the actors' roles as teachers and students was largely met in interactions between NATO and pro-reform Czech and Romanian elites.

In the discourse articulated by NATO officials during collective briefings and accession dialogues, the alliance was depicted as an essentially Western institution, which

---

[48] Chris Donnelly, quoted by Dragsdahl 1998, available at ⟨http://www.basicint.org/pubs/Papers/BP28.htm⟩. Accessed 21 June 2005.

[49] See "NATO Membership: Will There Be a Language Barrier?" Radio Praha, 11 March 1999. Available at ⟨http://archiv.radio.cz/nato/english5.html⟩. Accessed 21 June 2005.

[50] Author's interview with a senior NATO official, Brussels, 24 April 2000.

[51] Author's interview with a member of the Defense Planning and Operations Division, confirmed by senior EAPC officials, 6 February 2000, Brussels.

had always worked to defend the values of freedom, democracy, the rule of law, and liberal individual rights. The West and its institutional expressions were portrayed in a relation of opposition to the authoritarian ("repressive," "rigidly hierarchical," and "fear-based") communist system created by the Soviet Union. In other words, through the use of particular predicates (verbs and adjectives attached to nouns, such as "freedom-loving" versus "repressive"; and "based on consensus and the norms of consultation" versus "fear-based" and "rigidly hierarchical"), the NATO discourse defined a coherent subject, the West, defined by superior attributes of freedom, stability, and progress.[52] The idea was that "differences and national variations" occurred against the background of "common Western values," and were set against the inferior other—the communist world.[53] It was in its capacity as embodiment of a—presumably superior—community of values that NATO could now become engaged in teaching the correct norms of liberal democracy to the Central and Eastern Europeans.

In the course of interactions with NATO representatives, Czech actors were told that, while they had enacted important reforms, they had failed to learn a key principle of liberal democracy: it was unacceptable to isolate society from debates and decision-making processes in the field of security.[54] NATO advisers insisted that the hierarchical-defense institutional arrangements being built in the Czech Republic represented a deviation from the liberal-democratic model of governance. That is, in the NATO discourse, the Czech Republic appeared in a position of becoming vis-à-vis the superior West: while it was more advanced than other former communist countries, it had not yet reached the end of its journey of transition to democracy. The concern to lead socializees away from allegedly flawed definitions of liberal democracy was even more pronounced in the case of Romania. In interactions with reformers from Bucharest, NATO representatives sought to delegitimize Romanian understandings of appropriate norms of civil-military relations, by portraying them as undemocratic.[55] Teaching occurred within individual accession dialogues, within consultations with foreign and defense officials, and—since 1999—within Membership Action Plan (MAP) programs.[56] The creation of the MAP was informed by a perceived need for a more comprehensive system of monitoring and providing feedback to aspirant countries in their journey to potential NATO membership.

Even as they were told by NATO advisers that many reforms were still needed, Czech actors received assurances of their significant progress. By contrast, the Romanians were told that they were in a more precarious position. Given their particularly difficult communist legacy, the danger was that, unless Romanian reformers

---

[52] On predicate analysis, see Milliken 1999, 231–33.

[53] This idea of diversity within a fundamental Western unity was expressed by all the NATO officials that I interviewed in Brussels and Prague.

[54] According to my interviewees, including NATO representatives and Czech officials involved in the accession dialogue, this issue was stressed by NATO both prior to, and after, the July 1997 NATO Summit.

[55] Author interviews with senior Romanian officials from the ministries of Foreign Affairs and Defense, 30 March–5 April 2000, Bucharest; and with senior NATO Euro-Atlantic Partnership Council (EAPC) advisers, 24 April 2000, Brussels.

[56] MAP also provides for the establishment of a clearinghouse for coordinating security assistance, and enhanced defense planning that establishes and reviews agreed-upon planned targets.

learned true democracy and moved quickly to reconstruct their country accordingly, the chance to transcend the past could be endangered. As a NATO official put it, "Romania is at an important crossroads. After seven years of stagnation, it finally has the chance to do what [others] did a long time ago: fully embrace change. But if Romanians waste this chance, they might not recover for a very long time."[57] In other words, similar to the narrative presented to Czech reformers, the discourse articulated by NATO representatives to the Romanian elites depicted a universally valid model of state-society relations—involving transparency and democratic accountability, including in the sensitive area of defense—a model presumably known and promoted by the alliance.[58] In relation to that model, Romania appeared in an ambivalent position; moreover, a position that was inferior to other transition states of Central and Eastern Europe.

In addition to teaching elites, NATO was systematically engaged in socializing younger Czechs and Romanians, in civilian as well as military circles. The assumption underlying these activities was that the education of a new generation of liberal elites was necessary if the norms of liberal democracy were to be (re)produced in the future.[59] Since the end of the Cold War, countless courses, seminars, and workshops for young civilians and military officers were organized at the Partnership Training Centers, NATO's Defense College, the Geneva Center for Security Policy, the Marshall Center, the Partnership Coordination Cell, and various defense academies in Western countries. The explicit goal of these educational programs was not simply to provide military training, but, more broadly, to expose military personnel and civilians from NATO's partner countries to the values and norms of Western-defined democracy, human rights, and the rule of law,[60] and to teach them to define national identity and interests within the framework of those norms. The Marshall Center's mission statement reflects a prevailing belief in NATO's decision-making circles: that "the current [post–Cold War] environment provides a unique opportunity to fashion a world for the 21st century truly different from the centuries of conflict that characterized the nation-state system since its inception. The Marshall Center exists to help educate those leaders from the Atlantic to Eurasia who will forge a brighter future for all our nations."[61]

Developed as a branch of the Marshall Center, the College of International and Security Studies targets both senior military and civilian defense officials and younger people, and explicitly seeks to produce graduates expected to use their knowledge and expertise, as gained through the College's courses on democratic defense, to manage security issues in their countries in accordance with liberal-democratic norms and

---

[57] Author's interview with a NATO official from the Political Affairs division, 28 April 2000. Brussels.

[58] British Advisers' Report (formulated at the request of the Romanian Government): *A Strategic Analysis of the Evolution of Romanian Politics of Security,* Romanian Ministry of National Defense, Bucharest, 1998, 15–17.

[59] This was confirmed by NATO officials from SHAPE and the Euro-Atlantic Partnership Council, as well as PfP teachers who led courses targeting young Central and East European civilians and military officers. Author's interviews, November 1999 – April 2000, Brussels, Mons, and Vienna.

[60] Sava 2002, 49–56.

[61] Mission Statement quoted in ibid., 52. See also Kennedy 1998.

procedures.[62] Also centered at the Marshall Center, but as an independent organization, the PfP Consortium is "dedicated to strengthening defense and military education and research through enhanced institutional and national cooperation."[63] There are currently more than 260 defense academies, institutes, think tanks, universities, and research centers located in allied countries and in partner states. Established in 1998 as part of a U.S.-German initiative, the Consortium has grown into a massive forum for education in the liberal-democratic "spirit of the PfP." Most of the institutions that are part of the Consortium offer a variety of courses targeting military personnel and civilian defense experts at various levels of seniority, and seek to turn them into actors who have understood and internalized NATO's ways of thinking and attitudes about security, broadly defined, and who can be relied on to take these teachings back home. Those courses depict Western liberal-democratic norms in the area of security as the correct foundation of a modern democratic polity, in contrast to alternative (communist and nationalist) norms, seen as an obstacle to progress and a threat to domestic and international freedom and security.[64] In addition, with NATO's financial support— and often with the participation of security experts from NATO's member states— several branches of the PfP Consortium have been established in Central and Eastern Europe. The new programs established in Eastern Europe target both civilians and military personnel and are aimed at disseminating a Western-style democratic culture on security issues, to replace the Soviet-style culture on national security.

For its part, NATO's Parliamentary Assembly (PA) has conducted more than a hundred seminars and workshops, with the aim of diffusing knowledge about the normal functions of parliamentary defense and security committees, and, more generally, principles of democratic control of the military. For instance, the Rose-Roth program of cooperation with the parliaments of Central and Eastern Europe was initiated in 1990 with the explicit aim of strengthening the development of parliamentary democracy in the former communist countries. The Rose-Roth Initiative consists of a series of seminars designed to: "promote the development of appropriate civil-military relations, including the democratic control of the armed forces"; to "familiarize legislators with key security and defense issues"; to "share expertise and experience in parliamentary practice"; and "to help the development of a parliamentary staff structure in CEE parliaments" and thus provide Central and East European parliamentarians with administrative assistance comparable to their western counterparts.[65] More broadly, as Flockhart has shown, social learning takes place through the PA's seminar presentations and committee work, in which the Assembly presents a common Euro-Atlantic interpretation of key foreign and security issues, teaching Central and East European actors to interpret situations, identify problems, and formulate solutions within the framework of Euro-Atlantic norms, rules, and procedures.[66] Thus, like the PfP Consortium, the NATO Parliamentary Assembly has been involved in the diffusion of a

---

[62] Ibid.

[63] See the PfP Consortium Web site at ⟨http://www.pfpconsortium.org⟩. Accessed 21 June 2005.

[64] For a more detailed analysis, see chaps. 4 and 5 in Gheciu 2005.

[65] See the Rose-Roth Mission Statement. Available at http://www.nato-pa.int/default.asp. Accessed 21 June 2005.

[66] Flockhart 2004.

new, Western-based habitus, teaching the Central and Eastern Europeans new ways of thinking and acting in the field of security. In other words, the condition of systematic education that I mentioned above was met in the socialization of Czech and Romanian reformers and potential next-generation leaders by NATO representatives.

The dynamics of the educational activities carried out by NATO came closer to the constructivist—rather than the rationalist—logic. Those activities were explicitly aimed at teaching students to regard Western-defined norms as the correct foundation of a progressive society; they did not simply provide information about the conditions attached to NATO membership. Equally importantly, the NATO/PfP educational activities targeted diverse groups, rather than being directed only at Central and East European actors with decision-making power. Within the framework of the NATO/PfP educational programs, Central and East European participants occupied the role of students being exposed to a new culture—to new ways of understanding the world and thinking about building postcommunist polities. As indicated in the mission statements of these programs, as well as in the statements issued by some of their organizers, the interactions between NATO representatives and Czech and Romanian socializees were aimed at disseminating new ideas and presenting them as the correct way of making sense of the world, identifying problems, and finding solutions to those problems. The seminars and workshops organized within the PfP Consortium, at the Marshall Center, at the NATO Defense College, or by the NATO Assembly, were not about promising instrumental rewards to Central and East European socializees in exchange for their compliance with NATO-prescribed rules and norms. In fact, it is difficult to see how a system of incentives might have operated within the framework of those programs. For instance, it is unclear why—or how—the allies might have offered to reward those Central and East European socializees for learning new norms, when many of them did not have decision-making power (hence, were in no position, at that time, to introduce changes in the actions and policies of their countries).

Persuasion

In addition to, and often against the background of, systematic teachings, NATO representatives engaged in specific instances of persuasion. Among the techniques of persuasion (or types of persuasive appeals) used by NATO actors, especially important were consistency, authority, and social proof. *Consistency* involves linking prescribed reforms to norms that are accepted by socializees as unproblematic.[67] Linked to this, also frequently used were *authority* appeals, involving efforts at persuading actors to adopt specific reforms by pointing to the special expertise of NATO on a given question, or/and invoking the moral reliability of an institution that embodied the liberal-democratic community. Finally, NATO officials sometimes resorted to *social proof,* seeking to convince Czechs or Romanians to promote a series of legal and institutional changes by pointing to examples of established and even emerging democracies who had set up similar institutions. This argument posits that if everyone

---

[67] See, for example, Cialdini 1993; and Searing 1995.

followed a similar course of action, then it must be the right thing to do, because everyone else could not be wrong.

While teaching and persuasion were sometimes used in tandem, in other cases these two mechanisms of socialization were mobilized separately. For instance, vis-à-vis younger students involved in PfP-related courses or in educational programs at Western institutions, the focus appears to have been especially on teaching them new ways of conceptualizing the world and new dispositions for acting in that world.[68] In interactions with proliberal actors, however, NATO's attempts at persuasion often represented a way of taking socialization a step further: in addition to teaching them Western-defined norms, NATO representatives also tried to convince those actors to subscribe to a particular interpretation of how those norms were to be translated into practice in particular situations. They sought to persuade Czech and Romanian reformers of the importance of a series of institutional and legislative changes—reforms that were, nevertheless, still being ignored or even resisted in Prague and Bucharest. The argument put forward by NATO was that those prescribed changes represented the correct way to implement liberal-democratic norms.

In the period leading up to, but also following, the Madrid Summit, NATO advisers who participated in accession dialogues and informal consultations in Prague sought to persuade Czech decision makers to pursue key legislative reforms in the areas of national emergency and conscription—which were still governed by communist laws.[69] NATO representatives reportedly relied on consistency appeals: Czech decision makers were told that the lack of legislative change generated ambiguity in the definition of mandates of different governmental branches. That created problems of accountability and transparency: within the existing legislative framework, it was not clear which branch of government had the right to do what in situations deemed to constitute "national emergencies." In addition to the obvious problem of lack of transparency and accountability, the uncertainty associated with that situation also entailed the danger of abusive suspension of basic individual rights in the name of an alleged national emergency. Or, according to NATO representatives, such threats to the basic freedoms of citizens were inconsistent with the norms of liberalism—hence, they had to be resolved by an emerging liberal-democratic polity.[70] Authority appeals were also important in that context: it was often pointed out that Czech decision makers should trust the advice being provided by NATO officials, as the latter had, in their countries, acquired significant expertise in balancing requirements of legislation that ensured effective military responses to crises, with the need to protect individual rights.

As in the Czech case, NATO also sought to persuade Romanian policymakers to pursue specific reforms to change state-society relations in the area of defense.

---

[68] Author's interviews with teachers/graduates of the Marshall Center, the Geneva Center for Security Policy, and NATO's Defense College; as well as with three SHAPE officers involved in PfP courses, November 1999 – February 2000, Geneva, Brussels and Vienna.

[69] Author's interviews with two senior NATO officials, international staff (Political Affairs division), 29 November 1999, Brussels.

[70] Author's interviews with a senior NATO official, international staff, 28 April 2000, Brussels; and with a member of the Czech Senate Committee for Defense, 19 April 2000, Prague.

There, too, persuasion occurred against the background of teaching: having taught Romanians the "correct" norms of liberal democracy, NATO representatives tried to convince them to accept a particular interpretation of the application of those norms. In the case of Romania—regarded as a "laggard" compared to the Central Europeans—attempts at persuasion were even more frequent, and sought to affect more issues than in the Czech Republic. NATO's evolution into a more comprehensive agent of socialization was facilitated by two institutional innovations: the Membership Action Plan, and the appointment of permanent Western advisers to Romanian, and other East European, defense ministries. These innovations enhanced NATO's ability to closely monitor—and guide—the reform process in candidate states.

In 1997–98 consultations with Romanian members of parliament and defense and foreign affairs officials, NATO recommended the formulation of new legislation on the state of emergency, as well as legislation governing defense planning.[71] Western advisers mobilized the consistency technique, pointing to a basic tension between the norms of liberal democracy accepted by Romanian reformers, and the lack of a legislative framework aimed at limiting the power of the President to suspend basic individual rights in an emergency. Social proof appeals also appear to have been used, the argument being that established democracies had long accepted the importance of societal scrutiny of defense-related decision making. The idea was, if other states sharing the same values had taken this step, then it must be the right thing to do.[72]

Western advisers working within the framework of the MAP also sought to promote several institutional reforms, particularly targeting the restructuring of the Defense Ministry, the institutionalization of channels of communication with society, and the reform of the Interior Ministry. For instance, NATO officials argued that a militarized Ministry of Interior was a serious obstacle to the Romanian reform process, especially because that ministry had been a key instrument of repression under communism.[73] Through consistency appeals, NATO advisers insisted that it was imperative that Romanian politicians restructure the Interior Ministry in accordance with liberal-democratic principles.

Beyond Elite-Level Socialization: Educating the Public

In some instances, NATO sought to educate Central and East European publics into accepting a particular definition of national identity and of reasonable political goals. A case in point was the public relations campaign designed to enhance Czech support for membership in NATO. In the Czech Republic, as late as 1997, the level of public support for membership was low (under 50 percent).[74] This reflected disagreements among political parties regarding the desirable future trajectory for their

[71] Author's interviews with Romanian defense officials and security-related NGO member, March 30–April 5, 2000, Bucharest; and with an adviser from NATO's Euro-Atlantic Partnership Council, 24 April 2000, Brussels.
[72] Author's interview with an adviser from NATO's Political Affairs division, 24 April 2000, Brussels.
[73] Author's interviews with Romanian delegates to NATO, 17 February 2000, Brussels.
[74] Sarvas 1999, 18.

country. While 90 percent of the supporters of the liberal Civic Democratic Alliance were in favor of NATO, the level of support was around 45 percent among Social Democrats' supporters, and remained predictably low among those associated with the Communist Party and the nationalist Republican Party (respectively, 7 percent and 10 percent).[75]

These divisions were founded on different conceptions of Czech national identity. For the liberal coalition, NATO membership was tied to the idea of "return" to the Euro-Atlantic world. From that perspective, common historical roots and shared values made integration into Western institutions seem normal.[76] By contrast, communist and nationalist groups stressed the importance of cultivating the uniqueness of Czech society. For them, the key international others with whom the Czech Republic had historical and cultural affinities were not Western states, but Slavic nations. For communists and nationalists, entry into NATO would entail an unacceptable loss of sovereignty.[77] Between those extreme poles, the Social Democratic Party proposed a partial integration into Western structures, in a way that would not endanger the "unique Czech national character." The Social Democrats' vision translated into proposals for a Scandinavian status, aimed at limiting the loss of sovereignty. In concrete terms, that entailed the submission of the question of NATO membership to a referendum. In essence, as late as 1997 pro-Western actors in the Czech Republic were facing widespread domestic skepticism about the desirability of joining NATO, and a strong public view that it was not in the country's interest to take on the obligations associated with NATO membership (for example, sending Czech soldiers to defend other states, accepting allied troops in the Czech Republic, and, potentially, enhancing the military budget in the context of a perceived lack of military threats to the country).[78]

Given that Czech leaders attributed that public opinion climate to long-term communist propaganda, NATO advised an informational campaign to educate the public in understanding the appropriate relationship between their country and the Atlantic organization.[79] NATO's Media Office then worked with Czech policymakers and media representatives, and with domestic nongovernmental organizations (NGOs) linked to NATO, to organize various educational activities.[80] This resulted in an intensive media campaign, which ran from the end of 1997 until March 1998, and included TV and radio programs, public seminars, and newspaper articles. The campaign sought to promote a particular interpretation of national identity, to lead the Czech public to accept if as the natural, commonsense definition of their identity, and, on this basis, to persuade them that NATO membership was not only desirable, but also, quite simply, "normal." During the course of several months, Czechs were exposed to daily messages stressing the idea of a natural belonging of their country

[75] Ibid.
[76] Ibid., 7–8.
[77] Ibid.
[78] For a useful analysis, see Sarvas 1999, 32.
[79] Author's interviews with Czech foreign affairs and Ministry of Defense officials, 11 April 2000, Prague.
[80] Author's interview with an official from NATO's Press Office, 29 November 1999, Brussels; and with a media officer from the Czech Ministry of Defense, 20 April 2000, Prague.

in the West, and challenging the alternative interpretation of the Czech Republic as occupying a special position between the East and the West, as well as the interpretation stressing a special identification with the other Slavic nations. In other words, one particular condition of education (systematic interaction between teachers and students) was met in that case, as there was an intense media campaign involving newspapers, the radio, and television programs.

Some Czechs did not regard NATO as a legitimate teacher of norms, and some of them—particularly nationalist and socialist groups—associated the organization with Western imperialism, and with an American conspiracy to master the world.[81] Reformers in Prague transcended this problem of legitimacy by having charismatic domestic politicians (for example, President Havel) convey the message to ordinary Czechs. Also, during the public relations campaign, popular Czech actors and musicians provided "flashy" pro-NATO testimonials, arguing that "NATO will boost our independence and help us gain international respect."[82] It was through the establishment of the transnational network that the condition of recognition of the authority of teachers was fulfilled in the case of this public relations campaign. Several pro-NATO television infomercials featured a chessboard with the Czech Republic as a pawn, subject to a long history of international aggression, great-power manipulation, and domestic oppression under Soviet-sponsored communism. Against this background of historical tragedies, voice-overs presented NATO as a trustworthy source of stability, progress, and security. This was achieved by telling NATO's history—presented as a story of strength against communism, cooperation, and respect among the allies united around shared values and successful protection of the Western civilization against a multitude of threats.[83]

The discourse put forward by the pro-NATO campaign invoked a natural affinity with the Western world, depicted as a "messianic" figure which "will help us achieve political stability."[84] The Czech Republic's return to that messianic entity was justified by reference to history and basic shared values. President Havel's statements remain particularly powerful expressions of this view of Czech identity as inextricably linked to the West, and an integral part of Europe. In his words, "NATO entry meant the acceptance of principles of human rights, parliamentary democracy, and free market economy."[85] In response to the widespread public reluctance to take on the obligations entailed by the Washington Treaty, President Havel sought to present those obligations as duties associated with the identity of the Czech Republic as a member of the Western civilization. In his words, in a situation in which NATO is "an alliance which protects a certain civilization circle with its cultural tradition and responsibility,"[86] acceptance of the duties of membership represents nothing less than the Republic's "determination to meet its share of responsibility for the freedom of nations, human

[81] See Culik 1999; and Sarvas 1999, 30–33.
[82] Dasa Obereigner, "Czech Republic: Focus on EU, NATO," Central Europe Online, March 1998. Available at http://archive.tol.cz/transitions/archmarl.html. Accessed 21 June 2005.
[83] Ibid. See also Pecina 1999; and Zajicova 2000.
[84] Zajicova 2000.
[85] Stroehlein 1999.
[86] Havel, quoted by Hybner 2001, 52.

rights, democratic values and peace in Europe."[87] In other words, the pro-NATO campaign sought to redefine the issue of NATO membership as not simply a choice to join a defensive alliance, but also as a defining moment in Czech history—the moment at which the Czech people had the responsibility to affirm their belonging in the West, and to take on the duties associated with that identity.

Effects of NATO's Socialization Practices

NATO's teaching and persuasion had a significant impact on Czech and Romanian actors. In several instances, following interactions with NATO representatives, Czech and Romanian socializees redefined their views regarding the correct norms for governing their polities and the basic purpose of key domestic institutions, repositioned the national self in the international arena, and reconceptualized the kinds of domestic and international goals and practices seen as consistent with the liberal-democratic identity. How does one know that this was not simply the result of actions by domestic forces, or by other international actors? As I have shown, in the early 1990s there was a tension between definitions of liberal democracy held by Czech and Romanian reformers, and definitions that prevailed within NATO. In the area of security, it was in the aftermath of the socialization carried out by NATO—broadly recognized by both parties as a process of learning—that Czech and Romanian actors adopted the Western-defined vision of liberal democracy. As far as international actors are concerned, in the period covered by this study, NATO was by far the institution most deeply involved in defense-related Czech and Romanian reforms.[88]

Following interactions with NATO representatives, there was a significant shift in the Czech reformers' views of liberal democracy, in particular involving a redefinition of correct norms and institutions in the field of security. The new view was reflected both in the public discourse articulated by proliberal reformers in Prague, and in more private comments, with the new norms now being presented as natural, common-sense aspects of a liberal-democratic polity. The new discourse on defense was articulated vis-à-vis different audiences and in diverse forums. These ranged from official declarations on the reform of the armed forces (in which the NATO-prescribed model of democratic control of the military and the integration of the armed forces into society was portrayed as the only reasonable way of governing this area of society), to statements issued in the course of workshops and seminars aimed at teaching schoolchildren, university students, and the public at large the new norms of defense.[89] In a similar vein, in interviews conducted by the author in April 2000,

---

[87] Havel, quoted by Jolyon Naegele, "NATO: Havel Backs Continued RFE/RL Broadcasts from Prague," 26 February 1999. Available at ⟨http://www.rferl.org/features/1999/02/RRU. 990226134718.html⟩. Accessed 21 June 2005.

[88] See also Sava 2002.

[89] For details on the principles of reform of the armed forces, see the Czech Defense Ministry's Web site at ⟨http://www/army.cz/reforma/english/docs/reforma.htm⟩. Accessed 21 June 2005. The workshops, seminars, and briefing tours on defense issues in the context of Czech integration into NATO are often organized by the Public Relations Dept. of the Czech Ministry of Defense in cooperation with the Public Information Office of SHAPE, or by Czech NGOs working in cooperation with various branches of

defense and foreign affairs officials all argued that transparency, accountability, and societal involvement were a "normal" and "necessary" aspect of institutional arrangements governing defense in a democratic society.[90]

The new view regarding desirable state-society relations also informed a series of legislative changes, most of which were enacted in 1998 (especially a new Constitutional Act on National Security), and throughout 1999 (a package of defense-related laws to complement the Constitutional Act). In other words, rather than engaging in purely rhetorical action, Czech reformers took a series of steps aimed at embedding the new norms of security into the institutional and legislative fabric of their society—and continued that process even after the carrot of NATO membership had been promised and subsequently granted. The actions taken by the Czech policymakers are important because they indicate an effort to promote the society-wide internalization of new norms. Thus, new laws and institutions have the effect of (re)drawing the boundaries of normal arrangements and practices in a society.[91] The new legislative package was designed to redress problems that had been identified by NATO advisers in the course of individual accession dialogues and related informal consultations. For instance, the new legislation regulates the conditions under which military and security forces operate in times of crisis, seeking to limit the threat of abusive suspension of the right to property or freedom of movement through the declaration of a national emergency state.[92]

Another important area of change concerns the role of societal actors in the formulation of defense policies. At the end of 1997, the Defense Ministry approved the *Conception of Relations and Communication of the Defense Department with the Public,* which led to the creation of a public relations department in the ministry, and institutionalized consultations with Czech NGOs. Finally, in 1999 the ministries of defense and foreign affairs embraced the Western-suggested goal of institutionalizing a defense community, consisting of societal actors who would cooperate with governmental agencies in formulating and monitoring defense-related reforms.[93] In essence, Czech reformers moved away from their initial model of postcommunist polity, involving top-down civil-military relations and the virtual exclusion of civil society from debates and decision-making processes concerning defense issues, to a model consistent with NATO's prescriptions of correct norms in the area of defense. This is significant, for it reveals a change in the prevailing definition of key

NATO or the Atlantic Treaty Association. For more information on these activities, see Hybner 2001, 35–40, and the Czech Ministry of Defense Web site ⟨http://www.army.cz/scripts/detail.php?id=823⟩. Accessed 21 June 2005.

[90] Author's interviews with foreign affairs officials, 12 and 19 April 2000; with officials from the Ministry of Defense, 20 April 2000; and with a former assistant to top foreign affairs officials, 18 April 2000, Prague.

[91] On this, see Cortell and Davis 2000.

[92] Hoskova 1999, 8.

[93] According to Jaroslav Janda, the Deputy Director of the Czech Institute of International Relations, the goal of the security community was: "to contribute to the development of the civic and social consciousness of the responsibility for safety, defense and protection of both the citizen and the state, and to spread the knowledge on how to improve the defense system of the Czech Republic." Quoted by Hybner 2001, 42.

characteristics of the Czech polity (involving relations between state and civil society, and the attributes and purpose of key postcommunist institutions).

The legislative and institutional reforms aimed at implementing liberal-democratic norms in the field of security—some of them seeking to redress the specific problems identified by NATO—continued after the Czech Republic had acceded to the alliance. For example, at its session on 29 August 2001, the Czech government approved documents on the preparation of the reform of the armed forces, and stated that the key governing principle of the armed forces will continue to be civilian management and democratic control. Thus, "the integration of the Armed Forces into the democratic society will go on and become more profound."[94]Among other things, the reform documents provide for further improvements in the communication and consultation with the public, continuation of the process of civilianization of the Ministry of Defense, the establishment of a more efficient and transparent (liberal) economic management of the defense sector, and the adoption of more legislative acts to reflect the new (liberal-democratic) identity of the Czech Republic and its new role as a NATO member.

In some instances, pro-reform Czech decision makers requested NATO's aid in overcoming domestic obstacles encountered in the process of reform. The relationships involved in such situations can be usefully conceptualized as transnational networks, in which Central and East European political actors and Western officials acted on the basis of shared understandings regarding "correct" norms.[95] Scholars interested in transnational coalitions have documented the ways in which, through participation in such coalitions, domestic actors are sometimes able to put pressure on (norm-violating) governments to enact change. In my research, what was especially interesting was that transnational networks often involved reformers within the policymaking apparatus in the Czech Republic and Romania.

In the Czech case, an interesting instance of transnational networking occurred, as I have shown, during the 1997–98 educational campaign organized by NATO representatives and Czech reformers. Following that, the level of public support for membership in NATO rose to between 55 and 65 percent in March 1998.[96] In a situation in which the choice to join NATO was presented, in domestic debates, as a choice about the nature and desirable future of the Czech Republic, that shift represented a significant moment in the postcommunist definition of national identity. Specifically, it marked an important victory for the view of the Czech Republic as belonging—completely and naturally—in the Western community over the view of the country as occupying a unique position between East and West (and, therefore, requiring a special, "Scandinavian" status), and over the view of a primary identification with Slavic nations. As noted above, joining NATO would have been an unacceptable course of

---

[94] See "Reform of the Armed Forces of the Czech Republic: Objectives and Principles." Available at http://www.army.cz/reforma/english/docs/reforma.htm. Accessed 15 January 2004.

[95] On transnational coalitions, see Evangelista 1999; Keck and Sikkink 1998; and Risse, Ropp, and Sikkink 1998.

[96] Author's interview with an official from the Office of the Media, Ministry of Defense, 20 April 2000, Prague. While some polls indicated 65 percent support for NATO membership, others reported a lower level of support—around 55 percent. On this, see also Sarvas 1999b, 18.

action within the worldview that defined the West as the imperialist world, bent on exploiting the Czech Republic.

NATO's socialization practices had similarly important effects in Romania. Following consultations, collective briefings, workshops, and individual accession dialogues, Romanian reformers redefined their vision of a liberal-democratic society, and reconceptualized their goals regarding the kinds of domestic institutions that should be established. The change was not confined to their discourse, but came to be inscribed in key documents adopted by the Romanian government, including the 1999 *National Security Strategy* and the *White Book of the Government on Romania and NATO.* Contrary to their initial position, in 1999 Romanian policymakers argued that it was essential to enact reforms that would give a stronger voice to civil society, because this was a normal dimension of building liberal democracy. According to them, "in a modern democracy, defense should be the business of the entire society."[97]

Romanian reformers also took a series of steps aimed at embedding the new vision in the legal and institutional fabric of their society. Through governmental decrees issued in 1999, new laws on the organization and functioning of the Ministry of Defense, as well as on the state of emergency, came into effect. They both served to bring about changes advised by NATO. For instance, in January 1999 a special executive ordinance defined limited mandates for different government branches in a national state of emergency, established Western-style procedures for the declaration, continuation, and end of the state of emergency, and limited the right of the authorities to suspend individual freedoms even in that special context.[98] In addition, another ordinance issued in August 1999 sought to address the problem of Defense Ministry's isolation from society. The ordinance required the ministry to inform and cooperate on a permanent basis with other ministries and departments, as well as with NGOs."[99]

In addition to these legislative measures, Romanian policymakers carried out a series of institutional reforms, including further restructuring of the Defense Ministry (for example, via the creation of the function of Ombudsman and the establishment of a Western-based system of personnel management, aimed at limiting the practice of political appointments and nepotism and establishing selection, training, and promotion criteria for career management in accordance with NATO practices and standards). At the same time, a series of steps were finally taken in the direction of reforming the Ministry of Interior, and turning it into a more transparent institution. The 1999 Romanian Annual National Plan in the area of defense provided for the restructuring of the police and the *gendarmerie,* and the retraining of its members, in an attempt to make these institutions compatible with their Western counterparts.[100]

---

[97] Romanian Government 1999, 129.
[98] Romanian Government, "Ordonanta de Urgenta 1/21.01.1999 privind regimul starii de asediusi regimul de urgenta (Emergency Ordinance Regarding the Regimes Governing the State of Siege and the State of Emergency)," printed in Monitorul Official al Romaniei, 22, 1999, 1–10.
[99] Romanian Government, "Ordonanta 41/11.08.1999 privind organizarea si functionarea Ministerului Apararii Nationale (Ordinance Regarding the Organization and Functioning of the Ministry of National Defense)," printed in Monitorul Oficial al Romaniei, 388, Art. 2.
[100] Planul National Anual (Annual National Plan), 48–49.

Like their Czech counterparts, Romanian reformers sometimes acted within transnational networks, seeking NATO's aid in overcoming domestic opposition to Western-prescribed courses of action. An interesting case of this involves the Romanian participation in the NATO bombing campaign in Kosovo in 1999. The Romanian government accepted NATO's definition of the Kosovo crisis as a conflict between the progressive, modern values of liberal democracy and the barbarity embodied in the Milošević regime. According to NATO's representation of the situation, only a country that was not truly committed to the norms of liberal democracy could fail to support the Western military intervention. In a similar vein, against overwhelming domestic opposition and in spite of significant economic costs that Romania could ill afford at that time, the Romanian government defined its country's participation in the allied operation as the only course of action that was consistent with its emerging liberal-democratic identity.[101] In other words, in that case the Romanians acted in conformity to the logic of appropriate action: in spite of obvious and immediate costs, the option of not supporting NATO was not seriously considered by the Romanian decision makers. Participants in the governmental discussions on the Kosovo crisis noted that the consensus was that support for the Western intervention was the only reasonable course of action for an emerging liberal democracy.[102]

In justifying their unqualified support for NATO intervention in parliament, Romanian decision makers framed their response precisely in the terms of value-based confrontation depicted in the Western discourse.[103] When the Romanian leaders explained in parliament why they wanted to grant NATO unrestricted access to the Romanian airspace, and do so for an unlimited period of time, they pointed out that, "the Kosovo crisis represents a conflict between democracy and barbarism. Failure to cooperate with NATO might lead the West to place us in the camp of non-civilized people, for only they would not be opposed to what Milošević is doing to Kosovar Albanians."[104] Both their official discourse and the more confidential statements indicate that in that instance, Romanian decision makers adopted the logic of appropriate action: it was inconceivable for a country that claimed to be a modern democracy to do anything other than support the allied efforts to protect Kosovars.[105]

As it was becoming increasingly clear that the Romanian government and pro-West societal actors were encountering significant domestic opposition, allied officials stepped in to help them. NATO allies resorted to a strategy of shaming the critics of war, by presenting opposition to the Kosovo campaign as an indication of support of "barbarity." For instance, Prime Minister Tony Blair pointed out in his address to the Romanian Parliament on 4 May 1999 that the only appropriate course of action for an emerging democracy was to take a firm stand against the actions of the Milošević regime. In his words, "This is a test for countries like Romania, on the front-line. . . this is a time for democracies, old and new, to stand up and be counted."[106] In addition,

---

[101] On the costs associated with that participation, see Gousseff 2000.
[102] Author's interviews with senior officials from the Ministry of Foreign Affairs, 7 April 2000, Bucharest.
[103] Gousseff 2002, 12.
[104] Speech by liberal deputy minister for foreign affairs, 22 April 1999, Bucharest; printed in Adevarul, 23 April 1999.
[105] Author's interviews with senior officials from the Ministry of Foreign Affairs, 7 April 2000, Bucharest.
[106] Romania Libera, 5 May 1999, 7.

allied officials sought to project the image of a link between compliance with NATO's expectations and instrumental rewards. Thus, in that same speech to the Romanian Parliament, Blair promised that the United Kingdom would support the start of the accession dialogues between the EU and Bucharest.[107]

A critic might argue that NATO's pedagogic practices reflect no more than a case of instrumental learning on the basis of pregiven identity: Czech and Romanian pro-reform elites had decided they wanted to build liberalism, so it was a sensible thing for them to learn how to be "good liberals" from the institutions of the Western world.[108] But this argument tends to misrepresent the dynamics of the process of learning that was involved in this case, the competition between different interpretations of the correct model of democracy, and the role of identity-based trust and authority involved in the selection of a particular model. Initially, as I have shown, the Czech and Romanian reformers' conception of liberal democracy conflicted, in important ways, with the NATO-prescribed norms of liberal-democratic governance. The change in the definition of the true meaning of liberal democracy was not automatic; it was the result of social communications in which the teachers—recognized as such and trusted by virtue of their identity—played a key role. In a broader perspective, the importance of identity-based trust was reflected in the problems encountered by NATO in interactions with Czech and Romanian groups (for example, communists or nationalists) who did not recognize it as the reference group, and hence as a legitimate teacher of norms. Accordingly, those actors articulated a different vision of the "good" polity, and advocated norms and policies that did not conform to NATO's prescriptions.

Second, the rationalist vision of instrumental learning overlooks the extent of NATO's involvement in reshaping the orientation of Czech and Romanian societies. Thus, in the course of pedagogic activities targeting publics and future elites, NATO promoted a particular vision of national identity and portrayed the accession to NATO as a normal—indeed, necessary—course of action given that identity. In essence, in cooperation with Czech and Romanian reformers, NATO was involved in efforts to cultivate a particular type of rationality in those countries, so that certain conceptions of national identity and certain definitions of interest would come to be widely recognized as correct. In PfP courses and educational campaigns targeting the public, NATO sought to delegitimize nationalist and communist worldviews—which involved different definitions of the distinctiveness of the Czech Republic and Romania, and presented the integration into NATO as a threat to sovereignty—as an irrational course of action.

Scope Conditions and Socialization

The education of Czechs and Romanians by NATO was facilitated by a particular set of social relations, in which the parties' mutual recognition of their respective roles as teachers and students was essential. There was a prevailing collective understanding

---

[107] Ibid.
[108] See Ziim and Checkel, this volume.

within NATO that Central and East European actors could learn "correct" liberal democracy, and that, given its identity and expertise, the alliance could act as teacher in such a process of learning.[109] In addition, there was a shared allied view that the establishment of liberal democracy in Central and Eastern Europe would be a key factor of European stability.[110] Regarding Central and East European socializees, the political elites that represented the Czech Republic and Romania in interactions with the organization, as well as most of the younger students involved in PfP and other educational programs, accepted their role as "students" in the process of learning from Western institutions how to build a new kind of state. By virtue of its identity, NATO was recognized as an organization that embodied significant knowledge about liberal-democratic norms in the field of security, and that could be trusted not to use its significant material resources in pursuit of a hidden agenda of domination in Central and Eastern Europe.

By contrast, in the Czech case, it was much more difficult for NATO to teach new ideas and norms to communist or nationalist groups. From the perspective of those actors, what was needed was not the complete (re)construction of Czech society on a Western model. Rather, the process was one of reasserting unique elements of Czech national character. Nationalists and communists repeatedly argued that integration into Euro-Atlantic structures threatened to bring the Czech Republic under the exploitative influence of the West. From that perspective, the West appeared as a potential threat to the Czech identity, rather than an authoritative guide in the process of postcommunist reconstruction of the Czech polity. Similarly, in the Romanian case, several political parties and movements—particularly the socialists and the nationalists—did not see Westernization as the right way of (re)constructing the identity of their country.[111] For instance, the Party of Romanian National Unity's (PUNR) vision of the future relied on a particular (nationalist) reading of the Romanian past as a blueprint for the future. Accordingly, the idea that Western agencies might shape new domestic institutions was unacceptable.

A related scope condition involved NATO's ability to secure recognition in the eyes of its socializees as an institutional expression of the West. As President Havel insisted, NATO represented "a key democratic structure" of the West.[112] It was the acceptance of that identity of the alliance that enhanced its legitimacy as an educator, and led Czech policymakers to repeatedly appeal to NATO for advice and invite it to help shape the process of reform of defense policies and institutions. As noted above, this continued after the issue of an invitation to the Czech Republic, and even following its accession to NATO.

In the Romanian case, as I have shown, a similar acceptance by liberal decision makers that NATO was an institutional expression of the Western world led them to recognize the organization as a legitimate educator. This led these Romanian decision makers to invite NATO to play complex roles in the identification of national defense

---

[109] See also Williams 2001.

[110] See Risse-Kappen 1996; Williams and Neumann 2000; and Gheciu 2005.

[111] See the political platforms of the PUNR and the Greater Romania Party, available at http://www.romare.ro/partid/doctrina. Accessed 21 June 2005.

[112] Cited in Ulrich 2000, 79. This view was confirmed by senior Czech liberal politicians.

goals and reform priorities (for example, NATO advisers became directly involved in writing the 1999 *Annual National Plan,* and the *White Book of the Government on Romania and NATO).*[113] Such actions simply cannot be regarded as trivial gestures of compliance with Western expectations. On the contrary, they involve an unusual act of ceding sovereign decision-making power through the reliance on NATO to identify goals and priorities in an area (national defense) traditionally regarded as essential to the survival and freedom of the state. The alliance was able to participate in the postcommunist reconstruction of the Romanian polity even in a situation in which it did not promise NATO membership in exchange for Romanian adoption of Western norms of good governance.

An additional condition that facilitated the education of Czech and Romanian actors was the ongoing, systematic interaction between socializers and socializees. Recent institutional innovations created numerous forums within which NATO had ample opportunity to interact with, and shape the understandings of, Central and East European actors. Western advisers who worked with Czech and Romanian officials argue that, even within the category of pro-reformers, there is a significant difference between those who were systematically educated into Western ideas, and those who only participated in a few short sessions of socialization. The former tend to subscribe to norms taught by NATO, and to define problems and identify solutions within the framework of those norms, to a greater degree than the latter.[114] In the case of younger students ("next-generation elites"), there is, reportedly, a similar difference between those who graduated from long-term educational programs, and those who only attended a couple of seminars and workshops.[115]

Vis-à-vis Czech and Romanian actors who had come to subscribe to the normative framework taught by NATO, it was easier for the organization to conduct successful persuasion. In those situations, NATO had the advantage of a shared normative framework within which duties could be invoked, and reasonable actions—by reference to collective understandings—could be defined. Indeed, NATO succeeded, in several cases, in convincing Czech and Romanian reformers to change their attitudes vis-à-vis a series of reforms.

Yet there were also cases in which, although socializees had adopted norms taught by NATO, they were not persuaded that the correct interpretation of norms applicable to a given situation was that prescribed by NATO. One relevant case was the difficulty encountered by a British NATO adviser in convincing Czech officials to set up an integrated emergency security system, thus ending a situation of excessive decentralization of various security services. The Czechs argued that, while a centralized system might be a good solution in established liberal democracies, it was

---

[113] Author's interviews with members of the Romanian Mission to NATO, and with an official from the Romanian Ministry of Defense, February–April 2000, Brussels and Bucharest.

[114] Confirmed by NATO advisers who participated in accession dialogues and consultations at the ministries of defense in Prague and Bucharest, and military officers who work with PfP graduates. Author's interviews, 5 April 2000, Bucharest. For the Czech Republic, relevant also were author's interviews with NATO/PfP teachers attending a PfP workshop in Vienna, 18 November 1999.

[115] One problem with the evidence on systematic interactions is that it does not enable one to assess the importance of intensive—relative to extensive—exposure to socialization, because instances of intensive socialization also tended to be extensive in duration.

inappropriate in the specific case of their country. Given the particular history and persisting communist mentalities in those institutions, they argued, recentralization would recreate some of the authoritarian bureaucratic tendencies of the past.[116] In that case, the problem was one of breakdown of authority, in a situation in which the persuadees perceived a tension between the liberal norms to which NATO was formally committed, and the particular solution prescribed in response to a given problem—a solution that appeared to the Czech reformers as involving a return to communist-style arrangements. Accordingly, the Czechs argued for an application of norms of liberal democracy that differed from NATO's interpretation of the same norms. The British adviser was unable to persuade them that centralization in that particular area was needed, and his attempt at persuasion failed. Interestingly, in the end the Czechs did come to recognize the need for greater centralization in this area. However, this change occurred as a result of a domestic process of learning by doing: the 1997 floods made it painfully clear that the lack of a coordinated approach—more broadly, the lack of clear definition of duties and powers of state bodies—was undermining the country's ability to respond effectively to crises. Following the floods, the government finally established a Security Council (BRS) to improve coordination in the area of security, broadly defined.[117]

In a broader perspective, it is also important to keep in mind that even when NATO succeeded in (re)shaping the views held by Czech and Romanian actors regarding desirable institutions and correct norms of liberal-democratic governance, this did not always translate into direct change in the prevailing national discourse on security, or in the institutions and policies of their countries. In several instances, and in various ways, domestic politics complicated the international process of norm projection. Thus, NATO-socialized Czech and Romanian reformers encountered several domestic obstacles in their attempt to embed the new norms in the fabrics of their polities. At least two aspects of this problem were especially significant. Perhaps the most visible problem involved the marginalization of pro-reform actors socialized by NATO. This problem occurred at the level of political elites, particularly in the Romanian case, where many of the reformers associated with the proliberal coalition that governed the country in 1996–2000 were marginalized following the return to power of the socialists, led by President Iliescu. The same problem affected many young Romanian—but also Czech—civilian experts and military officers who graduated from Western defense academies and PfP courses, but who, upon their return home, were marginalized by older, more conservative superiors who perceived the younger, Westernized experts as a threat.

In addition, attempts at (re)shaping Czech and Romanian polities in accordance with NATO-prescribed norms were also complicated by problems of implementation of the new norms. In several instances, significant tensions persisted between, on the one hand, new laws and institutional arrangements, and, on the other hand, actual practices in the area of defense-related decision making. In the case of the Czech

---

[116] Mentioned by several Czech foreign affairs and defense officials; author's interviews, 19–20 April 2000, Prague.

[117] See Simon 2004, 59.

Republic, one relevant example concerns the relationship between the Ministry of Defense, Parliament, and the defense establishment. Following NATO's guidance, Czech decision makers initiated reforms aimed at enhancing consultation and cooperation among these different bodies. In so doing, they created the institutional basis for ending the past practice of isolation and secrecy shrouding defense policies. However, as late as spring 2000, the practice of interinstitutional cooperation in this area continued to be difficult, particularly below top-level contacts, where officials have been less exposed to Western-style socialization regarding the democratic control of the military. There, cooperation was hindered by persisting communist mentalities and practices, and a culture of mistrust on the part of civilians vis-à-vis military officers and vice versa.[118]

Similar problems occurred in Romania, where a culture of mutual civil-military mistrust, not unlike the Czech one, created obstacles in the reform process. In the eyes of many observers, the Romanian reform process was bound to be adversely affected by the socialists' return to power following the 2000 national elections. Yet it is interesting to note that the reforms carried out between 1996–2000, to a significant extent as a result of NATO's involvement, continued to have a positive impact on Romania even under the socialist government. The pro-West, pro-NATO discourse formulated by the 1996–2000 government, a discourse widely disseminated through the media and embedded in new strategic documents and defense-related legislation, portrayed Romania's liberalization, "return to Europe," and integration into Euro-Atlantic structures as the only course of action consistent with the true identity of the country.

That discourse shaped subsequent domestic political debates, making it difficult even for socialist political elites to advocate a different kind of future for Romania without appearing to favor a relapse into an anti-democratic past. The pro-West, pro-NATO discourse formulated by the 1996–2000 government, now embedded in key pieces of legislation, has redefined the boundaries of acceptable practices and institutional arrangements in a modern democracy. The Iliescu administration publicly subscribed to the Western-based liberal-democratic norms and principles of reform, including in the area of defense, and adopted and actively pursued the goal of integration into Euro-Atlantic structures. There was, then, an interesting shift away from the attitude characteristic of his first mandate, in which President Iliescu was adamant that Romania should strengthen ties with Russia and build a *sui generis* democracy, involving Euro-Atlantic integration only to the extent that it did not undermine that particular model of democratic polity.

In practice, the socialist government that came to power in 2000 was widely criticized for its corruption and for failing to take decisive action to carry out a series of reforms, and it is certainly true that corruption was a problem and the implementation of liberal-democratic norms was often quite slow.[119] Nevertheless, the Adrian

---

[118] See also Ulrich 2000, 87. This is similar to the problem of "cultural mismatch" identified by Checkel 1997. Keck and Sikkink 1998 reach a similar conclusion with respect to the ability of transnational networks to promote norm compliance. For a broader analysis of problems of norm implementation in the area of defense in the Czech Republic, see Simon 2004, especially Part II.

[119] For a more detailed analysis, see Gheciu 2005, chap. 5.

Nastase government repeatedly reiterated its commitment to the completion of the reform process and the integration of Romania into Western institutional structures. In the field of security, it is interesting to note that a series of goals formulated in 1996–2000 were actually achieved after the socialists' return to power.[120] In its foreign policy, Romania also continued to support the allies in their reconstruction efforts in the former Yugoslavia, and has contributed to the military campaigns and postwar missions in Afghanistan and, more recently, Iraq.[121]

The Romanians were rewarded for their reform efforts and their contribution to the wars in the Balkans and—more recently—the "war on terror" in November 2002, at the Prague Summit, at which the allies announced their intention to launch a second wave of enlargement, and included Romania on the list of countries expected to join as part of that second wave. In 2004, Romania finally achieved its goal of becoming a full member of NATO.

Conclusion

Some analysts have argued that NATO was successful in promoting liberal-democratic norms in those two countries because it prescribed things that Czech and Romanian reformist elites wanted to do anyway.[122] But this argument tends to overlook the fact that, initially, Czech and Romanian reformers did not share the vision of liberal democracy put forward by NATO. If one adopts the view of the Czech Republic and Romania as "liberal-minded states" that wanted to carry out NATO-prescribed liberal-democratic reforms in the first place, one loses sight of the systematic practices of teaching and persuasion through which NATO sought to—and often succeeded to—lead Central and East European elites to redefine their conceptions of liberal-democratic identity and interests. One also loses sight of NATO's deep involvement in a process conventionally attributed to sovereign authorities: that of shaping public opinion, and educating future generations of political and military elites into a particular definition of national identity.

Finally, let me briefly point to an important normative issue. In my analysis, I suspended the question of whether this process—which is carried out in the name of democracy promotion—is justified. Without trying to answer this here, it is worthwhile to point to a paradox of democracy promotion involved in NATO's activities. The implementation of NATO-prescribed norms did, I believe, lead to more transparent and inclusive arrangements in the former communist countries. At the same time, however, the process whereby these reforms were carried out was, in many ways, quite elitist. NATO conducted systematic socialization of political actors and military

---

[120] For an interesting analysis, see Barany 2003, chap. 4.

[121] In the presidential elections of 2004, the leader of the Democratic Party, Traian Basescu, defeated Adrian Nastase (the president of the ruling Social-Democratic Party) and subsequently managed to form a government around his Truth and Justice Alliance by appointing Rime Minister Calin Popescu-Tariceanu. The Alliance formed a government with the Humanist Party (now the Conservative Party), and the Democratic Alliance of Hungarians in Romania.

[122] I am grateful to Judith Kelley, Frank Schimmelfennig, and Michael Zürn for this point.

officers from target states and simultaneously sought to educate a new generation of elites into norms of Western-style liberal democracy. In some instances, NATO also tried to shape public opinion in Central and Eastern Europe. What seemed to be involved in these activities was a version of developmental democracy. According to that model, citizens—that is, in this case people perceived as carrying the heavy burden of socialist mentalities—require extensive guidance by enlightened elites to prepare them for self-governance. However, in the cases illustrated in this article, civic education was to be conducted not just by domestic actors, but also, to a large extent, by international institutions. Interestingly, one of the agents involved in this international socialization process was NATO—conventionally regarded as just a military alliance, which, by definition, would not become involved in domestic politics.

References

Adler, Emanuel. 1997. Imagined (Security) Communities: Cognitive Regions in International Relations. *Millennium* 26 (2):249–77.
———. 1998. Seeds of Peaceful Change: The OSCE's Security Community-Building Model. In *Security Communities*, edited by Emanuel Adler and Michael Barnett, 119–60. Cambridge: Cambridge University Press.
Adler, Emanuel, and Michael Barnett, eds. 1998. *Security Communities*. Cambridge: Cambridge University Press.
Asmus, Ronald. 2002. *Opening NATO's Door: How the Alliance Remade Itself for a New Era.* New York: Columbia University Press.
Barany, Zoltan. 2003. *The Future of NATO Expansion.* Cambridge: Cambridge University Press.
Barnett, Michael, and Raymond Duvall. 2005. Power in International Politics. *International Organization 59* (1):39–75.
Barnett, Michael, and Martha Finnemore. 1999. The Politics, Power and Pathologies of International Organizations. *International Organization* 53 (4):699–732.
Berger, Peter, and Thomas Luckmann. 1967. *The Social Construction of Reality: A Treatise in the Sociology of Knowledge.* Garden City, N.Y.: Doubleday.
Bourdieu, Pierre. 1990. *In Other "Words: Essays towards a Reflexive Sociology.* Stanford, Calif.: Stanford University Press.
———. 1991. *Language and Symbolic Power.* Cambridge, Mass.: Harvard University Press.
Bourdieu, Pierre, and J. C. Passeron. 1977. *Reproduction in Education, Society and Culture.* London: Sage.
Checkel, Jeffrey T. 1997. International Norms and Domestic Politics: Bridging the Rationalist-Constructivist Divide. *European Journal of International Relations* 3 (4):473–96.
———. 2001. Why Comply? Social Learning and European Identity Change. *International Organization* 55 (3):553–88.
———. 2003. 'Going Native' in Europe? Theorizing Social Interaction in European Institutions. *Comparative Political Studies* 36:209–31.
Checkel, Jeffrey T., and Andrew Moravcsik. 2001. A Constructivist Research Program in EU Studies? (Forum Debate). *European Union Politics 1* (2):219–49.
Cialdini, Robert. 1993. *Influence: Science and Practice.* 3d ed. New York: HarperCollins.
Cortell, Andrew, and James Davis. 2000. Understanding the Domestic Impact of International Norms: A Research Agenda. *International Studies Review* 2 (1):65–87.

Culik, Jan. 1999. Ten Years After Communism: The Great Czech Malaise. *Central Europe Review* 1 (1). Available at (http://www.ce-review.Org/99/l/culikl.html). Accessed 21 June 2005.

Donnelly, Chris. 1997a. Developing a National Strategy for the Transformation of the Defense Establishment in Post-Communist States. *Central European Issues* 3 (2):63–81.

———. 1997b. Defense Transformation in the New Democracies: A Framework for Tackling the Problem. *NATO Review* 45 (1):15–19.

Douglas, Mary. 1975. *Implicit Meanings: Essays in Anthropology.* London: Routledge and Kegan Paul.

———. 1986. *How Institutions Think.* Syracuse, N.Y.: Syracuse University Press.

Dragsdahl, Joergen. 1998. NATO Resists Pressures to Militarise Central Europe. BASIC Occasional Paper 28. Available at (http://www.basicint.org/pubs/Papers/BP28.htm). Accessed 21 June 2005.

Evangelista, Matthew. 1999. *Unarmed Forces: The Transnational Movement to End the Cold War.* Ithaca, N.Y.: Cornell University Press.

Finnemore, Martha. 1996. *National Interests in International Society.* Ithaca, N.Y.: Cornell University Press.

Finnemore, Martha, and Kathryn Sikkink. 1998. International Norm Dynamics and Political Change. *International Organization* 52 (4):887–917.

Flockhart, Trine. 2004. 'Masters and Novices': Socialisation and Social Learning through the NATO Parliamentary Assembly. *International Relations* 18 (3):361–80.

Gheciu, Alexandra. 2005. *NATO in the 'New Europe': The Politics of International Socialization After the Cold War.* Stanford, Calif.: Stanford University Press.

Gibson, James L. 1998. A Sober Second Thought: Persuading Russians to Tolerate. *American Journal of Political Science* 42 (3):819–50.

Gousseff, Catherine. 2000. L'effet Kosovo sur les nouveaux partenaires de l'OTAN. *Courrier des Pays de l'Est* 1001 (1):4–16.

Guzzini, Stefano. 2000. A Reconstruction of Constructivism in International Relations. *European Journal of International Relations* 6 (2): 147–82.

Haftendorn, Helga, Robert Keohane, and Celeste Wallander, eds. 1999. *Imperfect Unions: Security Institutions over Time and Space.* Oxford: Oxford University Press.

Hoskova, Mahulena. 1999. Civilian Control of the Military and Security Structures of the Czech Republic. Unpublished manuscript, Max Planck Institute for Comparative Public Law, Heidelberg, Germany.

Hybner, Jiri. 2001. *The Significance of the Washington Summit for Strengthening the Membership of the Czech Republic in NATO.* NATO-EAPC Fellowship Report, 1999–2001. Brussels: NATO HQ.

Jepperson, Ronald, Alexander Wendt, and Peter Katzenstein. 1996. Norms, Identity and Culture in National Security. In *The Culture of National Security*, edited by Peter Katzenstein, 33–75. New York: Columbia University Press.

Joergensen, Charlotte, Christian Kock, and Lone Roerbech. 1998. Rhetoric That Shifts Votes: An Explanatory Study of Persuasion in Issue-Oriented Public Debates. *Political Communication* 15:283–99.

Johnston, Alastair Iain. 2001. Treating International Institutions as Social Environments. *International Studies Quarterly* 45 (4):487–516.

Jupille, Joseph, James A. Caporaso, and Jeffrey T. Checkel. 2003. Integrating Institutions: Rationalism, Constructivism and the Study of the European Union. *Comparative Political Studies* 36 (1):7–40.

Katzenstein, Peter J., Robert O. Keohane, and Stephen D. Krasner. 1998. International Organization and the Study of World Politics. *International Organization* 52 (4):645–85.

Keck, Margaret, and Kathryn Sikkink. 1998. *Activists Beyond Borders: Advocacy Networks in International Politics.* Ithaca, N.Y.: Cornell University Press.

Kennedy, Robert. 1998. Educating Leaders for the 21st Century: A Snapshot of the Marshall Center for Security Studies. *NATO Review* 46 (4). Available at: ⟨http://www.nato.int/docu/ review/1998/ 9804-08.htm⟩. Accessed 21 June 2005.

Lauer, Robert, and Warren Handel. 1977. *Social Psychology: The Theory and Application of Symbolic Interactionism.* Boston: Houghton Mifflin.

March, James G., and Johan P. Olsen. 1989. *Rediscovering Institutions.* New York: Free Press.

———. 1998. The Institutional Dynamics of International Political Orders. *International Organization* 52 (4):943–69.

Milliken, Jennifer. 1999. The Study of Discourse in International Relations: A Critique of Research and Methods. *European Journal of International Relations* 5 (2):225–54.

Mutz, Diane C., Paul M. Sniderman, and Richard Brody, eds. 1996. *Political Persuasion and Attitude Change.* Ann Arbor: University of Michigan Press.

Payne, Rodger. 2001. Persuasion, Frames and Norm Construction. *European Journal of International Relations* 7 (1):37–61.

Pecina, Thomas. 1999. Arranged Marriage with Aborted Honeymoon? The Czech Republic and NATO. *Central Europe Review* 1 (5). Available at ⟨http://www.ce-review.Org/99/5/ pecina5.html⟩. Accessed 21 June 2005.

Powell, Walter, and Paul DiMaggio. 1991. *The New Institutionalism in Organizational Analysis.* Chicago: University of Chicago Press.

Reiter, Dan. 2001. Why NATO Enlargement Does Not Spread Democracy. *International Security* 25 (4):41–67.

Risse, Thomas. 2000. 'Let's Argue!': Communicative Action in World Politics. *International Organization* 54 (1):1–39.

Risse, Thomas, Stephen Ropp, and Kathryn Sikkink, eds. 1999. *The Power of Human Rights: International Norms and Domestic Change.* Cambridge: Cambridge University Press.

Risse-Kappen, Thomas. 1995. *Cooperation Among Democracies: The European Influence on U.S. Foreign Policy.* Princeton, N.J.: Princeton University Press.

———. 1996. Collective Identity in a Democratic Community: The Case of NATO. In *The Culture of National Security,* edited by Peter Katzenstein, 357–99. New York: Columbia University Press.

Roman, Petre. 1999. Building a Government-Opposition Consensus in the Field of Security Policy. In *Romania and Euro-Atlantic Integration,* edited by Kurt Treptow and Mihail Ionescu, 83–91. Iasi, Romania: Center for Romanian Studies.

Romanian Government. 1999a. *Programul National Anual de Pregatire a Integrarii in NATO (ANP) Conform Planului de Actiune Pentru Aderare (MAP).* Bucharest, Romania: Ministry of Foreign Affairs.

Romanian Government. 1999b. *White Book on Romania and NATO.* Bucharest, Romania: Ministry of Foreign Affairs.

Ruggie, John. 1998. What Makes the World Hang Together? Neo-Utilitarianism and the Constructivist Challenge. *International Organization* 52 (4):855–85.

Sarvas, Stefan. 1999. One Past, Two Futures?: The NATO Enlargement Debate in the Czech Republic and Slovakia. Harmonie Paper 4. Groningen, Netherlands: Center for European Security Studies.

Sava, Ionel Nicu. 2002. Western (NATO/PFP) Assistance to Build Democratic Civil-Military Relations in South Eastern Europe: The Case of Bulgaria, Romania and Slovenia. Manfred Womer Fellowship Report. Brussels: NATO.

Schimmelfennig, Frank. 2000. International Socialization in the New Europe: Rational Action in an Institutional Environment. *European Journal of International Relations* 6 (1):109–39.

———. 2003. *The EU, NATO and the Integration of Europe: Rules and Rhetoric.* Cambridge: Cambridge University Press.

Searing, Donald. 1995. The Psychology of Political Authority: A Causal Mechanism of Political Learning Through Persuasion and Manipulation. *Political Psychology* 16 (4):677–96.

Simon, Jeffrey. 2000. Transforming the Armed Forces of Central and Eastern Europe. *Strategic Forum* 172:1–8.

———. 2004. *NATO and the Czech and Slovak Republics: A Comparative Study in Civil-Military Relations.* Lanham, Md.: Rowman and Littlefield.

Stroehlein, Andrew. 1999. Promising Paradise. *Central Europe Review* 0 (23). Available at (http://www.ce-review.org/authorarchives/stroehlein_archive/stroehlein23old.html). Accessed 22 April 2005.

Terry, Deborah, and Michael Hogg, eds. 2000. *Attitudes, Behavior and Social Context.* Mahwah, N.J.: Lawrence Erlbaum.

Ulrich, Marybeth Peterson. 2000. *Democratizing Communist Militaries: The Cases of the Czech and Russian Armed Forces.* Ann Arbor: University of Michigan Press.

Walker, R. B. J. 1993. *Inside/Outside: International Relations as Political Theory.* Cambridge: Cambridge University Press.

Wallander, Celeste. 2000. Institutional Assets and Adaptability: NATO After the Cold War. *International Organization* 54 (4):705–35.

Wallander, Celeste, and Robert Keohane. 1999. Risk, Threat, and Security Institutions. In *Imperfect Unions: Security Institutions over Time and Space*, edited by Helga Haftendorn, Robert Keohane, and Celeste Wallander, 21–47. Oxford: Oxford University Press.

Waterman, Harvey, Dessie Zagorcheva, and Dan Reiter. 2002. NATO and Democracy. *International Security* 26 (3):221–35.

Wendt, Alexander. 1999. *Social Theory of International Politics.* Cambridge: Cambridge University Press.

Williams, Michael C. 1997. The Institutions of Security: Elements of a Theory of Security Organizations. *Cooperation and Conflict* 32 (3):287–307.

———. 2001. The Discipline of the Democratic Peace: Kant, Liberalism, and the Social Construction of Security Communities. *European Journal of International Relations* 7 (4):525–53.

Williams, Michael C., and Iver Neumann. 2000. From Alliance to Security Community: NATO, Russia and the Power of Security. *Millennium* 29 (2):357–87.

Zajicova, Darja. 2000. The Czech Media: Demythtified. *Central Europe Review* 2 (24). Available at: (http://www.ce-review.org). Accessed 22 April 2005.

Zanna, Mark, James Olson, and Peter Herman, eds. 1984. *Social Influence: The Ontario Symposium on Personality and Social Psychology.* Hillsdale, N.J.: Lawrence Erlbaum.

Zimbardo, Philip, and Michael Leippe. 1991. *The Psychology of Attitude Change and Social Influence.* New York: McGraw-Hill.

Part III

Critique, Conclusions and Extensions

7

Conclusions and Extensions

Toward Mid-Range Theorizing and Beyond Europe

Alastair Iain Johnston

The purpose of this essay is to reflect on the core analytical claims that the other chapters in this volume make about the processes and conditions under which socialization of state agents occurs in Europe, and to ask how these arguments could be extended, clarified, retested, and transported to other types of institutions in other parts of the world. Frankly, this is a daunting task. At best I can offer some suggestions about how to push some arguments further and why it might be worth doing so. In the first section of this chapter, therefore, I summarize the authors' core claims about scope conditions under which socialization is possible, and suggest where these can be extended, compared, and clarified. The second section looks more closely at one of the core mechanisms that establish the added value of both this project and, more generally, the concept of socialization in understanding international relations (IR): persuasion. It suggests how a focus on persuasion actually may suggest the need for more focus on strategic, or "thin rationalist," behavior. The third section looks at how the treatment of identity in this volume might be extended theoretically. The final section looks at issues involved in extending the claims of this collection to other parts of the world.

Core Analytical Claims

This is a diverse set of essays. At first glance, there appear to be some fairly large differences in whether the empirical evidence does or does not show socialization inside international institutions. Some authors argue that socialization in perhaps its truest sense—the internalization of new group norms through persuasion and/or communicative action—can be found in European institutions, though under certain scope conditions. Others appear skeptical about such claims and suggest that adaptation to the preferred norms of an institution (or of the actors who control the institution) is strategic, optimizing behavior. These apparent differences are useful because when considered together they suggest a rather long and rich list of scope conditions under which socialization can be hypothesized to work and not to work.

This is, perhaps, collectively the major contribution of this research. To date, with some more recent exceptions,[1] there has been a tendency to view strategic-choice effects and socialization effects as "either/or." An actor either adopts some set of norms deliberately so as to maximize some material payoff (for example, the economic benefits of inclusion in Europe; political survival in a government where others endorse these new norms), or the actor internalizes new values and attitudes semiconsciously through more or less hardwired responses to specific environmental stimuli in specific social-psychological environments, or through a reasoned reevaluation of the inherent normative goodness of old values. These essays collectively point out, however, that progress in understanding how actors change their interests and their behavior inside institutions will come from understanding the interaction of strategic behavior with social-psychological socialization mechanisms. This understanding is likely to come from so-called middle-range theories of socialization. These theories are both the most practical to test (because many have been developed in other subfields already) and the most likely to explain what IR theory has heretofore generally viewed as large macro changes in states as generalized wholes.

My argument here is that the skeptics actually help to refine the scope conditions under which persuasion is more likely to be operative. I do not believe that the skeptics intend to show or conclude that persuasion socialization is conceptually or empirically inconceivable. Elsewhere Kelley notes, for example, that the scope conditions for this kind of socialization are narrow, and thus that this particular process is relatively rare.[2] She suggests that persuasion is only likely when there is low domestic opposition to an institution's persuasion efforts. In her case—the convergence of domestic legislation concerning minority rights in newly liberated Eastern European states with European Union (EU) standards—the issue at stake is highly volatile, is contested, and touches on the identities of majority and minority populations. Linkage politics worked, persuasion alone did not. This is perhaps not so surprising. The arenas for effective persuasion, according to essays in this volume, are those in which intensive, face-to-face interaction is the primary mode of interaction. When national policies are the object of change, and when the political process involves massaging myriad interests of politicians and bureaucrats, this kind of small-group intensive interaction is unlikely to be the avenue of socialization in the first place. When the object of change is, however, the preferences, norms, and values of individual bureaucrats and key politicians, persuasion processes apparently do work.[3]

In this volume, Hooghe is also skeptical that persuasion-based socialization has much impact inside international institutions. For Hooghe, socialization within a state tends to trump international socialization because it occurs prior to the latter. Socialization within states, of course, does not necessarily undermine the internalization of

---

[1] Fearon and Wendt 2002.

[2] Kelley 2004.

[3] See Lewis, this volume. The case in Gheciu, this volume, also fits this pattern, even though the objects of change are ultimately national policies (civil-military relations). Her dependent variable is effects on those participating in NATO/Partnership for Peace (PfP) seminars (her informants). The link from this variable to national policies is less clear (for example, to the Romanian Democratic Convention) and it would not be surprising if strategic incentives were also used by newly socialized players to change positions of others in the policy process—from bureaucrats to politicians and legislatures.

pro-European norms. These norms may be inculcated at the national or subnational level through the internalization of pro-European ideologies or the development of a concept of identity that can incorporate both national and international allegiances. Hooghe's results suggest first that persuasion may in fact occur, but mainly at the national and subnational level (hence the internalization of political ideologies or national identities that support international norms). So the concept of socialization is still important in explaining outcomes. Second, she suggests that precisely because primacy matters, those who enter international institutions at a relatively young age are more likely to internalize the institution's norms than those older participants who were more socialized in national institutions. Whether youth is a conjunctural cause along with noviceness, or whether youth means a greater likelihood of socialization in pro-European norms at the national level, is unclear. But either way, the existence of socialization as a process that creates preferences is not disputed by Hooghe's research.

The Schimmelfennig argument is less clear, however, about the possibility of social- ization. At first glance, Schimmelfennig rules out the possibility that persuasion and/or communicative action have any causal impact in his cases. It is possible, of course, that he has picked two exceptions that do not undermine "the rule." But I think his cases implicitly reveal some interesting questions about the scope conditions for persuasion.

As one scope condition, Schimmelfennig implies that on issues related to identity change, where groups have developed deeply ingrained concepts of self and other, persuasion and communicative action are less likely to work. From some theoretical perspectives on identity (for example, social identity theory), this should not seem too surprising. In identity conflicts, ingroups are likely to be especially vigilant about the defection of members from the value systems that are deemed to characterize the ingroup. Internal dissent threatens the cohesion and positive valuation of the ingroup. "Deviants" will be considered threats to group norms, and there is considerable evi- dence that deviants are more often the targets of ingroup disciplining and coercion than devalued outgroup members.[4] This makes the ingroup more hypervigilant about, and resistant to, perceived efforts by norm entrepreneurs to "persuade" members of the group to reevaluate their attitudes toward out-groups. In addition, ingroups are likely to interpret these efforts at large-scale persuasion to be exercises in blaming them for the conflict. Identity blaming—the problem is X because your group has Y characteristics (as opposed to the problem is X because individual Y has done Z)—is also associated with the polarization of views and with resistance to the message from outside norm entrepreneurs.[5] It may be no coincidence, therefore, that much of the dissent about the efficacy of socialization comes from analyses of identity conflicts.

---

[4] Marques 2001.

[5] Romer et al. 1997. Granting that issues such as political rights in highly polarized identity environments are too sticky and too resistant to attempts to inculcate ideas that appear to threaten the dominant ingroup, this, of course, does not rule out the role of persuasion in inculcating the identity norms that make resistance to persuasive attempts to change these norms effective in the first place. This underscores the obvious, but not trite, point that socialization theories may help explain resistance to resocialization at time $t + n$. In other words, the absence of evidence of socialization at time $t + n$ does not refute the phenomenon of socialization at time t. One does not have to immediately cede the floor to a strategic material argument in the absence of evidence of resocialization.

Relatedly, Schimmelfennig also hypothesizes that persuasion requires the presence of a "liberal-minded" interlocutor. This is a testable argument about persuasion. But it could be explored and refined further. One direction would be to ask what exactly is a liberal-minded interlocutor? Why are liberal-minded actors more susceptible to persuasion than illiberal ones, especially on issues related to identity?[6] Is it possible that liberals are especially prone to persuasion/socialization, more so than authoritarian interlocutors, for example? If so, why? One possibility is that the essence of liberalism is tolerance and reason—openness to new, but convincing evidence, presented in particularly rigorous fashion. This draws close to a Habermasian argument about the preconditions for communicative action. In this regard, political strategizing and optimizing incentives may be required to create the conditions (democracy) under which the interlocutors are liberal in orientation.

But this argument about liberalism, tolerance, and persuasion could also draw on older research on the relationship between authoritarian personalities, conservative ideology, cognitive simplicity, and resistance to new information. Put bluntly, authoritarian personalities and ideologies are likely to have simplistic cognitive constructs, to be more resistant to disconfirming information, and to embody low levels of trust toward others, all conditions that are not conducive to persuasion.[7]

Another possibility is that liberalism, at least in its Anglo-American form, also stresses the authority of law and legal precedent. Here the effect of precedent goes beyond merely reminding actors of the legal costs of norm violation.[8] Rather, in terms of persuasion, one hypothesis might be that legal precedent is authoritative, and authoritative sources of ideas are more likely to be persuasive than nonauthoritative sources.[9] But there is another possible micro-process that derives not from the authoritativeness of precedent, but its "precedent-ness." Precedent cues concerns about consistency. There is also powerful evidence, in the psychological literature on persuasion, for the drive to be seen as acting consistently with one's identity. This increases, all things being equal, a willingness to engage in pro-norm behavior.[10] Precedent also invokes the notion that when something is settled, there is a presumption that other subsequent but similar issues are settled the same way (*stare decisis* in legal terms). Internalization of this norm thus makes more persuasive those arguments that claim situation X requires behavior Y because it is similar to preceding situations. Implied here, too, is the notion that to be consistent is to be just, for inconsistency leads to arbitrariness, a feature of illiberal regimes.[11]

This is a roundabout way of saying that buried underneath the claim that liberal actors are more susceptible to persuasion are at least three possible

---

[6] Moravcsik and others have noted that human rights norms (indeed any new norms) are more likely to diffuse among those whose values are closest to those of the norm entrepreneur. But stated this way, the hypothesis technically does not limit norm diffusion to liberal targets, only like-minded targets.

[7] See Feldman and Stenner, 1997; and Jost et al. 2003.

[8] Alter 2002.

[9] See Axsom, Yates, and Chaiken 1987; Cialdini 1985 and 1987; Jorgensen, Kock, and Rorbech 1998; Mutz, Sniderman, and Brody 1996; Rule and Bisanz 1987; and Zimbardo and Leippe 1991.

[10] Cialdini 1985, chap. 3.

[11] Perell 1987.

mechanisms—reason and respect for alternative evidence, the authoritativeness of legal precedent, and consistency.

There is always the possibility, of course, that Schimmelfennig's empirical work has fundamentally undercut the major premise of the project. He got it right, and most of the other authors did not. They have observed processes that are not really there or are irrelevant or secondary, accounting for little of the variance especially when placed in a "linear regression equation"-type model that includes strategic incentives. I believe it is premature to concede this possibility. The other chapters provide fairly convincing evidence from a wide range of methods—interviews, participant-observation, case analysis, and quantitative analysis—that persuasion and social influence effects are apparent in these institutions to different degrees. One way of testing whether Schimmelfennig's claims undermine the findings of the project is to apply his methods/starting point to other cases, and vice versa. It might be worthwhile, then, to go over the same cases using different arguments to piece together the process. This might mean, for instance, taking Gheciu's dependent variable (convergence in attitudes and policies toward civil-military relations) and asking: "What does Lewis' work on intensity/quality have to say about which part of this process of change in this dependent variable?" or "What does Schimmelfennig have to say about the role of material (or political) rewards, or the political strategies that 'socialized' agents inside these countries used to push new policies through parliaments and bureaucracies?" Alternatively, a micro-analysis of Schimmelfennig's cases might focus on whether there is any variation at the individual and small group level in the propensity for one identity group to accept the norm of protecting the interests of another identity group. Do hypotheses about face-to-face interaction, deliberative institutional environment, intensity, exposure, authoritativeness of messenger, and so on, work at the micro-level in his cases?

Having referred to some of the scope conditions that, together, the articles in this volume reveal, let me summarize some of the important ones and add questions and suggestions for extensions. These overlap to some degree with those identified in the Zürn and Checkel article, though we develop different criticisms and extensions. My first condition maps onto their "properties of institutions" condition. My second, third, and fourth conditions map onto, but unpack further, their "properties of interaction between socializing and socialized agent." My fifth condition corresponds to their "properties of political systems." My sixth condition is similar to their "properties of the issues or objects of contention."

Institutional Design Features

There are characteristics, both formal and informal, of institutional design that contribute to socialization. As developed in the chapters, these include the following.

Degree of Agent Autonomy.   As Lewis notes about the EU's Committee of Permanent Representatives (COREPER), national representatives inside these meetings appear to have a fair amount of leeway to push forward, or retreat from, a national position. There appears to be a relatively weak norm of supervision by the "principal," even though the permanent representatives are supposed to be state agents *par excellence* in establishing the agenda of ministerial meetings. This leeway allows representatives to present a position, knowing that it is unlikely to sell, and to back down without fear of repercussions from, or monitoring by, the principal. It is unclear how precisely this feature of the institution evolved. Additional hypotheses need to be developed about when an institution allows this kind of agent autonomy. It may be an issue-specific feature of institutions. Institutions in which the agenda is highly technical or on a relatively new topic, where the principal is unsure or less aware of what its interests might be, are more likely to witness this kind of autonomy. Of course, this autonomy may have little to do with institutional design or issue-area. It may be nation-specific. In one of Lewis' cases, the agent's (for example, the French ambassador's) autonomy came from his seniority over his foreign minister.

Norms of Consensus, Trust, Reciprocity, and Compromise.   These norms help ensure that national agendas cannot be pushed so far that the institution logjams. In a sense, these norms presuppose that the legitimacy of the institution is so strong that state agents are unwilling to undermine it even on issues where they have strong and divergent state preferences. It is unclear, however, how these norms evolve from deliberate institutional design choices to start with. There is probably a relationship. For example, as one Chinese diplomat explained it to me in an interview in 1999, it took this official some time to adjust from the style of discourse in the United Nations (UN) Conference on Disarmament to the style of the Association of Southeast Asian Nations (ASEAN) Regional Forum. In the Conference on Disarmament, the primary arms-control treaty negotiation body of the UN, the language is often that of national interest, and the debating style is parliamentary. The purpose of the institution is to negotiate treaties, hence the discourse is generally about bargaining over the distribution of goods. The ASEAN Regional Forum (ARF) is less formal. It is a deliberative institution, and one in which the provision of information, in the form of Confidence Building Measures (CBMs), is one of its major purposes. Thus the language is more consensus-focused, the atmosphere more flexible. In addition, perhaps like COREPER, the norm of flexible consensus is quite strong. This means that chairs of ARF meetings (who must be from an ASEAN state) have a legitimacy that allows them to declare a consensus even when it is unclear one actually exists. State agents refrain from challenging a chair's authority. So one design-related difference may be distributive versus deliberative institutions. The latter is more likely to develop norms of consensus, trust, reciprocity, and compromise. At first blush, COREPER does not seem to fit this hypothesis because it is designed to set distributive-like policies for the EU, but also arguably has a deliberative function—to consider agenda issues for further discussion.

Organizational Characteristics.   A number of authors have pointed out that organizational features of the institution in which actors are being socialized may be important conditions for the effectiveness of the process. There are three features in particular:

- Organizational primacy: secondary organizations are less likely to socialize actors once their identities are established by primary (usually national) organizations (Hooghe). This suggests, however, that primacy effects, rather than most recent experience (recency effects), are critical in socialization. The literature is divided on this, however, and it would be worth testing these assumptions further. In effect, what are the scope conditions for this scope condition; that is, when does primacy and when does recency matter in organizational socialization?[12] It may be, of course, that some degree of hybridity is the result of socialization in primary and secondary organizations, in which case, any follow-on to this volume will have to develop specific hypotheses about hybridization.[13]

- Organizational function: the more compatible secondary sectoral organizations are with primary (national) sectoral organizations, the less likely there will be any resocialization—indeed the more likely the persistence of older values and attitudes. This is a variant of the argument in, say, the human-rights norms literature, in which actors with more compatible values are more likely to influence each other. The resocialization, however, is likely to be marginal because the actors share so many values in common.

- Organizational specialization: variation in the purposes of institutions will have different effects on the efficacy of socialization. Thus socialization effects could promote identification with a geographic space or with a problem-solving ideology, depending on the type of specialization in the institution. It would be worthwhile to develop more general hypotheses about whether these different specializations have systematic effects on socialization. Institutions that specialize in issues relating to identity and identity change (minority rights) may be less effective as socializing environments than other kinds of specializations, however.[14]

---

[12] In the cognitive and social psychology literature, the size of the temporal gap between first and last messages and the responder's recall is considered a scope condition for primacy or recency effects. Analogizing to organizational socialization, the amount of time spent by an actor in the primary and secondary organizations, and the amount of time between occupation in the primary and secondary organizations, may be critical to determining which has the greatest impact on some measurement of the actor's values.

[13] Related to the issue of hybridity is the possibility that different institutions and institutional purposes can have interactive effects, whereby there is a cumulative effect from participation in multiple but related institutions. Hooghe suggests that "it is extremely difficult—nigh impossible—for an international organization to substantively shift the views of mature recruits." Hooghe, this volume. However, in some instances agents are not participating in only one institution, but in a number of related institutions and subinstitutions as well. All this participation might have a cumulative effect. For example, the ASEAN Regional Forum only meets once a year. But its formal intersessional meetings occur a few more times a year, its related Track II activities (unofficial or nonofficial) meet even more frequently. All of these meetings generally have similar purposes, namely promoting ideas of cooperative security and multilateralism. In many instances the same people often show up to some or all of these activities. So in the case of Asian security institutions and their socialization effects, at least, one would have to take into account the myriad, related institutional environments in which officials are involved.

[14] Kelley 2004.

- Organizational identity: the institution needs to have a coherent identity with a clearly linked set of normative characteristics. Without this feature, the socialization effects of the institution will be diluted, or indeed nonexistent. This point comes across in an important comment by one of Hooghe's informants about obstacles to socialization inside the European Commission: "national tensions are transferred to the Commission, and that makes it impossible to have everybody agree *ex ante* on common objectives. There are no common objectives.... This is still a relatively young, expanding, and maturing institution, which has not yet found its own identity."[15]

Style of Discourse and Shared Language

Lewis raises the interesting question of whether merely a shared way of expressing ideas may help socialize new members of a group. While he does not develop this point theoretically, there is certainly a large literature that claims, at its most radical, that language constructs reality, and at its less radical, that language shuts off or delegitimizes some kinds of arguments more than others.[16] This possibility suggests one socialization process that none of the articles here really deals with in any detail, namely mimicking.

Mimicking is a mechanism whereby a novice initially copies the behavioral norms—including discursive practices—of the group to navigate through an uncertain environment (in this regard it might be considered along with Checkel's notion of cognitive role playing and Zürn and Checkel's discussion of cognitive dissonance as part of a process of cognitive short-cutting that socialization can induce). But mimicking differs from rational strategic adaptation. It is a somewhat efficient means of adapting to uncertainty prior to any detailed ends-means calculation of the benefits of doing so. That is, mimicking, unlike strategic emulation, does not mean searching for and copying exemplars, or the most successful actor in the group. It is rather a satisficing first step designed simply to be able to participate in the group by following its most basic rules, even before the actor has a clear sense of what its interests might be that need maximizing.[17] The benefit of following these rules need not be to acquire the rewards that other people appear to be acquiring. Indeed, with mimicking, it is not clear what these rewards might be. Rather, actors assume there has to be some reward at some point, otherwise why would all others be acting in a more or less similar fashion. In a sense, actors have no preference over means, and only vaguely formed preferences over ends. They will do anything necessary, and quickly, to survive in a new environment. Mimicking provides a novice with the modal procedures, models, norms, languages, and (perhaps) preferences that, immediately on entry, seem necessary to survive, based on the supposition that everyone else seems to be surviving.

---

[15] Hooghe, this volume.

[16] For the classics in the linguistic construction of thinking, see Whorf 1956; and Sapir 1956. See also Gumperz and Levinson 1996; Dalby 1990; Doty 1993; Ochs 1986, 2–3; Waever 1990; Searle 1992; Bourdieu 1991, 49; Yee 1996, 94–97; Fierke 2002; and Fairclough 2003, 21–24.

[17] To some degree, the concept complements Checkel's notion of "cognitive role playing."

Mimicking can be reinforced by status concerns. That is, if one does not join an organization, then one may not just suffer a loss of material benefits, but may also be viewed by others as out of fashion, behind the times, and thus missing out on a status-enhancing experience. This can lead to choosing behaviors that may not be beneficial if the actor only behaved according to private information (because the private information is discounted in an uncertain environment).[18] Or at least, by the time the actor is certain through private information that participation could be disadvantageous for a particular interest (for example, military power), it has made commitments that make it costly to act on the private information (for example, status concerns, issue linkages, and so on). Thus, by mimicking, an actor can get locked into procedures, behaviors, and languages characteristic of the social environment. The lock-in or constraints occur on two levels—the new costs of backing out are high; the procedures, behaviors, and languages themselves constrain options inside the institution.

To be sure, mimicking stretches somewhat the concept of socialization, because pro-group behavior is only indirectly an effect generated by the nature of the social environment. Rather, it is a survival strategy in a particular social environment. That is, while mimicking is distinct from exogenously induced threats or punishments, and is not characterized by individual efforts to optimize long-run material well-being, it is not in the same class of causes as persuasion and social influence. The latter two are mechanisms that motivate. In mimicking, the mechanism that motivates can be survival under uncertainty.

On the other hand, choosing which groups to mimic involves a degree of prior identification. Moreover, mimicking prosocial behavior can lead to the internalization of norms through repetition. Or, alternatively, by mimicking an actor goes on record as behaving in some particular way. It may then be loathe to deviate from this precedent for status and image reasons. Many of the procedural constraints, work habits, and standard operating procedures, including discursive practices, that actors develop to minimally function inside an institution come from mimicking the behavior of others in the group. These can then limit legitimate forms of participation in the institution.[19] Mimicking can also lead to acceptance of the inter-subjective norms of the group governing basic communication. In other words, mimicking can achieve basic agreement on legitimate ways to resolve conflicts even though no Habermasian communicative action has taken place.[20] In short, mimicking could be both a condition for, and effect of, more direct forms of socialization.

---

[18] Hirshleifer 1995, 191.

[19] See Holland 1996, 29; Cialdini, Kallgren, and Reno 1991, 203–4; Hirshleifer 1995; and Biddle 1985, 162.

[20] James notes that communicative action involves agreement on the medium through which discussion of conflict takes place. This agreement—like learning a common foreign language—comes before all other communication—see James 1998, 7–11. Hence socialization, whether via persuasion or social influence, requires a basic level of communicative cooperation to begin with. I do not disagree with this argument. But there is no reason why this basic agreement need be achieved through discussion and argumentation that two or more equal, empathetic actors eventually find convincing. Mimicking the language, procedures, and habits—the parameters of this medium of communication—can lock an actor seeking to survive under uncertainty into such agreement as well.

Related to mimicking is the question of behavioral templates and how these affect actor behavior. Gheciu implies that much of the "teaching" or persuading in her cases appears to involve agents from the North Atlantic Treaty Organization (NATO) offering legal, organizational, and normative templates for reorganizing civil-military relations. So what is doing the socializing—the way in which these templates are offered and discussed by NATO? Or the templates themselves? There is perhaps an over-determination problem here: when a "teacher" says, "this is the way you should do X, if you have identity Y" (normative persuasion) and also says, "here is a method for acting Y-like" (template), it may be unclear which has the greatest impact on pro-group behavior.[21] But if templates are critical, why do they constrain on actor behavior? Are the "constraints" only ideational—the templates themselves embody concepts of identity and interest? Or are the effects institutional (the templates prescribe the construction of new organizations, say, with all of the concomitant incentives to optimize material or social or psychological interests)?

Exposure

Both Lewis and Gheciu raise the question of the intensity, duration, and quality of exposure to counterattitudinal messages as critical variables explaining the success of persuasion. There is some dispute over precisely how intensity or duration are independent of other elements of exposure, such as the autonomy of the agent, the authoritativeness of the persuader, the content of the message, and the cognitive characteristics of the persuadee, among other possibilities.

The quality of exposure is also somewhat illusive in meaning. But there appear to be at least three subelements to the "quality" variable. One is the consistency of the message. Another is social proof. A third is a focus on consistency between verbal commitment and action, a consistency that would highlight the hypocrisy of noncompliance with new norms. These latter two elements, however, imply a degree of optimizing, "logic of consequences" calculation by the target of the message. That is, as the literature on consistency suggests, there can be two ways in which actors decide to conform to a norm. In the first, actors compare the required behavior against a list of behaviors considered appropriate to the identity the actors believe they hold. Consistency theory suggests that it is the internal cognitive discomfort that hypocrisy generates that leads to changes in behavior. The second possibility is that conformity arises from calculating the relative status benefits (back patting) and status costs (shaming, opprobrium) of acting in ways consistent with the new norms.

How these more detailed micro-processes might be tested is a tough empirical problem. It probably requires moving more systematically into the details of social group

---

[21] One of the U.S. Coast Guard's jobs is to provide templates for developing countries to set up coast guards. These templates include draft legislation governing the surveillance of territorial waters. For a lot of small littoral states, their coast guards are their navies. So the U.S. Coast Guard literally provides models for setting up claims to being an ocean state with a navy. In Gheciu's case, then, is it the face-to-face process of teaching or the existence of templates that is primarily responsible for eliciting new norms of behavior?

interaction where individual and personality type are the critical units of analysis. There is likely to be a certain distribution in the sensitivity to appeals to consistency and social status across individuals inside institutions. This distribution will determine whether there is large- or small-scale compliance, and whether there are obvious tipping points in the group as to how many others have to first demonstrate compliance before the rest of the group does.[22] Specifically, one would have to determine this distribution for some sample of European agents before their participation in European institutions.

Noviceness

In Gheciu's chapter, the noviceness of those being exposed to counterattitudinal messages (to whom she refers colorfully as "baby generals") is a critical scope condition. Hooghe finds the same thing, except that noviceness combines with youth to encourage socialization for officials in the European Commission. This is believable because these are actors most likely to experience "primacy effects," in which early experience and information will have out-of-proportionate effects on inferences drawn from later experiences and information.[23] New states (specifically their decision makers and often their agents acting inside institutions for the first time) literally have had to determine what their foreign policy interests are on a range of novel issue-areas. They have to decide in which of myriad social environments in IR they should participate (for example, which institutions, which communities of states—middle power or major power; developed or developing). They also have to decide which competitive and cooperative relations to foster.[24]

But while novices may be more susceptible to persuasion and communicative action, this is not the only route to socialization. Novices are also more likely to mimic. As I noted above, while it is strategic behavior, mimicking is not necessarily optimizing behavior. At one level it is survival behavior, doing what is minimally necessary to survive in a new environment by copying what most other actors are doing. At another level, however, it can be behavior that maximizes self-valuation by demonstrating competence in a new environment. Some literature on organizational culture argues that actors have a desire to appear to be competent in their own eyes. This is done by adopting the trappings of competence in their field of endeavor— the discourse, symbolic practices, and even physical appearances that are presumed to indicate competence. This is sometimes called auto-communication.[25] Thus

---

[22] This draws from the threshold model of social action in Granovetter 1978, 1420–43. The empirical problem is measuring the distribution in willingness to comply before exposure to the institution and its normative message. Modeling this process would also require taking advantage of agent-based modeling techniques.

[23] See Choi 1993, 52–53.

[24] See, for instance, the argument in Chafetz, Abramson, and Grillot 1996. The authors argue that the debate in the Ukraine in the 1990s over whether to sign the Non-Proliferation Treaty (NPT) was in large measure a debate over whether Ukraine's identity was that of a great power (hence it could legitimately keep and develop nuclear weapons), or a middle European power (in which case it should denuclearize and join the NPT).

[25] Broms and Gahmberg 1983.

mimicking and auto-communication may feature more prominently in the conformist behavior of novices than in nonnovice actors inside an institution.

Domestic Variables

One of the important features of this project on European socialization is its sensitivity to the domestic or national political constraints on the socialization of state agents inside international organizations. Clearly the pace, process, and outcome of socialization inside one environment will be affected by socialization in a previous environment. Actors are usually not blank slates when they enter new social environments, though the degree to which "fresh and beautiful characters" can be written on new entrants will vary.[26] There are domestic and organizational sources of resistance to socialization that, in combination with socialization processes inside institutions, should lead to hybrid socialization outcomes. Or, alternatively, as some chapters here argue, domestic political structures could militate against international socialization entirely.

National Socialization Versus International Socialization. A number of essays (Beyers, Gheciu, Hooghe) raise an interesting, although understudied question: Why is it that national allegiances and / or allegiances to national-level organizational and bureaucratic interests remain strong in the face of supranational socialization processes? Beyers invokes three institutional reasons connected to socialization in national bureaucracies as well. Yet the answer is not as obvious as one might expect. After all, there are powerful discourses inside some national bureaucracies in many of these countries in favor of further integration, and in favor of the notion of "Europeanness." Moreover, many of these individuals spend considerable time away from national and organizational environments when they operate in European bureaucracies.

So what is it about these particular national levels of allegiance that seems so powerful? An answer to this question might suggest why the project finds a "European identity deficit." In principle there are a range of hypotheses (not all of which will apply to European states today, though this will depend on the demographics of some state agents in European institutions)[27]:

- Primary and primacy effects: state agents' first and most intensive period of socialization occurs inside the main institutions of state socialization (for example, education systems) and from exposure to the myriad symbols of state sovereignty—national anthems, passports, political participation in national rather than supranational collective expressions of a will (voting), and so on. Thus it should not be surprising that the strongest allegiances are to the state and its definitions of interest.

---

[26] To paraphrase Mao Zedong's comment about peasants being similar to blank sheets of paper.
[27] Some of these are raised in Hooghe, this volume.

- Intensity effects: socialization by institutions at the state level is more powerful because of the time spent in them and by the often zero-sum presentation of national allegiances (one cannot be both patriotic and internationalist).

- Boundary policing: it should not be surprising that policing ingroup identity is easier whether at the national and / or national organizational level or at the supranational or international organizational level. It is common in most types of ingroups to have formal and informal methods for punishing those with excessively liminal identities.[28] These mechanisms can include discourses that draw clear lines between the traits that the ingroup is expected to exhibit, in contrast to those of the outgroup. These discourses are signaling devices: those who do not exhibit these traits or who exhibit hybrid, liminal traits, will be exposed to peer pressure, physical coercion, threats, sanctions, and so on. Different groups have different membership rules.[29] The concept of treason, and its legal, economic, political, and personal sanctions, is a long-standing policing tool used against liminal identities at the national level. Different states have different definitions of treason. But in general, many have come to expect violations of national allegiances to be among the least easily forgiven of many kinds of social identities, and the kind of violation that brings down the power of the state on the heads of individuals and groups.[30]

But this raises an implication for this project, underexplored here. Perhaps one of the reasons for an underdeveloped supranational identity is that European-level mechanisms for policing identity are more or less absent. There are no powerful European-level institutions, for instance, that "punish" agents for holding liminal or cross-national and cross-regional identities.

This raises another possibility. Perhaps there is little policing by either national institutions or European institutions of the identities of those who participate in supranational organizations precisely because no contradiction is seen between having memberships in both groups. This is perhaps the true innovation in European identities—a discourse that reduces the incompatibility between the national and the supranational levels of identity. Indeed, arguably the essence of Western Europe's liberalism is that multiple identities are legitimate. This leads to the proposition that the key identity change for most state agents inside European institutions is not the emergence of a supranational identity as much as the emergence at the national level of identities that do not view a supranational identity as a particularly competitive "other."

There is a third possibility (raised by Hooghe's chapter), namely a hybridization process whereby national and international socialization, combined, produce variants of each level of norms. Acharya calls this "localization": norm-takers "build congruence between transnational norms—including norms previously institutionalized in

---

[28] See Burke and Tully 1977, on the effects of sex stereotyping on ostracism and bullying.

[29] Fearon, 1999.

[30] In contrast, in most liberal democracies defection from what in the past were quite rigid identity groups—for example, religious allegiances, sexual orientations, and class—does not carry these sorts of state-sanctioned penalties, at least not as much as it has in the past.

a region—and local beliefs and practices."[31] Acharya discusses some of the scope conditions under which hybridization (or localization) might occur. Unfortunately, however, the literature is quite spare when it comes to a priori determining when and under what conditions a new norm comes mostly from national or mostly from international level socialization.

The State-Society Relationship.   Schimmelfennig suggests that when populations are weakly mobilized (because of underdeveloped party systems), political elites are under less bottom-up pressure to conform to demands for normative changes from other states or international institutions. Transnational mobilization is less likely on these sorts of normative issues. By default, then, material incentives and disincentives are likely to be more effective in compelling political elites to change domestic policies. Moreover, variation in compliance through socialization will also depend on how liberal or illiberal these political elites are to begin with. It would be worth exploring these hypotheses further, however, because I think the causal arguments could go in a number of different directions. Mansfield and Snyder argue, for instance, that in newly democratizing states with underdeveloped party systems, the population can actually be overmobilized, particularly through appeals to nationalism.[32] This can, over time, constrain political elites (via blowback in nationalist ideologies). Following this line of argument, the reason for resistance to nonmaterial incentives for normative conformity may have more to do with society-level resistance to socialization attempts than political elite resistance. Conversely, a weak society, and low political mobilization, may give political elites the political space to endorse and push through new norms (embodied in legal and political reforms, say) that are being promoted by outside actors.[33]

Issues

The essays in this volume look at socialization in a wide variety of issue-areas in which European institutions have some jurisdiction—minority rights, civil-military relations, domestic elections, EU agenda setting, and so on. As I noted, the evidence for socialization, especially of the persuasion / communicative action kind, looks weakest on identity and ethnic conflict issues. Yet if Gheciu is right, it seems that these socialization processes worked quite well when it came to something as fundamental to political reform inside states as how the coercive arm of the state relates to the political arm (for example, civil-military relations in Eastern Europe). So it would seem worthwhile to categorize issue-areas more systematically according to their hypothesized effects on socialization.

In a sense, the chapters in this volume, together provide a rich list of scope conditions, a list of potentially relevant independent and intervening variables that could be

---

[31]   Acharya 2004, 241.
[32]   Mansfield and Snyder 2002.
[33]   See Risse-Kappen 1995.

tested on a shared set of dependent variables. While this project is important precisely because of the wide range of socialization phenomena it is trying to explain, pushing the causal hypotheses further would require one or both of two different projects: (1) a project in which these hypotheses and scope conditions were more systematically retested on the dependent variables in the various articles in this volume (for example, testing for Gheciu's micro-processes on Schimmelfennig's dependent variables); and (2) a project that tests each of these independent and intervening variables on a shared dependent variable.

This latter type of project would have to be clearer about what the relevant dependent variables were for testing the effects of socialization processes. It is clear that socialization research is at an early stage. Like the early stage of contractual institutionalist research, the goal is more or less to show that it happens, that it has ontological validity, in a sense, and, somewhat more vaguely, that it "matters" because one is seeing changes in preferences and interests that could not be explained otherwise. But, as with institutionalist theorizing, the next step is to show how much it matters and why. By definition, then, the next stage will involve looking at a range of different dependent variables to see how far socialization extends into different arenas and types of human political behavior. Thus there is nothing wrong with socialization theorizing dealing with a range of different dependent variables. I can think of several discrete dependent variables and one highly complex dependent variable (more properly, an "emergent property").[34]

The list of discrete dependent variables might include the following (some of these come from individual chapters):

- The effects of socialization on the identities and preferences of individual, human agents / actors. This is essentially the dependent variable of many of the essays in this volume.

- The foreign policies of states (in which case the link between individual socialization, mediated by state foreign policy processes, and state policy becomes a critical variable). In a sense, Schimmelfennig looks at this dependent variable.

- The evolution of the international institution itself—its organizational structures, normative structures and ideological message, and its performance as an agent in the socialization of human actors.

- The quantity and quality of interstate cooperation and integration in some functional area.

- Variation in regional organizational / normative structures around the globe.

- Variation in the institution's capacity to channel or focus "bottom-up," social-movement pressure on states.[35]

---

[34] All of these, of course, could at some point be independent variables as well.

[35] For instance, UN summit meetings in the 1990s were increasingly designed to allow nongovernmental organization (NGO) pressure to be placed on state delegations. The ASEAN Regional Forum and its NGO Track II partner, the Council on Security Cooperation in the Asia-Pacific, however, are highly elite-based, with no avenues for mass "peace and security" NGOs to participate.

The "emergent property" captures, basically, how the integration of all these discrete variables affects agent-structure constitution across time and space. That is, perhaps the end point of this research should be to close the loop that connects institutions-as-normative-agents vertically to the teaching and learning at the human agent level within states, and from there to the effect of horizontal interaction of multiple agents at the single state level, and from there to the creation of "hybrid" identity / interests in particular states, and from there to the effects of these new hybrid interests on interstate relations, and from there to the effects of these interstate interactions back to the organizational and normative structure of institutions at time $t + n$.

Many of the essays in this project are focused on how participation in institutions changes identities, interests, normative models, notions of appropriateness, and so on, in individuals as national agents. In a sense, this project thus picks up where Finnemore's "teaching" left off and looks at the kinds of resistances (individual, organizational, ideological at the state level) to teaching inside institutions. This is important, but it is only one part of the entire structure-agent relationship that is of interest to the sociological turn in IR.

Actually conducting empirical research that captures the "emergent property" effects of socialization within institutions is, of course, the hard part. In principle it would require, I think, large-scale cooperative projects where the life cycle of one institution (and its normative structure) is followed for a few iterations. Individual researchers would look at the institution and its ideology at time t; the institution's impact on socializing state-level agents at $t + 1$; state-level agent responses at $t + 2$; state-level agent interaction within a state's foreign policy process at $t + 3$ (agent-principal interaction); interstate interaction at $t + 4$; state-institution interaction at $t + 5$; and changes in institution and ideology at $t + 6$; with this process repeated over a few iterations.

There are costs for untenured scholars to engage in this kind of collaborative work. It would be important, I think, to present to the IR theory community a bold, long-term research plan showing precisely where such disparate studies as work on socialization in security ideologies in Eastern Europe and work on the Europeanization of a Belgian bureaucrat fit into a project on the mutual constitution of agents and structures.

Persuasion and 'Thin Rationalism'

As I noted earlier, persuasion is, in a sense, the trump card for demonstrating the added value of socialization approaches. This is because, if shown, persuasion suggests that preferences and identities do change and that they change in the absence of material incentives and disincentives. This does not undermine logic of consequences arguments about identity or preference change; it only establishes that there are places where argument and emotion help explain changes in actor motivation. But persuasion may also be fairly rare. Obviously at some point agents have to internalize a set of norms and values. It just is not clear that the independent effects of persuasion as opposed to consequentialist calculus can be separated out all that neatly, even if one adopts the micro-focused analysis that some of the chapters do here. Checkel suggests that the essays in this volume show the value of a "thin rationalist"–constructivist synthesis.[36] I agree with his critique of Risse, Ropp, and Sikkink that the incorporation of sharp, thin rationalist arguments can end up highlighting the more unwieldy, speculative and "soft" persuasion arguments that have been constructivism's trademark.

But I think it is also important for socialization theorists to point out that the thin rationalism they have in mind is in many respects fundamentally different from that used by more mainstream institutionalism. Contractualism has almost entirely neglected social thin rationalism in favor of material thin rationalism. Yet when one speaks of "normative pressure" in IR, one is talking about conformity for rational reasons but under conditions that are entirely "social." The "sociality" of this thin rationalist calculus comes in two forms.

First, actions (conformity to group norms) designed to maximize social status markers may be a "consequentialist" choice, but such a choice can only be made in a social environment in which members of a community are rewarding appropriate behavior with status markers. There has to be some common understanding between the actor and the community about the value of these markers as well.[37]

Second, because actors tend not to engage in audience shopping—they tend not to easily shift loyalties from group to group depending on which group maximizes status markers—this suggests a certain stickiness that is not captured by the materialist thin rationalism of contractualism. This stickiness is likely rooted in a sense of obligation to the social group or, perhaps more correctly, in at least some degree of identification with the values of the group. Otherwise, as noted, one would expect little stickiness in the search for status maximization. Thus, in the case of status maximization at least, the consequentialist calculus is still fundamentally different from side payments or sanctions of a material form provided by one actor or one institution acting as an agent. Expressed differently, social status cannot be a private side payment as technology transfers can be. Social status has to come from a community, not an autonomous privileged or powerful actor on the side. One could get a gold star from a friend for one's homework. But this will have no status value unless the star is bestowed publicly and comes endorsed by a valued social group. Moreover, one has to have some modicum of identification with this social group so that one does not go off looking for other groups that will give one larger or more golden stars (to press the metaphor perhaps too far!).

Another issue related to the status of "thin rationalism" in the study of socialization concerns strategic agency. No research project can do everything at once. But any follow-on to the agenda set by this volume might explicitly test for both the amount of strategic agency in the socialization story and the amount of unintended socialization in any strategic agency story. For instance, one might actually expect deeply socialized actors to be especially strategic in their behavior. Fundamentalists and true believers often have a particularly amoral approach to strategy, given their strong beliefs in the

---

[36] Checkel, this volume.
[37] I outline the social influence argument and the role of social back patting and shaming in more detail in Johnston 2001.

correctness of their cause and in the utter lack of legitimacy in the cause of others. At the most extreme, if one believes that the outgroup is devoid of moral capacity and that it thus threatens one's existence, then any and all means are justified in dealing with the outgroup. I am not suggesting that true-believer European supranationalists are Leninists when it comes to tactics and strategy. I am simply suggesting that the more deeply committed one is to a principle, oftentimes the more likely it is that one will behave strategically in an "ends justify the means" way. One might actually expect to see a U-shaped relationship, with degree of strategic calculation on the y axis, and true opportunism to true belief on the x axis. One sign of both shallow and deep socialization in new values may in fact be highly strategic behavior designed to promote these values. Therefore, strategic behavior, per se, does not necessarily undermine the possibility of prior socialization.

Socialization and Identity Change

The "strong" or maximum constructivist claim about pure socialization is that persuasion leads not just to change in causal arguments, or even principled ideas, but in identities and then in interests. Often the invoked "theory" of identity that links identity change to behavior is role-theoretic, that is, actors literally act out behaviors considered appropriate to the new roles they have internalized. While the essays in this volume go farther in delving into the mechanisms behind socialization than any study of which I am aware, I think it is important to push further into the mechanisms of identity change and normative conformity. This requires more specificity, first, about the logical range of identity change possible. The chapters as a whole suggest that actors, after exposure to an international institution, could discover that:

- Their primary identification is with the institution's interests first, and with national interests second.
- There is no fundamental conflict between identification with the institution's interests and with national interests, as was believed before.
- Their primary identification is with a new ideology and its associated practices.

Next, one would want to ask: what are the mechanisms that link particular institutional designs with particular types of identity change? As Checkel notes, for instance, the duration and intensity of exposure to an institution may actually lead to two distinct routes to identity change.[38] The frequency of proactive participation may lead to more intensive identification with the institution through the processes that Cialdini referred to under the rubric of "consistency theory."[39] Actors will tend to believe more strongly that they are a certain type of person if they are asked to make increasingly strong public statements in favor of some cause. This might be the function of frequent oral presentations to a group. In addition, having "informal contacts outside the formal

[38] Checkel, this volume.
[39] Cialdini 1985, chap. 3.

committee meetings" could also lead to higher levels of identification with the group. This process might be explained by network theories, "social liking" theories, or "status enhancement" theories, all of which suggest that more informal, face-to-face interaction increases the likelihood that individuals will do things they believe will be liked by liked others.

There are at least three issues here. The first is what kind of identity change one should expect from participation in international institutions. Unpacking the content of identity, one could argue that identities are composed of four somewhat overlapping components or dimensions: normative or constitutive beliefs and practices, beliefs about the social purposes of the group, beliefs about the group's relationship to other groups, and cognitive processes or worldviews.[40] Which dimensions of identity content is socialization in institutions more likely to change? Which behavioral practices do actors believe are constitutive of group identity? How do actors define the purposes of the extant ingroup? The entativity of other social groups with which the agent interacts? Or the cognitive models with which the agent understands how the world works? Gheciu's research suggests, for instance, that socialization mainly involves changing constitutive norms, and perhaps cognitive worldviews. In Hooghe's case, one of the main dependent variables is preferences about supranationalism—in essence, peoples' beliefs about how the EU should be constituted. In Beyers' case, the focus on role identity combines elements of change in constitutive norms and social purposes. In Lewis' case, identity change inside COREPER appears to mean a change in constitutive norms and in cognitive worldviews. But one could also imagine that a group's constitutive norms, social purposes, and cognitions may remain static, while beliefs about who the outgroup is could change. One could also imagine a change in constitutive norms without a change in social purpose or in perceived outgroups. The point is simply that if the socialization literature continues to work with a relatively unproblematized and blunt notion of identity, it is possible that null findings for one element of identity (such as constitutive practices) might obscure positive findings for some other elements of identity (a Type II error). One would thus run the risk of miscoding the effects of institutions on actors inside of them.

The second issue concerns the theories of action that link identity to behavior. Role theory is not the only way to think about the link between identity and action. Social identity theory provides a different theory of action. The authors in this volume use different theories of action. Beyers uses a role-theoretic notion of identity. Gheciu implies some kind of social identity theory in which identity expresses taken-for-granted characterizations of self and other. Yet these are two different theories with two different kinds of empirical evidence that "identity" matters. Role theory stresses the relevance of the content of identity to the kinds of actions considered appropriate. Social identity theory (SIT), in its basic form, downplays the importance of the content of identity in favor of the competition-inducing effects of having an identity, regardless of its content or characteristics. The former basically proposes that norms of appropriate behavior provide notions of self-efficacy and self-esteem. The latter suggests that evidence of identity change would involve changes

[40] Abdelal et al. 2005.

in conceptions of "ingroupness," new definitions of boundaries, changes in self-valuation as new allegiances are created, and action motivated by a desire to maximize group valuation.

So, if one focuses on how socialization affects identities and, in turn, behavior, ideally both the role-theoretic understanding of this relationship and SIT-based understandings should be tested against each other. It may be that SIT is actually empirically wrong when applied to European institutions. But it seems to be a powerful argument when one looks at the effects of socialization in other kinds of institutions (national, military, clubs, gangs, and so on). One wonders what it is about European international institutions that makes the effects of induction into their ideological and normative environment best captured by role-theoretic and not SIT-based processes.

The third issue has to do with the methods for observing identity change. The conclusion is this: regardless of whether one is conducting interviews, surveys, or textual content analysis, the trick is to isolate the characteristics that respondents believe are central to the group identity they believe they have, the intensity with which they identify with the group, the degree of difference they believe exists between own-group characteristics and other-group characteristics, and the appropriate behaviors associated with these different identity memberships.

Showing appropriateness is an exceedingly hard thing to do. As it is used in constructivist literature, appropriateness can mean at least three different things. First, it can mean that behavioral alternatives were never actively considered by agents with one identity, while agents with another might actively consider them. If one were using cognitive mapping, this would mean that because of internalized notions of appropriateness, entire cause-effect relationships would simply not show up in the maps because the actor was not consciously thinking about alternative ways of achieving some desired end.

Second, appropriateness could mean that behavioral alternatives are considered for a moment but are heavily discounted because they are considered useless or normatively objectionable (or they are considered useless because they are normatively objectionable).

The third possibility is that a behavior is chosen because it is considered appropriate for maximizing social rewards. The actor knows from experience that there is a severely limited range of behaviors that will be rewarded by the group socially; thus, alternatives are never considered. Behavior is automatic and optimizing at the same time.

These three different possibilities basically capture the difference between deep socialization / internalization (taken-for-grantedness where actors are simply unaware of their habits of group conformity) versus somewhat deep internalization (appropriateness where inappropriate options are consciously rejected) versus social influence.[41] What are the ways of getting at these differences? Hopf suggests that scholars

---

[41] This is somewhat similar to Hopf's distinction between logics of habit, the logics of appropriateness, and the logics of consequences. See Hopf 2002. The main difference is that at least one manifestation of socialization—social influence—works only because the influencer and the influenced view the bestowal and acceptance of status markers in instrumental ways. The influencer uses them to extract compliance; the influenced uses them to satisfy a psychological need for status recognition. In this

draw up a kind of highly inductive inventory of identity terms and references in popular culture, for instance. These references should help capture assumptions about self and other that are habitual and unquestioned.[42] Another possibility is cognitive mapping. Cognitive mapping entails breaking down selected texts from a decision-making process into all of their component cause-effect relationships.[43] The technique can help uncover the deep structure of an argument—the presence or absence of certain cause-effect assumptions, and the consistencies and inconsistencies across cause-effect arguments. The consistent absence of certain cause-effect relationships related to particular strategic choices might indicate that these choices are simply cognitively inconceivable. Another method might involve close participant-observation, with prior training in clinical psychology interview techniques to observe reactions (as Kull did so effectively in his study of nuclear war-fighters in the Reagan administration[44]).

One final comment about identity: Does one really need to show that supranational loyalties have emerged to show that socialization in institutions has been effective? I am not a Europeanist, but my sense is that among the ideological messages that European institutions are trying to promote, particularly in the East, are liberal values of tolerance and diversity. This means, I assume, that evidence of a changed identity could also include new understandings of national identity, not just supranational identity. Identification with "European-ness" could be manifest in acceptance that multiculturalism is a legitimate part of one's national identity; a strengthened commitment to one's local democratic institutions. This point is taken up by Beyers. There are two components to this argument, however: (1) that changes in national identity come from intensive participation in European institutions; and (2) that changes in national identity come before participation in these institutions—that national-level policies of integration actually change national-level conceptions of identity, such that European supranationalism becomes compatible with national identity. Indeed, some of the new work on nationalism argues that national identity emerges from and/or alongside local identities that accommodate national allegiances as a natural extension, rather than the elimination, of local identities.[45]

One way of getting at this question of whether national-level socialization is incompatible with the emergence of supranational identities would not be to look for evidence of socialization in supranational values, but to look for evidence (or the absence) of national policing against supranational values. As noted earlier, social-psychological work on how ingroups harass liminal identities suggests that powerful, though indirect, evidence of identity change is whether the ingroups detect and punish, police, or discipline these people. So, too, national bureaucracies may be alert to the possibility of supranational identity formation. These bureaucracies should only be so if they perceive there to be a tension or competition between the two. If there are

---

regard, I would agree with Checkel, who notes that socialization mechanisms should not a priori exclude elements of strict rationality and bounded rationality. See Checkel, this volume.

[42] Hopf 2002, chap. 2.
[43] Axelrod 1976.
[44] Kull 1988.
[45] See Confine and Skaria 2002.

no such efforts, then perhaps this means there is no perceived contradiction between the two levels of identification.

Empirical Extensions Beyond Europe

One could argue that European institutions constitute a relatively easy case for showing the processes and effects of socialization. The conventional wisdom has it that they are the most complex, most legalistic, most bureaucratized, most focused on the active inculcation of liberal values across national boundaries, and so on. If so, do the findings suffer from a *sui generis* problem? On the one hand, it would seem obvious that this is potentially a major problem, because nowhere in the world are interstate relations so bound up with international institutional commitments. The degree of European integration at the interstate, substate, and nonstate levels creates an overdetermination problem, depending on one's dependent variable. If the dependent variable is, for instance, "identification with European-ness" or "preference for multilateral solutions to national problems," there are so many routes through which individuals, even in government positions, could be exposed to the ideology and identity of "European-ness" (personal contact; travel; national education systems; experience in the EU; experience in those portions of the national bureaucracies designed to interact with the EU, the media, and so on, the intensity and extensiveness of which exceed any other region in the world except perhaps North America), that it would be hard to disaggregate the separate effects of all these possible socialization experiences at the microlevel. In addition to these multiple channels of socialization, the low level of interstate security threats suggests that identity socialization at the national level will be a weaker counterweight to supranational socialization than in other parts of the globe.

On the other hand, this *sui generis* feature of the European case could help generate at least one powerful theoretical argument. That is, precisely because Europe, compared to other regions and their institutions, may be an "easy" or "most likely" case for socialization arguments, if socialization arguments, in essence, fail in the European case, this is a fairly telling blow to the whole theoretical approach. If not in Europe, where?

Because socialization arguments, for a number of the authors in this volume, do not fail in the European context, the obvious question is, where else might they work? Unfortunately the field of comparative regional institutional studies is almost nonexistent in IR. Few specialists in the international relations and international institutions of different regions of the globe have sat down to compare whether socialization processes are limited to the "rich" institutional life of European interstate relations. This cross-regional dialogue has just begun in the academic community with a project on "Crafting Cooperation: The Design and Efficacy of Regional Institutions in Comparative Perspective," a project jointly sponsored by Harvard University and the Institute for Defence and Strategic Studies in Singapore. The project brings together people who specialize in both IR and area studies to examine similarities and differences in Asian, European, Latin American, African, and Middle Eastern regional institutions. It is too early to tell whether any systematic cross-regional differences exist, in part because in some regions institutional design is dynamic. Southeast Asian institutions (ASEAN ARE, for instance)—widely viewed as deliberately "underinstitutionalized" and based on informal, elite-based consensus-driven deliberation on issues that exclude domestic governance questions—may be changing in more intrusive and bureaucratized directions. Some Latin American institutions are as formally complex as some European institutions, yet the practice of solving disputes inside them often tends to rely on informal elite interaction.[46]

My first reaction, as an Asianist, to the question of whether there might be useful comparisons or extensions of the arguments in this volume to institutions in Asia, was envy. First, there is virtually no one doing work that is similar theoretically or empirically to this project on European institutions. The best work in this regard is being done by Acharya. It is hard for one individual, however, to go into the level of empirical detail and to employ the range of theoretical and methodological tools that, combined, these chapters provide. There is, as far as I am aware, no systematic effort to examine how intensity or quality of exposure to ASEAN or the ARF, for instance, has affected the attitudes and allegiances of key participants, or how issue-area or institutional design may have a systematic effect on the propensity of actors to endorse values distinct from their national government. The systematic study of institutions and socialization in the Asia-Pacific has been underdeveloped.

My work focuses on the mechanisms of mimicking, persuasion, and social influence, with an empirical focus on China's participation in international security institutions such as the ASEAN Regional Forum, the Comprehensive Test Ban Treaty negotiations, the Conference on Disarmament in Geneva, the Protocol II of the Conventional Weapons Convention, and the Ottawa Treaty on antipersonnel landmines. It has taken me about 120 interviews over about eight to ten years to gain a partial understanding about some of the issues raised in this volume's essays. These interviews, and my analysis of discourses of multilateralism over time in Chinese foreign policy, suggest that one may be seeing in some instances similar processes to those described by Gheciu and Lewis. That is, there is some evidence that those individuals most directly exposed to intensive social interactions with individuals and groups that are strong proponents of regional security dialogues in the Asia-Pacific, for example, are more likely to have a positive attitude toward multilateralism than those who have not had this exposure. The nature of these security dialogues—deliberative, exploratory, and, for some, multilateralist activists an opportunity to "teach" new norms of security—seems to facilitate this socialization process.[47]

Still, to be honest, the richness and robustness of these conclusions about Chinese participants in regional security dialogues leaves something to be desired compared to the data on Europe. Access to bureaucrats who can be systematically interviewed or sampled for survey-style protocols is hampered by the fact that many of the relevant countries in the Asia-Pacific are authoritarian regimes in which foreign policy issues are off limits to public and academic debate.

---

[46] On the ASEAN Regional Forum, see Tan et al. 2002. On Latin America, see Dommguez 2002.
[47] For a summary of this research, see Johnston 2003.

Having said that, I think there is a reasonable chance of doing cross-regional surveys and interviews on institutions and identity, comparing Europe with non-authoritarian Asia-Pacific, North American, and South American institutions. Depending on the variables of interest, these contrasts could control for external threat environment, internal social-political stability, level of development, the temporal space that a region is in, the macro-historical diffusion of institutional models, colonial history and postcolonial ideology, as well as formal and informal rules of the institutions.

It is quite possible, of course, that what appear to be broad interregional differences in institutional design and effects disappear if one looks at specific processes within institutions across regions. I was struck, for instance, by potential similarities between the ASEAN Regional Forum and COREPER in terms of the effects of small-group interaction, particularly the role of persuasion in effecting changing views of "national interest." Indeed, I think that Lewis' research methods in analyzing COREPER might be usefully reproduced in an analysis of the ARF and its Track II companion, the Council on Security Cooperation in the Asia Pacific. Another interesting study, inspired by Hooghe's distinction between national (or primary) and international (or secondary) affiliations, might be cross-regional comparisons in attitudes toward regional institutions between national bureaucrats in foreign ministries with no exposure to or responsibility for these institutions, diplomats whose responsibility is to participate in these institutions, and the professional Track II academics and think tank members whose main responsibility is to generate ideas for the Track I multilateral institutions in the region. In the Asia-Pacific region, at least, one would expect the first group to exhibit the lowest level of support for multilateralism, and the last group to exhibit the highest level.

I am also intrigued by potential comparisons among the effects of socialization processes on state agents from countries that are not far removed from the political and strategic culture of Marxist-Leninist systems—undemocratic and hard realpolitik. Here, comparisons between Gheciu's Eastern European cases and Chinese, Vietnamese, or North Korean diplomats would be instructive. Obviously the starting conditions are different—China is not officially eager for interactions on civil-military relations, or seminars on conflict management from the Organization for Security and Cooperation in Europe (OSCE). But the processes Gheciu describes, if transportable in some politically acceptable fashion, seem to *be prime facie* evidence in favor of intensive military-to-military engagement between the United States and its allies and China.

The major problem in doing any of these comparisons, of course, is access to diplomats or state agents. In the ARF case, for instance, some delegations allow academic participant-observers (Canada and Australia), while others (China) clearly do not.

Conclusion

One of the standard, usually valid, criticisms of any new analytical approach in international relations is the academic version of "where's the beef"—what does it tell us about the empirical world and the empirical puzzles that have been central to IR as a subfield? Theorizing about socialization in IR has been criticized for being long on meta-theory but short on testable hypotheses and empirical analysis. This criticism has not just come from those who are fundamentally skeptical of the "sociological" turn in IR, but also from its sympathizers.[48]

This volume has responded to this criticism, and admirably, in my view. To do this it has gone to mid-range theorizing, eclectically borrowing hypotheses from other subfields and testing them on a "most likely case" to see whether it is worth going further with the concept of socialization. In general, this is a smart research strategy for a novel approach in IR. It avoids alienating much of the field with another debate about meta-theory.[49] By examining Europe first, it also can quickly establish whether or not pursuing socialization theory further is a dead end or not, given the most-likely-case status of European IR in this regard.

Specifically, the chapters show the value of using mid-range theories about exposure effects (for example, primacy, recency, intensity), persuasion, social influence, cognitive role playing, and identity for analyzing the real-world policy implications of the social effects of human interaction inside different institutional environments. These essays have outlined a range of scope conditions under which each of these different mechanisms are hypothesized to work—conditions that range from the nature of state-society relations to the degree of "noviceness" of actors to the length of time actors have been exposed to new social environments.

In a sense, the chapters collectively show that what is called a sociological turn is really a sociological and psychological turn. It remains to be seen whether this particular application of psychology in IR will meet the same fate as the application of psychology in comparative foreign policy analysis—namely being looked down upon by the field as a whole in favor of pristine deductive theorizing. But I suspect not, for at least three reasons. First, the socialization research agenda, while focused thus far on fairly narrow and discrete empirical cases (for example, attitudes toward civil-military relations in Eastern Europe) actually addresses perhaps the most fundamental issue in IR, that of the origins and evolution of actor preferences.

Second, the socialization approach is, I believe, sustained methodologically and ontologically by the growing realization in the social sciences in general that outcomes are often the nonlinear emergent properties of multiple adaptive agents. In other words, whether it falls under the rubric of complexity theory, agent-based modeling, or parallel processing, there is a growing willingness to accept that endogeneity is a "fact" of politics and IR, and thus agent-structure interaction is a more insightful, if

---

[48] See Checkel 1998.

[49] I do not think that these meta-theory debates should stop, however. There is a danger that the field, having started with debates that assumed the complete incommensurability of rationalist and constructivist approaches, may swing to the other extreme, to the view that there is complete complementarity. At least in terms of research practice, rationalists have tended to start from a materialist ontology; constructivists from an ideational one. It is hard to see how these two can be easily reconciled. The fault line, then, is not so much rationalism versus constructivism, but the rationalist tendency to default to maximizing material interest versus the constructivist tendency to default to ideational appropriateness as the keys to understanding human behavior. These two starting points may indeed be incommensurate and it is important to understand, therefore, the implications of both for IR research.

still hard to execute, mode of analysis than the traditional linear regression-type mode. (I include in this latter mode the standard comparative case study method as well.) This ontology requires micro-analyses, precisely what these articles do by focusing on the study of individuals in small groups. Perhaps this is the start of applying the agent-based modeling concept to case-based empirical analysis. (I will return to this in a moment.)

Third, the socialization approach—particularly as developed in this volume— does not exclude a priori any "theory" of human action—such as strategic optimization, strategic satisficing, normative appropriateness, identity role playing, and habituation. While those working with this approach are most likely to be labeled constructivists or fellow travelers, this obscures the fact that they are more inclusive about motivation, hence about the methods of analysis and the range of empirical data used in IR, than both what is usually labeled "the mainstream" (versions of realism, and international political economy) and what is labeled the "marginalized" (postmodernism).

If this volume is a good start to the empirical analysis of socialization mechanisms, what is the next step? I do not intend to recap all the criticisms and suggestions for extensions that Checkel, Zürn and Checkel, and I have listed in our chapters.[50] But I have pulled out three related clusters of suggestions.

First, socialization research needs to focus more on comparison with other regions, other periods of time, and other socialization environments. For instance, beyond how European institutions might encourage socialization to be more supportive of institutional cooperation or new ideas about democratic notions of civil-military relations, scholars need to look more at how different levels of resistances to socialization might lead to hybrid or localized normative change.[51] It is clear from this project that prior to socialization in or by international institutions, national agents are socialized in their national-level organizations. How does national or local-level socialization filter or affect inter-, supra-, or transnational socialization attempts? Related to this is the question of socialization and noncooperative behavior. Not to be too repetitive, but I think that the general complaint against constructivist-related research on identity, normative, or social-psychological change in agents—namely, that this work focuses too much on cases of cooperation that mainstream IR believes are less central to traditional concerns about war and peace—is not entirely inaccurate. Constructivism has to argue that realpolitik behavior is norm- and identity-driven as well. How, then, is realpolitik socialization to be understood? What are the detailed mechanisms by which agents come to believe that it is natural, acceptable, and appropriate to act in realpolitik fashion? Unsuccessful socialization in cooperative norms at time t could very well mean successful socialization in realpolitik norms at time $t - n$.

Second, socialization research needs to think more about methods. This goes beyond investigating the value, for instance, of testing one author's propositions on another author's cases, as I suggested earlier about the essays in this volume. It includes a more fundamental look at how to access the most difficult, though most

[50] See Checkel, this volume; and Zürn and Checkel, this volume.
[51] See Acharya 2004.

central, piece of the socialization puzzle: how does one show changes in how agents understand their identities and preferences after they have been exposed to socialization environments? How does one show appropriateness or habituation in decision making? How does one show change in the content of agent identities? How does one show the depth of socialization (how does one show changes in the tradeoffs that agents would make under realistic conditions before and after socialization experiences)? There may be some potentially promising methods outside of the traditional toolbox of mainstream international relations (for example, cognitive mapping to show the absence of certain choices in the cause-effect arguments of actors after their socialization; semantic-differential analysis of changes in the content of agents' beliefs about their identity, among others).[52] But these will need to be tested and calibrated.

Third, socialization research needs to think more about research design. I do not mean by this simply the problems of case selection, the selection of appropriate methods, and alternative hypothesis testing. What I mean is how to research the endogeneity at the heart of socialization claims—agents interacting with agents producing changes in normative structures, which in turn resocialize or differently socialize agents and so on. This kind of research will rest on two key steps. The first is to figure out the prior distribution among relevant agents of their susceptibility to persuasion, in their sensitivity to image/status markers, of their willingness to brave policing by the ingroup in order to hold on to liminal identities. This distribution will affect the speed, depth, and content of socialization, that is, whether one should expect a strict reproduction of prior norms, their hybridization or localization, or their complete rejection. How does one measure this prior distribution?

The second step is to figure out how to empirically test this endogeneity process. The analogical method is agent-based modeling using computers. How does one organize a research project whereby all relevant agents and their iterated interactions with each other and with the emergent property (normative structure) are traced empirically systematically over time and space? The empirical data requirements are intimidating to say the least. Pragmatically it would require multiple researchers with multiple skills working on the same research puzzle. It would, in short, require lab-like research workshops, producing multiauthored research products. Unfortunately the social sciences are not set up for rewarding this kind of research financially or in terms of career opportunities, especially for untenured faculty. Atomized, individual research on a case of socialization here or a case of socialization there only covers one small part of the entire endogeneity processes.

The bottom line, then, is that moving forward in analyzing socialization in international relations requires a much more fundamental rethinking of how research is conceptualized and conducted in IR. Indeed, it requires the resocialization of a field.

---

[52] For examples of how these and other methods might be applied to the analysis of identity and identity change, see Abdelal et al 2005. Some useful tools have actually been used in comparative foreign policy analysis for some time (for example, cognitive mapping and other forms of cognitive-linguistic analysis, and content analysis), but many IR scholars are not routinely exposed to these methods.

References

Abdelal, Rawi, Yoshiko M. Herrera, Alastair Iain Johnston, and Rose McDermott. 2005. Identity as a Variable. Paper presented at the Harvard Identity Project Conference, December, Cambridge, Mass.

Acharya, Amitav. 2004. How Ideas Spread: Whose Norms Matter? Norm Localization and Institutional Change in Asian Regionalism. *International Organization* 58 (2):239–75.

Alter, Karen. 2002. Delegating to International Courts: Why, How, and the Problems in Doing So. Paper presented at the Conference on Delegation to International Organizations, Park City, Utah. Available at ⟨http://www.internationalorganizations.org/alter.PDF⟩. Accessed 22 June 2005.

Axelrod, Robert, ed. 1976. *The Structure of Decision: The Cognitive Maps of Political Elites.* Princeton, N.J.: Princeton University Press.

Axsom, Danny, Suzanne Yates, and Shelley Chaiken. 1987. Audience Response Cues as a Heuristic Cue in Persuasion. *Journal of Personality and Social Psychology* 53 (1):30–40.

Biddle, Bruce J. 1985. Social Influence, Self-Referent Identity Labels and Behavior. *Sociological Quarterly* 26 (2):59–86.

Bourdieu, Pierre. 1991. *Language and Symbolic Power*, edited by John B. Thompson. Cambridge, Mass.: Harvard University Press.

Broms, Henri, and Henrik Gahmberg. 1983. Communication to Self in Organizations and Cultures. *Administrative Science Quarterly* 28 (3):482–95.

Burke, Peter J., and Judy C. Tully. 1977. The Measurement of Role Identity. *Social Forces* 55 (4):881–97.

Chafetz, Glenn, Hillel Abramson, and Suzette Grillot. 1996. Role Theory and Foreign Policy: Belarussian and Ukrainian Compliance with the Nuclear Nonproliferation Regime. *Political Psychology* 17 (4):727–57.

Checkel, Jeffrey T. 1998. The Constructivist Turn in International Relations Theory. *World Politics* 50 (2):324–48.

Choi, Young Back. 1993. *Paradigms and Conventions: Uncertainty, Decisionmaking, and Entrepreneurship.* Ann Arbor: University of Michigan Press.

Cialdini, Robert. 1985. *Influence: The New Psychology of Modern Persuasion.* New York: Quill Books.

————. 1987. Compliance Principles of Compliance Professionals: Psychologists of Necessity. In *Social Influence: The Ontario Symposium on Personality and Social Psychology*, Vol. 5, edited by Mark P. Zanna, James M. Olson, and Peter Herman, 165–84. Hillsdale, N.J.: Lawrence Erlbaum.

Cialdini, R. B., C. A. Kallgren, and R. R. Reno. 1991. A Focus Theory of Normative Conduct: A Theoretical Refinement and Reevaluation of the Role of Norms in Human Behavior. In *Advances in Experimental Social Psychology*, Vol. 24, edited by Mark P. Zanna, 201–34. New York: Academic Press.

Confine, Alon, and Ajay Skaria. 2002. The Local Life of Nationhood. *National Identities* 4 (1):7–23.

Dalby, Simon. 1990. American Security Discourse: The Persistence of Geopolitics. *Political Geography Quarterly* 9 (2):171–88.

Dominguez, Jorge I. 2002. Latin America's Long March toward International Cooperation: The Jigsaw-Puzzle Approach to the Design of Regional Institutions. Paper presented at the Crafting Cooperation: A Comparative Study of the Design and Efficacy of Regional Institutions conference, October, Harvard University, Cambridge, Mass.

Doty, Roxanne Lynn. 1993. Foreign Policy as Social Construction: A Post-Positivist Analysis of US Counterinsurgency Policy in the Philippines. *International Studies Quarterly* 37 (3):297–320.

Fairclough, Norman. 2003. Political Correctness: The Politics of Culture and Language. *Discourse and Society* 14 (1):17–28.

Fearon, James. 1999. What Is Identity (as We Now Use the Word)? Unpublished manuscript, Stanford University, Stanford, Calif.

Fearon, James, and Alexander Wendt. 2002. Rationalism vs. Constructivism: A Skeptical View. In *Handbook of International Relations*, edited by Walter Carlsnaes, Thomas Risse, and Beth Simmons, 52–72. London: Sage.

Feldman, Stanley, and Karen Stenner. 1997. Perceived Threat and Authoritarianism. *Political Psychology* 18 (4):741–70.

Fierke, K. M. 2002. Links Across the Abyss: Language and Logic in International Relations. *International Studies Quarterly* 46 (3):331–54.

Granovetter, Mark. 1978. Threshold Models of Collective Behavior. *American Journal of Sociology* 83 (6):1420–43.

Gumperz, John, and Stephen Levinson, eds. 1996. *Rethinking Linguistic Relativity.* Cambridge: Cambridge University Press.

Hirshleifer, David. 1995. The Blind Leading the Blind: Social Influence, Fads, and Informational Cascades. In *The New Economics of Human Behavior*, edited by Mariano Tommasi and Kathryn Ierulli, 188–215. Cambridge: Cambridge University Press.

Holland, John. 1996. *Hidden Order: How Adaptation Builds Complexity.* Boston: Addison-Wesley.

Hopf, Ted. 2002. *Social Constructions of International Politics: Identities and Foreign Policies, Moscow, 1955 and 1999.* Ithaca, N.Y.: Cornell University Press.

James, Michael Rabinder. 1998. Communicative Action and the Logics of Group Conflict. Paper presented at the 84th Annual Meeting of the American Political Science Association, September, Boston.

Johnston, Alastair Iain. 2001. Treating International Institutions as Social Environments. *International Studies Quarterly* 45 (4):487–515.

———. 2003. Socialization in International Institutions: The ASEAN Way and International Relations Theory. In *International Relations Theory and the Asia-Pacific*, edited by Michael Mastanduno and G. John Ikenberry, 487–516. New York: Columbia University Press.

Jorgensen, Charlotte, Christian Kock, and Lone Rorbech. 1998. Rhetoric that Shifts Votes: An Exploratory Study of Persuasion in Issue-Oriented Public Debates. *Political Communication* 15 (3):283–99.

Jost, John T., Arie W. Kruglanski, Jack Glaser, and Frank J. Sulloway. 2003. Political Conservatism as Motivated Social Cognition. *Psychological Bulletin* 129 (3):339–75.

Kelley, Judith. 2004. International Actors on the Domestic Scene: Membership Conditionality and Socialization by International Institutions. *International Organization* 58 (3):425–57.

Kull, Steven. 1988. *Minds at War: Nuclear Reality and the Inner Conflicts of Defense Policy Makers.* New York: Basic Books.

Mansfield, Edward, and Jack L. Snyder. 2002. Democratic Transitions, Institutional Strength, and War. *International Organization* 56 (2):297–337.

Marques, Jose, Dominic Abrams, and Rui Serôdio. 2001. Being Better by Being Right: Subjective Group Dynamics and Derogation of Ingroup Deviants When Generic Norms Are Undermined. *Journal of Personality and Social Psychology* 81 (3):436–47.

Mutz, Diana C., Paul M. Sniderman, and Richard A. Brody. 1996. Political Persuasion: The Birth of a Field of Study. In *Political Persuasion and Attitude Change*, edited by Diane C. Mutz, Paul M. Sniderman and Richard A. Brody, 1–16. Ann Arbor: University of Michigan Press.

Ochs, Elinor. 1986. Introduction. In *Language Socialization Across Cultures*, edited by Bambi B. Schi-effelin and Elinor Ochs, 1–13. Cambridge: Cambridge University Press.

Perell, Paul. 1987. Stare Decisis and Techniques of Legal Reasoning and Legal Argument. *Legal Research Update*, Nos. 2, 3. Available at: ⟨http://legalresearch.org/docs/perell.html⟩. Accessed 22 June 2005.

Risse-Kappen, Thomas, ed. 1995. *Bringing Transnational Relations Back In: Non-State Actors, Domestic Structures, and International Institutions.* Cambridge: Cambridge University Press.

Romer, Daniel, Kathleen H. Jamieson, Catharine Riegner, Mika Emori, and Brigette Rouson. 1997. Blame Discourse versus Realistic Conflict as Explanations of Ethnic Tension in Urban Neighborhoods. *Political Communication* 14 (3):273–91.

Rule, Brendon Gail, and Gay L. Bisanz. 1987. Goals and Strategies of Persuasion: A Cognitive Schema for Understanding Social Events. In *Social Influence: The Ontario Symposium on Personality and Social Psychology*, Vol. 5, edited by Mark P. Zanna, James M. Olson, and Peter Herman, 185–206. Hillsdale, N.J.: Lawrence Erlbaum.

Sapir, Edward. 1956. *Culture, Language and Personality*, edited by D. G. Mandelbaum. Berkeley: University of California Press.

Searle, John. 1992. *The Social Construction of Reality.* Cambridge, Mass.: MIT Press.

Tan, See Seng, Ralf Emmers, Mely Caballero-Anthony, Amitav Acharya, Barry Desker, and Kwa Chong Guan. 2002. *A New Agenda for the ASEAN Regional Forum.* Singapore: Institute for Defence and Strategic Studies.

Waever, Ole. 1990. The Language of Foreign Policy. *Journal of Peace Research* 27 (3):335–43.

Whorf, B. L. 1956. *Language, Thought and Reality*, edited by J. B. Carroll. Cambridge, Mass.: MIT Press.

Yee, Albert S. 1996. The Causal Effects of Ideas on Policies. *International Organization* 50 (1):69–108.

Zimbardo, Philip G., and Michael R. Leippe. 1991. *The Psychology of Attitude Change and Social Influence.* Boston: McGraw Hill.

8

Getting Socialized to Build Bridges

Constructivism and Rationalism, Europe and the Nation-State

Michael Zürn and Jeffrey T. Checkel

As a scientific term, the concept of socialization originated more than 100 years ago—in the first issue of the *American Journal of Sociology*.[1] It later became a central term in sociology through the work of Durkheim, who saw it as the process through which individuals develop from the stage of being driven by instinct to being a sociable human being.[2] Socialization research in general has, since then, been marked by a definitional paradox. The closer the definition gets to the common-sense meaning of socialization—actors internalize norms and standards of behavior by acting in social structures—the more it runs into operational problems. The more operational the definition, the more detached socialization research becomes from its original sociological meaning, and the more it becomes the study of soft power.

This volume revisits the concept and links it to international relations (IR) by focusing on international socialization. It links to debates in IR theory by adopting a definition that allows for both sociological and rationalist accounts of norm adoption: socialization is the process of inducting actors into the norms and rules of a given community.[3] Whereas this definition cannot overcome the general paradox, it is nonetheless open both to the introduction of novices into common standards through the impersonal power of structures, and to the deliberate use of soft means of influence. It thus fosters a dialogue between constructivists and rationalists, specifically over the possibility of building bridges between different theoretical schools.

Bridge building has indeed become trendy. Panels are built around the theme at many national and international conferences. Courses may devote one or more weeks to its epistemological and practical implications. In publishing forums, one encounters a growing number of scholarly writings either wholeheartedly endorsing the idea, or strongly criticizing it.[4]

---

[1] Ross 1896.
[2] Durkheim 1922.
[3] Checkel, this volume.
[4] Compare Katzenstein, Keohane, and Krasner 1998; with Zehfuss 2002.

This volume is part of this trend. Contributors apply a form of positivist epistemology that advocates methodological pluralism. The chapters adhere to an abductionist logic, which emphasizes the dialogue between theory and data.[5] Authors were encouraged to be open-minded in the interpretation of their data, ignoring the philosophical objection that different theories cannot be comparatively tested from an outside perspective. More specifically, they were asked to pinpoint the mechanism (s) through which the principles of international institutions become translated into member behavior and to theorize their scope conditions. Research designs were kept as rigid and transparent as possible.

All these injunctions, for better or worse, push in the direction of bridge building. To give away our punch line, we think it is mostly for the better. At the same time, there is much to criticize. Like the other contributors, we organize our thoughts around this central bridge-building theme, but we expand its reach. In particular, while assessing it in the context of the rationalist-constructivist debate, we also use the concept as a springboard for addressing and reconciling two other tensions evident throughout the empirical studies—that between Europe and the nation-state, and that between substantive theorizing and normative assessment.

Having internalized the notion of bridge building, we advance three arguments, each of which follows a "both/and"—rather than an "either/or"—logic.[6] First, while socialization research has typically been construed as constructivism's home turf,[7] this volume's emphasis on mechanisms and scope conditions reveals that rational choice has much to contribute here as well. We develop this claim by undertaking a "double interpretation" of each essay, which allows us to advance more fine-grained arguments connecting the two social theories. While we do not negate the competitive aspects of the rationalist-constructivist debate, we argue that for some time to come, it may be worthwhile to focus efforts on the search for complementarities.

Second, while there are good conceptual reasons for expecting a predominance of international socialization in Europe, the empirical cases instead suggest that effects of socialization are often weak and secondary to dynamics at the national level. We make sense of this puzzle by thinking more explicitly in longitudinal terms, by drawing on work on European identity, and by noting that students of European socialization— as well as integration—have much to gain by "bringing the domestic back in." We call for studies that explore both the Europeanization of national identities and the importance of prior national socialization for European processes.

Third, while our collaborators have demonstrated the empirical and theoretical benefits of combining a social ontology with a positivist epistemology, this comes at a cost, with normative perspectives neglected. This matters—and all the more so in a Europe marked by supranational constitution and polity building. Socialization dynamics may well take us beyond the nation-state, but their legitimacy and governance

---

[5] With abductionism, the meaning of given data is explored with the help of different theories and then extended to a generalization, which in turn can be tested again. See Pierce 1878; Josephson 2000; and Schneider 2003.

[6] See Beck 1993, 9–23, for a general defense of a "both/and" logic in times of the pluralization of borders and identities.

[7] Contrast Hurrelmann 2002, 22; with Waltz 1979, 126–27.

implications bring us back—forcefully—to it. The tendency to strictly separate empirical from normative discourse, and the other way around, seems to us outdated in times when the national foundations of both empirical and normative theories are challenged.

We proceed in the following manner. In the next section, we reflect on the contributors' use of causal mechanisms and scope conditions, both of which are central to the framework of this volume. Our main criticism concerns the somewhat inconsistent use of these concepts across the articles, which makes it hard to interpret the results of the different authors cumulatively. In addition, we build further on the empirical contributions to develop some conceptual issues linked to research on international socialization.

In the second section, we summarize the major findings of the volume and engage in a "double interpretation" of all the cases. More specifically, this means that we interpret each of the identified causal mechanisms and scope conditions from both a rationalist and constructivist perspective. On the basis of this exercise, it may be easier to find the right places for building bridges between the approaches, and thus lay the groundwork for more complex theorizing.

In the third section, we reflect on the volume's central dependent variable, the degree of international socialization in Europe. We speculate on why the amount of socialization appears less than expected, and use this "nonfinding" to build bridges of a different sort—between Europe and the nation-state, and between socialization research and domestic politics.

The final section turns from the empirical and substantive theoretical to the normative. In particular, the focus on individual decision makers in several of the essays brings the normative implications of socialization through international institutions into the open. While the process of inducting actors into the international community would appear to be highly desirable, it is, normatively speaking, more ambiguous than it first seems. What would it mean in terms of democratic legitimacy if agents were socialized through institutions that lie outside the jurisdiction of their principals? What, on the other hand, is the role of socialization in building a polity beyond the nation-state? How can bridges be built and connections be made between the "postnational" world that may be developing, and conceptions of governance and democracy grounded in national experiences?

On Causal Mechanisms and Scope Conditions

The idea of causal mechanisms has gained prominence in the past decade or so. Recent contributions in both the philosophy of science and applied science, especially in the literature on the effects of international regimes, have elaborated on it. A common motive for invoking "mechanisms" is to clarify what happens between a cause and its effect, that is, to analyze in detail how the former relates to the latter.[8] Building on such insights, the introduction to this volume discusses socialization mechanisms,

[8] Hovi 2004.

244 International Institutions and Socialization in Europe

specifying two advantages to thinking in this way. For one, rather than relying on vague notions such as learning, this focus helps to theorize and empirically document specific socialization mechanisms. Moreover, the emphasis on mechanisms contributes to the much-needed development of middle-range socialization approaches.

It is hardly surprising that there are different definitions of such causal mechanisms.[9] Theorists who work in the tradition of methodological individualism conceive causal mechanisms as accounts for macro-processes in terms of their individual components. For instance, Stinchcombe defines a mechanism as a piece of scientific reasoning that is independently verifiable and that provides knowledge about a component process at a lower level.[10] A somewhat broader definition again includes the elements of independent verifiability and a component process, but does not restrict its function to the provision of micro-foundations for social explanations.[11] Such a broader definition seems to be favored in recent literature on international environmental regimes. Young and Levy identify six behavioral pathways by which international regimes affect behavior, and Stokke and Vidas use the term "mechanism" to point to an intermediate process between the design of a regime and its consequences.[12]

In this volume, the term *causal mechanisms* refers to the intermediate processes along which international institutions may lead actors toward accepting the norms, rules, and modes of behavior of a given community. Mechanisms connect things; they link specified initial conditions and a specific outcome.[13] As an example, arguing and persuasion can be seen as a causal mechanism that is triggered by the appropriate institutional design and that leads to a change in the interests or behavior of the actors concerned. Of course, this causal mechanism can only be triggered under certain scope conditions, for instance a high degree of credibility on the part of the institution and its community in the eyes of the addressee. In other words, a causal mechanism that leads to socialization will be triggered under certain circumstances.

Accordingly, the empirical essays in this collection face two challenges: to establish how socialization happens (identify the socialization mechanism) and under what conditions (identify the scope conditions). The underlying assumption of this formulation is that certain features of international institutions trigger causal mechanisms, which in turn cause socialization. The general causal framework is summarized in Table 1.

The framework has been adapted somewhat in the different essays. Indeed, the contributions suggest a number of different approaches for studying socialization (see Table 2)—a diversity that leads us to highlight four conceptual implications. The first addresses whether structures or agents trigger socialization. A second points to the need to move from an inventory to a typology of socialization mechanisms. The third concerns the appropriate target of socialization studies in international relations—individuals or states? The fourth concerns scope conditions.

---

[9] See Hovi 2004 for an excellent discussion.
[10] Stinchcombe 1991, 367. See also Elster 1998, 45–47; and Schelling 1978, 32–33.
[11] See Bunge 1997, 414; and Mayntz 2003, 4–5, for example.
[12] See Young and Levy 1999; and Stokke and Vidas 1996.
[13] Checkel, this volume.

Table 1. *The General Framework*

Trigger	*Mechanisms*	*Effect*	*Scope conditions*
International institutions	–Strategic calculation –Role playing –Normative suasion	Socialization (inducting actors into the norms, rules, and modes of behavior of a given community, either in the form of role playing or via internalization)	–Institutional design/setting of the interaction –Properties of the actor to be socialized –Properties of the socializing actor

Socialization through Structures or through Actors

All contributions treat international institutions as the trigger or as the independent variable, the effect of which is socialization. Each essay thus examines international institutions and how their existence may induce socialization. In this sense, all contributions see international institutions as triggers of socialization mechanisms—in most cases implicitly, however. Furthermore, a closer look reveals two different notions of triggers. One is the notion of international institutions as social environments, the mere membership of which evokes the socialization of actors (see the essays by Beyers, Hooghe, and Lewis). Other contributors—Gheciu and Schimmelfennig—have another outlook. They focus on different activities that are carried out by international institutions vis-à-vis states that are not yet members, but may wish to become so.

This difference in outlook—international institutions as (part of) social environments that structure interaction and subsequently identities, as opposed to international institutions as actors—reveals a tension in the chapters. Indeed, one may argue that, in a sociological reading, only the former conceptualization refers to socialization in its "truest sense," while the latter is about the exertion of soft power or the eliciting of compliance by a given actor. The latter notion—international institutions as actors—overlooks that any specific socialization is frequently the unintended result of an interplay of "activities" by many different outside actors. In this commonsense understanding, it is those who become socialized who are the "actors," not those who socialize (who are the structure). Sociologists sometimes use the term "self-socialization" to emphasize that socialization processes in modern times can no longer be adequately grasped by examining only the socializing structure.[14] Framing the agent-structure relationship so that there is a focus on the socializing structure only, therefore, seems to be somewhat one-sided.

In any case, this difference does not correspond with the difference between constructivist and rationalist approaches. Whereas Gheciu puts forward an argument in favor of constructivism that treats international institutions as actors, the analyses of Beyers and Hooghe—which are hard to categorize in terms of constructivism

---

[14] Zinnecker 2000.

Table 2. *The Cases as Presented in the Articles*

Author	Trigger	Mechanism	Effect	Scope conditions
Beyers	Institutional membership	—	Allegiances and supranational role conceptions	Intensity and length of contact; domestic experiences
Hooghe	EU Commission membership	—	Supranational attitudes; attitudes towards Commission autonomy and Commission agenda setting	Individual characteristics; domestic organizational variables; types of norms
Lewis	COREPER membership	Strategic calculation, role playing, normative suasion	Change of interests, "layering" of identities	Issue density/intensity; insulation
Gheciu	Security institutions	Teaching and normative suasion	State identities and definitions of interest (indicated by implementation of liberal military norms)	Presence of a pedagogic agent; Eastern European self-definition as student; systematic interaction
Schimmelfennig	Membership conditionality by international institutions	Strategic calculation (rewards and punishments); social influence	Behavioral change in line with the requirements of the institution (sustained compliance)	Strength of domestic opposition

or rationalism—consider international institutions as environments. This rather seems to indicate that the agent-structure problem is familiar to both theoretical approaches.

The "culprit" here is positivism. Virtually all forms of IR rationalism, as well as the conventional constructivism invoked in this volume, embrace it as an epistemology. As a result, scholars are forced into an "either/or" resolution of the agent-structure problem. Either they choose structure (and look at its effects on agents) or agency as the starting point of their analyses. The simultaneous study of the mutual constitution of structure and agency barely seems possible. Within a positivist epistemology, it seems that one is forced to favor one or the other perspective. In fact, it is still possible to remain open-minded on the issue and acknowledge both relationships; however, this leads to a sequential approach as a solution to the structure-agent problem.[15]

From an Inventory to a Typology of Socialization Mechanisms

While the introduction to this volume puts forth three principal socialization mechanisms—strategic calculation, role playing, and normative suasion—a closer look at each essay reveals a quite disparate understanding of what constitutes one.[16] For example, Beyers and Hooghe are cautious in using the term *mechanism* at all (and do so only as a synonym for independent variable), although they implicitly conceive the process of socialization as cognitive role playing, or what Johnston refers to as *mimicking.*

The processes that come closest to the concept of socialization mechanism as developed in the introduction are the ones identified by Gheciu, Lewis, and Schimmelfennig, who mainly refer to persuasion and teaching on the one hand, and incentives and strategic calculation, mostly in the form of conditionalities, on the other.[17] At first sight, this essentially reduces the number of socialization mechanisms to the well-known binary distinction between arguing and bargaining.[18] *Arguing* here refers to empirical and normative statements put forward with the intention of being valid and truthful and with the purpose of changing beliefs, whereas *bargaining* consists of threats and promises, the effectiveness of which depends on their credibility. The objective of bargaining is to change behavior through the manipulation of constraints.[19]

Given this dichotomy, however, it is hard to fit in the third mechanism mentioned by Checkel, that is, cognitive role playing or—to use Johnston's terminology— mimicking. The relationship between arguing and bargaining, on the one hand, and role playing, on the other, remains somewhat unclear. This tension is evident in Lewis' carefully argued study on socialization in the European Union's (EU's) Committee of

---

[15] Carlsnaes 1992. See also our elaboration of "dynamic" approaches to the study of European socialization in the third section.

[16] This section has benefited greatly from discussions with Frank Schimmelfennig.

[17] See also Kelley 2004. Lewis, alone among the contributors, explicitly theorizes and documents the third, role-playing mechanism at work. See below.

[18] See Elster 1992 and 1998; and Risse 2000.

[19] See Saretzki 1996; and Zangl and Zürn 1996, 352.

Permanent Representatives (COREPER).[20] While he does a good job documenting role playing at work, it is not clear in the end if such behavior is (passively) induced by the particulars of the institutional setting, or (actively) promoted by the arguments of COREPER colleagues ("this is the way we behave in this institution"). The former is indeed role playing as defined in the introduction; the latter, however, is parasitic on underlying dynamics of arguing and persuasion.

Further complicating matters, some of the authors use—at least implicitly—the concept of *social influence*. Social influence refers to a class of processes that elicit pro-norm behavior through the distribution of social rewards and punishments.[21] Under this definition, is social influence just the same as bargaining,[22] or is it different? If it is different and thus a fourth mechanism, how does it relate to the other three? These issues may be clarified by combining the clearly defined dichotomy of preferences (the focus of arguing) versus constraints (the focus of bargaining) with a second one—socialization through actors versus socialization through structures. Accordingly, international institutions can be conceived as actors who use persuasive tactics or carrots and sticks, or conceived as providing a social environment that channels social influence and induces certain role enactments. The combination of these two fundamental distinctions leads to a fourfold typology of socialization mechanisms (see Table 3).[23]

There still remains another issue. If one sees internalization as the end point of socialization, then arguing seems to be the only process that leads directly to it. The other three mechanisms point to changes that clearly come to a halt before full internalization has taken place, which is a little odd.[24] Often, bargaining or role enactment take place at the beginning of a process that eventually leads to something like complete socialization. As an example, due to external constraints and role enactment, significant sections of the German political elite after World War II behaved in a way that was compatible with the requirements of the newly emerging democracy. At least some of them, and the political elite as a collective, had internalized democratic values only two decades later. While constraints may have been the most important starting point of this process, it went further after a time.

It may therefore be necessary to also look at secondary socialization mechanisms, or secondary links in the causal chain that are triggered by the primary link. The notion of causal mechanisms as such can surely include causal chains with more than one link connecting the trigger with the effect. A complete account of socialization mechanisms therefore requires the study of both primary and secondary mechanisms. Most contributions to this volume and the typology of mechanisms given in Table 3, however, focus on primary mechanisms only.

[20] Lewis, this volume.
[21] Johnston 2001, 499.
[22] Checkel, this volume, seems to imply this when he writes: "While incentives and rewards can be social (status, shaming) as well as material (financial assistance, trade opportunities), one might expect both to play some role in the socialization process."
[23] See also Schimmelfennig 2003.
[24] Indeed, the distinction made in the volume's introduction between Type I and Type II internalization directly hints at this tension. Checkel, this volume.

Table 3. *A Typology of Socialization Mechanisms*

What gets changed? What induces change?	Constraints	Preferences
Actor	Bargaining	Arguing
Structure	Social influence	Cognitive role playing

What kind of secondary mechanisms might be conceivable? We point to just one possibility. According to cognitive dissonance theory, actors who—for ulterior reasons—act in a certain manner and need to justify these activities to themselves and others, begin to internalize the justification even if they were initially critical of it.[25] For example, a government (and its agents) that subscribes to an international compromise which also requires arms reductions on its own side, will often defend it as good and necessary. As a result, a cognitive dissonance will arise between what is justified and argued for, and what is thought of in secret.[26] Human beings have a tendency to resolve this dissonance by adapting their preferences to the behavior; that is to say, preferences are influenced by behavior.[27]

This cognitive dissonance mechanism can potentially be part of two of the three mechanisms discussed by Checkel in his introduction. It can follow strategic adaptations of behavior because of given constraints (see the examples above) and it can follow a temporary role enactment. In sum, a complete typology of socialization mechanisms needs to distinguish different primary mechanisms (as suggested in Table 3), and, furthermore, requires a similar typology of secondary mechanisms, plus the relation between the two. To this end, it may be worthwhile to combine psychological theory and rational choice. This is another plea for the "both/and" logic. It also indicates that there is still some work to do.[28]

Corporate and Personal Socialization

Socialization is the assumed effect in the framework here. Nevertheless, with respect to the dependent variable, there arises a division of the essays into two camps. While Schimmelfennig essentially focuses on behavioral changes in the direction of norm-compliance of states (that is, a corporate actor), Beyers and Hooghe inquire into individual allegiances and role conceptions.[29] The former approach is straightforward. It takes up the volume's definition of socialization and practically transforms it into a purely descriptive variable. The latter approach deals better with the agency problem. There are indeed good reasons for focusing on the socialization of individuals in small

---

[25] Festinger 1957.
[26] Zürn 1992, 144.
[27] The theory of cognitive dissonance has similarities to, but is nevertheless different from, the "civilizing force of hypocrisy." See Elster 1998.
[28] Johnston, this volume, provides further support for our argument here, with his similar call for more attention to psychological theory, in his case by constructivists.
[29] Gheciu and Lewis are partial exceptions to this categorization. See below.

groups. After all, states as unitary actors do not participate in negotiations and do not talk to each other, while state agents do. It therefore certainly makes sense to focus on the extent to which the organizational setting might account for an individual actor's allegiance and preference formation.

There are, however, substantial problems with such an approach as well. Most importantly, a complete account of a socialization process in world politics ought to include an analysis of the effects of resocialized agents on decision making in national foreign policy. The decisive question is thus whether a changed allegiance and the supranational role conception of a participating individual do indeed necessarily translate into pro-norm behavioral changes in states.

The Gheciu and Lewis essays take up the latter challenge—and demonstrate the difficulties involved in pulling it off. Let us be clear. Although Gheciu and Lewis both provide studies that are superb examples of process tracing—documenting how individual allegiances (and, in Gheciu's case, identities) are transformed—the trick is to connect such micro-dynamics to the macro level of state politics and policy. In each case, this connection is largely made by establishing correlations. That is, changes in individual identity or allegiance are shown to precede later shifts in policy that are consistent with them. For sure, this is an important first step. However, it would need to be followed by additional process tracing to establish causality. Furthermore, the latter move, by reaching into the national arena, would need explicit grounding in some theory of domestic politics.[30]

Scope Conditions

We now turn to the scope conditions. The goal here is to identify the conditions under which international institutions trigger certain mechanisms that lead to socialization. The list of such conditions suggested in the case studies is impressive. They include institutional features such as the principle of specialization or isolation from domestic politics (Lewis), the strength of prior beliefs (Hooghe), the length of participation (Beyers, Hooghe), the intensity of contact (Beyers, Lewis, Gheciu), a teacher-student relationship (Gheciu), and the strength of the domestic opposition (Schimmelfennig).[31] This list can be grouped under four more general headings:

- properties of the international institutions (be it as structure or as actor) that trigger socialization;[32]

- properties of the political systems and agents that become socialized (for example, the strength of domestic opposition);

- properties of the issues or norms regarding which socialization takes place (for example, minority rights or democratic procedures); and

- properties of the interaction between socializing and socialized agents (such as intensity of contact, style of discourse, or a teacher-student role distribution).

---

[30] See Lewis, this volume; and Gheciu, this volume. We return to, and amplify, the domestic-politics/ socialization nexus in the third section.

[31] See also Kelley 2004.

[32] See also Johnston, this volume.

Although the list of scope conditions can hardly be comprehensive, the ones identified here are interesting and telling, and the general approach seems convincing to us. Only two remarks are in order.

First, it is remarkable that we learn little about the properties of the actors and structures that trigger socialization. Whereas the properties of the actors who are, so to speak, undergoing socialization are obviously important (especially the role of domestic opposition), no properties of the actors encouraging socialization are systematically identified, with the exception of some more or less implicit references to power and credibility.

Second, with the exception of Hooghe's contribution, there is almost no mention of issue properties as conceivable scope conditions. While Hooghe argues that large or abstract values facilitate socialization, there are in fact good reasons to believe that socialization is easier with respect to superficial, as opposed to deeper, norms. Socialization, as used in common language and in the sociological literature, refers not only to abstract norms, but also to specific social expectations—for example, dress codes. With respect to the international sphere, it could be argued that the diplomatic code as behavioral standard gets socialized more easily than basic norms such as human rights or the rule of law. Further research is necessary to close this gap.

The Double Interpretation of Socialization and Future Directions in Research

In our reading of the cases (see Table 2), a number of promising findings are revealed. We highlight the most important ones here.

- All four socialization mechanisms we identified (see Table 3) do indeed play a role; that is, international institutions can—depending on their design and on scope conditions—trigger quite different socialization processes.

- Changes in individual allegiances are most likely to take place in highly issue-specific international institutions with a primary affiliation of all individual members and which are relatively isolated from domestic politics.

- For changes in individual allegiances, intensity of contact and career level are much more important than duration of contact.

- For individual actors in international relations, arguing seems to be the most important socialization mechanism.

- Socialization of individual actors in the direction of Europeanization can also take place at the national level. Indeed, dynamics at this level often seem to dominate those within European institutions.

- The socialization of states is most likely to take place where opposition to change is weak and the socialized state sees itself as a student in a teacher-student relationship.

- For states, arguing and bargaining seem to be the most important socialization mechanisms. They often coincide with attempts at social influence, and their individual effects are hard to distinguish.

How do these findings affect the debate between constructivists and rationalists? At first sight, one could assume that constructivists are winning on their home turf. Since socialization is a "constructivist theme," it is hardly surprising that the majority of contributions favor constructivist (Lewis and Gheciu) or at least sociological institutionalist (Beyers and Hooghe) explanations of socialization. Only one article—by Schimmelfennig—sees bargaining as the decisive mechanism for a pro-norm change of behavior. However, this is not the whole story.

As Fearon and Wendt have pointed out, there are different ways of framing the constructivist-rationalist divide. There is an ontological reading, according to which rationalism and constructivism are different sets of assumptions about what social life in general comprises. For our purposes, there are good reasons for putting this interpretation aside. A second reading sees the divide in empirical terms, "as a disagreement about substantive issues in the world, like how often actors follow a logic of consequences or logic of appropriateness."[33] A third, pragmatic reading sees the divide as one between analytic tools or lenses with which to theorize about world politics.

We start with the third reading and establish to what extent each of the constructivist and rationalist interpretations in this volume can be complemented with an interpretation from the other side. We thus verify whether or not they are compatible with one or both theories. The strategy we intend to apply may be labeled "double interpretation," meaning that empirical findings about causal mechanisms and scope conditions need to be interpreted once from the perspective of constructivism, and once from the perspective of rational choice. With the findings, we may be able to locate more precisely points at which bridge building between the theories is most promising.

At the same time, this exercise can contribute to the constructivist-rationalist debate in its second, empirical reading. Some philosophers defend the notion of the incommensurability of theories.[34] Theoretical concepts and models only make sense of the empirical world. Theory thus comes before empirical evidence, and exactly for this reason validates the exercise of double interpretation. It follows that any attempt to decide the competition between theories on the basis of empirical evidence would be doomed to failure.

While in philosophical terms this point of view is certainly on target, we should not read it as an argument in favor of an "anything goes" mentality. True, the judges of scientific truth are the disciplinary communities who ultimately decide on the basis of communicative action and not positivist notions of verification and falsification. However, the community discourse on rationalist and constructivist theories needs to be nourished with additional insights informed by positivist methodology.[35] At the end of the day, it should be the most important input for deciding scientific debates. It is therefore worth pondering over research designs that could help to discriminate between rationalist and constructivist accounts in terms of explanatory

---

[33] Fearon and Wendt 2002, 52–53.
[34] Kuhn 1962.
[35] See also Jupille, Caporaso, and Checkel 2003, 19–24. On the connection between epistemology and bridge building, see Checkel 2004.

power. By applying a double interpretation strategy, we should therefore be able to locate not only promising areas for bridge building, but also the decisive and certainly quite fine differences that need to be identified before the competitive aspect of the constructivist-rationalist debate can be resolved through empirical studies.

Beyers and Hooghe

These two essays focus on individual agents. The authors inquire into the conditions under which individual allegiances, role conceptions, and behavior change so that international institutions are no longer merely instrumental, but gain a value of their own. In this view, international institutions become "people-processing organizations"—to borrow a term from sociology that refers to formal organizations that socialize people.[36] Indeed, both authors provide evidence of such changes—the affirmation that agent socialization does to some extent take place is an important finding in itself. However, they are less successful in the empirical identification of socialization mechanisms. While Beyers uses the term only sparingly, Hooghe employs the concepts of scope conditions and causal mechanisms more or less interchangeably, both as independent variables in her research design.

We consider these analyses of the conditions under which individual actors get socialized to be interesting starting points. Yet a necessary next step would be the explicit identification of, and testing for, causal mechanisms—and especially cognitive dissonance in this case. To the extent that individuals are expected to behave as prescribed by the international institution (role enactment or mimicry), these agents have to adapt to such expectations and justify this adaptation to themselves, to peers, and possibly also to principals at home. As a result, they may later adapt their preferences to these justifications, in this way reducing cognitive dissonance.

This particular secondary socialization mechanism can indeed be doubly interpreted—both in line with constructivism and in line with thin rationalism. It is compatible with constructivism in that it emphasizes both the possibility of preference change as a result of interactions and the power of the logic of appropriateness. Acting in accordance with role expectations may lead to the internalization of these expectations.

It is also compatible with thin rationalism, or the intentional version of rationalist theory, which argues that agents act on the basis of beliefs and preferences, though these vary from actor to actor and from one issue to another and need to be assessed empirically. It follows from this two-step procedure that the development of preferences is not part of rational-choice theory, but indeed exogenous to it.[37] Preferences can then, in a second step, be traced back to arguing, to domestic politics, to material interests, to principled beliefs, and so on. This two-step procedure sees the reduction of cognitive dissonance—and a resulting change in preferences—as one of a number of possible effects of an international institution.[38]

---

[36] See also Barnett and Finnemore 2004.

[37] See Elster 1985, 4; Zürn 1992, 123–36, and 1997; and Moravcsik 1993.

[38] As our comments here suggest, we do not accept the oft-heard argument that the measurement of agent preferences—"getting inside heads," as it were—is an impossible task. See Zürn 1997; Johnston 2001; and Checkel 2003, for further discussion.

The scope conditions identified by these studies can also be interpreted in various ways. As evidence supporting their view, constructivists may point to the finding that career level (seniority) and intensity (but not necessarily duration) of contacts promote the development of new allegiances. Especially when the intensity of contacts is examined in more detail, as done by Beyers, it may be seen as a proxy for arguing. Thin rationalists, on the other hand, may see the importance of prior beliefs and domestic experiences—as emphasized by Hooghe—as support for their view. If one really has strong beliefs about national interests, then colleagues at the international level can talk until they are exhausted and still not carry any weight. Changes take place only if beliefs and preferences are indifferent and the attitude toward domestic politics is negative, or if there is already a positive disposition toward European institutions acquired on the national level.

Yet these are loose connections. Thin rationalists may respond to constructivists by pointing to oral presentations as a proxy for intensity of contacts. Oral presentations, it could be asserted, may reduce cognitive dissonance. If one makes arguments publicly, the likelihood that one internalizes and finally believes these arguments will increase. Constructivists, in turn, may respond that the intensity of beliefs and preferences indeed varies, and a strong belief is harder to change then a weak one. This, so the argument could go, in no way questions the power of arguing and persuasion. On the contrary, differences in the strength and nature of beliefs are what constructivism is all about.

In conclusion, it seems fair to say that the findings in the essays by Beyers and Hooghe are compatible with both constructivism and rationalism, and the double interpretation of these findings is quite easy to carry out. The question then arises of whether their findings suggest directions for further studies that may facilitate a clearer empirical judgment between constructivist and rationalist accounts. We see three possibilities.

First, Beyers and Hooghe assess changes in allegiances basically by asking the individual agents directly. This approach does have its drawbacks, but also has its advantages. In any case, it may be helpful to go a step further and ask the agents more about their perception of the process of change. One could ask to what extent arguments, the quality of decision making, the value of the institution itself, concern to defend the institution at home, routine, or the pleasures of Brussels caused the change in allegiances. To be sure, asking agents directly would distort the result in favor of constructivist logic—in general most people prefer to say that they are guided by good arguments and dislike saying that they have been bribed—yet a good interview technique could help to shed additional light on this process of change.[39]

Second, the counterintuitive finding that the length of time spent within the institution does not correlate significantly with changed allegiances—a central finding for both Beyers and Hooghe—is important. Hooghe even shows that prior national experiences are much more important than length of service in the European Commission. Why are those who have worked in an institution for a long time sometimes

<hr>

[39] See also Checkel 2003, 213–14, which offers an empirical operationalization of this process-oriented interview technique.

even more skeptical toward it, and why do they believe that their allegiances have not changed?

Is the change of allegiances a short-term phenomenon ensuing from the euphoria of having made it to the international scene? Do old-timers know how decision making really happens and therefore reject the idea of arguing taking place? Or is their internalization so thorough that they do not even notice it anymore? Studies into questions such as these may add important insights to the constructivist-rationalist debate.

Third, the strength of prior beliefs and different evaluations of the national political system are obviously important determinants for a change of allegiances. This raises the question of who is chosen for these positions. Hooghe points to the possibility that there is a tendency to choose (nationally socialized) Europeanists over stubborn nationalists. But why should selfish states do so? When do they choose whom? Answering these kinds of questions could provide an important link between micro-processes at the agent level and macro-processes at the level of the national political systems.[40]

Lewis and Gheciu

It is hardly surprising that Beyers and Hooghe can be double-interpreted fairly easily, as neither takes the constructivist-rationalist divide as a direct starting point. In contrast, the articles by Lewis and Gheciu both offer accounts of socialization that explicitly seek to build on constructivist theory. Is a double interpretation in such cases still possible? Lewis shows convincingly that within COREPER, a decision style has developed that goes beyond strategic adaptation. He points to the isolation of COREPER from domestic politics and its informal style as scope conditions for this process. Gheciu demonstrates persuasively that over time and as a result of teaching, decision makers in the Czech Republic and in Romania have adopted liberal military norms, indicating a new identity.

How would rationalists account for these findings? In the case of COREPER, one could argue that what one sees is an institution that has been rationally designed to engineer compromises. Ultimately, control remains with the states, which make final decisions in the Council of Ministers. This mechanism could be described as *Odysseus reversed.* Instead of tying oneself up to increase the credibility of threats and avoiding the call of the sirens,[41] the agents are deliberately freed to a significant extent from their national ties to increase both the zone of agreement and the problem-solving capacity of all actors. It then becomes more understandable that a permanent representative can be branded—as Lewis notes—a permanent traitor, but not be withdrawn from his position; there is an "unwritten, global, permanent instruction to 'find solutions.'"[42] The scope conditions identified by Lewis are also compatible with this interpretation.

---

[40] More generally, and as we argue in the next section, such dynamics highlight the central importance of explicitly linking the domestic and international in socialization studies.

[41] See Schelling 1960; and Elster 1979, respectively.

[42] Lewis, this volume.

If the principals want to create an institution that is good at crafting compromises, it makes a lot of sense to isolate it from domestic politics (delegation) and to establish a high issue-density so that linkages can be made easily.

In Gheciu's study, the argument is that the North Atlantic Treaty Organization (NATO) educated and persuaded elites in the Czech Republic and Romania to adopt liberal military norms. Because NATO membership was, according to her account, ambiguous in terms of instrumental benefits, guaranteed membership as an incentive cannot reasonably explain these changes. Rather, she argues, it is necessary to adopt a constructivist approach, "conceptualizing socialization as a process in which the socializer (NATO) has targeted—and sometimes affected—changes in the definitions of identity and interest held by the socializees."[43]

Rationalists are certainly forced onto the defensive by this excellent and carefully executed study. From their point of view, however, it is quite telling to learn that "proliberal elites tended to represent both countries in interactions with NATO. Those elites identified with the Western community and, hence, recognized it as a source of expertise on—and key forum for recognition of—those new identities."[44] Given these facts, thin rationalists could argue that the learning taking place was essentially on the basis of preexisting identities and preferences. If elites have decided they want to be good liberals, it is merely instrumental to then learn what this means in behavioral terms. Thus in this thin rationalist account, we see instrumental learning, which is a sensible thing for any rational actor to do. It is much in line with this interpretation that NATO officials tried to convince nonliberals by pointing to the merits of a pro-NATO policy change even within the socializees' normative framework.[45]

To summarize this rationalist account: Gheciu demonstrates convincingly that learning took place. She also correctly points to the scope condition of a teacher-student relationship. However, the prior role conceptions are suggestive of preexisting identities, which rendered any learning that took place instrumental. Moreover, because student-teacher relations (the scope condition) are seldom seen in international relations, even this kind of instrumental learning is likely quite rare.[46]

So, even these two excellent studies, with their clear-cut constructivist arguments, can be confronted with plausible rationalist explanations. The double interpretation works here as well. Given this state of affairs, we see four directions for future research. First, most constructivist studies lack a clear and operational definition of identity change. Both Gheciu and Lewis use proxies for it that are so far removed from the essence of the concept that there remains room for rationalist explanations of the findings. The competitive aspect of the constructivist-rationalist debate would thus benefit from attention to this issue.[47]

[43] Gheciu, this volume.
[44] Ibid.
[45] Gheciu, this volume. More generally on instrumental—or what is sometimes called simple—learning, see the excellent discussion in Levy 1994.
[46] For this reason, it is certainly useful to inquire into possible empirical extensions beyond Europe, as Johnston does in this volume.
[47] Here, IR constructivists could benefit from recent methodological advances in empirical research on European identity. See, especially, Hermann, et al. 2004.

Second, thin rationalists who do not work on the assumption of perfect information can often characterize a given change in preferences over outcomes as attributable to belief change, while desires (deeper values) remain constant. To the extent that rationalists can develop operational definitions that clearly distinguish changes in beliefs from changes in desires, the competitive aspect of the constructivist-rationalist debate again would gain.[48]

Third, the teacher-student constellation so accurately described by Gheciu is worth further attention. On the one hand, it would be useful to have an inventory of such teacher-student constellations, because they amount to a form of role playing that is highly atypical for any conception of international relations. Although one's initial reaction may be to consider such constellations as highly unusual (thus strongly restricting the generalizability of Gheciu's findings), a closer look might reveal that they occur more often and therefore require further analysis. Has anarchy been overcome in such situations? Can a strong divergence of interests be expected in teacher-student relationships? Should cooperation and institution building not be extremely easy in such an environment?

On the other hand, and especially from a contructivist point of view, it would be highly interesting to study the development of a teacher-student relationship. How did it come about? How stable is it? While rationalists can explain preference change in a given teacher-student relationship with instrumental learning, they would probably have a hard time explaining the emergence and acceptance of this distribution of roles as such.

Finally, Lewis' story of decision making in COREPER, in which representatives of nation-states at times give a lower priority to injunctions from their governments for the sake of a cooperative effort to solve problems at the supranational level, raises questions about the relation between task assignment through principals and decision-making style in international institutions. Thinking more systematically about this relation could also help to clarify the debate between constructivists and rationalists. Do democratic states create institutions that are allowed to ignore the short-term interests of the principals in order to foster longer-term gains? How does that affect the decision-making style of these institutions and the allegiances of the agents involved in decision making? Are these delegations functionally similar to national constitutions, which also withdraw some decisions from the regular, democratic process of decision making and place them in the realm of law or technical expertise?

Schimmelfennig

Analyzing the process through which Western international institutions affect Eastern European countries striving for membership, Schimmelfennig is the rationalist counterpart to Gheciu and Lewis. In particular, he demonstrates that the use of incentives by international institutions such as the EU, the Organization for Security and

---

[48] For one move in this direction, see Moravcsik's attempt to empirically operationalize insights from Bayesian updating theory, as applied to the rationalist/constructivist debate over European integration. Checkel and Moravscik 2001.

Cooperation in Europe (OSCE), and the Council of Europe has been successful in changing human rights and democracy norms in Central and Eastern Europe. While these institutions also used persuasive means to move the target countries to pro-norm behavior, these efforts were much less successful when applied without incentives, especially if domestic opposition to the change was strong.[49] Moreover, Schimmelfennig demonstrates that social influence by means of transnational channels has not had significant effects. To support this largely rationalist story, he provides the reader with strong qualitative and quantitative data.[50]

A constructivist reinterpretation would begin with two observations. First, persuasion is at times successful. For example, Schimmelfennig acknowledges the presence of socialization attempts by means other than rewards, yet points to restrictive scope conditions for their effectiveness.[51] Put this way, constructivists can fit these findings into their theoretical model. No constructivist would deny that incentives are important, especially if their application is considered to be normatively appropriate; they insist, however, that rationalists have significant problems coming to grips with arguing.[52]

Second, and in our view more importantly, the incentives used here are essentially membership incentives. Indeed, Schimmelfennig speaks about "political rewards." The question therefore arises of why membership is sometimes considered an incentive on the part of the socialization targets, for after all, there is considerable variation among elites in Eastern (and Western) Europe on its desirability. In other words, before membership can be used as an incentive, the decisive change has already taken place. The targets of socialization must be convinced that membership is beneficial to them. Moreover, the effectiveness of these rewards seems to depend, in turn, on the strength of liberal parties in the target countries. It could therefore be argued that liberal policies are adopted if the new elites of a formerly authoritarian regime wish to become liberal and therefore seek membership in liberal international institutions. The role of ideas in this interpretation is obvious.

In sum, while Schimmelfennig shows the importance of incentives as a socialization mechanism, their success is dependent on the construction of a certain relationship between those involved in the process and the diffusion of ideas that leads to valuing membership. Incentives are constructed as well.[53]

The double interpretation thus works in both directions. Even the most rigorous, well-written studies on socialization mechanisms are open to alternative theoretical interpretation. It is therefore not easy to establish real competition between the two schools. Although Schimmelfennig's study has already gone some way in carefully testing competing hypotheses, the constructivist rebuttal suggests two directions for further research.

---

[49] On the role of domestic opposition, see also Kelley 2004.
[50] Lewis and Gheciu—in keeping with constructivist proclivities—rely solely on qualitative techniques.
[51] Schimmelfennig, this volume.
[52] Mueller 2004, 397–401, which builds on and summarizes an earlier debate in the German IR journal *Zeitschrift für Internationale Beziehungen.*
[53] Our critique here could be applied to Kelley's recent work as well. See Kelley 2004.

First, thin rationalism is open to nonmaterial preferences. In this strand of rationalist theory, any kind of motivation and desire—be it material or nonmaterial, egoistic
or altruistic—can determine preferences. Through this conceptual move, many seemingly well-grounded criticisms of rationalism can be rejected. However, to remain
a complete theory, thin rationalism should be able to explain the formation of such
value-driven preferences without reference to processes of arguing and deliberation
and without reference to the normative structure of the social environment. Failing
this, thin rationalism would be forced to accept that it can only serve as an explanatory
tool if preferences are given, and that rationalism and constructivism are necessarily
complementary.[54]

Second, for Schimmelfennig, the norms directed at his target countries are clearly
compatible with the identity for which they strive. While he does his utmost to demonstrate that incentives have been decisive for pro-norm behavioral change, it would be
most challenging to identify constellations in which the socializing institutions reward
behavior that is incompatible with the identities that the new elites strive to attain.
In such situations, rationalist and constructivist theory would indeed come up with
competing hypotheses. The fact that it is hard to think of such situations indicates that
identities and interests often go together, suggesting a large degree of compatibility
between thin rationalist and moderate constructivist theorizing.

Summary

All of our double interpretations point to the same conclusion. Given the current state
of the art in socialization research, we are not really able to judge whether constructivists or rationalists are right. In this sense, it is more telling and adds more to our
understanding when both constructivist and rationalist lenses are used. Moreover, the
double interpretation seems a necessary step to identify issues and dimensions on
which rationalism and constructivism come to clearly competing predictions. These
need to be identified so that we can discriminate more sharply between different
theoretical accounts. Still, we believe that the "both/and" logic could apply even
then, to the extent that the two theoretical perspectives complemented each other:
the constructivist perspective would then focus mainly on the explanation of preferences, and the rationalist perspective on the explanation of behavior with given
preferences.[55]

The National/Supranational/Socialization Nexus

There are good historical and theoretical reasons for expecting a predominance of
international socialization in Europe. Historically, and compared to Asia, a distinct, more intense form of regionalism has developed in postwar Europe. This

---

[54] See also the discussion of "strategic social construction" in Finnemore and Sikkink 1998.
[55] In bridge-building parlance, this is an argument about "temporal sequencing." See Jupille, Caporaso,
and Checkel 2003, 22–23.

has facilitated the creation of a community, with common norms and rules, without which socialization would be impossible.[56] Theoretically, the IR literature on transnationalism and the sociological literature on organizations both suggest that value and preference change—by some measures, the hallmarks of socialization—are more likely in institutionally thick environments.[57] With its dense network of regional organizations, Europe easily qualifies as the thickest institutional environment beyond the nation-state anywhere on the globe.

So, Europe is a most likely case for socialization dynamics. Some of the preceding empirical essays, through carefully argued studies, do indeed demonstrate a strong and unambiguous role for socialization spurred by European regional organizations. However, given the volume's most-likely-case design, equally if not more important are the "nonfindings" reported, with several authors documenting cases of minimal socialization, in which its effects are clearly secondary to dynamics at the national level. To make sense of this somewhat unexpected pattern of results, we draw on three insights and literatures—time scale, European identity, and domestic politics.

Time Scales

Recall that the endpoint of socialization is internalization, which in turn can be subdivided into Type I (adoption of new roles) and Type II (adoption of new interests or possibly identities). Internalization—of either type—is not something that occurs overnight. Yet most contributors to this volume work with empirical materials that cover at most a three- to four-year period. It thus may simply be too early to detect measurable signs of internalization.

If we stop here, the news for the volume's dependent variable is good. That is, if we wait long enough, stronger evidence of socialization is likely to appear.[58] Unfortunately, such an interpretation is undermined by Hooghe's contribution. In her study of the European Commission, she explicitly controls for this time variable by building a longitudinal element into her design. Her finding: socialization effects do not increase with time, or certainly not as strongly as one might expect. At a minimum, this indicates that the overall theoretical framing, as well as future work on international socialization, must deal more carefully with time elements. Johnston's discussion of recency effects and Hooghe's analysis of primacy make first, important, moves in this direction.[59]

European Identity

Social identities refer to shared representations of a collective self. They depend on collective beliefs that the definition of the group and its membership is shared by all those in the group. With weak social identities, the welfare of the collective is part

---

[56] Hemmer and Katzenstein 2002. See also Adler and Barnett 1998.
[57] See Weber 1994; Risse-Kappen 1995, chap. 1; and Barnett and Finnemore 2004.
[58] Indeed, this is the motivating idea behind the so-called contact hypothesis. See, for discussion, Beyers, this volume; and Checkel, this volume.
[59] See Hooghe, this volume, figs. 1–3; and Johnston, this volume.

of individual preferences. Strong social identities are said to exist when individual interests are subordinated to the collective; there is a willingness to make sacrifices for its well-being.[60]

Given these definitions, it is easy to see why postwar Europe, and especially the EU, have fascinated students of social identity change. As Hooghe reminds us in her contribution to this volume, the EU Commission has what is virtually a constitutional mandate to promote the collective European interest.[61] More generally, prominent Europeanists have argued that, with its densely institutionalized structure, Europe and the EU would seem an ideal laboratory and "social soil within which actors' preferences might be transformed."[62]

Despite such promising raw material, work on European identity—until recently— has made for a frustrating read. There was a surplus of normative analysis (the kind of identity Europe ought to have), much of it very good,[63] and a paucity of substantive findings (the changes in European identity that had actually occurred). Moreover, with the latter, unclear research methodologies led to a situation in which scholars could study the same entity—the EU, say—and come to completely opposite conclusions regarding its identity-shaping potential.[64]

Recent years have seen a welcome change, however, with normative analyses increasingly complemented with rich, methodologically rigorous empirical studies. The conclusion of this work is unmistakable. It is simply too early to talk of an independent, robust, superordinate, and strong European social/collective identity. Instead, the central finding—all the more striking because it has been reproduced across various disciplines (political science, social psychology, anthropology, and sociology) using different methodologies—is that any putative European identity is still dominated by its national counterparts or, better said, coexists side by side with them. More specifically, the identity construction "game" is not zero sum, in which European identities grow at the expense of national ones, but positive sum, in which we may be witnessing an evolution to "national identity first, European identity second."[65]

In at least two ways, this work on European identity relates to and reinforces the findings in this volume. In one way, if we speak specifically about the EU, it is clear that Brussels has only secondary effects on core attitudes and loyalties. For students of European identity, this leads to the positive-sum outcomes described above. For contributors here, it is reflected in the extraordinary strength of national-level socialization experiences. Be it Beyers on the European Council, Hooghe on the Commission, or Lewis on COREPER, national factors play a central role. Moreover, these scholars—just like their counterparts studying European identity—go to great

---

[60] See Zürn 2000, 192; and Hermann and Brewer 2004, 5–6. Needless to say, socialization could be a primary mechanism through which individuals come to hold such "shared representations."
[61] See Hooghe, this volume.
[62] See Jupille and Caporaso 1999, 440.
[63] Fossum 2003, for example.
[64] Compare Wessels 1998; and Laffan 1998.
[65] See Checkel 1999; Risse and Maier 2003; Hooghe and Marks 2004a, 416–17; and, especially, the essays in Hermann, Risse, and Brewer 2004.

lengths to theorize and document the nuanced interplay between the national and European levels. It is not "either/or," but "both/and."

Consider in more detail Lewis' findings on COREPER. The individuals making up COREPER are the permanent representatives of member states to EU institutions. As such, they are exemplars of state agents; they articulate and defend national interests across the spectrum of EU affairs. Yet Lewis uncovers far more than the straight-forward bargaining one would expect if these diplomats viewed themselves only as defenders of state interests. Instead, the permanent representatives also internalize group-community standards, which then become part of an expanded conception of the self. However, this collective culture does not trigger shifts of loyalty or transfers of allegiance. To quote Lewis:

> Thus the identity configuration of EU permreps appears, even at first glance, more subtle and complex than zero-sum notions of loyalty and allegiance. In COREPER, what one sees instead is the cognitive blurring of sharp definitional boundaries between the "national" and "European" frames, and a shared sense of responsibility to deliver both at home and collectively. . . . [T]he pattern of socialization found in COREPER does not lead to the creation of a new overarching supranational identity, but rather to a more complex configuration of identity than is typically acknowledged.[66]

This is a quintessential "both/and" argument. Members of COREPER do indeed never forget that they are permanent representatives of particular states. At the same time, their self-understanding of the "national" is partly redefined through their joining the COREPER community—that is, through their socialization. For these diplomats, it is not Europe or nation-state, but both.[67]

Domestic Politics and European Integration/Socialization

The importance of domestic politics is a second way that the findings in this volume and work on European identity reinforce each other. In both cases, they play a key, if undertheorized, role. Depending on the author and his/her disciplinary and epistemological orientation, we see European identity or socialization experiences being shaped decisively by a wide array of domestic factors—deeply entrenched social discourses, previous bureaucratic experience, or the structure of national institutions, for example.[68]

This point leads directly to our main argument as to why the volume as a whole, given its most-likely-case design, did not "see as much socialization as expected." Here, we broaden our critique to the larger literature on European integration, of which arguments about European socialization are but one part.[69] This broadening does not affect the underlying claim. Simply put, for research on European integration and

---

[66] Lewis, this volume.

[67] See also Laffan 2004.

[68] Specifically on European identity, see the findings reported in Risse and Maier 2003.

[69] Much of the early neofunctionalist and more recent supranationalist theorizing on integration, while using a different analytic language, was and is greatly preoccupied with the same "dependent variables" of value-identity-interest shifts as scholars of socialization. Haas 2001.

socialization to consolidate and build on its recent achievements, sustained attention must be devoted to theorizing and linking the domestic and European levels. Once again, it is not "either/or," but "both/and."

A brief review of the literature highlights the challenges. To start, consider those two integration "warhorses"—neofunctionalism and intergovernmentalism. Both focused overwhelmingly on the European level, seeking to explain supranational loyalty transfers or interstate bargaining, respectively. More recent approaches— supranationalism, policy networks, and institutional analysis—have continued the European-level focus, albeit with a broader range of dependent variables (from the emergence of European governance structures to the multilayered nature of European policymaking, say).[70]

In all of this work, systematic attention to, let alone explicit theorization of, domestic politics is notable mainly by its absence. For sure, the domestic is present in integration theory. As Haas argued many years ago, "nationally constituted groups"—largely in the form of political elites—play a central role in integration.[71] Such a focus, however, is not the same as a theory of domestic politics. Indeed, it is telling that one recent review of the history of theories of European integration contains not a single reference to domestic politics.[72]

Work on Europeanization, liberal intergovernmentalism (LI), and arguments about multilevel governance are partial exceptions to the neglect of domestic politics in integration theory. Europeanization research shifts the focus to the national level, exploring the domestic impact of EU institutions and policies. LI starts the analysis with the specification of domestic interests. In neither case, however, do we get a theory of domestic politics, or of how they might be linked conceptually to the European level. Both schools also offer largely structural readings of the domestic setting—for example, the well-known goodness-of-fit argument by students of Europeanization,[73] or Moravcsik's domestic actors, whose interests are structurally dictated by their country's position in the global political economy.[74]

Proponents of multilevel governance go a step further, arguing that the European and national levels are becoming so deeply interconnected that it makes little analytic sense to give pride of place to one level over the other. The domestic is interpenetrated by the supranational—and vice versa. In our bridge-building language, theirs is a "both/and" argument.[75]

Unfortunately, a social-theoretic choice of an "either/or" type limits the impact of this important analytic move. Simply put, while taking the domestic level—and its integration with Europe—more seriously, scholars of multilevel governance build their arguments overwhelmingly on rational-choice foundations: theories of trans- action costs and informational asymmetries, as well as principal-agent frameworks.

---

[70] Wiener and Diez 2004 provide a concise overview of the various integration theories.
[71] Risse 2005, 293, quoting from Haas 1958.
[72] Wiener and Diez 2004, chap. 1.
[73] Cowles, Caporaso, and Risse 2001, chap. 1. See also Heritier, Knill, and Mingers 1996, chaps. 1 and 4.
[74] Moravcsik 1998.
[75] See Kohler-Koch and Eising 1999, chaps. 1 and 2; Hooghe and Marks 2001, chap. 1; and Kohler-Koch 2003, chap. 2.

The dominant institutional metaphor and empirical focus is European institutions as constraint; they induce actors to adopt certain strategies or shape their behavior.[76]

Developments in the international/European socialization literature have followed a similar trajectory, with initial neglect or bracketing of domestic politics being followed by greater attention to them.[77] Consider several examples from the present volume. In her study of NATO and socialization, Gheciu argues that noviceness plays an important role in determining the likelihood of successful socialization. Using a more explicit domestic politics language, we would simply argue that noviceness is all about measuring the degree of national bureaucratic or cultural embeddedness of particular individuals. Schimmelfennig theorizes that socialization outcomes are heavily influenced by the structure of domestic party constellations. In their quantitative studies of socialization by EU institutions, Beyers and Hooghe exercise great care in controlling for the independent effect of domestic factors, be these prior national bureaucratic experiences, exposure to federal national structures, or the like.[78]

Although we applaud such moves "to bring the domestic back in," more needs to be done.[79] At this point, the tendency is too often for "ad hocism" to prevail, in which domestic factors are added, but unguided by some broader and overarching theoretical argument. Such arguments—be they about elites, institutions, or pluralism—are readily found in work on comparative politics, a point made forcefully over a decade ago by Milner.[80] More recently, Cortell and Davis have argued that "[f]urther research into the relationship between the effects of socializing forces on the international system and states' domestic politics is required because it remains poorly understood."[81] If students of international relations are going to push comparativists to give up an exclusive focus on "methodological nationalism" in which national political systems are compared as if they were independent of each other, then it is only fair to ask that integration/IR theorists reciprocate by systematically building arguments about domestic politics into their approaches.[82]

In making these connections to the domestic, we would urge students of European/international socialization to adopt a "both/and" perspective, in which factors across different levels of analysis—national and European, in this case—are dynamically integrated. Dynamic here means that one goes back and forth across levels, emphasizing the simultaneity of international and domestic developments. This stands in contrast to an additive or residual variance approach—for many years the norm among IR theorists—in which the researcher explores one level at a time, explaining as much as possible there, before considering factors at other levels.[83]

To see this difference, we return to Hooghe's contribution.[84] Her central finding is that much of the European-level socialization we see in the EU Commission is in fact a

---

[76] This is especially true of the work by Hooghe and Marks. See Checkel 2001 for details.
[77] Compare Finnemore 1996; or Finnemore and Sikkink 1998; with Cortell and Davis 2000.
[78] See, respectively, Gheciu; Schimmelfennig; Beyers; and Hooghe, all this volume.
[79] Of course, such criticisms could easily be extended to the broader IR literature. Gourevitch 2002.
[80] Milner 1992.
[81] Cortell and Davis 2000, 83–84.
[82] Zürn 2002, 248.
[83] See Mueller and Risse-Kappen 1993; and Moravcsik 1993.
[84] Hooghe, this volume.

product of prior, national socialization. The approach here is basically additive, which suits her design well. Yet an intriguing possibility is that those national-level experiences are themselves enmeshed with, and shaped by, European factors. A dynamic integration of the two levels could better capture such interplay.[85]

We well appreciate that there are complicated methodological issues involved in any such move. After all, to argue and show that A is a cause of B requires that something be held constant. Yet on our reading, these are (resolvable) issues of operationalization and method, and not (insurmountable) questions of epistemology.[86] Indeed, while using different language, Risse has recently made precisely the same argument in regards to empirical research on European identity. In what he calls a "marble cake" model, the various components of an individual's identity cannot be separated on different levels; rather, different components—German and European, say—"influence . . . mesh and blend into each other."[87]

Such a dynamic approach would benefit research on European socialization in two ways. First, an emphasis on simultaneity and cross-cutting influences would keep the focus on process, where it should rightly be, given existing biases toward structural accounts in the literature. After all, socialization, in its formal, definitional sense—the induction of actors into the norms and rules of a given community—is nothing if not a process. By stressing the latter, scholars will also be pushed to better explicate the micro-mechanisms of socialization—a gap in the literature and one the essays in this volume have already begun to fill.

Second, a dynamic, cross-cutting approach might better alert scholars of socialization to an understudied element in their analyses—feedback effects. What happens to the socializing agents or structures themselves—the EU Commission and Council, NATO, COREPER, and the OSCE in this volume—when they attempt (and perhaps fail) to socialize a target group? There is a tendency—reproduced in the chapters considered here—for the causal arrows to point mainly in one direction: from socializer to socializee. To take one example, it would be a fascinating follow-up study to Gheciu's exploration of NATO's socialization role to consider the effect on NATO if her "baby generals" talked back, thus reversing the causal arrows.[88]

Our arguments on continuing and taking further the turn to domestic politics in socialization research find support in three closely related literatures. Among IR constructivists, there is now a growing recognition that, as Hopf so nicely puts it, "constructivism [starts] at home," which in more operational terms means that "domestic society . . . must be brought back into any constructivist account of world politics."[89]

Within the field of European studies, two similar trends are at work. Scholars of integration are coming to recognize that the EU—and theory about it—is to some extent becoming a victim of its own success. The deepening of integration during the

---

[85] See also Risse 2005, 305.
[86] See Martin and Simmons 1998, 749; and Katzenstein 2003, 737–39, for other recent analyses that resonate with our thinking.
[87] Risse 2005, 296. See also Risse 2004, 251–52.
[88] See also Johnston, this volume, on "emergent property" effects.
[89] Hopf 2002, 1, 278. See also Checkel 2004.

past decade and the current process of constitutionalization have spawned increasing domestic political resistance to, and mobilization against, the European project. In turn, this has led prominent theorists of integration to add a strong domestic politics–politicization element to their arguments.[90] In addition, new work on Europeanization emphasizes domestic cultural context, theorizing and documenting how religious communities that are at once both deeply national and transnational are likely to affect the degree of Europeanization in an enlarged EU.[91]

Interestingly, in both cases, the addition of an explicit domestic element leads these analysts to evince more pessimism, be it about the future path of integration ("domestic support for European supranationalism is as weak as it has ever been") or the likely degree of Europeanization ("religion, as a political force, appears more likely to hinder the further integration of the European continent than to advance it").[92]

In sum, and to return to the central question motivating this section—why the volume did not see as much socialization as expected—we would argue that the problem is not poorly crafted designs or methodologically suspect research. Instead, like their integration and Europeanization counterparts, students of socialization would appear to be operating with an underspecified theoretical apparatus, especially at the domestic political level.

Effective and Legitimate Governance beyond the Nation-State

There remains one—important—issue that has largely been ignored in this collection. It is mainly a normative one that raises questions of accountability and legitimacy. Simply put, in terms of democratic legitimacy, socialization beyond the nation-state would appear to be both good and bad at the same time.

As long as the analysis of international cooperation was based on rationalist cooperation theory, it was relatively easy and convincing to maintain that cooperation was worth striving for and thus normatively unproblematic. The claim was neither that international cooperation is sufficient for a normatively acceptable world nor that each instance of international cooperation advances global goods. The claim was merely that the management of urgent global problems could not be successful without international cooperation. On these grounds, it was easy to defend such cooperation and regimes on grounds of legitimacy—in normative terms and in terms of social acceptance.[93] In sum, international cooperation was not everything, but, without international cooperation, all was for naught.

Things change decisively when it comes to more in-depth cooperation, the delegation of authority to more or less supranational agents, and the socializing effects of these much more intrusive international institutions. In the case of the EU, supranational agents such as the European Court of Justice and the European Commission

---

[90] Hooghe and Marks 2004b. See also Wiener and Diez 2004, 238–46.
[91] Byrnes and Katzenstein 2006. The communities are the Catholic, Orthodox Christian, and Islamic.
[92] See Hooghe and Marks 2004b, 15; and Byrnes and Katzenstein 2006, 304, respectively.
[93] Keohane 1984, 7, for example.

do have almost a monopoly in interpreting given norms and rules. To the extent that norm interpretation also involves an element of rule setting, European institutions have the power to decide against the will of a given state.

In this way, European institutions undermine the principle that external interventions can only take place with the consent of affected states. This dilemma becomes even more accentuated if the agents working in European institutions are socialized to support European norms at the expense of the norms of the national political system. These developments raise understandable doubts: Does the functioning of international institutions such as the EU, but also the World Trade Organization (WTO) and other organizations, still meet democratic standards?

In addition, democratic criteria seem to be violated when there are no identifiable decision makers who are directly answerable for false decisions about rule setting made at the international level. As opposed to rule interpretation, national actors still play a key role in European rule setting. However, supranational actors like the European Commission and the European Parliament play an important role in this decision-making system as well. The European Commission, however, is not accountable to national communities, and election campaigns for the European Parliament focus mostly on current national issues, but rarely on European questions. Moreover, the inscrutability of international decision-making processes gives the national executive decision makers an additional advantage over others in terms of information. By pointing to European norms that need to be implemented even if the government does not agree, national decision makers can exploit their linking role between the different levels.

The most sophisticated defense of the legitimacy of the EU is put forward by scholars such as Kahler and Moravcsik.[94] They defend the functioning of international institutions by conceptualizing them as agents that deliver certain services to the principals, which are democratically elected governments in this case. In this view, international institutions have only delegated authority from the national political systems and thus possess indirect legitimacy.

This line of democratic defense of international institutions weakens significantly, however, when the national representatives in international institutions—those who are supposed to exercise control—develop allegiances to them that are stronger than their national ones. This would mean that socialization effects blur the principal-agent distinction. The ironic description of the German representative at COREPER as *ständiger Verräter* (permanent traitor) instead of *ständiger Vertreter* (permanent representative) highlights this point as well.[95] To the extent that national agents develop distinctive identities and supranational allegiances, they become detached from their national constituency. A significant accountability problem arises in this way. What may be celebrated by international relations theorists as the deepening of international institutions may easily be dismissed by normative theorists as undemocratic. While the effectiveness of international institutions may benefit from socialization processes, citizen participation and control may be degraded.[96] Some of

---

[94] See Kahler 2004; and Moravcsik 2002.
[95] Lewis, this volume.
[96] See, in general, Dahl 1994; and Scharpf 1997.

the societal resistance to the EU and its more intrusive decisions needs to be explained against this background.[97]

Most analysts therefore agree that the democratic legitimacy of international institutions is clearly inadequate. However, those who demand the reform of international institutions to make them more democratically accountable are confronted with yet another objection. According to the so-called skeptics, the mere possibility of democratic processes beyond the nation-state is questioned because the EU and other international institutions cannot meet the social prerequisites for democracy. In this view, democratic legitimacy is only possible within the framework of a *demos,* that is, a political community with some sense of common identity. In the absence of such a community, the professional confrontation of incompatible interests prevails completely in international institutions, while the common search for a sound solution, which is a necessary democratic requirement, is lacking completely.

It is against the background of this objection that socialization through international institutions becomes interesting in democratic terms. Contrary to the objection of the skeptics, socialization harbors the potential for identity building and deliberation beyond the nation-state. Given that international institutions increasingly contain supranational elements and features such as socializing power—an identity-forming effect that usually only national political institutions possess—it indeed makes sense to inquire into the opportunities to democratize these institutions themselves.[98] Democracy for the new millennium must involve citizens who are able to gain access to the political process, and mediate between the social, economic, and political processes on national terrain and flows that cut across and transform traditional community borders.

The findings in this volume show that the issue of democratic legitimacy should be taken into account. Whereas there is no strong socialization on the European level detached from the national level, double identities evolve and some arguing certainly takes place. The implications of these processes are twofold and, again, best captured by a "both/and" logic. They increase the problems that intrusive international institutions have in terms of democratic legitimacy. At the same time, they carry the potential to democratize these institutions. In any case, with the expansion of international institutions, their normative evaluation becomes much more complicated. While these issues have been neglected in the debate between constructivists and rationalists, they certainly deserve more attention.

Conclusion

This volume brought together Europeanists and IR scholars to study socialization, with a view toward contributing to the debate between rationalists and constructivists. On the whole, this endeavor has been successful. The studies are empirically rich and theoretically subtle, and all address innovatively and open-mindedly a number of decisive issues in the rationalist-constructivist debate. Although, as we argued in

[97] See Zürn and Neyer 2005.
[98] For example, see Held 1995; Zürn 1998; Keohane and Nye 2000; and Eriksen and Fossum 2000.

the first and second sections, the theoretical framework is not applied absolutely consistently, the case studies address each other in dialogue and together come up with a number of interesting findings.

The most important result is that different socialization mechanisms take place and are effective. Socialization can come about via different pathways—a complexity best explained by seeking complementarities and points of contact between rational choice and constructivism. However, the extent of the socializing effect depends on scope conditions: The socialization of states is most likely to take place when opposition to change is weak and the socialized state sees itself as the student in a teacher-student relationship. Moreover, institutional design and domestic politics play significant—if undertheorized—roles.

While the foregoing articles contribute to the rationalist-constructivist debate, they certainly do not resolve it. We have argued that all the stories told in this volume are open to double interpretation. There is a constructivist and a rationalist account for all the cases, which supports the notion of the constructivist-rationalist debate—in pragmatic terms—as one between different analytical tools or lenses for explaining social events, and weakens the notion of the debate as a theoretical battle that can be resolved through empirical research. At the same time, all the studies in this volume are extremely instructive and indicate directions for further fruitful work, some of which could help to distinguish more clearly the different empirical predictions of rationalism and constructivism.

For Europeanists and students of the EU, the volume's findings remind us that the development of European institutions—compared to their national counterparts—is a relatively new undertaking. National-level socialization at times competes with, and often dominates, European processes. Research on European/international socialization will thus go astray if it fails to theorize this complex interplay between the domestic and the international.[99]

Overall, then, our plea for "both/and" theorizing surely makes life harder—for IR scholars and Europeanists as well. The intellectual, data collection, and methodological challenges of linking constructivism and rationalism, Europe and the nation-state, normative and positivist theory, should not be underestimated—as our comments and criticisms above suggest. Yet, and especially after so many years of so many (unproductive) paradigm wars, the payoff—in terms of developing arguments that capture and explain the world as it really is—could be immense.

References

Adler, Emanuel, and Michael Barnett, eds. 1998. *Security Communities*. Cambridge: Cambridge University Press.

Barnett, Michael, and Martha Finnemore. 2004. *Rules for the World: International Organizations in Global Politics*. Ithaca, N.Y.: Cornell University Press.

Beck, Ulrich. 1993. *Die Erfindung des Politischen*. Frankfurt, Germany: Suhrkamp.

---

[99] Surveying the broader literature on international institutions, Martin and Simmons have recently come to exactly the same conclusion. Martin and Simmons 1998, 747–57.

Bunge, Mario. 1997. Mechanism and Explanation. *Philosophy of the Social Sciences* 27 (4):410–65.

Byrnes, Timothy, and Peter Katzenstein, eds. 2006. *Religion in an Expanding Europe.* Cambridge: Cambridge University Press.

Carlsnaes, Walter. 1992. The Agency-Structure Problem in Foreign Policy Analysis. *International Studies Quarterly* 36 (3):245–70.

Checkel, Jeffrey T. 1999. Norms, Institutions and National Identity in Contemporary Europe. *International Studies Quarterly* 43 (1):83–114.

———. 2001. Constructing European Institutions. In *The Rules of Integration: Institutionalist Approaches to the Study of Europe*, edited by Gerald Schneider and Mark Aspinwall, 19–39. Manchester, England: Manchester University Press.

———. 2003. 'Going Native' in Europe? Theorizing Social Interaction in European Institutions. *Comparative Political Studies* 36 (1–2):209–31.

———. 2004. Social Constructivisms in Global and European Politics: A Review Essay. *Review of International Studies* 30 (2):229–44.

Checkel, Jeffrey T., and Andrew Moravcsik. 2001. A Constructivist Research Program in EU Studies? Forum Debate. *European Union Politics* 2 (2):219–49.

Cortell, Andrew, and James Davis. 2000. Understanding the Domestic Impact of International Norms: A Research Agenda. *International Studies Review* 2 (1):65–90.

Cowles, Maria Green, James A. Caporaso, and Thomas Risse, eds. 2001. *Transforming Europe: Europeanization and Domestic Change.* Ithaca, N.Y.: Cornell University Press.

Dahl, Robert A. 1994. A Democratic Dilemma: System Effectiveness versus Citizen Participation. *Political Science Quarterly* 109 (1):23–34.

Durkheim, Emile. 1922. *Éducation et sociologie.* Paris: Alcan.

Elster, Jon. 1979. *Ulysses and the Sirens: Studies in Rationality and Irrationality.* Cambridge: Cambridge University Press.

———. 1985. *Sour Grapes: Studies in the Subversion of Rationality.* Cambridge: Cambridge University Press.

———. 1992. Arguing and Bargaining in the Federal Convention and the Assemblee Constituante. In *Rationality and Institutions: Essays in Honour of Knut Midgaard*, edited by Raino Malnes and Arild Underdal, 13–50. Oslo, Norway: Universitetsforlaget.

———. 1998. A Plea for Mechanisms. In *Social Mechanisms: An Analytical Approach to Social Theory*, edited by Peter Hedström and Richard Swedberg, 45–73. Cambridge: Cambridge University Press.

Eriksen, Erik Oddvar, and John Erik Fossum, eds. 2000. *Democracy in the European Union: Integration through Deliberation?* London: Routledge.

Fearon, James D., and Alexander Wendt. 2002. Rationalism versus Constructivism: A Skeptical View. In *Handbook of International Relations*, edited by Walter Carlsnaes, Beth Simmons, and Thomas Risse, 52–72. London: Sage Publications.

Festinger, Leon. 1957. *A Theory of Cognitive Dissonance.* Stanford, Calif.: Stanford University Press.

Finnemore, Martha. 1996. *National Interests in International Society.* Ithaca, N.Y.: Cornell University Press.

Finnemore, Martha, and Kathryn Sikkink. 1998. International Norm Dynamics and Political Change. *International Organization* 52 (4):887–917.

Fossum, John Erik. 2003. The European Union: In Search of an Identity. *European Journal of Political Theory* 2 (3):319–40.

Gourevitch, Peter. 2002. Domestic Politics and International Relations. In *Handbook of International Relations*, edited by Walter Carlsnaes, Thomas Risse, and Beth Simmons, 309–28. London: Sage Publications.

Haas, Ernst B. 1958. *The Uniting of Europe: Political, Social and Economic Forces, 1950–57*. Stanford, Calif.: Stanford University Press.

———. 2001. Does Constructivism Subsume Neo-Functionalism? In *The Social Construction of Europe*, edited by Thomas Christiansen, Knud Erik Jorgensen, and Antje Wiener, 22–31. London: Sage Publications.

Held, David. 1995. *Democracy and the Global Order: From the Modern State to Cosmopolitan Governance*. Cambridge: Polity Press.

Hemmer, Christopher, and Peter Katzenstein. 2002. Why Is There No NATO in Asia? Collective Identity, Regionalism and the Origins of Multilateralism. *International Organization* 56 (3):575–608.

Heritier, Adrienne, Christoph Knill, and Susanne Mingers. 1996. *Ringing the Changes in Europe: Regulatory Competition and Redefinition of the State. Britain, France, Germany.* Berlin: Walter de Gruyter.

Herrmann, Richard, and Marilynn Brewer. 2004. Identities and Institutions: Becoming European in the EU. In *Transnational Identities: Becoming European in the EU*, edited by Richard Herrmann, Thomas Risse, and Marilynn Brewer, 1–24. Boulder, Colo.: Rowman & Littlefield.

Herrmann, Richard, Thomas Risse, and Marilynn Brewer, eds. 2004. *Transnational Identities: Becoming European in the EU*. Boulder, Colo.: Rowman & Littlefield.

Hooghe, Liesbet, and Gary Marks. 2001. *Multi-Level Governance and European Integration*. Lanham, Md.: Rowman & Littlefield.

———. 2004a. Does Identity or Economic Rationality Drive Public Opinion on European Integration? *PS: Political Science & Politics* 37 (3):415–20.

———. 2004b. The Neofunctionalists Were (Almost) Right: Politicization and European Integration. Paper presented at the ARENA Research Seminar, October, ARENA Centre for European Studies, Oslo.

Hopf, Ted. 2002. *Social Construction of International Politics: Identities and Foreign Policies, Moscow, 1955 and 1999*. Ithaca, N.Y.: Cornell University Press.

Hovi, Jon. 2004. Causal Mechanisms and the Study of International Environmental Regimes. In *Regime Consequences: Methodological Challenges and Research Strategies*, edited by Arild Underdal and Oran Young, 71–86. Boston: Kluwer Academic.

Hurrelmann, Klaus. 2002. *Einführung in die Sozialisationstheorie*. 8th ed. Weinheim/Basel: Beltz.

Johnston, Alastair Iain. 2001. Treating International Institutions as Social Environments. *International Studies Quarterly* 45 (4):487–515.

Josephson, John R. 2000. Smart Inductive Generalizations are Abductions. In *Abduction and Induction: Essays on Their Relation and Integration*, edited by Peter A. Flach and Antonis Kakas, 31–44. Dordrecht, Netherlands: Kluwer.

Jupille, Joseph, and James A. Caporaso. 1999. Institutionalism and the European Union: Beyond International Relations and Comparative Politics. *Annual Review of Political Science* 2:429–44.

Jupille, Joseph, James A. Caporaso, and Jeffrey T. Checkel. 2003. Integrating Institutions: Rationalism, Constructivism, and the Study of the European Union. *Comparative Political Studies* 36 (1/2):7–40.

Kahler, Miles. 2004. Defining Accountability Up: The Global Economic Multilaterals. *Government and Opposition* 39 (2):132–58.

Katzenstein, Peter. 2003. Same War–Different Views: Germany, Japan and Counterterrorism. *International Organization* 57 (4):731–60.

Katzenstein, Peter, Robert Keohane, and Stephen Krasner, eds. 1998. International Organization at Fifty: Exploration and Contestation in the Study of World Politics. *International Organization* 52 (4):645–1061.

Kelley, Judith. 2004. International Actors on the Domestic Scene: Membership Conditionality and Socialization by International Institutions. *International Organization* 58 (3):425–58.

Keohane, Robert O. 1984. *After Hegemony: Cooperation and Discord in the World Political Economy.* Princeton, N.J.: Princeton University Press.

Keohane, Robert O., and Joseph S. Nye. 2000. Introduction. In *Governance in a Globalizing World,* edited by Joseph S. Nye and John D. Donahue, 1–41. Washington, D.C.: Brookings Institution Press.

Kohler-Koch, Beate, ed. 2003. *Linking EU and National Governance.* Oxford: Oxford University Press.

Kohler-Koch, Beate, and Rainer Eising, eds. 1999. *The Transformation of Governance in the European Union.* London: Routledge.

Kuhn, Thomas. 1962. *The Structure of Scientific Revolutions.* Chicago: University of Chicago Press.

Laffan, Brigid. 1998. The European Union: A Distinctive Model of Internationalization. *Journal of European Public Policy* 5 (2):235–53.

——. 2004. The European Union and Its Institutions as 'Identity Builders.' In *Transnational Identities: Becoming European in the EU,* edited by Richard Herrmann, Thomas Risse, and Marilynn Brewer, 75–96. Boulder, Colo.: Rowman & Littlefield.

Levy, Jack. 1994. Learning and Foreign Policy: Sweeping a Conceptual Minefield. A Review Essay. *International Organization* 48 (2):279–312.

Martin, Lisa, and Beth Simmons. 1998. Theories and Empirical Studies of International Institutions. *International Organization* 52 (4):729–58.

Mayntz, Renate. 2003. Mechanisms in the Analysis of Macro-Social Phenomena. MPIfG Working Paper 03/3. Cologne, Germany: Max Planck Institute for the Study of Societies.

Milner, Helen. 1992. International Theories of Cooperation Among Nations: Strengths and Weaknesses. A Review Essay. *World Politics* 44 (3):466–96.

Moravcsik, Andrew. 1993. Integrating International and Domestic Theories of International Bargaining. In *Double-edged Diplomacy: International Bargaining and Domestic Politics,* edited by Peter B. Evans, Harold Jacobson, and Robert Putnam, 3–42. Berkeley: University of California Press.

——. 1998. *The Choice for Europe: Social Purpose and State Power from Messina to Maastricht.* Ithaca, N.Y.: Cornell University Press.

——. 2002. In Defense of the 'Democratic Deficit': Reassessing Legitimacy in the European Union. *Journal of Common Market Studies* 40 (4):603–24.

Mueller, Harald. 2004. Arguing, Bargaining and All That: Communicative Action, Rationalist Theory and the Logic of Appropriateness in International Relations. *European Journal of International Relations* 10 (3):395–436.

Mueller, Harald, and Thomas Risse-Kappen. 1993. From the Outside In and From the Inside Out: International Relations, Domestic Politics and Foreign Policy. In *The Limits of State Autonomy: Societal Groups and Foreign Policy Formulation,* edited by David Skidmore and Valerie Hudson, 25–48. Boulder, Colo.: Westview.

Pierce, Charles S. 1878. Deduction, Induction, and Hypothesis. *Popular Science Monthly* 13 (8):470–82.

Risse, Thomas. 2000. 'Let's Argue!': Communicative Action in World Politics. *International Organization* 54 (1):1–39.

————. 2004. European Institutions and Identity Change: What Have We Learned? In *Transnational Identities: Becoming European in the EU*, edited by Richard Herrmann, Thomas Risse, and Marilynn Brewer, 247–71. Boulder, Colo.: Rowman & Littlefield.

————. 2005. Neo-Functionalism, European Identity, and the Puzzles of European Integration. *Journal of European Public Policy* 12 (2):291–309.

Risse, Thomas, and Matthias Maier, eds. 2003. *Europeanization, Collective Identities and Public Discourses—Draft Final Report submitted to the European Commission.* Florence, Italy: European University Institute and Robert Schuman Centre for Advanced Studies.

Risse-Kappen, Thomas, ed. 1995. *Bringing Transnational Relations Back In: Non-State Actors, Domestic Structures and International Institutions.* New York: Cambridge University Press.

Ross, Edward A. 1896. Social Control. *American Journal of Sociology* 1 (5):513–35.

Saretzki, Thomas. 1996. Wie unterscheiden sich Argumentieren und Verhandeln? Definitionsprobleme, funktionale Bezüge und strukturelle Differenzen von zwei verschiedenen Kommunikationsmodi. In *Verhandeln und Argumentieren. Dialog, Interessen und Macht in der Umweltpolitik*, edited by Volker Prittwitz, 19–39. Opladen, Germany: Leske & Budrich.

Scharpf, Fritz W. 1997. Economic Integration, Democracy, and the Welfare State. *Journal of European Public Policy* 4 (1):18–36.

Schelling, Thomas C. 1960. *The Strategy of Conflict.* Cambridge, Mass.: Harvard University Press.

————. 1978. *Micromotives and Macrobehavior.* New York: Norton.

Schimmelfennig, Frank. 2003. Internationale Sozialisation: Von einem "erschöpften" zu einem produktiven Forschungsprogramm? In *Die Neuen Internationalen Beziehungen: Forschungsstand und Perspektiven in Deutschland*, edited by Gunther Hellmann, Klaus-Dieter Wolf, and Michael Zürn, 401–28. Baden-Baden, Germany: Nomos.

Schneider, Volker. 2003. Komplexität und Policy-Forschung: Über die Angemessenheit von Erklärungsstrategien. In *Die Reformierbarkeit der Demokratie. Innovationen und Blockaden*, edited by Renate Mayntz and Wolfgang Streeck, 291–317. Frankfurt/New York: Campus.

Stinchcombe, Arthur L. 1991. The Conditions of Fruitfulness of Theorizing About Mechanisms in Social Science. *Philosophy of the Social Sciences* 21 (3):367–88.

Stokke, Olav Schram, and Davor Vidas. 1996. Effectiveness and Legitimacy of International Regimes. In *Governing the Antarctic: The Effectiveness and Legitimacy of the Antarctic Treaty System*, edited by Olav Schram Stokke and Davor Vidas, 13–31. Cambridge: Cambridge University Press.

Waltz, Kenneth N. 1979. *Theory of International Politics.* New York: McGraw-Hill.

Weber, Steven. 1994. Origins of the European Bank for Reconstruction and Development. *International Organization* 48 (1):1–38.

Wessels, Wolfgang. 1998. Comitology: Fusion in Action. Politico-Administrative Trends in the EU System. *Journal of European Public Policy* 5 (2):209–34.

Wiener, Antje, and Thomas Diez, eds. 2004. *European Integration Theory.* Oxford: Oxford University Press.

Young, Oran R., and Marc Levy. 1999. The Effectiveness of International Environmental Regimes. In *The Effectiveness of International Environmental Regimes: Causal Connections and Behavioral Mechanisms*, edited by Oran Young, 1–32. Cambridge, Mass.: MIT Press.

Zangl, Bernhard, and Michael Zürn. 1996. Argumentatives Handeln bei internationalen Verhandlungen. Moderate Anmerkungen zur post-realistischen Debatte. *Zeitschrift für Internationale Beziehungen* 3 (2):341–66.

Zehfuss, Maja. 2002. *Constructivism in International Relations: The Politics of Reality.* Cambridge: Cambridge University Press.

Zinnecker, Jürgen. 2000. Selbstsozialisation. *Zeitschrift für Soziologie der Erziehung und Sozialisation* 20 (3):272–90.

Zürn, Michael. 1992. *Interessen und Institutionen in der internationalen Politik. Grundlegung und Anwendungen des situationsstrukturellen Ansatzes.* Opladen, Germany: Leske & Budrich.

———. 1997. Assessing State Preferences and Explaining Institutional Choice: The Case of Intra-German Trade. *International Studies Quarterly* 41 (2):295–320.

———. 1998. *Regieren jenseits des Nationalstaates. Globalisierung und Denationalisierung als Chance.* Frankfurt, Germany: Suhrkamp.

———. 2000. Democratic Governance Beyond the Nation-State: The EU and Other International Institutions. *European Journal of International Relations* 6 (2):183–221.

———. 2002. From Interdependence to Globalization. In *Handbook of International Relations*, edited by Walter Carlsnaes, Beth Simmons, and Thomas Risse, 235–54. London: Sage Publications.

Zürn, Michael, and Juergen Neyer. 2005. Conclusions—The Conditions of Compliance. In *Law and Governance in Postnational Europe: Compliance Beyond the Nation-State*, edited by Michael Zürn and Christian Joerges, 183–217. Cambridge: Cambridge University Press.

Index

For EU product safety concerns, contact us at Calle de José Abascal, 56–1°,
28003 Madrid, Spain or eugpsr@cambridge.org.

www.ingramcontent.com/pod-product-compliance
Ingram Content Group UK Ltd.
Pitfield, Milton Keynes, MK11 3LW, UK
UKHW010034140625
459647UK00012BA/1368